SHATTERED DREAMS

SHATTERED DREAMS

THE FAILURE OF THE PEACE PROCESS IN THE MIDDLE EAST

1995–2002

CHARLES ENDERLIN

TRANSLATED BY SUSAN FAIRFIELD

OTHER

Other Press • New York

Copyright © 2002 Libraire Arthème Fayard, *Le rêve brisé: Histoire de l'échec du processus de paix au Proche-Orient 1995–2002*

Translation copyright © 2003 Susan Fairfield

Book Design: Kaoru Tamura

Production Editor: Robert D. Hack

This book was set in 12 pt. Plantin by Alpha Graphics of Pittsfield, New Hampshire.

10 9 8 7 6 5 4 3 2

Library of Congress Cataloging-in-Publication Data

Enderlin, Charles.
　[Rêve brisé. English]
　Shattered dreams : the failure of the peace process in the Middle East, 1995–2002 / Charles Enderlin ; translated by Susan Fairfield.
　　p. cm.
　Includes index.
　ISBN 1-59051-060-7 (hc.)
　1. Arab-Israeli conflict–1993—Peace.　2. Israel–Politics and government–20th century.　3. Palestinian Arabs–Politics and government–20th century.　I. Title.

DS119.76 .E5913 2003
956.05'3–dc21

2002032173

*To Lara, Sonia, Raphaëlle, and David Benjamin,
my children*

When big dreams are shattered, a lot of blood flows.

Milan Kundera

If all the partners in the peace process do not unite against the angel of death that is terrorism, all that will be left of this ceremony is a souvenir photo, and soon rivers of hatred will flood the Middle East.

Yitzhak Rabin

Washington, September 28, 1995

CONTENTS

LIST OF MAPS AND PHOTOS

Introduction

Exhausted after ten hours in the air, Avi Gil, chief of staff for Israeli Foreign Minister Shimon Peres, was stretched out asleep in the aisle between the two rows of seats in the small private plane. Suddenly the other passengers heard him cry out in his sleep. He was obviously having a vivid dream of Warren Christopher, the American secretary of state, furiously berating the Israeli delegates coming to meet with him at Point Magoo on the California coast: "Why did you use these dumb Norwegians? We have a perfectly good ambassador in Tel Aviv. We're going to wreck this dumb accord!" Everyone burst out laughing, and Gil woke up.

It was August 27, 1993. Gil was traveling with Peres and the head of Norwegian diplomacy, Johan Holst. His nightmare showed how afraid he was of the Clinton administration's possible reaction to the news they were bringing Warren Christopher: in secret negotiations held in Oslo, an Israeli delegation had just concluded an accord with the Palestine Liberation Organization (PLO).

These negotiations marked a 180-degree turn away from the policy of all Israeli governments since 1967, which had viewed the PLO as one of the primary enemies of the Jewish state. Throughout this time, Israel had asked Washington to be its ally by not recognizing the PLO. And now, without involving the United States, an Israeli government had reached a major agreement with the Palestinians.

Their faces showing no reaction, Warren Christopher and the State Department's special coordinator for the Middle East, Dennis Ross, listened during the Point Magoo meeting as Holst and Peres defended American policy toward Norway and Israel and then presented the Oslo accords. Silence. The secretary of state turned to Ross. "Dennis, what do you think?" Ross: "I think it's terrific! It's a historic agreement. It crosses an extraordinary threshold. Psychologically we have just gone . . . we have made unbelievable progress."[1]

What American diplomacy had just received on a silver platter was a peace process no one in the Middle East had expected. The Oslo accords would be signed in a ceremony at the White House two weeks later. The United States was to be their principal guarantor.

The atmosphere in the Middle East was changing, bringing visions of more rapid economic development and new hope to people in this part of the world, and all the more so because relations between Israel and the Palestinians were noticeably improving. The same was true of peace between Israel and Jordan in the following year. All these negotiations took place without the direct participation of the United States. Yitzhak Rabin, the Israeli prime minister, believed that the parties concerned should resolve matters by themselves, without foreign intervention.

His assassination changed everything.

In the years that followed, the Clinton administration tried to save the peace process by getting more and more involved in the talks—until they failed, not coincidentally, when Clinton left the White House. No longer just a sponsor, the United States became a mediator, sometimes also a party to the talks, torn between the need to keep its neu-

---

1. Enderlin, 1997, pp. 652–653. See also http://www.pbs.org/newshour/bb/ politics/ross.

tral role as an intermediary and, under pressure from internal American politics, the need to maintain its traditional support for its Israeli ally.

After Rabin's assassination and the election of Benjamin Netanyahu, I quickly became convinced that, given the way the negotiations were being conducted, they would end in failure. The gap between the reality on the ground and the official positions of the negotiators was getting wider from one day to the next. In the refugee camps of Gaza and the West Bank, and in the so-called development towns in Israel, I was told again and again that life had become harder since 1996. "If they want to make peace," the Palestinians would ask me, "why are they speeding up construction in the settlements and on our territory? Why do we have to pass through so many military checkpoints?" To which the Israelis would retort, "Why are they staging attacks in our country, when we're prepared to sign an agreement and evacuate some of the settlements?" Rabin had wanted to usher in an era of adaptation to peace, a period of economic development and peaceful relations. But now the region was marking a slow countdown toward a foreseeable disaster: the bloody tragedy that is ripping the Middle East apart.

In writing this book, I came up against a problem of distrust and secrecy. The issue was not the negotiators, almost all of whom opened their doors to me, but rather their method. They were constantly afraid of leaks that could reach their respective publics and interfere with their task. As a result, from 1996 on there are almost no official transcripts for the various talks. Some "non-papers" did circulate, but they were often denied, sometimes even destroyed. All that remains of the conversations themselves are personal notes made by one side or the other. To reconstruct some of the negotiations, I had to find notes taken in real time by as many participants as possible and then cross-check them, keeping in mind the credibility of each informant.

When Ehud Barak decided to risk everything in order to reach a final agreement on peace between Israel and Palestine, I came to believe that this method wasn't enough. A chapter of history was opening, and I couldn't make do with written notes alone. Several top-level negotiators agreed to speak in front of my camera as soon as possible after each important meeting, on the understanding that I would not broadcast or publish anything they told me before the end of 2001. They were Saeb Erekat, Yasir Abed Rabbo, Abu Ala, and Hassan Asfur on the Palestinian side; Gilead Sher and Yossi Beilin for the Israelis; and Miguel Angel Moratinos, the European Union's envoy to the Middle East. These filmed interviews were the basis for a documentary series, part of which was shown on the public television program *Frontline* in June 2002. The complete series was shown on the French television station France 2 in November of that year.[2]

These accounts were supplemented by interviews, also on video, held in 2001 and 2002 with most of the actors on the Israeli–Arab and Israeli–Syrian stage since November 1995. There were the leaders: Yasir Arafat, Shimon Peres, Benjamin Netanyahu, and Ehud Barak. Then the region's top-ranking figures: Amr Moussa, Osama al-Baz, and Muhammad Bassiouny in Egypt, and Walid al-Moualem and Ryad Daoudi in Syria. In the United States: Madeleine Albright, Samuel (Sandy) Berger, Dennis Ross, Martin Indyk, and Robert Malley. In Israel: Yitzhak Mordechai, Amnon Lipkin-Shahak, Uri Savir, Oded Eran, Israel Hasson (the first such interviews he had ever granted), and Gidi Grinstein. On the West Bank and in Gaza: Mohammed Dahlan, Jibril Rajoub, and Marwan Barghouti, who, as I

---

2. This project, parallel to the book, was made possible thanks to the talent and courage of Dan Setton, the director-producer, and Tor Ben Mayor, the director-editor, two outstanding professionals.

write, is being held prisoner after being captured by the Israeli army. In Paris there was Leila Shahid, and in Tel Aviv Terje Larsen, the United Nations representative to the Middle East.

The Wye River summit in 1998 was reconstructed with the help of the participants' notes as well as interviews with them that I filmed in 2000, 2001, and 2002. The Camp David summit, for which there is likewise no transcript, was reconstructed through accounts filmed during the weeks following the meeting, as well as through the notes that several participants, Israeli and Palestinian, took in real time. A close associate of Bill Clinton has been kind enough to look over my work and offer comments. Several other people have taken me into their confidence under the seal of anonymity. They contributed significantly to my investigations. Where no reference is cited for a given remark, the source is one of these confidential communications or my own on-the-scene reporting.

In the last months of the year 2000, as the peace process was rapidly going under, some of my Israeli and Palestinian contacts called and asked me to videotape them. "You are my witness," they said. I thank them all, especially Gilead Sher, who has allowed me to cite freely from his own book on the negotiations he conducted on behalf of Ehud Barak from 1999 to 2001; Miguel Angel Moratinos, whose analyses and advice were of great value to me; and Robert Malley, who was kind enough to share his comments.

Danièle Kriegel-Enderlin, my wife, has been my companion on this occasionally difficult journey. Without her, this book would never have seen the light of day.

Charles Enderlin
Jerusalem
September 30, 2002

Translator's note: The transliteration of Arabic and Hebrew names was made in accordance with the most common current practice and, in given cases, with the way the person in question prefers to spell his name in English.

Chapter 1

Shalom, Chaver

The rally is over. Under loudspeakers blaring rock music, Kings of Israel Square in Tel Aviv has turned into a huge disco floor. Thousands of young people are singing and dancing their joy. And what a surprising evening this has been: after months of lethargy, the peace camp has just demonstrated its power in the face of the right-wing nationalists and the settlers. Yitzhak Rabin, the prime minister, and Shimon Peres, his minister of foreign affairs, looked deeply happy. Didn't Rabin himself try to strike up "The Song of Peace"? That would have been unthinkable only a few years ago. The ex-general, Israel's "Mr. Security," here at a peace rally!

We are the last television crew still on the scene. Jean Frydman, who organized the evening with Shlomo Lahat, the former mayor of Tel Aviv, promised me that he would bring Shimon Peres over to the gate at the top of the stairs. He isn't there. The cameraman and the soundman look at me sourly. They've been invited to a stag party by someone who works for France 2 in Jerusalem, and once again I'm making them stay until the crowd has dispersed.

I'm feeling uneasy. For months now, I've had the sense that something is going to happen. During the recent violent demonstrations against any concessions to the Palestin-

ians, religious extremists have been telling me, "This process isn't going to make it through to completion. People
are getting weapons together." In the Jewish settlement of
Hebron, I'd noticed papers tacked on doors, little posters
with the declaration made by Rabbi Zvi Yehuda Hacohen
Kook, the spiritual leader of the Gush Emunim movement,
after the 1967 conquest of the West Bank and East Jerusalem: "The Torah forbids us to give up even an inch of the
land of Israel. May the hand that signs concession agreements be cut off!"[3]

It is 10:30 P.M. on this November 4, 1995. No sign of
anything unusual. Suddenly, at the top of the stairs, the police break into a run. My crew follows them. A few minutes
later, the soundman calls to me, "Someone shot at Rabin;
I hear he's been wounded." It happened behind the city
hall. I rush over. An ambulance is parked on the right. Over
to the left, dozens of plainclothes and uniformed police are
subduing a young man, pinning him against a wall. Jean
Frydman goes back up the stairs leading to the parking lot
where the drama unfolded. He calls out to me in French,
"A young Jewish terrorist fired three bullets at Rabin. He's
lightly wounded."

The guests and performers who are still standing around
the VIP platform are in a state of shock. Israeli radios are
beginning to broadcast bulletins about what, by agreement,
is still being called a rumor of an assassination attempt
against the prime minister. I call Paris. The news is not on
the wire, and I transmit it to the Jerusalem bureau of Agence
France-Presse, the news service. Then I get a message on
my beeper: "Avigdor Eskin informs you: the *pulsa denura*
prayer has been granted." I had filmed this oddball, Eskin,
a few weeks earlier in Jerusalem, in front of the prime minister's residence. Along with two rabbis, he had been recit

---

3. Enderlin, 1997, p. 257.

ing that cabalistic incantation, a prayer for someone's death. The death in question was Yitzhak Rabin's.

The bulletins are getting more precise by the minute. Rabin is in Ichilov Hospital, apparently gravely wounded. The prognosis is dire. Then, on the way back to Jerusalem, I get a call from my oldest daughter. One of her friends, a nurse at Ichilov, has just told her about the death of the prime minister.

A few minutes later, the radio broadcasts live the statement of Eytan Haber, Rabin's top aide. It's official. Yitzhak Rabin is dead. For the first time in the history of the State of Israel, a head of government has been assassinated because he was conducting peace talks. What comes to my mind are the Israeli–Egyptian peace negotiations of 1956, at which David Ben-Gurion had told the American envoy Robert Anderson, "We Israeli leaders aren't in danger of being murdered if we make peace with Nasser. Didn't Nasser say that he's the one who fears for his life?" In the space of a few hours, Israel has undergone a radical change.

And yet, apart from the climate of violence maintained by the Israeli right, everything was going relatively well. The interim accord with the PLO had been signed six weeks earlier at the White House. There had been no attack for several months, and Rabin, the military man, truly seemed to have changed. He was beginning to express a certain sympathy for the Palestinians. During the July 14 reception at the French embassy in Tel Aviv, he had "interviewed" the Gaza correspondent for France 2 at length. The prime minister of the State of Israel had asked Talal Abu Rahmeh if the atmosphere in Gaza was improving, if girls' skirts were getting a little shorter, that sort of thing.

It's hard for me to grasp what has happened. I had a meeting scheduled with Eytan Haber for the following day, Sunday, November 5, to set up an interview with Rabin for my next book.

WHO KILLED RABIN?

The country is in a state of shock. Hundreds of young people have gathered spontaneously at the scene of the crime. In Jerusalem, about twenty people, in tears, are humming songs and praying in front of the late prime minister's residence. A period of national mourning has begun. In Tel Aviv, the government convenes at the defense ministry. Shimon Peres is named interim prime minister. In the limousine taking him back to Jerusalem along with Uri Savir, chief director of the foreign ministry, and two bodyguards armed with machine guns, he remains deep in thought, saying only, "I feel alone. . . ."

And alone he is. He will be so for a long time.

The assassin's name is Yigal Amir. He is 27 years old, lives north of Tel Aviv, and is a student at Bar Ilan, the religious university. He tells investigators that he coldly decided to kill Rabin in order to prevent new concessions from being made to the Palestinians. Be that as it may, the heads of the security services must very quickly determine whether this man was acting on his own or was part of a plot threatening the stability of the country. The first searches are underway. Shin Bet, the intelligence service, establishes an internal commission of inquiry. Rafi Malka, Shin Bet's former chief of operations, has joined the investigation.

Shimon Peres had set up this commission, but he did not authorize it to investigate the assassin's motives or the climate of incitement to hatred in which the murder took place. Under these constraints, the conclusions issued two days later are purely operational: Shin Bet's protective service, which was supposed to ensure the safety of the prime minister, had been inadequately deployed, failing to cover Yitzhak Rabin's entire route and, in particular, leaving him without cover between the stairs and his car. Three high officials of the service are dismissed.

Reactions from abroad are beginning to reach Israel. In Washington, President Clinton issues an announcement: "A senseless act of violence has deprived the United States and the world of a statesman, a brave fighter for peace." He proclaims a gesture of national mourning: the American flag will be lowered to half-mast in the United States, on all its military bases, on all its ships, and in American embassies and consulates.

In Israel, prior to the funeral, which will be held twenty-four hours later on November 7, the bier has been set up on the esplanade of the Knesset, the Israeli parliament. Hundreds of thousands of weeping mourners file past the coffin.

Kings of Israel Square in Tel Aviv has been transformed into a giant commemoration. Walls, sidewalks, and telephone booths are covered with inscriptions, poems, and letters to Rabin. Adults and teenagers, the latter in great number, gather in front of the memorial candles.

The Rabin generation has just been born. In the years to come, it will lose strength.

Returning to her home in Ramat Aviv late in the evening, the widowed Leah Rabin finds several hundred Israelis of all ages who have come to express their support and offer her their condolences. Thousands of lighted candles cover the sidewalk. She addresses the crowd: "I'm sorry you weren't there when, every Friday, demonstrators from the right used to come and insult us. . . . But you are here this evening, and, for me and my children, that is encouraging. You're showing respect for my husband's memory in a very beautiful way. Thank you. I am truly grateful, and, in his name, I offer you my affection."

The security of all Israeli political figures is being beefed up. Benjamin Netanyahu, leader of the opposition, no longer goes anywhere without bodyguards armed with M16 rifles, their fingers on the trigger.

The ministry of foreign affairs has been devoting all its

efforts to the funeral: 4,000 dignitaries from all over the world are due to arrive tomorrow. Three special planes will bring the American delegation, led by Bill Clinton. King Hussein of Jordan has said he would come, as has the Egyptian head of state Hosni Mubarak, making his first visit to Israel. French president Jacques Chirac and Charles, Prince of Wales, are also expected. In the course of the night all retired ambassadors and diplomats, and all the reservists of the security services, return to their former posts.

Israel has never known anything like this. At Ben-Gurion Airport, near Tel Aviv, airplanes from eighty-six different countries are landing one after another. There is not enough room on the tarmac, and some have to take off again and land in other regional airports. The diplomats in charge of protocol learn of the arrival of some of the delegations from the control tower as flight plans come in.

The funeral will take place on Mount Herzl, where Theodor Herzl, the founder of Zionism, is buried. Everything is symbolic: even part of the Arab world will be there.

Hussein of Jordan can hardly hold back his tears. He has not been back to Jerusalem since the city was conquered in 1967 by Yitzhak Rabin, then commander in chief of the army. And for the first time since the visit of Anwar el-Sadat in 1977, Arab leaders have come to Jerusalem. In addition to Hosni Mubarak, Abdel Latif Filali, the Moroccan head of government, is here, as are several ministers from the Persian Gulf states, including Oman and Qatar.

In front of the coffin, Shimon Peres speaks to the late prime minister:

Last Saturday, the two of us stood side by side, holding hands. Together, we sang "The Song of Peace," and I could feel how thrilled you were. You told me you'd been informed of the risk of an attempted assassination during this impressive rally. We didn't know who the assassin would be, or about the enormity of the attack. But we knew that we should not fear death, that we could not hold back in the quest for peace. . . . I didn't know that these would be the final hours we would be working together in a mutual endeavor that knew no limits.

I sensed that a certain generosity of spirit was surrounding you, that suddenly you could breathe freely at the sight of this sea of friends who had come to support the path you had taken and to applaud you. . . . You had promised to change the priorities [in Israel]. And in fact [everything has changed]. New roads have been paved; unemployment has decreased and exports increased, as have investments; [the budget for] education has doubled; and science has progressed.

But above all, and perhaps here is where we can see the origin of all this, the powerful winds of peace have begun to blow.

Two agreements with our neighbors the Palestinians will enable them to hold democratic elections and will free us from the need to dominate another people, just as you promised.

A cordial peace with Jordan could transform the desert separating us into a meadow of hope for the two nations. The Middle East has reawakened, and a coalition for peace is taking shape: a regional coalition maintained by a worldwide coalition overseen by the leaders of America, Europe, Asia, Africa, and our region, standing before your newly dug grave.

His voice breaking with emotion, Rabin's faithful aide Eytan Haber then addresses the man for whom he had written hundreds of speeches:

Yitzhak, this is the last speech. There will be no others. For a generation, for more than thirty-five years, you have been my guide, my leader, and like a second father to me. Five minutes before the assassin fired his gun, you sang "The Song of Peace" from a song sheet that had been handed to you so that, as you always said, you wouldn't mumble the words. Yitzhak, you know you had a thousand good qualities, a thousand advantages, you were wonderful, but singing was not your strong point. You faked the words just a little bit during the song, and then you folded the page into four parts, as usual, and put it into your jacket pocket.

In the hospital, after the doctors and nurses wept, they handed me the paper they found in your jacket. It was still folded into four parts. Now I would like to read some of the words from the paper, but it is difficult for me. Your blood, your blood, Yitzhak, covers some of the words. Your blood on the page of "The Song of Peace." This is the blood that flowed from your body in the final moments of your life and onto the paper among the lines and the words. From this red page, from the blood that screams out to you, I would now like to read these words, which seem as though they were written only yesterday. After you sang there, and after you and peace were shot. This is the page:

Let the sun rise and give the morning light.
The purest prayer will not bring back to us
The man whose candle was snuffed out, who was bur-
ied in the dust.
A cry of pain won't wake him, won't bring him back.
No one will bring us back from the dead dark pit
Here.—Neither the victory cheer nor songs of praise
will help,
So: sing only a song for peace, do not whisper a prayer.
Better sing a song for peace, with a great shout.

Yitzhak, we already miss you.

Next King Hussein recalls the day when his grandfather was assassinated in the Al-Aqsa Mosque, a few miles from the place where he is standing. "When my time comes," he says, "I hope it will be like my grandfather's and like Yitzhak Rabin's." (His wish will not be fulfilled. He will die of cancer.) On Mount Herzl, the grandson of Abdallah of Jordan pronounces the eulogy of the man he had fought so bitterly and who had become his friend:

You lived as a soldier, you died as a soldier for peace, and I believe it is time for all of us to come forth and speak out openly, not just here today, but for all time to come. We belong to the camp of peace. We believe in peace. We believe that our one God wishes us to live in peace and wishes peace upon us, for these are His teachings to all the followers of the three great monotheistic religions, the children of Abraham.

Then Hosni Mubarak gives a short speech:

Yitzhak Rabin defied the prejudices of the past and dealt forthrightly with the most complicated of problems, namely the Palestinian question. The success he achieved in this regard has laid firm foundations of peaceful coexistence between Palestinians and Israelis in a climate of trust and mutual respect. These achievements have without a doubt established him as a true hero of peace. Only through our unwavering commitment to this goal can we truly honor the memory of this fallen hero. And I would say that the memorial message for Yitzhak Rabin is that we continue what he started. And that is the peace process.

It is obvious that Bill Clinton is deeply moved. He quotes the speech Rabin had given in Washington that past September 28, at the signing ceremony for the interim accord:

"First the good news," Rabin said. "I am the last speaker." But he understood the power of words and symbolism. "Take a look at the stage," he said in Washington. "The king of Jordan, the president of Egypt, Chairman Arafat, and we, the prime minister and foreign minister of Israel, on one platform. Please, take a good, hard look. The sight you see before you was impossible, was unthinkable, just three years ago. Only poets dreamt of it, and, to our great pain, soldiers and civilians went to their deaths to make this moment possible." Those were his words. Today, my fellow citizens of the world, I ask all of you to take a good, hard look at this picture. Look at the leaders from all over the Middle East and around the world who have journeyed here today for Yitzhak Rabin and for peace. Though we no longer hear his deep, booming voice, it is he who has brought us together again here, in word and deed, for peace.

Your prime minister was a martyr for peace, but he was a victim of hate. Surely we must learn from his martyrdom that if people cannot let go of the hatred of their enemies, they risk sowing the seeds of hatred among themselves.

And the president ends with a blessing in Hebrew: "*Shalom, chaver*": "Farewell, friend. May peace be with you." For several years to come, these words will unite the left in Israel.

In the international press, the focus is on Noa Ben Artzi, Rabin's granddaughter, who movingly expresses her grief in a very personal way:

Grandfather, you've always been our hero, and you still are. I want you to know that, in everything I've done,

I've always had you before my eyes. Your respect and your love have accompanied us every step of the way, and on every road. We lived in the light of your values. You have never abandoned us, and now they have abandoned you, my eternal hero, . . . and there is nothing I can do to save you, you who are so wonderful. . . .

That afternoon, Shimon Peres takes Bill Clinton back to the airport. Clinton tells the interim prime minister that he'd like to have a minute alone with him in his airplane:

Have you been kept posted? Yitzhak Rabin made an oral promise to us that he would agree to undertake negotiations on the basis of a full Israeli withdrawal from the Golan, that is, to the line of June 4, 1967, on condition that the Syrians agree to security arrangements that are satisfactory from Israel's point of view and to a full peace including an exchange of ambassadors and the opening of borders.

Peres is surprised: "No I wasn't informed," he said. "But all of Yitzhak's commitments hold true for me as well. I'm bound by all his promises."[4] Clinton leaves, satisfied. His intention is to take advantage of the atmosphere in the region after Rabin's murder and quickly get Israeli–Syrian negotiations back on track.

THE STATE OF NEGOTIATIONS

Yasir Arafat is conspicuous by his absence at the funeral. The Israelis have not allowed him to make this trip, judging that his presence would not only pose an insurmount-

---

4. Videotaped interview with Shimon Peres, October 8, 2001, Tel Aviv.

able security problem but would also arouse hostility in the Israeli political class. The PLO is represented by a delegation led by Abu Mazen, Arafat's aide.

The memory of the solemn signing of the interim accord exactly six weeks earlier in the White House is still in everyone's mind. This ceremony was truly one of hope, held in the presence of King Hussein, President Mubarak, the Spanish prime minister (as the European representative), and the Russian foreign minister. At that time, Rabin had addressed the Palestinians:

> We who have killed and have been killed, let us walk at your side towards a common future. . . . It is important to me to tell you, President Arafat, leader of the Palestinians, that together we must not let the land flowing with milk and honey be flooded with tears. Do not let that happen. If all the partners in the peace process do not unite against the angel of death that is terrorism, all that will be left of this ceremony is a souvenir photo, and soon rivers of hatred will flood the Middle East.

Arafat had made an equally stirring speech condemning violence, "not only because it is morally reprehensible, but also because it undermines Palestinian efforts toward peace and toward our political and national aspirations. . . . From this day forward, we proclaim that we shall do all we can to avert every threat, whatever its source, against the life of any innocent Palestinian, any innocent Israeli."

Arafat had not forgotten the anger that came over him when, on September 19 at Taba, in Egypt, he saw the proposed map of the West Bank as envisioned by the Israelis: the Palestinians were to receive some isolated mini-cantons in a sea controlled by Israel. In the end, though, after some slight modifications, he had agreed to the partitioning of the territory into three zones.

The seven large Palestinian cities would become autonomous: Jenin, Qalqilya, Tulkarm, Nablus, Ramallah, Bethlehem, and a part of Hebron. This would be Area A, covering 2 percent of the West Bank, and the Palestinian Authority would be in charge of its security and civil administration. In Area B, 26 percent of the West Bank, the Autonomous Authority would be in charge of administration but not of security, which would remain Israel's sole responsibility. Area C, 72 percent of the West Bank, would comprise military bases, all the settlements, and all state-owned land. Israel would continue to be sovereign there. In Hebron, because of the presence of 400 Jewish settlers living in the area of the Tomb of the Patriarchs, one sector of the city would be granted a special status, according to which Israel would keep the upper hand in matters of security. Moreover, none of the 150 Jewish settlements in occupied territory would be evacuated.[5]

Still, it was Arafat's hope that this move would increase the extent of the liberated territory sixfold, after the formation of the enclave of Jericho and the evacuation of 80 percent of the Gaza Strip in May 1994. And the agreement promised three new Israeli withdrawals from the West Bank, movements that were to occur eighteen months after the election of the Palestinian legislative council. Although the size of these withdrawals and their geography had yet to be determined, Arafat hoped to get virtually all of the West Bank in future negotiations.

A number of foreign leaders present at Rabin's funeral tell Peres that he must quickly follow through on the interim accord. He replies that this is certainly his intention.

The news of Rabin's death comes to Yossi Beilin in New York. He is devastated. The secret talks he has been hold-

---

5. See www.fmep.org.charts/chart98114.html.

ing with Abu Mazen had ended, four days earlier, in the drawing up of the Stockholm document, a plan for a definitive agreement between Israel and the Palestinians. The most important part of the work had been done in Sweden and Tel Aviv by Yair Hirschfeld and Ron Pundak on the Israeli side,[6] and, for the Palestinians, by two academics living in London, Ahmed Khalidi and Hussein Agha. The text was to be submitted to Rabin, Peres, and Arafat.

As Beilin later describes the document, two elements made it especially attractive to the Israelis. One was the creation of a Palestinian capital called Al-Qods at Abu Dis, east of the city limits of Jerusalem, the eastern part of the city remaining under Israeli control. The other was the resolution of the problem of the Palestinian refugees of 1948, who could now ask to be repatriated to the West Bank or Gaza, though not on Israeli territory. In addition, the vast majority of them would be compensated for the property they had left behind in Israel.

The Palestinians who took part in drawing up this document will give a somewhat different version of it. Yes, they will say, the issue during the first meetings was to create the framework for a definitive accord. But later on the Israelis suggested putting together a document aimed at supporting the electoral campaign of the Labor Party. According to Hussein Agha,

> it was a sort of peace platform, designed to avoid protests from the Palestinian side and to persuade the Israeli public that an agreement was possible. An agreement that would respect Yitzhak Rabin's famous lines in the sand:

---

6. Hirschfeld and Pundak were the two Israeli academics appointed by Yossi Beilin to begin the secret Oslo negotiations in 1993. The Palestinian Hassan Asfur, another Oslo veteran, took part intermittently in the discussions on the Stockholm document.

no withdrawal to the cease-fire lines before the Six-Day War; Jerusalem must remain the undivided capital of Israel; no foreign troops between the Mediterranean and the Jordan, the river marking Israel's secure boundary; no heavy influx of Palestinian refugees into Israel so as to preserve the nature of the state; retention of most of the Jewish settlements in the occupied territories.[7]

THE ULTRA-ORTHODOX CONDEMN RABIN

But what most preoccupies the new head of government is the scene in Israel itself. The emotion stirred up by Yigal Amir's act has faded, and the principal fault lines of Israeli society could well reappear. There can be no doubt that the encouragement of violence in religious circles and the nationalistic right was a major component of the atmosphere leading to Rabin's assassination. Shimon Peres has the file in his hands: judgments based on *halacha* (Jewish law), handed down by certain rabbis from the settlement movement, can be considered actual incitements to murder. This is why, on the advice of Avi Gil (his chief of staff) and Uri Savir, Peres decided to limit the work of the judicial commission investigating the circumstances of the assassination and did not authorize it to look at the problem of incitement to violence.

And yet the case against the religious right is strong. It turns out that the heads of the rabbinical council for the West Bank settlements had looked into ways to have the Rabin government condemned by the ancient definitions of *din rodef* and *din mosser*. According to religious law, a Jew

---

7. Interview with Hussein Agha, January 3, 2002, St. Anthony's College, Oxford University.

who betrays his community or endangers the lives of other Jews is a *mosser*. He must be condemned if he provides non-Jews with information about the community or sells or gives them Jewish property. Since the land of Israel is considered the sacred property of the Jewish people, the death penalty is applicable in this case. The term *rodef* refers to someone about to commit or abet a murder. His immediate execution is intended to save a Jewish life. According to strict Jewish law, this is the only situation in which a Jew is entitled to kill another Jew without a trial.

In February 1995, rabbis living in the settlements had sent the following memorandum to Israel's two chief grand rabbis, the grand rabbis of the country's major cities, and the members of the councils of Torah sages of the ultra-Orthodox parties:

Ever since the signing of the Oslo accord [August 19, 1993],[8] the number of Israelis killed in attacks has been three times greater than during the years of the Intifada. The more concessions this evil government makes to the Arabs, the more attacks there are in Israel, especially against the inhabitants of Judea–Samaria. There are no localities where people have not been killed or wounded. . . .

At the present time, with the implementation of the Oslo accord and the granting of land and roads to the Palestinian Authority, the danger has become even greater. Terrorists can plan attacks with impunity now that the territories have become autonomous. The government of Israel has equipped Palestinian police with rifles, and the police can shoot at vehicles carrying soldiers and citizens without being arrested. They are becoming bolder all the time. But this is not all. Hamas militants

---

8. For the texts of the Oslo and Wye River accords, see the Appendix.

opposing the accord are carrying out attacks without police intervention. Even the men of Fatah are mounting attacks. . . .

Men and women, dwellers in Judea–Samaria and other parts of Eretz Yisrael [the land of Israel], have asked us what judgment must be handed down against this evil government and against the man who is in charge of it.

Are they to be considered accomplices to the murders committed by the terrorists? They are in fact responsible for strengthening these terrorists, for having given them weapons, for having authorized the entry of Palestinian police into Gaza and Jericho, and this after they promised, at the signing of the accord, that peace would prevail. Yet the inhabitants of Judea–Samaria and the heads of the opposition had issued a warning, saying that murderers must not be trusted or taken at their word. . . . Are they not to be judged according to *halacha*? And, if it is proved that they are accomplices to murder, what ought to be the sentence?

And, the rabbis continued, "Should not the government and the prime minister be subject to the law of *din mosser*, since they are giving the land of Israel, the property of the people of Israel, to the gentiles?"[9]

At the same time, other religious leaders in the settlement movement, in particular Shlomo Aviner, rabbi of the Beit-El settlement on the West Bank and head of a Talmudic school in Jerusalem's Old City, had tried to calm this debate, fearing that the discussion of *din rodef* would have "dramatic consequences."[10]

---

9. Lior and colleagues, 1996, p. 121.
10. Sprinzak, 1999, p. 256.

Carmi Gilon is a specialist on Jewish extremism. The head of Shin Bet, he had handed in his resignation a few days after Rabin's assassination, but this gesture was refused by Shimon Peres. It was Gilon who, in 1984, had conducted the investigation of the Jewish terrorist network formed by militants from the settlement movement, militants who had launched attacks against the Palestinians and were planning to blow up the holy mosques of Jerusalem. Uneasy ever since the signing of the Oslo accords, Gilon was eager to meet with all the opposition leaders in parliament and ask them to calm down their followers: street violence, he explained, could end in political murder. At that time, Jewish terrorists were supported by only a few marginal plotters and were not yet being encouraged by the rabbis with street credibility. Thinkers from the religious right, Gilon was convinced, believed that the redemption of the Jewish people would come about through a gradual evolution, not a revolution.[11]

But Shin Bet was still anxious about the mounting level of unrest among ordinary Israelis since 1993. A few weeks before the murder of Rabin, Gilon had convened the country's leading journalists and asked them to lower the pitch. "They didn't think I meant it," he would say later. In May 1995, Shin Bet had even bought an armored Cadillac for the heightened security of the prime minister. A correspondent from a television channel filmed it when it arrived at the port of Haifa, noting sardonically, "A $250,000 Cadillac! Isn't a Chevy good enough for the head of government?" "You'll never get me into that car," Rabin had told Gilon. Like Peres, he refused to wear a bullet-proof vest. Gilon also "had a lot of trouble trying to convince the bodyguards that they had to face dangers other than Arab terrorism."

---

11. This comment and the following passages are from an interview with Carmi Gilon, September 5, 1999, Tel Aviv.

But now, according to Avi Gil, a common denominator for both right and left has to be found. The Jewish settlers living in occupied territory have to be reassured, but at the same time the religious contingent has to grant the Oslo process a certain legitimacy. This is why, as I learn in interviews with Gil and Peres, Beilin is preparing for discreet negotiations with the National Religious Party, and Peres will have several meetings with Benjamin Netanyahu, the leader of the nationalist right. A number of editorialists will later say that, in so doing, Peres saved the political career of the man who was to beat him in the next elections.

ARAFAT AND PERES CONTINUE THE PEACE PROCESS

For the time being, the Israeli government intends to show that the agreements with the Palestinians will be implemented to the last detail. On November 13, 1995, the army evacuates Jenin, in the north of the West Bank. That city's sizable jail, transferred to the Palestinian Authority, immediately becomes a place of pilgrimage for hundreds of former Palestinian detainees. Jibril Rajoub, head of preventive security for the Palestinians on the West Bank, spent long years there. He will choose not to take part in the visit.

On November 27, Ehud Barak begins his career as a diplomat. The former chief of staff did not get the defense ministry, which he had been coveting since Rabin's death, but was put in charge of foreign affairs. He arrives, late, in Barcelona, where he is to take part in the Mediterranean Conference. To his Spanish counterpart, Javier Solana, he declares straight out:

Ehud Barak is my name, and I want to be prime minister of Israel one day. I can't go back to my country with a declaration containing a paragraph enshrining the principle of land in exchange for peace and recognizing the Palestinians' right to self-determination. It's also unacceptable to mention the armed struggle of Hezbollah. . . . As far as I'm concerned, what's going on is terrorism. You have to modify this declaration.

Solana and Miguel Angel Moratinos, the director general of his ministry, look at one another, aghast. Shimon Peres in person had approved the text, but now everything will have to be renegotiated tonight. The Palestinians are furious: this document had been the subject of many discussions, and they were counting on it. But Farouk al-Shareh, the Syrian foreign minister, turns out to be accommodating. And, in the wee hours of the morning, the new resolution will be accepted by all.

It will, however, remain in the desk drawers of Middle Eastern diplomacy.

On December 7, Shimon Peres and Yasir Arafat meet at the Erez checkpoint, in the north of the Gaza Strip. The Israeli prime minister promises to pursue the implementation of the agreements. Israel is getting ready to free 1,000 imprisoned Palestinians, and the number of Palestinian workers authorized to come to Israel will now be increased to 9,500. But, most important, four days later the Israeli army withdraws from Nablus, where 1,200 Palestinian police are deployed.

On the 15th, in Washington, Secretary of State Warren Christopher announces that Syria is prepared to resume immediate negotiations with Israel. Bill Clinton has told Hafez el-Assad of Peres' willingness to reach a rapid agreement. In Cairo, the Fatah leader Hani el-Hassan is conducting secret negotiations with representatives of Hamas, so that they will not launch a new attack or issue an appeal for the boycott of the Palestinian elections slated for the following month. On the same day, the Israeli army withdraws from Bethlehem, which is transferred to the control of the Palestinian Authority. On December 24, Yasir Arafat goes there to attend Christmas mass, which, for the first time since 1967, is held without the presence of representatives of the Israel military authorities. Forty-eight hours later, Ramallah, the last large city on the West Bank, is handed over to Palestinian control.

THE ASSASSINATION OF "THE ENGINEER"

At the beginning of January, Peres meets with the heads of Shin Bet: Carmi Gilon; Israel Hasson, who is in charge of the West Bank; and Avi Diechter, who heads the Gaza branch. The security services have pinpointed the place in Gaza where Yehiah Ayyash is hiding. Nicknamed "the Engineer," this Islamist is considered public enemy number one by Israel. Leader of the Ezzedin al-Qassam commando unit, the armed branch of Hamas, he is the man who organized the first suicide attacks against the Israelis. He must be brought down.

In several meetings with Yasir Arafat, Gilon had advised him to incapacitate Ayyash, stating that he would thereby give the Israelis "the strongest evidence that he was fighting terrorism." Peres himself had made this request to Arafat, who replied, "Ayyash is not in Gaza; he's in Sudan!" Colonel Mohammed Dahlan, director of Palestinian security in Gaza, had finally admitted that the terrorist was indeed on his home turf, where, moreover, his mother, wife, and son still lived. Realizing that the Israelis were ready to move into action, he had strongly advised them against this.[12]

---

12. Mr. Dahlan maintains that he did not know exactly where in Gaza Ayyash was hiding.

The meeting with the men of Shin Bet takes place in Tel Aviv in the absence of the prime minister's political advisers, who are never allowed to participate in this type of discussion. When it comes to operations that are believed to have important political consequences—those being planned by the military or those the special services are getting ready to carry out—it is traditional in Israel for the head of government to be accompanied only by his aide-de-camp. And this operation is clearly going to have major repercussions on the talks underway with the Palestinians.

Peres very quickly sees that he has no choice. Israel Hasson believes that the Engineer poses a genuine strategic threat to Israel.[13] The bloody attacks he has organized over the past twelve months were aimed at overturning the peace process, and new suicide attacks could be disastrous. Peres approves the "neutralization" of Ayyash. "When you decide to fight terrorism," his advisers from Shin Bet tell him, "you have to be ready to pay the price. If you're afraid of the reactions, don't fight terrorism." "Buses might get blown up in this country," someone is reported to have said. "They're going to get blown up in any case," another participant in the debate retorted. Avi Gil will later use another argument: "What would Israeli opinion say if, after a terrorist attack, people learned that Peres had refused to liquidate Ayyash out of concern for the elections?" And besides, the suicide-bomber phenomenon had to be contained at all costs.

Sources inside the Israeli security services will deny reports that Ayyash was ready to give himself up to the Palestinian police. In Gaza, however, General Nasser Youssef has suggested that the correspondent from France 2 film and interview Ayyash at the moment of his surrender, which is to take place in the course of the following weeks. On

---

13. Videotaped interview with Israel Hasson, January 10, 2002, Jerusalem.

January 5, the Engineer is killed in the explosion of a port-
able phone. He was hiding in the house of a cousin of his,
who had fled to Israel several hours before the death.
Gaza holds what amounts to a national funeral for the
Engineer. A hundred thousand people throng the road along
which the cortege passes. All the Islamic leaders of Gaza are
there, together with representatives of the Palestinian Authority. Yasir Arafat offers his condolences in person to the
family of Israel's enemy. The Israeli right will be sure to
make use of these pictures: for them, this is the proof that
Arafat is not fighting terrorism. That very evening, graffiti
symbolizing the explosion of Israeli buses appear on the
walls of Gaza. But Hamas does not react immediately. The
Islamic organization will hold off until the Palestinian elections, which are to take place on January 20, 1996.

Carmi Gilon, the director of Shin Bet, has just been
warned by the judicial investigatory commission that he
could be considered partially responsible for the errors of his
service that permitted Rabin's assassination. Once again he
sends a letter of resignation, effective tomorrow, to Shimon
Peres:

A few days after the murder, I came before you and
before the government. Because of the failure of the security service that permitted the murder of the prime
minister, I handed in my resignation. . . . You did not
accept it. . . .

The heart of Shin Bet's activity concerns the Palestinian issue. The service is in the vanguard of the combat
against terrorism, even as it contributes to the dialogue
with the former enemy in order to establish security in
cooperation with the Palestinians in the context of the
new reality that has come about in our region. Among
the numerous missions it has had to accomplish, the service has had the aim of neutralizing Yehiah Ayyash, not

only to settle a bloody score but above all to cut off a hand that would have perpetrated many new attacks.

This time, Peres accepts the resignation. Carmi Gilon leaves the scene. In wiping out the Engineer, he feels that he has rehabilitated Shin Bet.

THE SYRIAN INTERLUDE

On December 4, 1995, Dennis Ross comes to Jerusalem to give Peres the details of the negotiations with Syria.[14] On the 11th, Clinton telephones Hafez el-Assad to tell him that Peres has confirmed the "deposit," Rabin's promise that he would accept a total withdrawal from the Golan if all of Israel's conditions in matters of security were respected and relations between the two countries normalized. For Damascus, this means that Israel is ready to withdraw to the line of cease-fire before the Six-Day War, that is, before June 4, 1967.

The history of this secret engagement on Rabin's part, which even those close to him were entirely unaware of, deserves to be told. In early November 1992, Rabin had declared for the first time: "The depth of the withdrawal will reflect the depth of the peace." The Americans undertook an analysis of this remark during their discussions, explaining that the formula meant: "A full withdrawal from the Golan will correspond to a full peace." According to the British journalist Patrick Seale, who had access to the letters and transcripts of the Syrian–American talks, on August 4, 1993 Secretary of State Warren Christopher sent Assad

---

14. Seale, 1999, p. 1. See also MEMRI, 1999.

a message from Rabin: "Negotiations could take place on the basis of full Israeli withdrawal, on condition that the Syrians agree to security arrangements that are satisfactory from Israel's point of view, and to full peace, including an exchange of ambassadors and the opening of borders." The Israeli prime minister added that this commitment must remain strictly confidential.

Rabin was also hoping for American involvement in the security arrangements, and he stipulated that the Israeli retreat from the Golan be spread out over five years. His expectation was that the peace treaty would be subject to a referendum in Israel. Assad accepted the principle of total peace in exchange for total withdrawal. But he called for the evacuation of the Golan in the six months following the agreement and demanded that the line of June 4, 1967 be mentioned explicitly.

Rabin refused. But, after Warren Christopher and Dennis Ross shuttled between Jerusalem and Damascus several times during the month of April, he finally gave Christopher the verbal promise demanded by Assad: there would be a retreat to the line of June 4, 1967. But Christopher was supposed to keep the promise "on deposit," to be used only if the Syrians met Israeli requirements with regard to security and the nature of the peace. Bill Clinton did not keep his word: to Rabin's great displeasure, he had described the "deposit" in a June 6, 1995 letter to Assad.[15]

The final contacts with Yitzhak Rabin in the Syrian matter were stormy. Dennis Ross worked out a compromise proposal involving total retreat from the Golan and establishment of American observers and detection posts on both sides of the border. But Rabin had flown into a rage, and the proposal was buried.

---

15. Seale, 1999, p. 1, and MEMRI, 1999.

The new Israeli–Syrian negotiations take place at Wye Plantation, part of the Aspen Institute in Maryland. The Americans want to calm down the atmosphere between the two delegations. Meals are to be taken in common, and the press will be kept at a distance. Shimon Peres, who hopes for an agreement, sends Uri Savir, director general of the foreign ministry in Jerusalem, to head the team of Israeli negotiators alongside Itamar Rabinovich, the Israeli ambassador. The Syrians have agreed in principle to intensive discussions, and Warren Christopher has the feeling that this time an accord is on the horizon.

The talks are to extend over ten weeks, concentrated in three series of meetings. The first begins on December 27, 1995. It is limited to civilians. Walid Moualem, Syria's ambassador to Washington, is accompanied by Michael Wabha, chief of staff for foreign minister Farouk el-Shareh, and by Ryad el-Daoudi, an expert on international law. In addition to Savir and Rabinovich, the Israeli delegation includes Yoel Singer, legal adviser to the Oslo accord, who takes up his job again; Yossi Vardi, a businessman specializing in regional projects; and experts from the planning department of the general staff and from the foreign ministry in Jerusalem.

The aim of this first round of talks is to define peace. Singer submits a document including eighteen points of possible agreement in a number of areas including telecommunications, cultural exchange, diplomatic and consular relations, and the canceling of all boycotts. At the end of several days of discussion, the Syrian position is clear: there is no question of entering into the details of normalizing relations with Israel. Moualem bridles at the formula specifying that "the two countries will have normal peacetime relations." The Israelis will have to be content with a new reality involving an exchange of ambassadors and the possibility of a route to Turkey passing through Syria.[16]

Savir sets forth Peres' vision of a Middle East in which peace will be based on accelerated economic development. He realizes that the Clinton administration has not prepared a file anticipating massive economic aid to Syria, although this is a crucial element in peace negotiations. As it happens, the White House is under pressure from Congress, where lobbyists from the Israeli right are solidly entrenched. Yossi Ben Aharon, director general of the prime minister's office during Yitzhak Shamir's administration, has won several senators over to the belief "that Israel has to be saved from itself and prevented from making concessions that would be disastrous for its security."

And, in fact, it will be very hard to get a green light for the deployment of American forces on the Golan, or even for aid to Syria, still considered to be a state that encourages terrorism. What Savir proposes, therefore, is setting up a group of private investors to undertake major projects in Syria. There will be a meeting on this subject on February 23, 1996. It will not have a sequel.

The Wye Plantation talks devoted to the military issue begin on January 24. They quickly reach an impasse. Savir, Rabinovich, and the Israeli generals—Uzi Dayan and Danny Yatom, who has become the head of Peres' defense department—understand that the exchanges Warren Christopher held in Damascus had no effect on the Syrian delegation, and that, in particular, there was no further intention of discussing the role of the Syrian army or the deployment of forces on either side of the border after the conclusion of an accord. Thus the talks focus on the only document on which the generals of the two parties have managed to reach agreement.

---

16. Rabinovich, 1998, p. 267.

Dated May 24, 1994, it is entitled "Aspirations and Aims of Security Arrangements." Here it is, in its sometimes murky formulation, as conveyed to me by one of my sources. Each word was the subject of lengthy discussion:

Security is a legitimate need for both sides. As far as security is concerned, no complaint should be made and no guarantee should be asked for at the expense of the other side.

Security arrangements should be equal, mutual, and reciprocal on both sides. The purpose of the security arrangements is to ensure a quality of overall security. In the context of the state of peace between Syria and Israel, and if during the negotiations on security arrangements it appears that the implementation of equality as a principle, as [far as] geography is concerned, with regard to a particular arrangement is impossible or too difficult, the experts of the two sides will discuss that difficulty, resolve it by modifying it or supplementing or subtracting from [it] by mutually agreed solutions.

The two sides acknowledge that security arrangements should be reached through mutual agreement and as such should be consistent with the principle of sovereignty and the territorial integrity of each side.

Security arrangements should be confined to the relevant areas on both sides of the boundary between the two countries.

As Walid Moualem, who is overseeing the Wye negotiation, notes: "In any case, the strategic balance cannot be assessed in one sector alone but must be considered in a larger perspective. Israel has a definite advantage over Syria by virtue of the superiority of its air force, its strategic relations with the United States, its nuclear capacity. . . ."[17] A debate on this issue, he says, would get nowhere.

In other areas more progress is made. Moualem will state, for example, that he is in accord with Savir on the schedule for the negotiations: both men are eager to finalize the points of agreement before June 1996, so as to draw up the peace treaty between Israel and Syria by September at the latest.[18] This is why, he will later report, he was unpleasantly surprised when, on January 25, 1996, Christopher informed him of Peres' decision to hold the elections that had been anticipated in Israel.

And the date Moualem mentions, January 25, is surprising. Peres wanted to know whether a historic summit with Hafez el-Assad could be organized in the near future, but Christopher did not ask Assad about this until February 5, in Damascus. Nevertheless, Peres understands that the Wye Plantation talks are going to go on for months, and he is afraid his popularity will suffer. On February 11, he decides that the Israelis will go to the polls not in November but on May 29, 1996.

This is how Dennis Ross describes the incident:

We wanted to establish a schedule for the negotiations, and our goal was definitely to finish within the year. But Shimon sent a message to Assad via our intermediary: Do you want to go fast and far, or slowly? Fast and far meant reaching a quick agreement and therefore a summit meeting with Assad. In that case, he was willing to push back the elections. If not, if they were still at the level of the negotiators, [Peres] had nothing special to

---

17. Rabinovich, 1998, p. 278.
18. Butler, 1997, pp. 81–94.

expect from the talks. Assad decided not to negotiate [directly with Peres].[19]

According to the American diplomats who meet with him, Assad is furious at the Israeli decision. He realizes that serious negotiations with Israel are going to be slowed down by the electoral campaign.

At Wye Plantation, however, new sessions of the talks are soon interrupted by the dramatic events unfolding in Israel.

HAMAS RETALIATES

On the West Bank and in Gaza, Hamas has sworn to avenge Ayyash but at first observes a truce—officially, it is said, so as not to disturb the Palestinian elections set for January 20. The Islamists are most certainly going to boycott the voting, but they ask their militants to put themselves on the voting lists in anticipation of future municipal elections in which they have decided to take part. Only Samikha Khalil, in her seventies but still La Pasionaria of the neo-Marxist Popular Front for the Liberation of Palestine, dares to defy Arafat and sets her sights on the presidency of the Palestinian Authority in the name of her opposition to the Oslo accord. She will make a respectable showing under the circumstances, but the head of the PLO will be elected with 87 percent of the vote.

Six hundred and seventy-two candidates have presented themselves to the voters, who must choose the eighty-eight deputies of the Palestinian legislative council. The voting takes place under the scrutiny of observers from the European Union, and participation is important: 86 percent of

---

19. Videotaped interview with Dennis Ross, February 10, 2002, Washington.

registered voters in Gaza go to the polls, 68 percent on the West Bank, only 35 percent in Jerusalem, where someone has started the rumor that people who vote will lose Israeli Social Security. Al Fatah gets fifty seats. The small Samaritan community of Nablus gets one deputy. Of the remaining seats, sixteen go to militants of Fatah, whose candidacies were not endorsed by Arafat. This is the first sign that local activists are becoming increasingly discontent with the leadership in Tunis, which is reluctant to share power with them.

In spite of everything, however, Arafat sees his legitimacy confirmed. At this time, the Authority controls 6 percent of the land on the West Bank and a bit more than two-thirds of the Gaza Strip.

On February 25, a suicide bomber blows himself up in a Jerusalem bus. There are twenty-six dead and forty-six wounded. A few hours later, at a hitchhiking station for soldiers near Ashkelon, another suicide volunteer dies while setting off his belt of explosives, killing one Israeli and injuring thirty-two others. Responsibility for the attacks is claimed by the "New Generation Yehiah Ayyash Brigade," an offshoot of the Ezzedin al-Qassam commando unit, the armed branch of Hamas, but one that is said to take orders from outside the country. The organization has chosen the timing deliberately: two years ago to the day, a Jewish terrorist, Baruch Goldstein, had staged a massacre at the Tomb of the Patriarchs in Hebron. Twenty-nine Muslims were killed.

Shimon Peres orders the cordoning off of Palestinian territories and halts the negotiations on the withdrawal from Hebron scheduled for May 15. The far right and other rightists demonstrate furiously in Jerusalem. Exactly one week after these attacks, there is a new explosion in a bus from the same line in Jerusalem: ten are dead, a dozen injured. Once again, the terrorist is a member of Hamas. The following day, a human bomb from Islamic Jihad sets off an explosion in the Dizengoff commercial center in Tel Aviv: fourteen dead, one hundred and fifty-seven injured. The leaders of the organization in Gaza are surprised by this attack against civilians; in past years, Jihad has been careful to choose only military targets. They contact headquarters in Damascus and are told, "Since Fathi Shikaki was assassinated, our policy has changed."[20]

Polls show a major drop in Peres' popularity. A victory by his challenger, Benjamin Netanyahu, is no longer out of the question. Swift measures have to be taken if new attacks are to be avoided. Military personnel, Shin Bet agents, and other experts come up with all sorts of ideas that, after ripe reflection, are dismissed. (One suggestion, for example, is to announce that the bodies of suicide bombers will be buried wrapped in the skin of pigs, an impure animal for Muslims.) Tsahal, the Israeli defense force, cordons off Palestinian areas even more tightly. As a result, 60,000 workers cannot reach Israel, and unemployment is rife.

Arafat realizes that his policy of entente with Hamas has failed, and that the suicide attacks may lose the elections for the Labor Party, his partners in the peace talks. He therefore orders his security forces to neutralize Hamas. On March 5, dozens of Islamist institutions—kindergartens, charitable organizations, mosques—are searched and placed under the control of his administration.

Persuading his men to fight for the security of the State of Israel was no easy task for Colonel Mohammed Dahlan:

All security work with the Israeli side is unpopular from the Palestinian point of view. It's especially com-

---

20. Shikaki had been murdered on Malta by Israeli agents on October 26, 1995.

plicated for personnel in preventive security, because 90 percent of the members, officers, and cadres of preventive security belong to Fatah, and they spent time in Israeli jails during the first Intifada. Nevertheless, we managed to convince those officers and those cadres that steps like these had to be taken in order to impose control and respect for the Palestinian Authority among the Palestinians.[21]

Israel Hasson, one of the leaders of Shin Bet, will later say that 2,000 militants were taken into custody. In his view, "The coordination with our services at that time was what it should have been."[22] In the territories it controls, the Israeli army arrests hundreds of suspects.

The Palestinians accuse Iran of promoting the terrorism of Hamas and Islamic Jihad. Western intelligence services confirm the link, and European diplomacy intervenes with Tehran. As Dennis Ross puts it, "We had information to the effect that the Iranians were encouraging this terrorism, and both the French and the Germans passed along the following message to them: 'If you want to have contacts with the outside world, terrorism in Israel must cease immediately.'"[23] And German chancellor Helmut Kohl addresses a personal letter to the Iranian president, a message that, if Shimon Peres is to be believed, achieves its goal.

But the external directorship of Hamas is located in Jordan. Mohammed Dahlan, the Palestinian head of security in Gaza, says he has proof that the attacks against the Israelis are planned in Amman. He informs George Tenet, director of the CIA, who visits the Palestinian territories on

---

21. Videotaped interview with Mohammed Dahlan, November 7, 2001, Gaza.
22. Videotaped interview with Israel Hasson, December 9, 2001, Jerusalem.
23. Videotaped interview with Dennis Ross, February 10, 2002, Washington.

March 9. Dennis Ross will meet Hussein of Jordan a few days later, hand him the file, and ask him to neutralize the Palestinian Islamist leaders in his kingdom.

Distressed about the implications of these attacks for the peace process, Bill Clinton and Hosni Mubarak organize a summit of "peacemakers" at Sharm el-Sheik on March 13. Never before has such a meeting been held in the Middle East. Bill Clinton, Russian president Boris Yeltsin, French president Jacques Chirac, John Major from Great Britain, Helmut Kohl from Germany, King Hassan II of Morocco, the Tunisian and Canadian prime ministers, emirs from the Gulf States, and leading diplomats from Saudi Arabia, Algeria, and other countries come together under the patronage of the Egyptian president to express their support for the peace process and for Shimon Peres, whom they are meeting publicly for the first time.

But the final image of this unprecedented meeting—kings, heads of state, and ministers hand in hand, the Israeli prime minister standing at center stage—will be totally misunderstood by the Israeli journalists at the summit: all they will see here, oddly enough, is a strategy aimed at the election. And with that, this extraordinary event will have no impact on Israeli opinion.

Bill Clinton does not let matters rest. No sooner is the summit over than he heads for Jerusalem on an official visit. The timing with regard to Peres' electoral campaign is perfect. A memorial ceremony at the tomb of Yitzhak Rabin, a meeting with Israeli high-school students, and similar events are broadcast on Israeli television with the prime minister appearing for hours on end at the side of the president of the United States. There is an unintended result: polls show that, if he were a candidate, Clinton would win the election in Israel.

As luck would have it, at this very moment the calendar reminds Israelis of the tragic assassination on November 4,

1995. For, on March 27, the trial of Yigal Amir, Rabin's murderer, comes to a close. Judge Edmund Levy, president of the court, reads the sentence:

The defendant before us, and people like him, are a terrible nightmare for all those who hope for democracy, whatever camp they may belong to. Nevertheless, this was not a political trial. . . . It is not the defendant's concept of the sanctity of the land of Israel that was judged, nor the issue of whether the measures adopted by the government of Israel since the signing of the Oslo accord were correct. The only question we had to answer was whether the defendant was guilty of the crime of assassination as defined by the Penal Code. We have replied in the affirmative.

The debate taking place in our midst is a difficult one, since it brings up fundamental issues for the State of Israel, not only for our generation but especially for future generations. All of us feel genuine and sincere anxiety for peace in the nation, on the one hand, and peace with our neighbors, on the other.

As is the custom in a democratic state, this debate must be conducted with firmness but also with respect for others and with tolerance, the latter being especially necessary when unpopular opinions are expressed by minorities. That is not all. The rupture within the heart of the nation will not be healed by words alone, but above all by acts, and in the first place acts by the leaders of all the political parties. These leaders must not fail to repeat, night and day, "Wise men, be careful of what you say."

Deciding unanimously, the three judges condemn Yigal Amir to life in prison for the assassination, a sentence to which another is added: six years for having wounded one of the former prime minister's bodyguards.

THE GRAPES OF WRATH IN SOUTH LEBANON

As far as security is concerned, cooperation with the Palestinian Authority is finally paying off. But although attacks in Israel have practically ceased, the situation in South Lebanon is getting worse. Tsahal, which occupies a safety zone there a dozen kilometers deep, has to deal with guerrilla warfare waged by Hezbollah, the pro-Iranian militia. On March 30, two Lebanese civilians are killed during an Israeli operation carried out by Tsahal on the border of the sector. Hezbollah responds by firing Katyusha rockets at northern Israel, wounding one civilian. On April 8, there is another incident: two Lebanese teenagers are killed by an explosive charge said to have been set by the South Lebanese Army, a military force under Israeli command.[24]

That night, twenty-five rockets are fired at Israeli territory. Thirty-six civilians are injured. The entire Israeli population has to seek shelter. The following day, a soldier is killed during a suicide bombing. For the general staff in Tel Aviv, the line has been crossed. The generals present Peres with the plan for an extensive military operation called Grapes of Wrath. South Lebanon is to be bombed from the air and on the ground, so that the population will retreat toward Beirut where, it is thought, the arrival of hundreds of thousands of refugees will induce the Lebanese government to put pressure on Hezbollah. Peres meets alone with the general staff. His advisors, who happen to be opposed to the operation, are not allowed to take part in the discussion.

Once again, Peres is quick to understand that he has no choice. If he rejects the plan, certain generals will be sure to let slip to the press that the prime minister is not giving

---

24. On the South Lebanon affair and Operation Grapes of Wrath, see Sigler (n.d.).

the nation's safety the highest priority, that he is not fulfill-
ing his duties, and so on. Coming right in the middle of an
electoral campaign, the effect would be disastrous. Besides,
a military success would burnish Peres' image, something
he greatly needs.

And so Operation Grapes of Wrath is launched on April
11, 1996. The massive bombardment of South Lebanon
begins. Tsahal issues a call to the inhabitants of forty-nine
villages, telling them to evacuate their homes at once, and
200,000 refugees flee the area. The Shiite military force responds by firing rockets at northern Israel, where the population is hiding in shelters. They will remain there for sixteen
days. In Beirut, several headquarters of Hezbollah are attacked by combat helicopters equipped with laser-guided
bombs.

The first blunder occurs two days later. A helicopter destroys a Lebanese ambulance, killing four children and two
women. Still, Peres decides to carry on with the operation
until his aim has been achieved. On April 16, still unable to
stop the rockets being fired every day onto Israeli soil, the
Israeli Defense Force (IDF) attacks the international airport
in Beirut. Four Lebanese civilians are killed.

After a telephone conversation with Rafiq Hariri, the
Lebanese prime minister, French president Jacques Chirac
sends his foreign minister, Hervé de Charrette, to the em-
battled region. April 18 is a day of catastrophe. Israeli shell-
fire falls on a base of the United Nations Interim Force in
Lebanon at Kfar Kana, where many Lebanese civilians have
taken refuge. This is a real slaughter: 102 people, among
them women and children, are killed. The IDF and the
Israeli government offer their regrets and excuses, explaining that there was a firing error. According to some versions
of the drama, the artillery was supposed to cover a special
unit of Israelis operating against a Hezbollah commando
force near the United Nations position.

Shimon Peres is in the middle of a press conference with Yasir Arafat at the Erez checkpoint when he gets the news. He immediately leaves for Jerusalem. A very worried Uri Savir makes the trip back in the helicopter of Amnon Lipkin-Shahak, the chief of staff, telling him only, "The peace camp just lost the elections." Grim faced, both keep silent.[25]

For Peres and his government, the pictures from Kana have the worst possible effect. The Clinton administration is even afraid of a new escalation of conflict in the Middle East. Secretary of State Warren Christopher arrives on April 20 to negotiate a cease-fire as quickly as possible. He shuttles back and forth among Jerusalem, Beirut, and Damascus. But French diplomacy is already at work. Thanks to France's privileged relations with Lebanon and Syria, Hervé de Charrette is developing a plan for an agreement that, after a few modifications, will ultimately be accepted by the Americans. Christopher, however, sends Peres a letter defining what he sees as Israel's right to self-defense.

Israel and Hezbollah promise not to aim at civilian targets or to launch attacks from areas with civilian populations. A committee in charge of military activities, bringing together representatives of Israel, Lebanon, and Syria, will meet regularly at Nakura, near the Israeli border, in the presence of French and American diplomats. A cease-fire is set for April 27. All in all, 154 Lebanese civilians have been killed and 350 wounded. In Israel, three women have been seriously wounded.

Politically, the chief victim of this operation is Peres' election bid. Benjamin Netanyahu, also campaigning hard, skillfully turns the Lebanese affair and the uncertain situation in Galilee to his advantage. Most important, however, is that

---

25. Videotaped interview with Uri Savir, December 9, 2001, Jerusalem.

the Arab community in Israel, profoundly shocked by the dreadful pictures from Kana, decides to boycott the elections. It is Shimon Peres who will lose these votes.

NETANYAHU'S VICTORY

Peres had met with Arafat at the Erez checkpoint on April 18 to explain that, given the approaching election, he would not be able to go forward with the Hebron withdrawal scheduled for May 15: there was no point risking new incidents with the Jewish settlers living in the City of the Patriarchs. Peres also asked Arafat to keep his word by putting to a vote the repeal of the articles in the Palestinian Charter calling for the destruction of Israel. Fine, the head of the PLO replied, but this meant that the members of the Palestinian National Council (PNC), comprising the majority of Palestinian organizations, would have to be able to go to Gaza. Among them were George Habash, Nayef Hawatmeh, and Abu al-Abbas, who had led the hijacking of the Achille Lauro in 1985. The news of the events at Kana was broadcast a few minutes after the meeting ended.

On April 25, Arafat does keep his word: the PNC meets in Gaza, with the aim of changing the Palestinian Charter. Although Arafat's chief opponents have not come, the presence of Abu al-Abbas and the famous airplane hijacker Leila Khaled creates a sensation. The key part of the debate takes place behind closed doors.

On May 4, Arafat writes to Peres:

In the framework . . . of our commitment regarding the peace process, and on the basis of mutual recognition between the Palestine Liberation Organization and the government of Israel, the Palestinian National Council, which has been meeting in the city of Gaza in an extraordinary session from April 22 to 25, 1996, has decided that the Palestinian National Charter is to be amended by the nullification of all its articles contrary to the letters exchanged between the PLO and the government of Israel on September 9 and 10, 1993.

The official translation of this resolution "reaffirms the desire to reach a just, lasting, and comprehensive accord as well as an historic resolution by means of an agreed political process." The PNC notes all the United Nations resolutions[26] concerning the Palestinian question; restates its commitments to the Oslo accord, the Cairo accord, and the interim accord; repeals all the articles contrary to mutual recognition between Israel and the PLO; and entrusts to its juridical commission the task of correcting the text of the Palestinian National Charter for presentation at the next session of the PNC.

For the Israeli right, this is not enough. The Palestinian delegates, it is said on that side of the chessboard, have not drawn up a precise list of the articles to be rescinded and have not voted on the new charter.

Surveys are predicting a narrow victory for Shimon Peres. The Clinton administration is getting worried. On April 30, Peres and Arafat are invited to Washington. The United States offers Israel $100,000,000 in aid to deal with its war on terrorism. Pictures of the handshakes at the White House are broadcast in Israel alongside news of the electoral campaign.

For Peres, though, this comes too late. The televised campaign has been disastrous. While the right was quick to broadcast pictures of the bloody attacks of February and March, Chaim Ramon, the Labor deputy in charge of the

---

26. For the text of United Nations resolutions pertaining to events discussed in this book, see the Appendix.

Peres campaign, has decided that his ads would not use scenes of violence contrary to the peace process. And the ads have hardly even mentioned the assassination of Yitzhak Rabin.

The Israelis go to the polls on May 29, 1996. They are to elect a new parliament, and, for the first time, will elect their prime minister by universal suffrage. The results are very close, and it is not until late at night that Benjamin Netanyahu learns he has won with 50.4 percent of the votes against 49.5 for Peres. The margin is 30,000 votes.

The Israeli Arabs boycotted the election en masse. The new prime minister benefited from the support of the ultra-Orthodox community, the settlement movement, and the right and far right, all of which had been mobilized in his favor. With thirty-four representatives in the Knesset, the Labor Party has lost six seats but remains the dominant factor in the chamber. Likud goes from forty to thirty-two representatives, but the Orthodox parties win twenty-three seats. The left, which had negotiated the Oslo accords, is no longer in power. From now on, Israel will be led by the principal opponents of the peace process.

Chapter 2

The "Iron Wall"

Benjamin Netanyahu knows he has no choice. The Oslo process has the support of the international community and two-thirds of Israeli public opinion, so he has to pursue negotiations with the Palestinians. But he will do so only on certain conditions:

> I've made the reciprocity formula clear. If Arafat gives something, he'll get something in return. And I've also decided to reduce the hidden dangers of the Oslo agreements. I was inclined toward a very limited accord. Rabin and Peres had promised Arafat that he would get all of the territories, with the exception of the settlements and the sectors in which there are military installations. This even before the end of the negotiations on the definitive status. That meant that Arafat could expect to get—as they'd probably told him in secret—95 percent of the territories. To my mind that was absurd and dangerous.[27]

27. Videotaped interview with Benjamin Netanyahu, January 20, 2002, Jerusalem. It should be noted that neither Rabin nor Peres ever promised Arafat an Israeli withdrawal of this magnitude.

This about-face in Israeli politics comes at the worst possible moment from Yasir Arafat's point of view. Tsahal has been imposing more blockades for reasons of security, and the economic and social situation on the West Bank and in Gaza has gotten considerably worse since 1994. In 1995, Palestinians lost seventy-three days of work and will lose eighty-two in the course of 1996. Unemployment, which affected less than 6 percent of the able-bodied population in 1993, is now reaching 29 percent. Average income has declined 17 percent.[28] Meanwhile, Jewish settlements have increased substantially, growing from 105,940 settlers in 1992 to 151,324 in June 1996. The number of Israelis living in the new Jewish areas constructed in the occupied territories has risen to 200,000, in an additional 50,000 units. Leaders of the Israeli left, in power at the time, had explained to their Palestinian counterparts that these constructions were being built only in limited sectors and would remain under Israeli control in the context of a definitive accord. The tax advantages granted to the settlers had been canceled. Yitzhak Rabin thought that once autonomy was established, the settlers would become discouraged and eventually start packing their bags.[29] He was mistaken.

Under these circumstances, the international community is afraid of a rapid collapse of the peace process and goes into action. What foreign leader, at this time, does not explain to Yasir Arafat that Netanyahu is in fact a pragmatist, that he, Arafat, would get more from Likud than from Labor, as was the case with Menachem Begin and Anwar el-Sadat? The list of people holding such conversations with the Palestinians is

---

28. See http://www.merip.org. See also the UNSCO reports at http://www.arts.mcgill.ca/mepp/unsco/.

29. Interview with Jacques Neriah, former diplomatic advisor to Rabin, March 10, 1998, Tel Aviv.

a long one, from the American emissary Dennis Ross to Shimon Peres, and includes King Hussein of Jordan, who had discreetly supported Netanyahu in his campaign. Even Hosni Mubarak will come around after several meetings with the new Israeli prime minister. Not until several months later will the Egyptian president change his mind and then, in private, call Netanyahu only "el Kazab" (the Liar).

WHAT DOES BENJAMIN NETANYAHU WANT?

Yasir Arafat has received an alarming report from Ahmed Tibi, his adviser on Israeli affairs. According to this Israeli Arab, a physician, Netanyahu sees the Palestinian problem only from the point of view of the struggle against terrorism. But the Palestinian authorities, won over by the arguments of their American contacts and the Israeli left, decide to ignore him.

And yet all one has to do is read what Netanyahu has written to know what he wants. An heir of Jabotinsky, Begin, and Shamir, the new prime minister cites ideological and strategic grounds for rejecting the principle of the creation of a Palestinian state on the West Bank and in Gaza. In *A Place among the Nations*, published in 1993, he had followed his Likud predecessors in proposing that the Palestinians be granted autonomy in the urban zones, with the understanding that the Israeli army would not only retain freedom of action throughout the whole of the territory but would also control all strategic positions. Later, "if the Arabs were to demonstrate clearly that they had adopted a genuine peacetime footing, Israel could consider offering citizenship to the Arab population of Judea and Samaria at the end of a cooling-off period of twenty years."[30]

---

30. Netanyahu, 1993, p. 353.

Does he feel obliged to implement a policy of territorial concessions, one that he had always fought? This is what he says on November 22, 1996, a few months after coming to power:

If you look carefully at what I've accomplished since I became president of the council, you'll see that I'm doing exactly what I promised the voters. Before the election, I said that, in spite of my reservations with regard to the Oslo agreements, I would not reject them, but I would also take my party's politics and platform into account. . . . You must understand that the Oslo accords constitute a poorly prepared framework. . . . Although they don't anticipate the nature of the final arrangement, they head in an unacceptable direction. And that's because Oslo is imbued with the assumption that the parties are willing to create a Palestinian state and [must] therefore define a framework that will not unduly alarm Israeli public opinion but, on the contrary, will very gradually, progressively, get it used to the desired result.

And he criticizes the policy of the Rabin government:

It's clear that when you [pursue a policy of withdrawal] to the lines of June 4, 1967 without receiving anything in return, you get praised and honored. I assure you that I, too, if I gave up half of Jerusalem, would get the same kind of awards and praise. . . . The real challenge for a statesman is to watch out for his interests by setting clear limits [for negotiation]. It's not surprising that, when you go from a policy of "concession after concession" to a policy of "give and take," the other party will not be satisfied.

The Arabs are going through a period of adaptation at this time, and it's only natural that they're trying to apply

pressure. . . . I can tell you, and this is not mere hypothesis but the result of factual knowledge, that these attacks
against us are motivated by two considerations. The first
is that every measure taken against us by the Arabs will
have the support of the West. Blame for every crisis will
be placed on Israel. The second is that the Arabs can
now divide Israeli society and get half of public opinion
to protest against the government.[31]

Netanyahu lends no credence to any of the arguments
put forth by the Israeli left when they say that, in the final
agreement, the Palestinian State will be demilitarized and its
airspace controlled by Israel. Nor does he believe that that
state can be kept from forming alliances with enemies of
Israel like Iraq and Iran, or that it can be persuaded to
abandon the idea of having two to three million Palestinian
refugees return to Israeli territory. For Netanyahu, it is unthinkable to make any commitments on fundamental issues
like these, simply because no sovereign state could comply
with such conditions.

Netanyahu, then, is faithful to his ideology. The West
Bank must be the "iron wall" behind which Zionism can
safely flourish. The Jewish settlements are the outposts of
Israeli defense. He will make only limited territorial concessions, and the Palestinians will just have to get used to the
idea that they will never be granted anything but circum-
scribed autonomy.

Yasir Arafat wants to know right away whether he can
negotiate with Netanyahu. On May 30, the day after the
election, Abu Mazen, second in command of the PLO, calls
Terje Larsen and asks to see him immediately. Larsen, the
UN representative in Gaza, had been the Norwegian media-

---

31. Shavit, 1996, p. 18.

tor of the secret Oslo negotiations. His wife, Mona, is the chargée d'affaires in the Norwegian embassy in Tel Aviv. A meeting is set for that very evening at the Larsens' home. When Abu Mazen arrives, accompanied by Mohammed Dahlan, the first thing he does is tell his hosts, "You've got to help us. We don't know anyone on the inside in this new government. We have to get a dialogue going with these people, and the sooner the better." The Norwegian diplomat makes contact at once with Netanyahu's circle. Secret negotiations begin.

But what concerns Netanyahu most of all are the Golan Heights. He assigns his chief political adviser, Dore Gold, an academic of American origin, the task of summarizing where matters stand with the Israeli–Syrian negotiations. The first issue is to determine the validity of the "deposit," the famous promise made by Yitzhak Rabin to the American secretary of state, Warren Christopher, and confirmed by Shimon Peres after the assassination of the prime minister.

Rabin, it will be recalled, had undertaken to withdraw from the Golan as long as all the conditions set forth by Israel were respected with regard to security and the nature of the peace with Syria. Gold finds only vague allusions to this promise in the files. So he consults Itamar Rabinovich and General Danny Yatom (the former head of Rabin's defense department, who had been named head of Mossad a few months earlier by Peres), in an attempt to get an answer to a fundamental question: Is Rabin's "deposit" binding on the new head of the Israeli government? He quickly establishes that this is not the case. The promise was an oral one, hypothetical and indirect.

At the end of August, Gold goes to Washington with Shimon Shapira, a colonel in military intelligence and Yatom's successor in the cabinet. The two men meet with Warren Christopher, who corroborates the existence of Rabin's "deposit" and explains that this was not a formal undertaking but an oral statement that the president of the United States could utilize in the context of the negotiations in progress. Dore Gold asks Christopher to confirm this in writing and suggests that Dennis Ross bring the document with him on his next trip to Jerusalem.

Ross comes to Israel as anticipated, but without the document requested by Netanyahu and his team. The talks are difficult. The Clinton administration must completely revise its strategy vis-à-vis Hafez el-Assad: the Israelis are demanding not only an explicit statement to the effect that Rabin's promise puts Israel under no obligation whatsoever, but also the complete annulment of the working document entitled "Aims and Principles of Security Arrangements."

As we know, this text, negotiated for better or worse at the request of the Syrians, had enabled military negotiations to resume at the beginning of the year between the chiefs of staff of the two countries, Amnon Lipkin-Shahak and Hikmat el-Shihabi, at Wye Plantation. Netanyahu and Gold also ask the Americans to confirm the letter of undertaking sent in 1975 by President Gerald Ford to Yitzhak Rabin, then Israel's ambassador in Washington. At that time, the United States had said that it would

> support the position that an overall settlement with Syria in the framework of a peace agreement must assure Israel's security from attack from the Golan Heights. The U.S. further supports the position that a just and lasting peace, which remains our objective, must be acceptable to both sides. The U.S. has not developed a final position on the borders. Should it do so it will give great weight to Israel's position that any peace agreement with Syria must be predicated on Israel remaining on the Golan Heights.[32]

---

32. Ford, 1975.

Several weeks later, the United States embassy will forward the expected document to Netanyahu, signed by Warren Christopher. "That day, I had the feeling I'd saved the Golan," Dore Gold will say.[33]

After three weeks of secret negotiations at the Larsens' home in Tel Aviv, Gold and Saeb Erekat have set up a timetable for the resumption of the peace process. On June 27, Gold makes a discreet trip to Gaza, where he meets with Arafat for the first time. An observant Jew, Gold recalls the evening: "To break the ice, Arafat invited me to dinner. 'Dore,' he said to me, 'it's fish, it's kosher, you can eat it.' Then he offered me yogurt with honey, and one of the Israeli experts who had come along with me whispered, 'That's so you'll find it harder to talk; it makes you sweat.'"

The political discussion takes place without incident in an atmosphere that is almost friendly. Gold hands Arafat a letter, the new Israeli government's assurance that it will pursue the dialogue with the Palestinian Authority. The letter also includes a list of violations of the accords by the Palestinians, especially in Jerusalem. Arafat replies that, at the time, Shimon Peres had promised him that PLO institutions in Jerusalem could continue to function. Not to mention the fact that he, Arafat, has his own list of Israeli violations to present. And he reminds his guests that he is still awaiting the Israeli redeployment from Hebron.

Nevertheless, contacts will be kept up. News of the meeting will make tomorrow's newspaper headlines.

On July 9, Bill Clinton receives in the White House the man he had hoped would not be elected. Benjamin Netanyahu, whom everyone calls Bibi, arrives as though on conquered territory. He has already met with his friends from the Republican right and fundamentalist Christian movements, enemies of the Democratic president, who is

---

33. Videotaped interview with Dore Gold, June 11, 2001, Jerusalem.

making the best of the situation: Israel is the ally of the United States, and a prime minister is always welcome in Washington.

At the end of their meeting, the two men state their agreement that "peace with security" is the best formula for resolving conflict in the Middle East. On this occasion Clinton will not mention the central principle set forth in the Oslo peace process: "land for peace." A few hours earlier, however, a White House spokesman had stated that the American administration would always consider this principle to be the basis for negotiations between the Israelis and the Palestinians.

To a question about a possible meeting with Yasir Arafat, Netanyahu replies that he would not preclude one, should he consider it necessary for peace. Clinton then presents his guest with a substantial gift: Israel will be linked with the American antimissile warning system. Back in Jerusalem, the Israeli prime minister will say, in a televised interview, "I gave President Clinton and the members of Congress the statistics on the growth of the Jewish population in Judea–Samaria and Gaza. It is 50 percent. This came about under a Labor government, not a Likud government. It's the result of a natural development."

On July 23, Netanyahu sends David Levy, his foreign minister, to meet officially with Arafat. The conversation takes place at the Erez checkpoint at the entry to the Gaza Strip. The long handshake between the two men delights television channels and the Israeli left: "It was almost worth losing the elections to see that. When I launched the Oslo process I never thought I would see David Levy shaking Arafat's hand!" exclaims Yossi Beilin.

On July 19, north of Ramallah, hundreds of Palestinians demonstrate against the seizure of forty hectares of farmland by the Israeli army. The inhabitants of Samua, near Hebron, are accused of sabotaging machinery used by Israeli contractors for building a road that will go through their land, and they are placed under a curfew. Ten days later, Avigdor Lieberman, director general of the office of the council in Jerusalem, announces a new program designed to spur the economy in the settlements. All the monetary advantages that had been canceled by the former government are restored, and, on August 2, the go-ahead is given for development of settlements in all the occupied territories, including the center of the West Bank, where the Labor Party had intentionally held back.[34]

The mastermind of this new policy is none other than Ariel Sharon, minister of the interior. With over $500,000,000 at his disposal, he has everything he needs to strengthen the settlements, create new ones, and stand in the way of any territorial concession to the Palestinians. The highway department and the administration of land surveys, which controls thousands of hectares of state-owned land on the West Bank and in Gaza, are answerable to him. He oversees the 1,500 kilometers of roads in Palestinian territory, roads he has every intention of developing so as to link the colonies to Israel and, at the same time, to isolate the various autonomous zones.

In addition, Sharon absorbs the ministry of energy and the water department, becoming their de facto director. He will utilize them to construct the electricity network and water pipelines supplying the settlements. The new government plans to increase the Jewish population in the occupied territories by 50,000 in four years.

On the West Bank, the Autonomous Authority is faced with mounting agitation. In Hebron a pamphlet is being circulated, signed by mysterious "Forces of Popular Commit-

---

34. On the policies of Israeli governments with regard to settlements, see Foundation for Middle East Peace, http://www.fmep.org.

tees for Palestinian National Solidarity." It is an appeal for a resumption of the Intifada, the Palestinian uprising that had raged almost ten years earlier with the aim of hastening the withdrawal of the Israeli army from the city. On August 1, after the death of a man being held in the Nablus prison, and serious incidents at Tulkarm, where the Palestinian police opened fire on protesters demonstrating in front of the prison, Hamas militants issue a call for an uprising against Israel and the Palestinian Authority. On August 15, at a meeting in Gaza, the Islamist organization takes aim at a new target and asks its fighters to attack the settlements.

Yet at the home of the Larsens in Tel Aviv, negotiations are still going forward in the presence of Saeb Erekat and Dore Gold (who will soon be replaced by Yitzhak Molho, Netanyahu's personal lawyer). Abu Mazen and Colonel Mohammed Dahlan, chief of preventive security in Gaza, are taking part in these talks, and so, on occasion, is Danny Naveh, a young wolf from Likud who has been made a government secretary. Down to the last detail, they prepare for the meeting between Arafat and Netanyahu.

This meeting takes place on September 4, 1996, in the Israeli part of the Erez checkpoint. Palestinian leaders recall that a door suddenly opened. Netanyahu rushed over to Arafat and took his hand, exclaiming, "Mr. President, we should have done this a long time ago!"

The two men approve the proposals drawn up by their negotiators concerning the form to be taken by the talks in the coming weeks. Arafat, who had hardly protested the development of certain settlements under the former government, asks Netanyahu to set a limit to new construction. "Out of the question!" shouts Netanyahu. "First of all, nothing in the Oslo accords prevents us from building. And besides, ideologically, we're different from the Labor Party, who, let me remind you, never gave up plans for these Jewish places." Arafat is shocked by his interlocutor's tone.

Yasir Abed Rabbo, who is present at the talk, interjects, "We haven't come here to listen to thoughts about differences between you and Labor." Tension is in the air. The joint press conference proceeds exactly as Erekat and Molho had expected. The next day, Arafat will be unpleasantly surprised to learn that, at a session of the central committee of Likud, Netanyahu had publicly declared that "there will never be a Palestinian State between the Mediterranean and the Jordan."

Joint commissions meet again, but the Palestinians quickly realize that no progress is being made. Netanyahu wants to renegotiate the agreement on the Israeli withdrawal from three-fifths of Hebron, a redeployment that has been slow to occur. Arafat refuses.

THE FIGHT OVER A "TUNNEL"

Soon Netanyahu makes his first big mistake. The Department of Religious Affairs had had an underground passageway along the Wailing Wall cleared during the 1980s, and now, on the night of September 23–24, 1996, Netanyahu authorizes the opening of its northern access.

This is the most sensitive part of Jerusalem. The narrow route that the press will incorrectly call a "tunnel" extends for 450 meters along what the Jews regard as the Western Wall of the Temple Mount, their most sacred site, where King Solomon is said to have built the first Temple and King Herod the second. For the Muslims, this is the retaining wall of Islam's third most holy place, the Haram al-Sharif, site of the Al-Aqsa Mosque and the Dome of the Rock. Here, according to Jewish tradition, is where the sacrifice of Isaac was to take place. Wrong, say the Muslims: it was Ishmael whom Abraham wanted to sacrifice, and not in Jerusalem but in Mecca. The rock, they say, actually shows the mark left by the iron shoes of Al-Bouraq, the Prophet Mohammed's mare, when he made his nighttime journey to Jerusalem.

The "tunnel" is supposed to end at the Via Dolorosa in front of the Convent of the Little Sisters of Zion. Previously, however, when visitors came to the end, they had had to turn around and go back the way they came. Now that the opening has been made, thousands of tourists and worshippers can use the passageway.

The plan had been dragging on for years. The Waqf, the administration of Muslim property, opposed any change in the status quo. As prime minister, Shimon Peres had unsuccessfully offered to transform Solomon's stables, under Al-Aqsa Plaza, into a mosque, if Muslim leaders would agree to the opening of the tunnel. Dore Gold will relate how Netanyahu took up this idea but, considering Israel to be sovereign in Jerusalem, neglected to consult with the Waqf.[35]

Ami Ayalon, head of the security service, and Defense Minister Yitzhak Mordechai are opposed to the plan.[36] But, under pressure from Ehud Olmert, the Likud mayor of the city, Netanyahu authorizes the operation. Neither the army nor Shin Bet is informed.

The operation takes place under cover of night. Around eleven in the morning, the Palestinians begin to demonstrate. For them, to touch the Wailing Wall is to attack the retaining wall of the holy mosques. The most insane rumors circulate: "The Jews are attacking Haram al-Sharif" is an example of one that can be heard here and there.

---

35. Videotaped interview with Dore Gold, June 11, 2001, Jerusalem.

36. Videotaped interviews with Yitzhak Mordechai (July 4, 2001, Jerusalem), Israel Hasson (July 2, 2001, Jerusalem), and General Amnon Lipkin-Shahak, then chief of staff (June 4, 2001, Tel Aviv).

Muslim authorities in Jerusalem hold an emergency meeting and announce that the opening of the passage is an attack on the holy site. The Palestinian people, Yasir Arafat declares, will not look on passively as their sacred grounds are being harmed. He calls for a general strike and demonstrations throughout the territories. In East Jerusalem, the police use military force to break up a gathering of Palestinian notables. Sheik Hassan Tahabub, minister of religious affairs of the Autonomous Authority, is among the eight people injured. That same evening, Arab television stations broadcast the pictures via satellite.

The confrontations take a much more dramatic turn the next day, September 25. At Ramallah, Marwan Barghouti, secretary general of Fatah on the West Bank, organizes a demonstration with the students of Bir Zeit University. It begins at eleven in the morning on the main road at the entrance to El-Bireh in North Jerusalem, where the Israeli army has set up a barricade. Dozens of young people immediately start throwing stones at the soldiers deployed along the road and surveying each side. The soldiers have tactical control of the situation, but they respond by shooting rubber-coated metal bullets. At this distance, forty meters or so, such bullets can be lethal. And so, in less than an hour, almost a hundred young Palestinians are wounded—some gravely, with a bullet in the head.

Israel Hasson, second in command at Shin Bet, is on the scene, along with Gaby Ofir, the general in charge of the sector. Hasson quickly understands how explosive the situation is:

A wave of young people is coming forward, throwing stones. The soldiers open fire, like shooting ducks. Young people are falling, are carried over to the ambulances. A new wave comes on, and it begins all over again. I can see the faces of the Palestinian police, and I turn to the general. I tell him this has to be stopped right away, because we're attacking the honor of the Palestinian Authority. They're not just going to stand there, and they might return fire with real bullets. Then the whole area will go up in flames. Ofir agrees. I rush to Jerusalem to meet with Moshe Katsav [the minister of tourism, who is in temporary command while Benjamin Netanyahu is in Europe]. Katsav is listening to me patiently when I get a message on my beeper: "There are violent exchanges of gunfire between the Israeli army and the Palestinian police at El-Bireh." Katsav looks at me suspiciously. He thinks I'm keeping something from him.[37]

Turmoil has erupted. Incidents pile up. At the end of the day, seven people are dead and 253 wounded on the West Bank. The region is about to collapse.

The following day brings even harsher fighting. At Ramallah, late in the morning, the funerals for the victims become one enormous demonstration of rage. Once again there is a confrontation at the El-Bireh barricade. Sixteen Palestinians are killed.

Another drama is unfolding at Nablus, an Israeli enclave within the autonomous territory and the place where tradition places Joseph's Tomb. The students at the Talmudic school there have been asked to stay in their respective settlements today. Around nine in the morning, hundreds of Palestinians throw stones and Molotov cocktails in an attack on the thirteen Israeli soldiers guarding the tomb. The soldiers respond by shooting rubber-coated bullets, followed by real ones. Palestinian police then load their Kalashnikovs and open fire on the same Israelis with whom, just a few

---

37. This and the following quotation are from a videotaped interview with Israel Hasson, July 2, 2001, Jerusalem.

days earlier, they had conducted joint patrols. Two Israelis are seriously wounded. Surrounded, the unit calls for immediate reinforcements. Five jeeps carrying thirty soldiers arrive an hour later without too much difficulty. But the intensity of the fighting increases, and Tsahal decides to send new reinforcements. A column of armored military trucks passes through the eastern suburbs of Nablus under steady fire. Six soldiers are killed.

In the Palestinian territories as a whole, the situation is deteriorating fast: one armed clash follows another. Benjamin Netanyahu has immediately returned to Jerusalem and given his approval to the measures taken by the defense minister. Tanks are deploying on the West Bank and in Gaza. Combat helicopters are taking off. The death toll increases from hour to hour.

Despite the fighting at the various roadblocks, the consul general of the United States, Edward Abington, manages to get to Yasir Arafat's office in Gaza. In contact with Dennis Ross in Washington, he tries to calm the situation. The Americans' greatest fear is that the peace process will collapse, with disastrous consequences for the region. Mohammed Dahlan, returning from Germany where he had been on an official visit, is now conferring at the Tel Aviv airport with the heads of Shin Bet and the military.

Yitzhak Mordechai gives the go-ahead to Uzi Dayan, the general in command of the central region: free the soldiers trapped in Joseph's Tomb and, if necessary, completely evacuate this holy place, since several wounded soldiers may die if they do not get treatment right away. Plans for an operation are drawn up: Nablus will be entered with tanks under cover of combat helicopters. If this happens, carnage is inevitable. Israel Hasson and Jibril Rajoub, head of preventive security on the West Bank, meet with Dayan outside the city. The general is persuaded not to intervene immediately.

Hasson and Rajoub go the scene of the fighting. Risking his life by interposing himself between the large crowd and the Israelis, Rajoub's deputy, Sameh Knaan, has managed to effect a cease-fire near the Tomb. Hasson is protected by the Palestinian's bodyguards. In this overwrought atmosphere, the three men organize the successful evacuation of the soldiers.

"When it was all over," Hasson relates,

I asked Rajoub what orders Arafat had given regarding the cease-fire. "Why don't you talk to him," he said to me. So I had a phone conversation with Arafat, who told me he wanted to speak with the prime minister. I said that wouldn't be a problem. But I was worried, because I didn't know whether Netanyahu would be willing. When I learned, a little later on, that the two men had spoken with one another, I felt enormously relieved but also somewhat ill. Ever since that day, I've suffered from slight diabetes. I'd taken a huge political risk.

At the end of the battle, the death toll is heavy: nearly eighty killed on the Palestinian side and fifteen Israeli soldiers. Hundreds have been wounded. The Clinton administration decides to bring Netanyahu and Arafat together in Washington. The Israeli prime minister flies out on September 30. After his plane has taken off, his advisers discover, to their horror, that they have forgotten to inform Dan Shomron about the trip. The former chief of staff is chairing the commission of experts that is supposed to follow negotiations with the Palestinians. He will catch a plane a few hours later.

Things go badly in Washington. On the morning of October 1, Yasir Arafat flies into a rage when he discovers a working document, drawn up by Dennis Ross, that he considers wholly inspired by the Israelis. Arafat is all for heading back to Gaza until Amr Moussa, the Egyptian foreign minister, persuades him to stay.

Discussions with the Americans continue throughout the day. Taking part on the Palestinian side are Nabil Shaath, Abu Mazen, and Saeb Erekat. King Hussein of Jordan is also present, and he spares no effort.

The summit meeting takes place at the White House on October 2. Arafat insists that Erekat and Abu Mazen be there at his side, and, though Dennis Ross objects to this arrangement, Erekat remains.

King Hussein, who is accompanied by his prime minister, then addresses Netanyahu: "At the Arab summit following your election, I declared publicly that you had to be given a chance. I thought you needed time. It seems that you are a man of strong ideological convictions. I hope that, in the end, you will have the wisdom and courage of Yitzhak Rabin. I have never been so worried for the region."

Arafat takes the floor and describes the difficulties confronting the Palestinians: the blockading of Gaza and the West Bank, the economic situation, the increasing opposition he has to deal with, the impasse in the negotiations. Netanyahu breaks in: "Believe me, I am a man of peace; I want to make peace."

Bill Clinton advises all those present not to let a historic opportunity go by. Ross then suggests that a tripartite meeting be held on October 6 in Gaza or Israel, and Arafat immediately agrees. He also asks that Clinton be the only one to speak at the upcoming press conference. As they leave the White House, Clinton insists that Arafat shake Netanyahu's hand. The picture will be televised worldwide. Everyone takes this as a sign that the crisis has been overcome.

On the way home, the Palestinians stop off in Morocco, where Hassan II has a long audience with them in the company of his adviser, André Azoulay, who has been closely following the Israeli–Arab negotiations. The events of recent weeks, the king declares, have confirmed his opinion of Netanyahu: "This man is definitely dangerous!" Hassan II will have no further contact with the Israeli prime minister.

ISRAEL WITHDRAWS FROM HEBRON

The Israeli army is analyzing the events following the opening of the "tunnel." Surprised by the intensity of the fighting, it decides to prepare for the worst: an uprising of the Palestinian population that may call for retaking the autonomous cities by military force. Experts have found that the infantry was poorly prepared; the soldiers were missing their targets too often, and the active and reserve forces need more training in marksmanship. Assault rifles will be equipped with sights. Plans are drawn up for an operation in which, should it prove necessary, control of the West Bank and Gaza can be regained. Operation Field of Thorns involves the following elements:

- Mobilization and deployment of armored and other land forces in the event of a massive Palestinian uprising.
- Massive reinforcement of Israeli Defense Force troops at points of friction.
- Use of armored vehicles and artillery to isolate major Palestinian population areas and to seal off Palestinian areas, including many in the A zones.
- Use of other forces to secure settlements, key roads, and terrain points.
- Use of helicopter gunships and snipers to provide mobility and suppressive fire.
- Use of extensive small arms, artillery, and tank fire to suppress sniping, rock throwing, and demonstrations.

- Bombing, artillery strikes, and helicopter and combat-aircraft strikes on high-value Palestinian targets and to punish Palestinian elements for attacks.
- Search-and-seizure interventions and raids into Palestinian areas in Gaza and the West Bank to break up organized resistance and capture or kill key leaders.
- Limited penetrations into Palestinian-controlled territory to destroy buildings and houses from which attacks have originated or to prevent future attacks, and to uproot trees from which mortar attacks have originated.
- Selective assassinations of suspected leaders and instigators of conflict, including through stand-off tactics such as drones and remote-controlled explosive devices.
- Use of military forces trained in urban warfare to penetrate into cities if necessary [the reference is probably to cities like Hebron, where there are Jewish enclaves].
- Arrest of Palestinian Authority officials and imposition of a new military administration.
- Introduction of a simultaneous economic blockade with selective cutoffs of financial transactions, labor movements, and food/fuel shipments.
- Selective destruction of high-value Palestinian facilities and clearing of strong points and fields of fire, and, from now on, near Palestinian urban areas.
- Use of Israeli control of water, power, communications, and road access to limit the size and duration of Palestinian action.
- Regulation and control of media access and conduct of a major information campaign to influence local and world opinion.
- Carrying out "temporary" withdrawal of Israeli settlers from exposed and low-value isolated settlements like Hebron.

- Forced evacuations of Palestinians from "sensitive areas."[38]

All this is just a plan by the general staff, meant to remain in a drawer for as long as the situation does not call for its implementation. On several occasions, however, Operation Field of Thorns will be mentioned by journalists and military sources. The spokesman for the Israeli army will confirm its existence in June 1997.

The Palestinians, too, have learned lessons from the recent confrontations. A number of Fatah militants found themselves on the front line, opposite the Israeli army. These men belong to the generation that led the Intifada in the late 1980s, and they are beginning to lose confidence in their negotiators. What they are increasingly coming to believe is that the Israelis are more likely to yield if they come up against violence. Thus, for Marwan Barghouti, head of Fatah on the West Bank, "the situation has changed since these events. One segment of the Palestinian leadership and some of our deputies think everything can be gotten through negotiation without pressure. I don't agree with them. I don't think they understand the situation."[39]

Tanzim, the secret armed organization of Fatah, is going to be revived. The challenge now is not just to be prepared to confront Tsahal, but also to gain gradual control of the movement as a whole, so as to lead the fight for the creation of a Palestinian state in all of the West Bank and Gaza, with Jerusalem as the capital. And, in the meantime, the aim will be to secure the release of prisoners still being held in Israeli jails.

---

38. Cordesman, 2001. The text is quoted verbatim.

39. Videotaped interview with Marwan Barghouti, November 11, 2001, Ramallah.

On October 15, Hussein of Jordan takes action and goes to Jericho, where he is received by Arafat. The image has a historic dimension. Hussein reviews a Palestinian honor guard, the very fighters he had confronted in September 1970. And all this occurs on the West Bank, the territory that had formed part of his kingdom twenty-nine years earlier.

However precariously, negotiations on the Israeli redeployment in Hebron are resumed. On October 6, Warren Christopher goes to Jerusalem and Gaza to tell Netanyahu and Arafat that an agreement on this redeployment absolutely must be concluded. But how? The Palestinians demand the implementation of the entire accord signed in the presence of United States representatives, while Netanyahu is eager to show public opinion in his country that he can achieve more than his predecessors. Dennis Ross is instructed to remain on the scene in order to follow the discussions. He will shuttle back and forth a number of times.

At first the talks get stuck in crisis after crisis, with Ross putting pressure now on one party, now on the other, cajoling, threatening, and announcing his imminent departure. On November 1, Saeb Erekat is in Cairo, where he presents Hosni Mubarak with a report on the state of the negotiations. Mubarak tells him that, at all costs, the Palestinians must not renege on the signed agreement; that would be too dangerous a precedent. The next day, Erekat is back in Jerusalem, meeting with Yitzhak Molho. But, once again, the discussion gets nowhere.

Erekat is getting more nervous by the hour. A heavy smoker, he finds he has only three cigarettes left in the pack he had bought that same morning, and it is only 11:30. "God is punishing me," he tells Molho. "Negotiating with you is a real trial. I'm going to quit smoking!" "I dare you to," says Molho. Erekat takes up the dare. And, with superhuman effort, he holds out during the coming sessions. Daniel Reisner, the judicial adviser of the Israeli defense ministry, will go to the trouble of bringing him fake cigarettes to help him get through his ordeal.

On December 16, the heads of security reach an agreement. Mohammed Dahlan, one of the negotiators, informs Erekat that he has a document signed by his Israeli counterparts, including General Shlomo Yanai. Before flying off to London, Arafat, who has been kept up to date, calls United States Secretary of State Madeleine Albright to tell her that he gives his approval.

Benjamin Netanyahu, for his part, has official business in Paris. Just before taking off, he reads the document and decides not to sign it. One short sentence disturbs him: each of the two parties will undertake to fight against its extremists. The only thing Netanyahu wants to hear about is how the Palestinian Authority will struggle against terrorism. On the plane, journalists who have gotten wind of the conclusion of an agreement witness the humiliation of General Yanai, a moderate, who is along on the trip. Everything will have to be renegotiated. As he lands in London, Arafat is surprised to learn what has happened.

Hussein of Jordan steps in on January 12, 1997, during an unannounced conversation with Netanyahu at the defense ministry in Tel Aviv. That same night he goes to Gaza to tell Arafat how the talks went. Actually, according to Dennis Ross, the main points of the agreement had been negotiated a week earlier by Abu Mazen and Yitzhak Mordechai, the Israeli defense minister, along with Netanyahu's lawyer, Molho. Mordechai had announced that he was not authorized to initial this text. "Then I won't sign it either!" Abu Mazen had declared. In the end, it was Dennis Ross who placed his signature on the document.[40]

---

40. This report and the following citation are from a videotaped interview with Dennis Ross, February 19, 2002, Washington.

The accord is submitted to the fifteen-member security cabinet, and Benjamin Netanyahu now begins a final bout of arm wrestling with the Americans. As Ross describes the episode, "I'm told that the meeting of the Israeli cabinet was interrupted because an American official, whose name is not mentioned, is supposed to have stated that Israel would not have the sole right to make decisions about the further redeployment from the West Bank. So, before ratifying the agreement, Bibi Netanyahu demanded a letter from us. The members of his government didn't believe what he told them, and so he wanted a letter from us."

And Netanyahu has this to say:

We were supposed to get a letter from the Americans stipulating that Israel, and Israel alone, would decide on the extent and place of future redeployments. As the debate was taking place in the cabinet, I discovered that we did not have such a letter. So I suspended the meeting, folded my arms, and said we were going to wait. Danny Naveh phoned the American ambassador to tell him: no letter, no ratification of the agreement. A little later, we got what we wanted. The letter was signed by Warren Christopher.

What a turnabout! The cabinet members were satisfied. I'd managed to knock down the Oslo accords. The Oslo process was no longer a one-way street in which Israel kept endlessly giving and giving [to the Palestinians]; from now on we had our foot on the brake. We were in command. But that's not all: I demanded that Arafat receive a copy of the letter, and we waited to have that confirmed before voting.[41]

---

41. This and the following passage are from a videotaped interview with Benjamin Netanyahu, January 20, 2002, Jerusalem.

The Israeli government approves the agreement by a vote of eleven to seven. Benjamin Begin, son of the former prime minister, resigns from his position as minister of scientific affairs. As he sees it, an axiom—no Likud head of government could give up an inch of the land of Israel—has just been shattered. Begin will become one of Netanyahu's primary enemies. The Knesset confirms the cabinet's vote the following day, January 16, 1997, with eighty-seven in favor, eleven opposed, and one abstention.

The nationalist right, Likud, is giving up part of Hebron, City of the Patriarchs! This is a major event. But how could Benjamin Netanyahu, heir to Zeev Jabotinsky, Menachem Begin, and Yitzhak Shamir, ever have agreed to a concession like this? "It was very hard for me," he explains:

I did not in fact give up the Jewish part of Hebron. We didn't give up the Jewish quarter and the holy site, the Cave of the Patriarchs. Nevertheless, yes, it was hard. The agreement had of course been concluded by my predecessor, but [in any case] I had an idea in mind. If I got reciprocity [of concessions] on Arafat's ten points, the Americans' letter, I would trade the Arab part of Hebron for the rest of Judea–Samaria.

Giving up territory is hard. This is a part of my land, a place where my ancestors, the prophets, and the kings of Israel lived, and where so many generations of Jews have dreamed of returning. So I was going to implement the agreement with the idea that the exchange would keep all, or nearly all, of Judea–Samaria.

The withdrawal from Hebron proceeds without a hitch on January 17. Arafat makes a memorable speech there, in which he congratulates himself on the vote in the Knesset. The Palestinians celebrate, convinced that they have achieved the impossible: extracting a territorial concession from Likud.

But, in February, they have a rude awakening. Construction of a new Jewish quarter is going to begin in South Jerusalem, between the town of Umm Touba and the autonomous Palestinian city of Beit Sahur on the hill the Palestinians call Djebel Abu Ghneim, from the name of a companion of the prophet Mohammed, and the Israelis Har Homa, which means "Hill of the Rampart."

The first requisitions of land from Djebel Abu Ghneim date from 1991, under the Shamir government, after which the Israeli supreme court blocked the project for several years. On February 13, 1997, the National Religious Party and the centrist Third Way movement threaten to quit the ruling coalition if work does not begin quickly, and on the 26th a ministerial commission authorizes the construction of 6,500 housing units on this hill.

For the Palestinians, this new settlement is a fait accompli contrary to the Oslo accord, proof that Benjamin Netanyahu will never make a concession on East Jerusalem. On March 7, they bring the matter before the United Nations Security Council. But the proposed resolution, put forth by the Arab countries condemning the Har Homa settlement, comes up against an American veto. On March 13, however, the General Assembly examines the issue and condemns Israel by a 133-vote majority.

To no avail. Five days later, Israeli bulldozers arrive on the hill. Work gets underway. Violent protests break out in the West Bank. By March 21, terrorism has returned. A charge explodes in a café of the A Propos chain in Tel Aviv, killing three Israeli women and injuring several dozen people. At Hebron and the entry to Bethlehem, incidents become a daily occurrence. Once again the peace process has been blocked.

For Jibril Rajoub, the construction at Djebel Abu Ghneim "led to the clinical death of the Oslo process."[42] As

---

42. Videotaped interview with Jibril Rajoub, December 1, 2001, Ramallah.

Saeb Erekat will say, "For the Palestinians, the settlements are the equivalent of blowing up a bus in Tel Aviv. [The settlements] are the ultimate threat. This is the land, this is the future. The settlements are being built to prevent us from having a future!"[43]

Benjamin Netanyahu will explain his position as follows: "Our commitment to unifying Jerusalem under Israeli sovereignty isn't a matter of cosmetics. I'd made it clear that I was going to do this. I was ready to face [the reactions]. . . . We would not have built the State of Israel if, at each stage, we had taken Arab protests into consideration. Jerusalem wasn't a part of the Oslo accords, and Israel had the right to act within the city limits of Jerusalem."[44]

Internally, the Israeli political scene is also in disorder. Netanyahu is now the subject of a formal investigation after his decision to name the lawyer Roni Bar-On to the position of legal adviser to the government. According to Israeli television, this nomination has the primary aim of protecting Arieh Deri, the head of the Sephardic Orthodox movement Shas, who has been accused of corruption. The attorney general's office will eventually close the file for lack of proof. Netanyahu proclaims this an artificial scandal, fomented by the elite elements in the country with whom he has always fought. His spokesman, David Bar Ilan, says that "the elitists, who, in Israel, are dominated by the Labor Party, decided to show a head of state who is not a member that he can't nominate anyone he wishes, contrary to what his predecessors did."[45]

As Netanyahu sees it, these elitists are responsible for the trend toward appeasement following the Oslo accords, a

---

43. Videotaped interview with Saeb Erekat, October 26, 2001, Jericho.

44. Videotaped interview with Benjamin Netanyahu, January 20, 2002, Jerusalem.

45. Agence France Presse, 1997 (wire story).

mood that has anesthetized one part of the Israeli public. The nation must now wake up, he says, and become aware of the dangers surrounding it. What he wants to do is wage battle on two fronts: externally against the Palestinians and the Arab world, who are demanding Israel's capitulation and inviting the country to give up its historic legacy and its security, and internally against the "defeatists" on the Israeli left, who are manipulated by Yasir Arafat.

In this battle Netanyahu's main weapon is communication. Schooled in American techniques of utilizing the media, the Israeli prime minister loses no opportunity to send the message "PLO equals terrorism." Thus, after the attack on the A Propos café in Tel Aviv, the office of the cabinet in Jerusalem gave several hand-picked journalists the minutes of a meeting held on March 9 in Gaza, during which Yasir Arafat had authorized Hamas to mount attacks.[46]

This theme, regularly repeated by Netanyahu and his spokesmen, convinces the great majority of leading editorialists in the Israeli press. Yet the Palestinian Authority is cooperating with Israeli security services in dismantling the network responsible for the attack in the town of Tsurif, near Hebron, in the sector under Israeli control. And General Amos Gilaad, head of the evaluation department of military intelligence, contradicts his prime minister:

We never said Yasir Arafat gave the green light [to Hamas]; we said that this was the understanding of the Islamist organizations. It could, of course, be asked in reply: What's the difference? The fact is that there was an attack. So how did the organizations understand that they had the green light? On the basis of a general feeling, statements that had been heard, and so on. . . . It's clear that the Palestinian Authority realizes today that terror-

---

46. Marcus, 1997, p. A13.

ism and the peace process can't co-exist. Nowadays I'm noticing a more intensive effort on the part of the Palestinian Authority to prevent terrorism.[47]

Netanyahu, then, is in disagreement with his own intelligence services. But this is not surprising. On several occasions, the people around him have let it be known that, sooner or later, he would have to replace the leaders of Mossad and Shin Bet, named by Shimon Peres, and the chief of staff, General Amnon Lipkin-Shahak, who was appointed by Yitzhak Rabin. Again those leftist Labor elitists!

FROM ONE DISASTER TO THE NEXT

Relations with Jordan are deteriorating. At the beginning of March 1997, King Hussein invites Yasir Arafat on board his personal airplane for the inauguration of the new landing strip that has just been built at Rafah. But Netanyahu forbids Hussein to overfly Israeli territory. The king is furious. On March 8, he sends a fierce letter to Netanyahu. The message is machine typed, and the king has initialed every page and corrected the text by hand. Extracts:

> You are piling up tragic actions. . . . You are pushing all Arabs and Israelis toward an abyss of disasters and a bloodbath. . . . You are not keeping the promises you made to me in person. . . . You cannot make promises to me and then go back on them. . . . And if, in spite of everything, I had taken off for Gaza, . . . would you have ordered my fellow pilots of the Israeli airforce to force me to land, or worse? You will never know how close I was to deciding to do that.

---

47. Mosko, 1997, p. 45.

Netanyahu replies, two days later, that he inherited "a moribund peace process" he has been trying to revive. "I was surprised," he adds, "by the personal attacks against me, and I can only conclude that you do not fully appreciate the situation in Israel."

On March 13, a new drama shakes the region. At Naharayim, on the border between Israel and Jordan, in an enclave open to tourists, a Jordanian soldier named Ahmad Daqamseh fires his automatic at Israeli schoolgirls. Seven girls are killed and five others wounded. Five days later, King Hussein comes in person to offer his condolences and, in the name of the people of Jordan, to apologize to the victims' families at Beit Shemesh, in West Jerusalem.

The Israeli public is profoundly moved by this unimaginable gesture of an Arab monarch kneeling to console a Jewish mother. In Jordan, however, not everyone will condemn these murders. The president of the lawyers' association, opposed to peace with Israel, will volunteer to defend Daqamseh. He will explain that the soldier, a very religious man, had been provoked by the schoolgirls.

The situation is becoming dangerously unstable, and the Americans are worried. Dennis Ross returns to the region. On May 14, 1997, he and Martin Indyk, the United States ambassador to Israel, meet with Saeb Erekat and Yitzhak Mordechai, who is accompanied by Yitzhak Molho. The exchange is tense:

Erekat: You're signing a death warrant for future generations of Jews. You belong to the most privileged generation of the Jewish people. You have everything: weapons, connections abroad. But you're ruining everything with these settlements. This is no way to make peace.

Mordechai (trying to calm his interlocutor): You'll see; with goodwill on both sides we'll reach an agreement.

Erekat: No one is so blind as the man who does not want to see! What are you going to do with us?

On July 30, 1997, two suicide bombers from Hamas blow themselves up in the heart of Mahaneh Yehuda, the Jewish market in Jerusalem. There are thirteen dead and 170 wounded, three of whom, seriously injured, will later die. The Israeli government suspends all contacts with the Palestinian Authority. Gaza and the West Bank are blockaded again.

At the beginning of August, Dennis Ross returns in an attempt to restart the negotiations. Jordan, too, gets involved. Crown Prince Hassan goes to Jerusalem for a series of conversations with Benjamin Netanyahu. A meeting is arranged between the king and the Israeli prime minister. This private conversation takes place in Akaba on August 13. Netanyahu announces that the talks went extremely well, but the next day the Jordanian press adopts another tone. To be sure, Hussein states, the discussion was fruitful; yes, the Israeli leader is a partner in peace, but the region is going through an extremely dangerous period. He issues an appeal for the lifting of the closure of Palestinian territories.

On September 4, 1997, around 3 P.M., there is another attack in Ben Yehuda Street. Right in the center of Jerusalem, three suicide bombers set off charges that they are carrying around their waists. The scenes are appalling. Five Israeli civilians are killed, and there are 200 wounded, most of them young people who had come to meet friends in this street very popular among pedestrians. Among the victims is Smadar Elhanan, granddaughter of General Matti Peled, one of the forerunners of the dialogue with the PLO and, with Arieh Eliav, founder of the first committee for peace between Israel and Palestine.[48]

---

48. See Enderlin, 1997, p. 370.

Peled had died two years earlier. Nurit Peled-Elhanan, Smadar's mother, knows Benjamin Netanyahu well; they had been classmates in a Jerusalem high school. Before the press, and personally confronting the prime minister, Ms. Peled-Elhanan blames the Israeli government for these attacks: "Israel is raising terrorists. My daughter's death is the direct result of the humiliation inflicted on the Palestinians. . . . We invented the suicide bombers. They are sacrificing themselves because we have made their lives valueless in their own eyes." Smadar's funeral takes place on September 8, in the presence of Shimon Peres and a representative of the Palestinian Authority.

On September 14, the planning commission of the Jerusalem district approves the construction of a Jewish settlement in the Palestinian quarter of Ras el-Amud, in an operation financed by the Jewish-American millionaire Irving Moskowitz, a friend of Netanyahu's. Against all expectation, however, Netanyahu lets it be known that he is opposed to this project. No one believes him. Besides, three Jewish families are moving into the building that very evening. They will leave on September 18, following an agreement worked out behind the scenes, and a dozen students from a Talmudic school will then live in the house. Moskowitz has a formal permit to construct 132 housing units, but these have been held up until the government reaches a final decision.

The Palestinians are not mistaken. To the east, on the Mount of Olives, is the Beit Orot settlement; further to the south, near the Hill of Evil Counsel, the Ras el-Amud settlement; below the ramparts, in the south, the Ir David quarter established in the Palestinian suburb of Silwan: all are intended to block access from the autonomous territories to the plaza of the Al-Aqsa Mosque and the Dome of the Rock. Even the territorial solution, continuity between Abu Dis in the east and the mosques in the west as envisaged by the Beilin–Abu Mazen agreement, has become impossible.

In Washington, the new Clinton administration has taken shape. Madeleine Albright has succeeded Warren Christopher as the head of American diplomacy. On September 10, 1997, she pays her first official visit to the Middle East, where, alongside her meetings with Benjamin Netanyahu, she discovers the Palestinian problem:

I went to a school for Palestinian students, and I think that, of all the encounters I've had as secretary of state, this was one of the hardest. The Palestinian students are asking very pointed questions. They're saying, "We don't know what the future holds for us," and I didn't have any good answers for them. The truth is that this meeting touched me, and it made me aware that there was much more I had to learn about the needs of the Palestinians.[49]

MOSSAD POISONS A HAMAS LEADER

On September 25, 1997, on a street in Amman, two Mossad agents inject lethal poison into Khaled Mashaal, a member of the political bureau of Hamas, whom Israeli intelligence suspects of being the head of the Ezzedin el-Qassam commando, the movement's armed branch. The operation has been poorly planned. One of Mashaal's bodyguards manages to track the assailants, who are running to find the rest of their team a few hundred meters further ahead. He alerts the police; the Israelis are caught. Some members of the team have time to seek refuge in the Israeli embassy, which is surrounded, but six Mossad agents are put in prison.

---

49. Videotaped interview with Madeleine Albright, March 28, 2002, Washington.

King Hussein is beside himself with rage. Forty-eight hours earlier, he had sent Netanyahu a letter informing him that negotiations with Hamas were a possibility. Netanyahu will say that he had not yet received the letter. That evening, Danny Yatom, head of Israeli intelligence, comes to Amman to ask Hussein to release his men. Furious, the king throws Yatom out, shouting, "How could you have done that? Just a few days ago you were my guests on my yacht, you and your family!" Yatom leaves, shamefaced.

And the affair is far from over. Mashaal is in the hospital, gravely ill. An antidote is needed. Hussein tells the Israelis that his reaction will be very severe if the Hamas leader dies. Netanyahu is afraid of a breach in relations between the two countries, and so, on September 27, an Israeli doctor sets out for Amman with a syringe containing the antidote. Mashaal is saved. All the Israelis implicated in this affair are permitted to leave Jordan, with the exception of the two agents involved in the attack.

The crisis must somehow be resolved. Benjamin Netanyahu and his minister of public works, Ariel Sharon, travel to Amman. The king refuses to receive them and sends his brother, Prince Hassan, to substitute for him in talks with the two Israelis. An accord is reached two days later by Sharon. Netanyahu will pay a high price: he will have to free Sheik Ahmed Yassin, the founder of Hamas, and seventy-three Palestinians and Jordanians who are serving prison sentences in Israel.

On October 1, the sheik is sent to Amman, where King Hussein receives him personally. The same day, the Israeli agents are set free. Yassin returns to Gaza, where 20,000 Hamas militants give him a hero's welcome with cries of "God is great!" and "Yassin, king of the Intifada!" Yasir Arafat looks sour but will come to welcome the Islamist leader later on. For the Israeli heads of security, the return of Yassin is a bad omen. According to the chief of staff,

General Amnon Lipkin-Shahak, "the reasons for his being set free against the advice of most of the security services, and his return to Gaza as a hero, have been a blow to the Palestinian Authority and strengthen Hamas."[50]

ASSAD ON A DIET

What is going on in Hafez el-Assad's mind? Daniel Abraham, the American billionaire owner of the big diet-food company Slimfast, who is also a fervent advocate of peace in the Middle East, pays a visit to the Syrian president on December 17, 1997. Congressman Gary Ackerman and Wayne Owens, co-founder of the Center for Middle East Peace, are part of the American delegation; Farouk al-Shareh, the Syrian foreign minister, is also present. The conversation opens with dietary matters:

Hafez el-Assad: Welcome, welcome. I see you've put on a little weight, although you manufacture diet food.
Daniel Abraham: I keep half of America slim.
Gary Ackerman: We're typical Americans. My [weight] predicament has been his fortune.
Abraham (to Assad): For sure, you wouldn't be a good customer.
Assad: I told you from the first meeting: don't encourage me, because I'm not going to buy.
Abraham: Fortunately for me, you don't need it. Gary buys a lot. . . .
Assad: Personally, I used to have a tendency to put on weight. I used to do exercises. About twenty-five years

---

50. Videotaped interview with Amnon Lipkin-Shahak, November 5, 2001, Tel Aviv.

ago, things changed, and suddenly I saw that I had a huge belly. I started to do two to three hours of exercises daily, every single day, and it was summer, and I was sweating intensely. . . . In less than a month I got rid of my strange belly. . . . I was in a rented apartment without all the equipment I needed, and I had them put in a punching bag. But I never disturbed my neighbors. I took precautions. At any rate, no fighting, no punching. We were working diplomatically.

Wayne Owens: It's a good sign, a good symbol. The fighting has stopped and you've quit punching. You're ready to make peace.

Assad (referring to Netanyahu): But another boxer has come along, and we need to make sure he's not punching where he shouldn't. We're very concerned that the new boxer not keep territory that isn't his. [The Israelis] are always saying "peace," and now we're finding out that they don't want to make peace.

Assad describes the circumstances that led him to agree to his country's participation in the Madrid conference of 1991. He then gives his version of the incidents on the cease-fire line before 1967: 98 percent of them were provoked by Israel, he states, and he recalls Moshe Dayan's confirming that it was the Israelis who initiated the attacks.[51] The American delegates reply that they have had talks with Netanyahu in Israel, and that he genuinely desires peace. Assad goes on to speak of the negotiations he conducted with Yitzhak Rabin and Shimon Peres:

---

51. Assad is referring to an interview Moshe Dayan gave on November 22, 1976 (Tal, 1997, pp. 2–6), in which he stated that over 80 percent of the incidents with Syria were provoked by the Israeli army. Dayan had asked Tal not to publish this interview until after his (Dayan's) death.

When Labor came to power in Israel, everything changed completely. We began to discuss things with logic and in a friendly atmosphere. Then, gradually, we got somewhere. Neither party imposed anything on the other. We reached an agreement on the idea that Syrian territory should be returned to Syria, and that this should be done up to the starting positions from which Israel had mounted its attack against Syria. When the delegations went their separate ways, they met with the Americans and told them that Syrian territory would be entirely restored to Syria.

I remember that I asked [the Americans] questions to clarify matters. "Does [Israel] intend to return all of the Golan?" They answered yes, all of the Golan. "Is Israel claiming any part of the Golan?" No! I was told that this was spelled out clearly and would remain on deposit with the president of the United States, and so we could get onto the other aspects of the peace process. [But this issue already covers] 80 to 85 percent of the peace process. The rest concerns security arrangements.

Then we decided on the framework within which we would negotiate security arrangements. We put four or five months into reaching an agreement on [the principles]. Because no party would be able to dominate the other. We both need security. This principle was set down on paper, and all parties have a copy. Then we discussed the application of these principles on the ground: the demilitarized zones, the international presence, the sectors with limited arms. The problem of warning and detection stations was the hardest. They offered to install a Syrian station on Israeli territory. This matter became a symbol; I don't think we need a warning system. In short, we didn't get to that point.

Israel also proposed the deployment of international forces on both sides of the border. Israel could control the deployment of forces on the ground by sending reconnaissance planes. We replied that the Americans [too] could provide images by satellite and plane and send reports to both parties. The United States wouldn't lie to Israel, even though it doesn't approve of Mr. Netanyahu. That's as far as we got. If it hadn't been for the upcoming elections in Israel, we could have wrapped it up in eight months.

Netanyahu doesn't acknowledge what was gained in these negotiations, though they were conducted with the legitimate Israeli government. Nowadays the Israelis are telling us, "We want to resume the talks." We say, "Let's pick up where we left off; we're ready." But Netanyahu refuses. . . . This means that we have to begin from square one. But we have no choice. We aren't about to rush into a war now.

Several members of the delegation then try to persuade Assad to undertake serious negotiations with Netanyahu: "If you and the prime minister meet, you'll be able to reach an agreement."[52]

Assad: Negotiations don't start at the top level. They start at a lower level. Failure at the top is a serious problem.

Ackerman: Your wisdom is showing forth at this late hour. At what level do you want to start?

Assad: Someone with similar experience and past. The others don't [lacuna in the transcript] peace. We're surviving, we are well. We've been adversaries for thirty or forty years. We'll wait. It is unreasonable to think peace can be established if it's not a just peace.

---

52. What follows, the document I obtained from my source, is the simultaneous translation into English of what was said at the meeting.

It has to be just. It is not reasonable to expect someone to impose his will on others. . . .

Yet, for eighteen months, all [Netanyahu's] decla-
rations have been going in that direction. We hear
what he says. He doesn't even trust the United States,
and the United States doesn't trust him.

Farouk al-Shareh: If he doesn't trust the United States
and doesn't accept the deposits they have, how can we
trust him? . . .

Assad: This is not the way to do it. At any rate, he always
repeats: "come to the table." It is true, I was a pilot
and flew high and fast, but not that fast. At any rate,
one goes back as a corpse in this case, by one's own
people, not from Israel.

Daniel Abraham: You said you have time. I'm 73. We
won't live forever.

Assad: You don't look 73. . . .

Abraham: Slimfast! But I'm getting on!

Assad: I didn't say that we weren't in a hurry to make
peace. But if the others aren't, then we aren't going to
be in a hurry either.

NETANYAHU, ARAFAT, AND MONICA

Keeping the peace process alive is one of the major objectives of American diplomacy. To this end, Dennis Ross
is visiting the Middle East more often. Martin Indyk, the
American ambassador to Israel, is talking with the protagonists. A summit is finally organized, and, on January 20,
1998, Netanyahu arrives in Washington.

In his first meetings, he learns that some of Clinton's
enemies have just declared war on the president. Newt
Gingrich, speaker of the House of Representatives and leader
of the Republican opposition, and Jerry Falwell, the far-right

preacher who considers the Democratic president a criminal, bring Netanyahu the good news: this time they're sure to have Clinton's hide, since he's involved in a new scandal, an adulterous affair with a certain Monica Lewinsky, a White House intern. The relationship has just exploded into public knowledge, and the administration will have all sorts of concerns beside putting pressure on Netanyahu.

Be that as it may, the prime minister has every intention of resisting American demands for a new withdrawal from the West Bank. Palestinian terrorism is at the top of his agenda. Over breakfast, Madeleine Albright tells him that Yasir Arafat will be able to combat the Islamist movements effectively only if he can bring his people evidence that the peace process is going forward. Likewise, a few hours later, Bill Clinton tells him he must decide on a withdrawal in double digits.

Netanyahu knows that the state department has been talking of 13 percent. The interim accord even anticipates a third redeployment, one he has no intention of carrying out. So he launches into a lengthy speech on the inadequacy of Palestinian security arrangements: those terrorists who move about freely in the autonomous region, those secret workshops where bombs are made, and so forth, ending with the need to make explicit changes in the Palestinian Charter—and, to that end, to demand a meeting of the Palestinian National Council.

Abu Mazen, who had been in Washington a few days earlier, replied in advance to this Israeli demand with a burst of laughter: "The PNC has more than 750 members! What does Netanyahu want? To bring them all together in Gaza? He thinks at least 200 of them are terrorists! Does he want them to be brought in by force? Does he want Habash?"

The suggestion is made that Arafat write a new letter to Clinton, repeating that all the articles of the Palestinian Charter contrary to agreements with Israel are null and void. He has already sent such a letter to the British prime minister, Tony Blair. But Netanyahu refuses. He wants a formal ceremony and is willing to give in on only one point: the identity of the Palestinian agency that will annul the charter.

Forty-eight hours later, Yasir Arafat meets with Clinton. But Clinton has other problems on his mind. The Lewinsky affair has become a scandal. The young woman's confidences have been taped and are in the hands of Kenneth Starr, the special prosecutor investigating infractions of the law by the president: Starr claims that Clinton lied under oath and in his televised statements.

All through his conversation with Arafat, Clinton is distraught. He gets up, leaves the office twice, comes back, apologizes, and so on. The Middle East is no longer the order of the day in Washington. Journalists invited to film the beginning of the encounter have not asked a single question about the peace process. All they are interested in now is the scandal.

Clinton nevertheless tries to encourage Arafat, who is quite depressed. He asks about the murderers of two Israeli civilians who, according to Netanyahu, were walking around freely in autonomous territory. Arafat explains that they are in prison, and that Stan Moskowitz, head of the CIA bureau in Tel Aviv, can come and verify this. Relations between the Clinton administration and the Palestinians are improving. As the months go by, they will take a downright friendly turn.

On April 16, 1998, Netanyahu has a new meeting with Hussein of Jordan, this time at Eilat. In the evening, after the summit, his office broadcasts reassuring news: the two leaders had a first-rate, amicable conversation. But the very next day Hussein sends Netanyahu a letter warning against the dangers that an impasse would bring to the Middle East. And Jordanian officials report how distressed the king was when Netanyahu spread out maps to show him the security problems the Jewish state would face if there were a new 13-percent withdrawal, such as the Americans are proposing.

The peace process has stalled, and Madeleine Albright tries to get it going again. On May 3, in London, she receives Abu Mazen and Abu Ala, the two Palestinian leaders, followed by Benjamin Netanyahu on May 5, but without success. Meanwhile, in Jerusalem, a man is demonstrating for peace in front of Netanyahu's residence: David Kimche.

Formerly third in command at Mossad, Kimche had been an architect of the 1982 war in Lebanon. Now in retirement, he is one of the founding members of the International Alliance for Israeli–Arab Peace, also known as the Copenhagen Group, which has been bringing together Palestinians, Jordanians, Egyptians, and Israelis since January 1997. Only a speedy agreement with the Palestinians, he believes, will avoid a regional catastrophe. So here he is on the sidewalk, installed in a tent along with a number of pacifists who, at the time, had protested the Lebanon operation.

The Americans continue their efforts. On September 28, as a sidebar to a session of the UN General Assembly, Madeleine Albright has a conversation with Netanyahu and Arafat in New York. The press conference afterwards is typical of its kind:

Albright: It was an important meeting, and I am very glad it took place. I won't discuss here the topics that were raised, but it was really important that we have this meeting.

Question: Will you have a three-way summit in the White House?

Albright: That hasn't been ruled out.

Question: Mr. Netanyahu, will you attend a three-way summit at the White House?

Netanyahu: I'll quote the secretary of state!

Question: Mr. Arafat, what are you doing to calm Israeli concerns about matters of security? Have you confiscated weapons? Dismantled terrorist cells?
Arafat: Ditto!
Question [to Netanyahu]: What was your response, sir?
Netanyahu: No.

The meeting at the White House takes place several hours later. Although the Clinton administration would like Netanyahu to accept the principle of a 13.1 percent withdrawal from the West Bank, the prime minister refuses: a security agreement must come first. Albright goes back to the Middle East on October 5 for a new round of shuttling between Arafat and Netanyahu—with no great success.

WYE PLANTATION

With an electoral campaign in the United States in full swing, and while impeachment proceedings are being readied in the House of Representatives, Bill Clinton decides to save the peace process. There will be a summit at the Aspen Institute at Wye River Plantation in Maryland. Benjamin Netanyahu lets it be known that he is reluctant to accept the invitation; the Palestinians, he says, must first present plans for security and combating terrorism. According to Palestinian analysts, this is a maneuver on Netanyahu's part to block the peace process.

On October 10, Mohammed Dahlan, the head of preventive security in Gaza, meets with Ami Ayalon, the head of Shin Bet, who tells him, "You and I have to urge our leaders to go to the United States. We have to prepare the ground for them." He suggests a meeting with Netanyahu. Dahlan calls Yasir Arafat, who gives him the go-ahead. He is received that very evening in the prime minister's private residence. Dahlan assures Netanyahu that the Palestinians will present a security plan.

The Palestinian leadership prepares and approves the document the very next day, with the understanding that it will be presented orally, and only orally, to the Israelis and the Americans. No hard copy will be handed over to them. On October 14, there is a meeting in Tel Aviv, where Mohammed Dahlan and Jibril Rajoub discuss their security plan with Yitzhak Mordechai, the Israeli defense minister. General Shaul Mofaz, from military intelligence, is there, as is Israel Hasson, the number two man at Shin Bet.

The Palestinian leaders present their protocol for the meeting. They are asked several times by the Israelis to demonstrate their good intentions by promising to work for security and stability. The protocol is signed: in principle, the matter is settled. The CIA representatives who have been following all these discussions are satisfied.

Yasir Arafat and Benjamin Netanyahu arrive in Washington on October 15, 1998. This time, the Americans have taken precautions. The Israeli prime minister will not have time to meet with his friends on the Republican right or with far-right fundamentalists. He is immediately taken to the White House and, after a brief ceremony, is placed in a helicopter heading straight for Wye Plantation.

Madeleine Albright is there, assisted by her Middle East team from the state department. The discussions on matters of security are led by George Tenet, head of the CIA, and Stan Moskowitz, head of the CIA bureau in Tel Aviv. Bill Clinton spends long hours conferring with one side and the other; Vice President Al Gore follows the talks from a distance.

On the evening of October 16, Yitzhak Mordechai and Ariel Sharon, who in the meantime has become the foreign minister, join Netanyahu and Nathan Shcharansky, the minister of commerce. The heart of the discussion is the Palestinian security plan. Meir Dagan, general in the reserves and adviser to the prime minister for the struggle against terrorism, rejects the document Mordechai had accepted a few days before. He demands a detailed plan, including a list of names of the Islamists and Palestinian police the Autonomous Authority agrees to arrest. Israel Hasson then explains to the defense minister that such a demand is not "professional," and that the Palestinians cannot satisfy it.

The next day, Sunday, Netanyahu, Sharon, and Shcharansky return to the attack: "No detailed plan, no negotiations." The collision occurs that evening. During a meeting with Clinton and the Palestinians, Bibi Netanyahu announces that the Israeli delegation is going to pack its bags unless there is an explicit tripartite agreement on security. For Mohammed Dahlan, this is out of the question. A Palestinian document presented orally to the Israelis and Americans is one thing, but definitely not a plan officially approved by Netanyahu, which would make him, Dahlan, the Israelis' collaborator. "So go ahead and leave!" Dahlan tells Netanyahu and stalks out of the meeting.

Another crisis. To prevent Netanyahu from acting on his threat, Bill Clinton and his advisers tell the Israelis—knowing this is not the case—that a detailed security plan exists and will be presented to them tomorrow. Yitzhak Mordechai, who is at the meeting, goes back to his quarters. He calls in Israel Hasson and General Yanai: "We asked the Palestinians to present their detailed plan. The Americans say they have one."

Hasson is thunderstruck: "Another plan with a detailed list of the people they should arrest?" "Yes," Mordechai answers. "Go find Tenet, and calm Dahlan down so he'll come and present it to us tomorrow."

Hasson understands that the aim of the maneuver is to avoid a major crisis. He goes to see Tenet, who has no idea how to get out of this predicament, and tells him he will do what he can to resolve matters with the Palestinians. His only condition is that, in the meeting on security he will be chairing tomorrow, he be allowed to speak whenever he asks to. The Shin Bet agent then goes to smoke the nargileh together with Dahlan in the wing of the Palestinian delegation. He tells him that, tomorrow, he must reply in the affirmative to all his questions.

The next day's meeting is one long fanfare on the part of Tenet and Hasson, who manage to get the original security plan passed. Each time Dahlan gets hot under the collar after one of Meir Dagan's questions, Hasson interrupts him and exclaims, "Abu Fadi [father of Fadi]!" to calm him down (Fadi is Dahlan's son). The Americans consider the security plan a fait accompli.

The next day brings a violent incident: a Palestinian hurls a grenade at Israeli civilians at Beersheva. Sixty-four people are wounded, three seriously. Netanyahu suspends all negotiations, except those concerning security. Clinton, who has canceled his appearance at a fundraiser in California, returns to Wye Plantation. After a few hours everything returns to normal. The terrorist turns out to be a former collaborator with Israeli intelligence and is said to have acted alone.

Hussein of Jordan arrives on October 20. He is undergoing treatment for cancer at the Mayo Clinic. Bald, his complexion waxy, he pleads passionately with Netanyahu and Arafat, begging them to go forward and arrive at an agreement. But, on the 21st, there is a major crisis.

Aviv Bushinsky, Netanyahu's spokesman, comes to the press center that has been set up in a nearby college and makes an announcement: since there is no Palestinian security plan, the prime minister is leaving the conference. Palestinian spokesmen come to give their reaction, and a journalist asks Ahmed Tibi, a doctor, how he interprets the Israeli gesture. "I'm a gynecologist, not a psychiatrist," is

Tibi's reply. From his room, Benjamin Netanyahu holds a phone meeting with Israeli consuls on duty in the United States. He tells them that the Americans at Wye Plantation are alarmed by his gesture: "I've got them by the balls!" he crows.

The diplomats are, to say the least, surprised. Clinton, who was due to return, cancels his plan. Madeleine Albright goes to see Netanyahu. It would be a pity if he left, she tells him; but, she adds, he is free to do as he wishes. A few minutes later, the American chief of protocol meets with Netanyahu to ask what type of ceremony he wants for his departure from Washington.

In the evening, the Israeli initiative misfires. Netanyahu finally decides to stay. The episode, abundantly covered by American television, will not improve the prime minister's image.

Bill Clinton returns to Wye Plantation on October 22 with the intention of finishing up. Everyone is brought together: Albright and her team, National Security Adviser Sandy Berger and his Middle East specialists, Tenet and Moskowitz from the CIA. Israelis and Palestinians are asked to go to the large room of the main building, which has been extended with a tent. In the middle is a table where the leaders will sit. In one corner, the drafting committee will write up the agreements reached by Netanyahu and Arafat. The rest of the delegations will sit further away. The meeting begins at 10:30 in the morning and will last twenty-one hours.

Clinton starts out with the problem of the Palestinian airport, built with the help of the European Union and the King of Morocco, near Rafah in the south of the Gaza Strip. "There is an agreement," he says, "and all that remains is to determine its international code, which will be Palestinian." Netanyahu's opening gambit is to refer to the number of Palestinian police, which he wants to see reduced, and the expense to which the implementation of the accord will put him. Clinton reassures him that he will get American aid.

The discussion returns to the issue of the airport. Israeli security will be permitted to search all the planes there; only Yasir Arafat's equipment will be considered off limits to Israeli agents. Arafat then explains that he sometimes borrows Saudi or Egyptian planes, put at his disposal by the leaders of those countries—and he would not like to have them searched by the Israelis. Well, why don't we set up a special three-way meeting just to discuss Arafat's plane, Netanyahu suggests. At this Yasir Abed Rabbo, who is present at the session, feels deeply humiliated. Ariel Sharon's smile is particularly galling to him.

Mordechai, who has personal contacts in Arafat's delegation, drops a word to Abu Ala to the effect that, from now on, the Palestinians should emphasize the issue of their prisoners held in Israel. Meanwhile, after the failure of his meeting with Netanyahu and Arafat, Clinton, together with Albright and Ross, is trying to find a solution to the problem of how large the Palestinian police force should be. The Americans suggest a compromise formula:

1. The force will be limited to 28,000 men, and American and Palestinian experts will then re-evaluate its needs in view of the threats facing the Palestinian Authority.
2. The CIA will increase its support of the Palestinian police by holding more frequent training sessions and supplying updated equipment.

Ariel Sharon, Abu Mazen, and Abu Ala are examining the question of the two safe corridors between Gaza and the West Bank. Only one, between Gaza and the Hebron area, has been negotiated, since at this point the Israelis are refusing to discuss the second, which is to end at Latrun. Sharon, who had seemed to show interest in the harbor project the Palestinians want to construct on the Gaza coast, is now reluctant to give his assent.

The discussions are getting nowhere. After lunch, Netanyahu comes over to chat with the Palestinians. "An agreement will definitely not be reached this evening," he tells them. "There's still the whole matter of security to be dealt with." "That file is closed," Saeb Erekat protests. "The negotiation is over." Netanyahu is visibly sorry to have let the CIA be the judge in this regard: the Americans have confirmed that Mohammed Dahlan, the chief of preventive security in Gaza, and Amin al-Hindi, head of Palestinian intelligence, have given them a satisfactory proposal accepted by Yitzhak Mordechai and his team. His voice tight, Netanyahu tells Erekat that Mordechai has not informed him of this. It is unclear whether Netanyahu knows what his defense minister has been up to.

It is 2:30 in the afternoon, and things must move forward. The leaders assemble in the middle of the room. Netanyahu suggests that each one reveal his priorities in the negotiation. Yasir Arafat immediately says, "The third Israeli withdrawal from the West Bank and the release of prisoners."

To which Netanyahu replies:

We want you to hand over the terrorists among you, the ones we've been looking for, or else put them in jail. At least then I'll be able to say that the matter has been settled. There is also the meeting of the Palestinian National Council [to abrogate the Palestinian Charter]. As for the first redeployment, it will take place in the north and south of the West Bank, and territorial continuity [between Palestinian enclaves] will be assured. You will see the maps one week after I've shown them to my cabinet, one week afterward. Regarding the third stage, I am not satisfied with the text Ross has prepared.

Netanyahu lets it be understood that he might free hundreds of prisoners, perhaps a hundred from Fatah and a hundred others who have not committed violent crimes and do not belong to Hamas. And then, he says, the problem of the Palestinian National Council must be resolved. Netanyahu does not know that his defense minister has discreetly suggested a solution to the Palestinians: Arafat would invite as many PNC members as possible to Gaza to meet with representatives of the Palestinian institutions in the autonomous territories: the executive committee of the PLO, the autonomous legislative council, and the like. Bill Clinton would attend the meeting, during which Arafat would put to a new vote his letter nullifying the articles in the Palestinian Charter that run contrary to the agreements with Israel. Arafat had immediately replied that he would accept such a formula. The idea was communicated to the Americans.

The three leaders examine the problem in the course of the afternoon, and it is Benjamin Netanyahu who suggests that the Palestinian institutions meet in Gaza with Clinton present. Arafat debates pro forma. But, under pressure from Ariel Sharon, Netanyahu soon changes his mind. Agreement on this point will finally be reached in the evening.

Haggling on the prisoner issue continues. The Israelis are ready to release 500 prisoners; the Palestinians demand 1,000. Another point of conflict is the strength of the Palestinian police force. Netanyahu wants to reduce it to 24,000; Clinton suggests 28,000. Arafat defends his position:

If you want me to ensure safety and order, you've got to let me have the means to do so! Have you ever supplied me with weapons when I had to face Hamas and

Jihad, when they were seizing control of the streets, and a coup d'état was given free rein for forty-eight hours, an incursion fomented by the Iranians, those same Iranians who gave our embassy in Tehran to Hamas?

It's up to me to decide how to respond to your demands when it comes to security, and with the number you're suggesting, 24,000 men, I couldn't meet your security requirements. I think that, as a former army captain, you should ask me to increase this number. Unless you expect me to mobilize schoolboys to prevent a takeover?

Netanyahu: I'm not familiar with this attempted coup d'état.

Yasir Abed Rabbo: I don't understand what you mean when you say that.

Ariel Sharon: It's not a police force you have; it's an army, with officers, regional commanders, chiefs. When we fought during the War of Independence, we had as many men as you do today, and we were facing seven Arab armies, seven countries. We have to take that into consideration, and I think this is what our prime minister means. We were around 30,000 to 35,000 fighters. . . .

This reasoning makes the American experts smile. It's hard to imagine the Israeli army, its air power, its armored vehicles, its nuclear deterrent, routed by 28,000 Palestinian soldiers armed with Kalashnikov assault rifles.

Sharon never addresses Arafat directly. He openly ignores him, while cordially greeting the other members of his delegation. Yasir Abed Rabbo, enraged by this lack of courtesy, does not return Sharon's overtures.

The negotiation limps along. At one in the morning, Israelis and Palestinians face off on the prisoner issue. Netanyahu has confirmed his offer to free 500 prisoners:

100 Fatah militants and 400 others, on condition that they are not members of Hamas. Abu Mazen ups the number to 1,000 and demands an increase in the freeing of militants imprisoned before the signing of the Oslo accord in 1993.

Clinton, Arafat, and Netanyahu once again sit down at the central table at the request of the Israeli prime minister, who offers a new suggestion. He is prepared to release additional prisoners in exchange for the arrest of General Ghazi Jebali, who is in charge of the Palestinian police and is accused by Israeli intelligence of having had a hand in a terrorist matter.

Arafat gets angry whenever he has to deal with a demand of this kind. So, when Netanyahu continues: "All you have to do is, every week, arrest eight of your officers who are being sought by us, until the forty-five we want [are in jail]," Arafat sees this as a provocation. He gets up and leaves the table. Clinton alone remains opposite Netanyahu. After several minutes he too gives up, throws the papers he has been holding onto the table, and shouts at Netanyahu, "It's sickening how you confuse the dead and the living. Up to now I haven't said anything, but now I'm going to." And he leaves the room.

All those present are petrified. Danny Naveh, the secretary of the Israeli government, mumbles something. For Sandy Berger, the national security adviser, enough is enough. Under the stunned gaze of the Palestinians, he turns to Naveh and says, "You must respect our president." A few minutes later, Madeleine Albright comes back into the room and asks Netanyahu to join Clinton, who wants to speak with him one on one.

Everyone is waiting. George Tenet keeps Arafat and the Palestinian delegation company. "You just about guessed right," he says to Mohammed Dahlan, who, since the beginning of the conference, has been predicting that Netanyahu would not sign an agreement.

It is 3 A.M. Clinton finishes his talk with Netanyahu and has met with Arafat. The crisis is over. The Israelis have come down a peg or two: they agree to the release of 750 Palestinian prisoners. But there is a price to be paid. Netanyahu has put back on the table his intention to build the new Jewish quarter on the hill of Djebel Abu Ghneim in South Jerusalem, as well as several roads going around Arab locales on the West Bank. Arafat and Abu Ala have raised strong protests. Netanyahu has even suggested a trade-off: if the Palestinians accept in principle the construction of the Jewish quarter of Har Homa in South Jerusalem, he will cancel the arrest warrant against General Ghazi Jebali. The idea misfires.

According to Dennis Ross, the negotiation on the prisoners held by Israel then proceeded as follows:

Arafat was alone. I was sitting next to President Clinton, who told him what he thought he, Clinton, could get [from Netanyahu] on this matter. The prisoners who had not committed crimes of violence. Those who had killed Palestinians, not Israelis. That would come to 300 on one side, 350 on the other. Maybe more, 750 in all. But Arafat had put nothing in writing. When Dahlan came to tell me that all prisoners released had to be political, I said, "This isn't what your boss agreed to with my president." And Dahlan said to me, "That's going to be a problem."[53]

By 5 A.M. an agreement seems to be in the offing. Netanyahu is hunched over the telephone with some of his ministers. Two hours later, the Americans heave a sigh of relief. It's done: the text has been drawn up and will be signed later that morning at the White House. Tenet turns to Dahlan: "You lost. He's going to sign!"

---

53. Videotaped interview with Dennis Ross, February 19, 2002, Washington.

"Hold on. It's not a done deal yet," Dahlan replies. Fifteen minutes later, events seem to prove him right. Netanyahu is saying that Clinton promised him the release of Jonathan Pollard, the American who is serving a long prison sentence after having been found guilty of spying for Israel.

Clinton never made any such promise. All he says he agreed to do was order a review of the case. George Tenet expresses his strong opposition to the freeing of a man whom the FBI and CIA consider a traitor. In the United States, the press and political circles react very negatively to this new crisis provoked by Netanyahu—who finally decides to do an about-face. The closing ceremony will take place at the scheduled time.

Bill Clinton thanks his colleagues and King Hussein of Jordan, who is manifestly weakened by his illness. The president congratulates the protagonists. He gives the floor to Benjamin Netanyahu, who says, "Today, the security of Israel and the entire region is better assured. Sacrifices have had to be made by both parties. This is an important moment in time. [We are offering] a future of peace and security to our children, and to the children of our neighbors, the Palestinians. We have seized the moment. . . ."

Netanyahu speaks for only a few minutes. The time of the Sabbath is approaching in Israel, and he would like to make his statement live on Israeli television. In a little over an hour that will no longer be possible. Clinton takes the microphone again in order to hand it over to Yasir Arafat. But he cannot resist a barb in Netanyahu's direction: "I can't picture you in a kaffiyeh!" This is an allusion to the posters distributed by the extreme right in Israel after the conclusion of the Oslo accord, showing Yitzhak Rabin wearing the traditional Arab headcovering.

Arafat makes a very long speech. The members of his delegation realize that, instead of choosing one text from among the three that were presented to him, he has decided to read all of them. Has he made a mistake? Or does he want to embarrass Netanyahu, who is in a hurry to end?

Hussein of Jordan takes the floor next. His statement sounds like a political last will and testament:

> I have great faith in God, and I believe that everyone lives out his destiny. . . . One great concern has been with me constantly all these years: a total commitment to the cause of peace. We quarrel, we reach agreements; we are friends, we aren't. But we do not have the right to determine the future of our children and our grandchildren by acting irresponsibly. There has been enough destruction. Enough death. . . . It is time that all of us together take the place our people deserve under the sun, we, the descendants of Abraham.

CLINTON IN GAZA

Back in Jerusalem, Netanyahu has to deal with a revolt by the toughest elements in his coalition government. Day after day he reports to the government group assigned to examine the accord. Finally, on November 17, the Knesset approves the text. Seventy-five members, of whom only thirty belong to the coalition, vote in favor. Two days later, the government gives its approval only to the implementation of the first phase of the accord, and that by a hairbreadth vote of six in favor, five against, and three abstentions.

On November 20, 1998, the Israeli army carries out a redeployment near Jenin in the northern part of the West Bank, where the inhabitants of the Jewish settlements are the least militant. The Palestinian Authority is granted control of 7.1 percent of territories for which it had formerly had only administrative responsibility. In addition, 2 percent of territories under exclusive Israeli control now come under Palestinian administration. In other words, the fully autonomous territories now represent 10 percent of the West Bank, in contrast to 3 percent previously, and the number of administratively autonomous zones reaches 18.6 percent.[54]

Two hundred and fifty Palestinian prisoners have been freed when the Authority suddenly discovers that 150 of them are guilty of ordinary crimes: auto theft and working without a permit. The families of political prisoners then begin a hunger strike. Demonstrations are held in the major cities of the West Bank and Gaza. In several places, violent incidents erupt between the Israeli army and young people throwing stones.

After a few weeks, Arafat's services will manage to quiet down what had become the "prisoners' intifada" in time for Bill Clinton's visit to Gaza. But there is still tension. The Authority has promised to confiscate weapons kept illegally by organizations and private persons. On October 25, the security service under Colonel Moussa Arafat had tried to occupy the Fatah offices in Ramallah, where militants of the Tanzim, the armed branch of Fatah, are staying. The operation collapses. During the exchange of fire, a young Palestinian is killed.

The confrontation goes on for several days, until Yasir Arafat orders the withdrawal of the security forces. The Tanzim have just won their first victory over the traditional leadership of the Autonomous Authority. Three weeks later, in the Balata refugee camp in Nablus, other militants will set fire to the Palestinian police station; the police had prevented the demonstrators from attacking the Israeli enclave at Joseph's Tomb.[55]

---

54. According to the Wye agreements, the Autonomous Authority was to receive partial or total control of 40 percent of the West Bank.

55. See, for example, Cordesman, pp. 163–164.

On November 24, Rafah Airport, in the south of the Gaza Strip, is officially opened by the arrival of Egyptian, Saudi, and Moroccan planes in the symbolic presence of the European emissary to the Near East, Miguel Moratinos, who makes the first Tel Aviv-to-Gaza flight.

Bill Clinton arrives in Israel on December 13, 1998. The atmosphere is, quite frankly, bad. In the past two weeks there has been renewed agitation in the Palestinian territories at the instigation of Fatah and the families of prisoners still being held in Israel. And several Israeli ministers have suggested that Clinton's visit be canceled, in the belief that his participation in the gathering of Palestinian agencies would be too great a concession to Yasir Arafat.

The peace process is stalled once again, especially since Netanyahu has decided to suspend implementation of the accords if the Palestinian Authority does not fulfill five conditions:

1. Give up the unilateral proclamation of the Palestinian State;
2. Give up the demand for the release of Palestinian prisoners guilty of violent crimes;
3. Mount an operation, under American control, to seize illegal weapons;
4. Furnish a list of Palestinian police. Cut this police force back to 30,000 men;
5. Furnish the first report of the commission against incitement to violence.

The American administration rejects these new Israeli demands. In Netanyahu's circle, it is being said that, in any case, no agreement with the Palestinians is possible: "Even if Yasir Arafat started to echo Zeev Jabotinsky, he wouldn't get an inch of extra land, because the far right won't let

Benjamin Netanyahu make concessions." The source of this remark prefers to remain anonymous.

Conversations between Madeleine Albright and Ariel Sharon are unable to ease the tension. Clinton will wear a forced smile during the official ceremonies: at this very time, in Washington, the House of Representatives is getting ready to vote on his possible impeachment.

But by the following day the scene and the mood have changed. The helicopters carrying Clinton and his entourage land on the runway of the Gaza airport and are met with a warm reception. Jewish-American officials breathe a sigh of relief: "It's good to finally feel welcome in this part of the world!" At a lunch provided by Arafat, Clinton sets the tone. He drops a phrase that will enrage the Israeli right: "For the first time in the history of the Palestinian movement, the Palestinian people and their elected representatives now have a chance to determine their own destiny on their own land. . . . I am proud to be the first American president here, standing side by side with the Palestinian people as you forge your future."

At five in the afternoon, the Palestinian agencies hold their meeting. Arafat, beaming, welcomes the American president, who then makes a major speech: "Peace must mean many things. Legitimate rights for the Palestinians, genuine security for Israel. But it must begin with something more fundamental: mutual recognition." Clinton mentions the children to whom Arafat introduced him, children whose fathers are imprisoned in Israel, as well as the Israeli orphans he had seen the previous evening at Netanyahu's house. This comparison will infuriate some Israelis. Haven't the Palestinians in question been jailed for acts of terrorism?

Clinton continues: "The Palestinians must recognize Israel's right to existence, the right of its people to live in safety today, tomorrow, and forever. Israel must recognize the right of the Palestinians to aspire to live in freedom today, tomorrow, and forever."

The next day, in the Israeli part of the Erez checkpoint, Netanyahu and Arafat face each other once again under the gaze of Bill Clinton, who has many other worries. Beside the prospect of impeachment proceedings, he is at this very time preparing an offensive against Iraq. The meeting goes badly and will not result in a joint declaration. Each of the participants, separately, speaks to the press. Ariel Sharon accuses the Palestinian Authority of flouting the law by stockpiling a large quantity of weapons.

Clinton goes off to Bethlehem, where he lights the Christmas tree in Manger Square. In the afternoon, he is the guest of Benjamin Netanyahu, who takes him to see Masada, the place where, 2,000 years earlier, Jewish zealots chose suicide rather than fall into the hands of the Romans. "I want you to see how strong Jewish determination is!" declares the Israeli prime minister.

The writer Meron Benvenisti is annoyed by this initiative: Isn't Netanyahu taking the risk of rekindling an old quarrel? "Is it right," Benvenisti wonders, "to glorify the actions of a group of disheartened zealots? Wouldn't it be more appropriate, instead, to praise the school of Yavneh and its sages, whose primary concern was rationality?"[56] Two millennia ago, Rabbi Yochanan Ben Zakkai refused to participate in the great revolt of the Jews against Rome and created a center for the study of biblical law at Yavneh. Its realism contrasted with the extremist ideology of the zealots.

Oddly enough, in the preceding months Benjamin Netanyahu has been keeping up the dialogue with Hafez el-Assad via several intermediaries. But Assad continues to

---

56. Benvenisti, 1998, p. 5.

refuse any direct secret negotiations with Israel. Ron Lauder, a Jewish-American millionaire close to Netanyahu, has agreed to mediate between Damascus and Jerusalem. Netanyahu's diplomatic adviser, Uzi Arad, a former head of analysis in Mossad, has taken on this portfolio.

The negotiations will make considerable progress. Netanyahu has accepted in principle the withdrawal from the Golan up to the ridge overlooking Lake Tiberias, but he is demanding an ongoing Israeli presence in warning and detection stations to be set up on Mount Hermon. The Lauder mission will capsize the day the Syrians ask him to bring a map showing how Netanyahu envisages the layout of the border. Let into the secret by Netanyahu, Ariel Sharon will demand the immediate cessation of these contacts.

Another odd episode takes place during a clandestine meeting between Netanyahu and Ehud Barak at the Mossad headquarters near Tel Aviv. Netanyahu offers the Labor leader a united national front, with the aim of pursuing the talks with Syria. Barak refuses.

Miguel Moratinos, the European emissary to the Middle East, also plays the role of mediator. His discussions in Damascus and Jerusalem have led to the drawing up of a working document.[57] Informal negotiations, sponsored by the European Union, are to take place, their goal being the resumption of bilateral talks under American auspices. Moratinos suggests that these discussions be based on a withdrawal of the Israeli army from the lines it occupies on the Golan Heights, in accord with Resolutions 242 and 338 of the UN Security Council. At the same time, Resolution 425, concerning the Israeli withdrawal from South Lebanon, will be implemented.

---

57. This is what is called a "non-paper," whose existence can, if necessary, be denied by the parties to it.

Security arrangements between Israel and Syria are to be discussed as well. The Syrians have agreed to consider the establishment of warning and detection stations on the ground, something they have rejected up to now. This is also the first time that a solution to the Israeli occupation of South Lebanon has been directly examined in such a context. But this dialogue, too, will fail, because of the radicalization of the political crisis in Israel and the planning of upcoming elections.

ELECTIONS OR PUTSCH?

On January 4, 1999, the Knesset votes to dissolve itself by a vote of eighty-five in favor, twenty-seven against. The right takes advantage of the occasion to get approval for a "law of reinforcement of the Golan," stipulating that any restitution of territories to Syria must be preceded by popular approval in a referendum and a majority vote of sixty-one members of parliament. Labor votes in favor, since they don't want to give the impression that they are ready to give up the Golan. The first round of elections for prime minister will take place on May 17; if no candidate has an absolute majority, there will be a second round on June 2.

The event that the Middle East had been expecting for weeks is announced on February 8 by the royal palace in Amman: Hussein of Jordan is dead. He had been brought home in great pain from the Mayo Clinic in the United States, where, several days earlier, a final attempt at a bone-marrow transplant had failed. The entire Arab world will attend the funeral, along with Israeli politicians in full force, majority and opposition alike. A few days before breathing his last, the Hashemite ruler had deprived his brother, Prince Hassan, of the title of heir apparent and designated his son, Abdallah, who now assumes power.

In March, the Kosovo drama rocks the political scene in Israel. Pictures of thousands of Muslim Kosovars evicted from their homes and thrown onto trains by rough Serbian soldiers scandalize the Israeli public, who are reminded of the Jewish genocide. But, to the great surprise of commentators from the daily press in Israel, Netanyahu is slow to condemn the Milosevic government and to approve the military operation being conducted by the United States and its European allies.

A controversy breaks out in the right-wing camp. Typical is this broadcast of March 29, 1999, on Arutz 7, the radio station of the Jewish settlers:

It is certainly unnecessary to explain to the listeners of Arutz 7 all about "hostile media." But did you ever realize that there is another group suffering from similarly hostile media? The Serbs, for example? Without condoning the terrible war crimes no doubt committed by the Serbs, we and they basically find ourselves in the same boat. The world press understates each of our respective sides, while it embellishes the Arab–Moslem case, and sweeps under the carpet its faults, crimes, and inherent dangers. Both the Serbs and the Israelis are given to American–European pressure on behalf of the Moslems. We were forced in Wye Plantation to give over portions of our homeland to the Arabs, and the Serbs are being forced right now to hand over a sovereign region of theirs, Kosovo, to the Moslem Albanians. The Serbs, in fact, call Kosovo their "Jerusalem"—would it be that we would learn from them how to stand fast in conviction and determination and strength when the time comes for us to fight for our Jerusalem.[58]

---

58. Ha'etzni, 1999. The translation is as it appears on the Arutz website.

Some of Netanyahu's cabinet ministers believe that Israel should not take sides; others, like Moshe Arens, fully support the international coalition led by the United States. Eventually, under fire from critics in the Israeli press, the government will issue a statement condemning massacres committed "by the Serbs or any other group, . . . from the point of view of both our history and our moral sense."[59]

Later, faced with denunciations in the American press, which cannot understand this attitude, and with the strong reaction of part of the Israeli public, deeply moved by pictures of the Kosovars' suffering, Netanyahu sends a medical team to Albania and even takes in a group of Kosovar refugees.

The Israeli electoral campaign is a long one, and some commentators will call it a "military putsch" carried out democratically. Dozens of generals and colonels of the reserve, supported by part of the defense establishment, mobilize to, in effect, overthrow Benjamin Netanyahu. For, in his three years in office, Netanyahu has managed the feat of quarreling with the army.

The antagonistic tone is set by Yitzhak Mordechai, the defense minister who had been relieved of his post on January 23, 1999. Very popular, especially among Jews of Middle Eastern origin, this former general had played a large part in Netanyahu's election in 1996.[60] On April 13, the two men confront one another on television. Netanyahu has decided to ignore Mordechai and attack Ehud Barak, who is not present. This is a mistake. The debate quickly turns into a domestic quarrel, but it is Netanyahu who gets the

---

59. Hockstader, 1999, p. A12.

60. After leaving the army at the beginning of 1996, Mordechai had come to Shimon Peres to ask for a post in civilian life. What he wanted was the directorship of Mossad. Peres told Mordechai that this position would not suit him.

worst of it. Mordechai hurls accusations at his enemy: "You are utterly devoid of honesty, decency, and integrity." One phrase is repeated several times, with all its insinuations: "You know that I stood in the way of certain things because they would have plunged the country into a very different situation from what we have today." And, when Netanyahu shows signs of nervousness, Mordechai lets loose with: "I know you. You don't have the patience to listen, not even during meetings of the security cabinet." As for reducing the intensity of terrorism, he goes on to say, Netanyahu has had nothing to do with it; it is the result of the ceaseless efforts of the army, the security services, and the defense ministry.

Netanyahu strikes back. "You have no ideals, no message to send," he says. "You're motivated by hate and the defense of your own personal interests." But in vain. This is the funeral of a regime.

The heads of the security services are sneering. For months, anti-Netanyahu anecdotes have been making the rounds of newspaper offices. It is said, for example, that Netanyahu used to summon Mordechai to the office of the cabinet and then keep him waiting long hours, and that meetings to which Mordechai had been invited were canceled at the last minute without his having been told. Reserve General David Agmon, who headed Netanyahu's cabinet for four months before being dismissed, says that "Bibi makes his decisions at random. He doesn't listen to experts. Part of his time is devoted to communications and manipulation of the press. He never makes a transcript after his meetings with foreign or Palestinian leaders."[61]

And it is revealed that Netanyahu had risked a major political crisis by suggesting the kidnapping of General Tawfiq al-Tirawi, an associate of Arafat's, in an autonomous Pal-

---

61. Interview with David Agmon, April 15, 1999, Tel Aviv.

estinian zone, on the grounds that he was behind the murder of people selling Palestinian land to Israelis. The head of Shin Bet, Ami Ayalon, had protested this plan, and his response had filtered down to the press: "You're crazy! That would lead to a break with the Palestinian Authority!" Plans to assassinate Ahmed Yassin in Gaza and to effect the escape from his Cairo prison of Azzam Azzam, an Israeli Druse found guilty of espionage in Egypt, had been considered but quickly abandoned under pressure from the heads of the security services.

Mordechai declares his candidacy at the cabinet office. He has joined the Center Party, a group formed by ex-Chief of Staff Amnon Lipkin-Shahak and several Likud dissidents. Netanyahu is becoming more and more isolated. To win the trust of an electorate always highly concerned with matters of security, he has only one general left to rely on for support: Ariel Sharon, who has a controversial past. His other remaining allies are the ultra-Orthodox and the far right, along with the settlement movement.

Running opposite him is Ehud Barak. The most decorated soldier in Israel's history, surrounded by an impressive group of former division commanders, chiefs of police, and heads of special services, Barak has everything it takes to reassure the public. For the military has mobilized not just against Netanyahu the man, but also against his political philosophy, against the idea that the Israeli-style "melting pot" has failed and given way to a society divided into tribes whose demands have to be catered to so that Netanyahu can remain in power.

In contrast, the generals are eager to see a pure product of original Israeli identity at the helm. A sabra[62] formed by the army would share the army's conviction that, beyond

---

62. Literally, a prickly pear, the term used familiarly to designate the native Jewish citizens of Israel.

political disagreements about the future of the Palestinian territories, Israeli society is held together by the passage of young immigrants and the religious, including the Orthodox, through the melting pot of military service.

Ehud Barak, then, is in effect conducting an electoral campaign and a military one at the same time. Although those closest to him are for the most part veterans of the Sayeret Matkal, the commando unit of the general staff, reserve officers are taking charge of the army of young volunteers of the Rabin generation, teenagers who, the day after the assassination, had promised to follow the path of peace. This is the group that will win the battle of posters and will take to the streets opposite the Likud militants and the Orthodox mobilized in favor of Netanyahu.

In Washington, Bill Clinton is anxiously watching the electoral campaign. His political advisers, and polls sent to him regularly by the local branch of the CIA, are not yet predicting a decisive victory for Barak.

May 4 is approaching, the critical date marking the end of the interim period stipulated by the Cairo accord. Yasir Arafat's intentions are not clear. Legally, the head of the PLO could consider himself free of any obligations and could proclaim the Palestinian State. But the Israeli government has announced that, should this happen, it will immediately annex all the territories of the West Bank and Gaza now under its control: a fatal blow to the peace process.

And so, on April 26, Clinton sends an unprecedented letter to Arafat:

As the leader of the Palestinian people, you have made historic decisions for peace. At this time it is critical that you stay that course and maintain the courage and vision that can help bring us closer to that goal. . . . Mr. Chairman, I know that your people have faced great difficulties in the past several years. Clearly, the Oslo process has not made the kind of progress we would have hoped to see. Much time has been wasted, and many opportunities lost. Oslo was based on the principle of mutuality and the critical role negotiations must play in realizing Palestinian aspirations. At the same time, the Palestinian–Israeli partnership, so essential to peacemaking, has been badly shaken.

The agreement we helped facilitate between you and Prime Minister Netanyahu at Wye carried with it a great deal of promise. The first phase was implemented. Unfortunately, the second and third phases have not been. The Palestinians have implemented many of their commitments for the second phase, and I appreciate your efforts, particularly in the security area where Palestinians are engaged in a serious effort to fight terror. It is important that you continue these efforts and fulfill all of your commitments. We will continue to work actively for implementation by Israel.

It is also critical that Palestinians and Israelis proceed with the important work of the permanent status negotiations. As agreed by the parties in the Declaration of Principles, "these negotiations shall cover remaining issues, including: Jerusalem, refugees, settlements, security arrangements, borders, relations, and cooperation with other neighbors and other issues of common interest."

As May 4 approaches, I also understand that you face enormous pressures and challenges in trying to realize Palestinian aspirations and keep hopes for peace alive. In your effort to deal with these challenges, I am asking that you continue to rely on the peace process as the way to fulfill the aspirations of your people. Indeed, negotiations are the only realistic way to fulfill those aspirations. . . . As I said in Gaza, I believe Palestinians should live free today, tomorrow and forever. . . .

For these negotiations to succeed, it is vital that the environment in which they occur be credible, serious and fair. The United States knows how destructive settlement activities, land confiscation, and house demolitions are to the pursuit of Palestinian-Israeli peace. . . .

Clinton adds that he will do all he can to strengthen the partnership between the United States and the Palestinians.

May 17, 10:30 P.M.: the voting booths have been closed for half an hour, and the first polls are predicting an overwhelming victory for Ehud Barak with 56 percent of the vote. Benjamin Netanyahu is about to concede defeat and congratulate his former chief of staff. What he will do now, he says, is take a break from politics for awhile.

Barak's is a victory not of a political movement but of a man, as the numbers suggest: he received three times as many votes as his legislative slate, "United Israel," although the slate brought together parliamentary candidates from the Labor Party, David Levy's Guesher Party, and religious moderates from Meimad. The Israeli parliament has been fragmented into fifteen units, and the major parties have lost ground: Likud has only nineteen seats left and Labor twenty-six. Shas has taken a leap forward with seventeen members.

The new prime minister will form a very large coalition, bringing together sibling rivals like the National Religious Party, Shas, and Meretz.[63] Single-handedly, he will undertake negotiations with Syria, Lebanon, and the Palestinians. This former chief of staff will pursue the peace process out

---

63. Shas is a Sephardic Orthodox movement, Meretz a small party that challenges Labor from the left.

of patriotism, convinced that, strategically, it is in the best interest of the country to do so, but he will make no concessions, either to Arafat or to Syria, when the security of Israeli is at stake. He will stand firmly against the left, for whom peace cannot be gained unless Israel takes risks and shows generosity, evacuating certain settlements in Gaza and the West Bank and accepting a solution for East Jerusalem. It will not be long before the Israeli peace camp discovers that it has backed the wrong candidate.

Chapter 3

Building Mistrust

May 17, 1999, 11 P.M. Benjamin Netanyahu is not waiting for the official results. Standing before his tearful militants, he acknowledges defeat:

> Thank you, my friends. I congratulate Ehud Barak on
> his victory. This is how it is in a democracy. . . . We have
> almost completely checked terrorism and restored per-
> sonal safety in Israel, we have imposed the principle
> of reciprocity, we have pursued the peace process and
> reduced unemployment. . . . I think the time has come
> for me to get back to my family, my wife, and my chil-
> dren, and to decide about my future. I am hereby inform-
> ing you of my intention to resign from the leadership of
> Likud.

The left is celebrating for the first time since November 4, 1995, that magical evening that ended so tragically
with the assassination of Yitzhak Rabin. In the square that
bears Rabin's name today, tens of thousands of Israelis
have gathered. Young people are dancing and singing. The
nightmare is over, they are saying; we'll have peace again.
Ehud Barak does not arrive until 3 A.M. He thanks all those

who voted for him and issues an appeal for national unity: "The time has come to make peace among us. Whether we are traditionalists, secular, ultra-Orthodox, or religious, we must not be one another's enemies. . . . I know that this victory would not have been possible without your support, and it would not have been possible without the support of many Likud backers [who voted for me]. I appreciate that and am committed to being the prime minister for everyone."

Barak says that he will ask all the political parties to join his governmental coalition, including, he says, the Sephardic Orthodox Shas. At this point, there is some booing from the crowd. Barak continues:

> The time for [making] peace has come. Not peace from a position of weakness, but peace in strength and security; not peace by giving up security, but peace that will bring security. We will move quickly toward a separation from the Palestinians by drawing four lines in the sand: once and for all a unified Jerusalem, under our sovereignty, as the eternal capital of Israel; in no case will we withdraw to the 1967 borders; no foreign army on the west bank of the Jordan; most of the settlement dwellers in Judea–Samaria to be housed in settlement units under our sovereignty. As I have promised, any final accord will be submitted to a referendum. When all is said and done, it will be you, the people of Israel, who will decide.

Discussions on the formation of the new government begin twenty-four hours later. Barak has asked Gilead Sher to be his representative to the various political parties. Forty-six years old, the son of a diplomat, a former journalist, and a colonel in the reserves, this brilliant lawyer is a fervent supporter of the peace process. And, most important, he has the wholehearted trust of Ehud Barak, despite the latter's famously suspicious nature.

THE UNLIKELY ALLIANCE WITH
THE RELIGIOUS PARTIES

As the new prime minister sees it, he faces a crucial choice: making the country's internal problems his priority, or relaunching the peace process so as to reach a definitive agreement with the Syrians and the Palestinians. In the first case, he must form a government of national unity with Likud. The religious parties would be neutralized, and Barak could keep his campaign promises to end exemption from military service for ultra-Orthodox youth, reduce the budgets of Talmudic schools, offer free education to everyone aged three and over as well as free university education, and establish a large-scale program of job creation. But the alliance with Likud, newly headed by Ariel Sharon, would automatically mean the blocking of the peace process. Barak therefore decides to form a coalition with the left and the religious parties.

On June 25, the National Religious Party and Yisrael Ba'Aliyah, Nathan Shcharansky's Russian-language movement, reach an agreement with Barak. The next day, Meretz, a left-wing branch of the Labor Party, joins the new government. Its head, Yossi Sarid, will be the minister of education. Foreign affairs will go to David Levy, the Likud dissident who, after a number of quarrels with Netanyahu, had finally joined the slate presented by Barak. Yitzhak Levy, head of the National Religious Party, wants the ministry of construction and gets it. He will be the settlers' de facto representative in the cabinet. Shlomo Ben Ami, who had won the Labor primaries, will be the minister of homeland security. It is hard for him to accept this appointment: at 56, this well-known history professor never dreamed he would be directing the Israeli police. The ultra-Orthodox are promised that the issue of drafting their yeshiva[64] students will be examined by a commission, and they sign an agreement with Barak.

The new government is presented to the Knesset on July 6. It consists of eighteen members, to whom five others will be added when, on August 5, the law limiting the number of ministers is amended. Yossi Beilin is named minister of justice. He was the architect of the 1993 Oslo accords together with Shimon Peres, the former foreign minister to whom Barak is anything but generous now: he offers Peres the ministry of regional cooperation, a virtual sinecure.

The personal relationship between Barak and Peres is dreadful. And besides, the new prime minister wants to keep all the former Oslo negotiators away from the peace process; to his mind, they made too many concessions to the Palestinians when the interim accord was drawn up. As minister of the interior at the time, in September 1995, to Yitzhak Rabin's great displeasure, Barak had even abstained when the accord was voted on by the government. Peres will not be involved in the negotiations until the end of the year 2000.

Seven weeks have gone by since the elections, and Yasir Arafat is champing at the bit. Barak's inaugural speech before the Knesset did nothing to calm his fears. True, the prime minister had stated that his priority was to conclude "a peace of the brave" and end the conflict that had dragged on for a century in the Middle East. "I understand not only my people's suffering but also the suffering of the Palestinian people," he had said. Yet his four firm principles were explicitly spelled out in the coalition agreement.

---

64. Yeshivas are Talmudic schools.

Abu Mazen, second in command of the PLO, expressed his dissatisfaction that very day in an interview on an Arab satellite television station: "If this is all Barak can offer, there will be no negotiations on the final status." And the Palestinians were distressed by a speech the prime minister had made the day before, in which he said he hoped to go ahead simultaneously with implementation of the Wye River agreement and negotiations on the final status of the Palestinian territories. "There is no question of accepting any delay whatsoever in the implementation of the accords that have been signed," Saeb Erekat had declared. "We aren't stupid!"

Then comes another gesture that enrages the Palestinians. Instead of meeting with Arafat immediately after taking office, Barak instead goes off to Alexandria to talk with Hosni Mubarak on July 9.

The Egyptian president, delighted to be rid of Benjamin Netanyahu at last, gives Barak a warm welcome: "This is a golden opportunity to advance the cause of peace. I have high hopes, but give this man time, two months, to get his bearings to the point where he can go straight ahead, firmly, in the direction of peace." Barak replies that he is "determined to use all means necessary to find the path on which we can move ahead, though without endangering the security or the vital interests of Israel."

Two days later, in the Israeli part of the Erez checkpoint at the northern entrance to the Gaza Strip, the meeting with Arafat finally takes place. Barak, who arrives first, greets the head of the PLO in front of the television cameras: an embrace, followed by a long handshake. But when the discussion gets underway a few minutes later, it will be strained. Barak says he wants to go straight to negotiations on the final status: "If we haven't reached an agreement in six months, we can go back to the implementation of the Wye River accord and the interim accord."

Arafat: The two have to be done at the same time: implementing Wye and the other accords, and beginning negotiations on the definitive status.[65]

Barak: No! No! Think about it!

Arafat: My mind is made up. I don't want that. Implement Wye right away! It's an agreement that Netanyahu made.

Barak: Give it some thought!

Arafat accepts the principle of establishing a permanent secret liaison with the prime minister: Yossi Ginosar, formerly number two at Shin Bet, who had already served in this capacity under Rabin, will be Barak's personal envoy to Arafat.

Barak leaves for the United States, where Bill Clinton is awaiting him. He is to make a stopover in London to meet with Tony Blair. After the takeoff at Tel Aviv, the Franco-Israeli businessman Jean Frydman passes him a message: "French leaders will not appreciate being left out on this first trip made by the head of the Israeli government, especially since he's taking the trouble to meet with the British prime minister." And so, from his plane, Barak phones Jacques Chirac and Lionel Jospin.

On July 15, at the White House, it's love at first sight between Clinton and Barak. Their meeting lasts two and a half hours. Clinton promises his guest that "America will walk beside you on the road to peace and will do whatever it can to help." Barak promises to implement all the accords that have been signed, including Wye River, but announces that he intends to complete negotiations on the definitive status in fifteen months. Clinton then invites Barak and his wife to have dinner at Camp David with him and Hillary.

---

65. Arafat is afraid that Barak will not surrender the territory the Palestinians are expecting before such a time as there may be a final agreement. He wants to be sure that the interim agreement will be implemented.

In private, Barak will say on this occasion that a treaty with Syria would be more important for Israel, from the strategic point of view, than an accord with the Palestinians, who pose only a weak threat.

The evening ends at 1 A.M. In the days that follow, Barak is received by Congress and also by the secretary of the treasury; he promises the latter that he will reduce Israel's request for economic aid over a period of six years. The visit is a success. Clinton, who in his day had managed to escape the draft during the Vietnam era, is full of admiration for this Israeli general: "I feel like a child with a new toy," he will say.

All this worries Arafat even more, and Danny Yatom, Barak's security adviser, soon finds it necessary to issue a clarifying statement: the Palestinians will not have to wait fifteen months to see the planned Israeli withdrawals on the West Bank.

On July 27, there is a new meeting at Erez. The Palestinians make it clear that they are feeling testy. Barak is still claiming that the negotiations on the final status and the implementation of the Wye accord must occur simultaneously. For Arafat, this means that the Israelis do not want to go ahead with the third redeployment from the West Bank before signing a definitive agreement. Once again, the meeting has not been prepared for; there have been no preliminary contacts. Eventually Arafat agrees to put off a decision for two weeks. Gilead Sher and Saeb Erekat are charged with examining the question. Erekat is instructed to do nothing but listen to Sher's arguments for the time being.

SHARM EL-SHEIK

On July 29, Ehud Barak makes another trip to Egypt, where Hosni Mubarak has promised to help him. On the same day, the first meeting of the negotiators takes place in a hotel in Jerusalem. Sher is accompanied by General Michael Herzog and Colonel Daniel Reisner, a jurist in the army's legal division. From the outset, Sher states that Israel will stand by the commitments made in the Wye River accord, including the planned redeployment on the West Bank. He does, however, ask for a revised timetable for the implementation of the accord.[66] Erekat replies that he believes Ehud Barak "to be an upright and sincere man." But, he says,

we have no more leeway. Palestinian society has lost all hope for peace. Over the past years it has been literally suffocated and humiliated. We are ready to begin negotiations on the definitive status, but there is no question of integrating them into the implementation of the Wye River accord. You can't say that time stopped in November 1998, and that you're now asking for twenty-two weeks to implement this accord, instead of eleven weeks.

Mohammed Dahlan, head of preventive security in Gaza, is taking part in the discussion. He reminds the others that the Autonomous Authority has continued the battle against terrorism, even under the Netanyahu government. "And," he adds, "we're shocked by the fact that you want to renegotiate the accord reached by the preceding Israeli government. If Arafat were to accept such a proposal, I would resign."

But as the weeks go by, an atmosphere of trust develops between Sher and Erekat, and progress is substantial. Barak

---

66. According to Sher, Barak was afraid that implementation of the Wye River timetable would create political problems for him in Israel itself. See Sher, 2001, p. 43.

makes some concessions, and, under pressure from the Egyptians and the Americans, so does Arafat. On August 20, Osama al-Baz, Hosni Mubarak's political adviser, arrives in Israel to add his contribution. From this date on, some of the talks will take place at the residence of the Egyptian ambassador to Israel, Muhammad Bassiouny.

On September 3, Dennis Ross is in Ramallah to put the finishing touches on the agreement with Yasir Arafat. The signing is planned for September 4 in Egypt, and Mubarak's staff announces an opening ceremony in Alexandria. The European emissary Miguel Moratinos, who has been following the negotiations closely, is present, and the international press rushes to the city—in vain. After a day of waiting, it turns out that Erekat and Dahlan are furious: they find that too few Palestinian prisoners are likely to be freed by Israel. The crisis will be resolved behind the scenes by Yossi Ginosar and Osama al-Baz, who, from Bassiouny's residence in Herzlia, will negotiate the final points of the accord by telephone.

Not until very late on Saturday, September 4 will the "Memorandum of the Implementation of the Timetable of Commitments and Accords Signed and the Resumption of Negotiations on the Permanent Status" be signed in Sharm el-Sheik. Barak has gotten what he wanted.

The first phase of negotiations on the definitive status is to end on February 13, 2000 with the conclusion of a framework accord, the final version being planned for September 13 of that year. The Israelis agree to go ahead with the following redeployments on the West Bank: on September 5, 1999, 7 percent of Zone C, under total Israeli control, will be transferred to Zone B, the set of territories placed under Palestinian responsibility except in matters of security. On November 5, 1999, 2 percent of Zone B will become part of Zone A, under total control of the Palestinian Authority, and 3 percent of Zone C will become part of

Zone B. On January 20, 2000, 1 percent of Zone C will become Zone A, as will 5.1 percent of Zone B.

On this date, exclusive Israeli control over the West Bank will be reduced from 72 percent to 59 percent of the territory. The Palestinian Authority will control an additional 11 percent of the area.

These three phases are part of the second stage of the redeployment initially planned in the accord of September 28, 1995, so-called Oslo II. No clause of the Sharm el-Sheik agreement bears on the third stage initially planned, which has still not been discussed. This agreement also provides for the freeing, on September 5, of 200 Palestinian prisoners held in Israeli jails, with an additional 150 to be released on October 8. These are Palestinians who committed armed attacks before the signing of the Oslo accords on September 13, 1993 and were arrested before the Cairo accord of May 4, 1994.

The agreement on the establishment of safe corridors for the southern route (between Gaza and a checkpoint situated at the southwest edge of the West Bank) is scheduled to be signed on October 1, while negotiations on the northern route (between Gaza and a checkpoint situated west of Ramallah) are to be concluded before October 5. In addition, Israel will permit the construction of the harbor in Gaza.

The ceremony takes place in the presence of President Hosni Mubarak, King Abdallah of Jordan, and Madeleine Albright, who has come with the entire American peace team. The mood is one of reconciliation. Yossi Ginosar is working to improve the relationship between Saeb Erekat and Nabil Shaath, the two Palestinian negotiators who had been in disagreement during the talks. Israeli, Egyptian, and Jordanian officers shake hands, often for the first time in five years. But many commentators express doubts about the planned timetable. Nahum Barnea, editorial writer for the major daily *Yediot Ahronot,* entitles one of his articles "Barak: Peace is an Order!"[67]

The next day, September 3, 1999, the Barak government approves the accord by a vote of 21 to 2. At the same moment, two booby-trapped cars explode, one in Tiberias, the other in Haifa. Three Palestinians—the ones who set the bombs—are killed. On September 9, Israel frees 199 Palestinian prisoners. The two-hundredth inmate chooses to remain in jail out of solidarity with his comrades.

The symbolic opening of negotiations on the definitive status of the Palestinian territories takes place on the 13th, at the Erez checkpoint. Before the cameras, Abu Mazen and David Levy, the Israeli foreign minister, shake hands. And that is where matters will rest for now, since Barak has still not named his delegation to these talks. As a sign of protest against the plan for Palestinian prisoners in the Sharm el-Sheik accord, Mohammed Dahlan refuses to take part in the ceremony.

A few days later, at the home of Jean Frydman in Savyon, Ehud Barak and Yasir Arafat get together for a friendly dinner. The prime minister is accompanied by his wife and some family members. Arafat has come with several leaders, including Yasir Abed Rabbo. Barak will tell his friend, Frydman, who has been detained abroad, that the evening was a success. Among other things, the two heads of state recall the battle of Karameh in 1968, in which they both took part, Barak as an ordinary soldier, Arafat as head of the Palestinian fighters.

Gilead Sher has a major problem. Elyakim Rubinstein, the government's legal counsel, does not want him to head the Israeli delegation on the definitive status. A lawyer from outside the civil service, Rubinstein says, should not nego-

---

67. Barnea, 1999a, p. 1.

tiate in the name of the Israeli government. Several top ju-
rists disagree and suggest that Barak bring the matter before
the Supreme Court. But the prime minister is not about to
arm wrestle with the man who is serving as his attorney general. Exit Gilead Sher, who decides not to go against
Rubinstein. Barak's advisers start looking for someone else
to lead official negotiations with the Palestinians.

TOWARD A DEFINITIVE RESOLUTION

On September 16, Arafat names Yasir Abed Rabbo, the
Palestinian minister of culture and information, to head his
delegation to the talks on the definitive status. Nabil Shaath;
Faisal al-Husseini, the minister in charge of Jerusalem af-
fairs; Nabil Kassis, who was one of the delegates to the 1991
Madrid conference; and Akram Hanieh, who is close to
Arafat, will accompany him.

That same day, Barak receives a report from the defense
ministry concerning forty-two new settlements that have
been created on the West Bank without authorization. According to experts, ten of these are "illegal," and an eleventh
has been built on a firing range. Barak will reach an agreement with the settlement council: thirty settlements will be
"legalized" and will get construction permits in the framework of existing plans for development; the others will be
evacuated. This compromise is unacceptable to the young
militants of the settlement movement, who declare that they
will not go along with any evacuation. The left, from within
the Barak government, protests only mildly against the creation of new settlements.

On October 5, the agreement on the safe corridor between Gaza and the West Bank is concluded, and ten days
later Israel frees 151 prisoners. One hundred and nine are
Palestinians, the rest Arabs of other nationalities. On the

West Bank and in Gaza, more had been expected. According to a poll taken by an institute in Nablus, only 18 percent of Palestinians say they trust Barak, down from 29 percent in July.

The safe corridor between Gaza and the West Bank is opened on October 25. It is an immediate success. For days, hundreds of young Gazans have been waiting for permits to make the almost one-hour bus trip to Hebron and, from there, to what is for them the city of light, Ramallah, which most of them have never visited. Once in Ramallah, however, they are in for a major disappointment: the inhabitants of the West Bank, convinced that the newcomers will ruin the labor market by accepting low salaries, do not look kindly on their arrival. After a few days, hundreds of penniless teenagers are walking the streets of the city, sleeping in doorways, and breaking into mosques to find a place to stay at night. The Palestinian police will finally have to use force to send them back to Gaza.

On November 3, Bill Clinton, Ehud Barak, and Yasir Arafat meet in Oslo to commemorate the granting of the Nobel Peace Prize to Arafat, Yitzhak Rabin, and Shimon Peres. The three leaders draw up the schedule for the coming negotiations. A framework accord is to be signed before February 13, 2000, the final document before September of that year. Ehud Barak announces that his delegation will be led by Oded Eran, the Israeli ambassador to Jordan; General Shlomo Yanai from the planning department of Tsahal; Daniel Reisner; Allan Baker, a lawyer from the foreign ministry; and Pini Medan, formerly of Mossad. The United States will be following the talks closely and making contributions from time to time. The possibility of a summit on the Camp David model, in the coming January or February, is mentioned. But, most important, it is decided to establish a secret channel of negotiations parallel to the official talks. Reserve General Uri Saguy is given the Syria portfolio.

Oded Eran and Yasir Abed Rabbo hold their first negotiating session on November 8 in Ramallah. Eran agrees
that Resolution 242 of the United Nations Security Council will be the starting point of the talks. Abed Rabbo starts
moving his pawns right away: East Jerusalem, occupied in
1967, falls within the provisions of the United Nations resolutions, the settlements in the occupied territories are illegal, Israel must withdraw to the 1967 borders, the refugee
problem must be solved in the context of Resolution 194 of
the UN General Assembly, and an agreement on the shar-
ing of water must be reached on the basis of the principle
that each nation has the right to control its natural resources. And Abed Rabbo demands damages and interest
for all the actions committed by Israel that were contrary to
international law.

The next day, Ehud Barak and Yasir Arafat take part in
the meeting of the Socialist International in Paris. Their
conversation lasts barely a quarter of an hour. Arafat is furious. The Israeli prime minister has said in a press conference that, as he sees it, Resolution 242 does not refer to the
West Bank, since, he says, the annexation of this territory
by Jordan in the 1948 war was not recognized by the international community.

On November 10, the Israeli army and police evacuate
dozens of militants from the settlement movement who are
occupying an unauthorized settlement in Havat Maon,
near Hebron. The settlers resist and are taken away by
force. Pictures broadcast that evening on Israel television
give a foretaste of what would happen if evacuations of the
large settlements on the West Bank and in Gaza were to
be ordered.

The Barak government approves the plan for the next
redeployment from the West Bank, starting the following
day. But when Arafat finds out about the map of what the
Israelis are proposing, he flies into a rage and rejects it.

PEACE WITH SYRIA IS AT HAND

December is Syria month. The first signs of a thaw had appeared five months earlier. At that time the British journalist Patrick Seale, who is close to Hafez el-Assad and wrote his biography, had paid a visit to Israel. On June 23, he had published interviews with Assad and Barak in an Arab daily put out in London. The two men exchanged compliments:

> *Assad:* Barak seems to be a strong and sincere man. As the election result shows, he has a great deal of popular support. It's clear that he wants to make peace with Syria. He's proceeding skillfully. . . .
>
> *Barak:* The only way to establish a lasting and comprehensive peace in the Middle East must involve an accord with Syria. Such an accord would be the keystone of peace in the region. There can be no doubt that it is President Hafez el-Assad who built the Syria we see today.[68]

Assad had informed the American peace team that he intended to negotiate an accord in short order. There is quick agreement on the principle of secret Israeli–Syrian meetings, in the course of which all the problems between the two countries will be put on the table. Dennis Ross reports: "When I asked Assad in December what level he wanted to negotiate on, he said, 'What do you want?' I said, 'Foreign ministers.' He said, 'OK.' For seven and a half years, he'd been refusing political negotiations. I took this to mean that he was ready to conclude an agreement. And Barak was impatient to negotiate."[69]

---

68. Seale, 1999, p. 1.
69. Videotaped interview with Dennis Ross, February 19, 2002, Washington.

But before the talks begin on a formal basis, with the participation of Farouk al-Shareh, the Syrian foreign minister, a secret preliminary meeting takes place in Berne that September under the auspices of Dennis Ross. Uri Saguy has two days of meetings with Ryad el-Daoudi, the legal counsel for foreign affairs in Damascus. "We really defined the essential problems of our relations with Syria," Saguy would say later. "The border; the question of the line of June 4, 1967; water. The discussion was frank, direct. It was about substance, not form."[70] Saguy phones Barak on a secure line and tells him about the progress thus far: "We have partners for peace. An accord is in sight."

Ross then sets up a meeting in Washington between Saguy and General Ibrahim Omar, who is highly placed in Syrian military intelligence. The two men have something in common, since they both fought on the Golan in 1967. The discussion is fruitful, and Saguy is increasingly convinced that peace with Syria is within arm's reach.

Then, on December 12, *Yediot Ahronot* publishes a survey taken in the Knesset: 54 deputies are against a withdrawal from the Golan, 53 in favor. According to the newspaper, there are three ministers among the reluctant members: Shlomo Ben Ami, Mathan Vilnai, and Amnon Lipkin-Shahak. The next day, Ehud Barak delivers a speech in the chamber, announcing that Israel is ready to sign a peace agreement with Syria—but at a price. Only 47 deputies support him. In front of the Knesset building, the right is holding a demonstration, 10,000 people strong. Three ministers address the crowd, harshly criticizing any prospect of an agreement with Syria: Nathan Shcharansky and Yuli Edelstein from Yisrael Ba'Aliyah, the Russian-language party, and Eliahu Suissa from Shas.

---

70. Videotaped interview with Uri Saguy, March 25, 2002, Tel Aviv.

In Syria, however, there is a new mood of conciliation. The Israeli press publishes photos of posters put up on walls in Damascus: "We have made war with honor, we will make peace with honor." And Farouk al-Shareh declares, "At this point I am optimistic and believe that a few months will be all we need for [reaching] an agreement." But before leaving the next day for Washington, where he is to meet with the head of Syrian diplomacy, Ehud Barak announces that he does not intend to set a time limit for the conclusion of an accord. "We'll talk about principles, not maps," he says. Ariel Sharon, leader of the opposition on the right, is severely critical of the prime minister: "Assad is a tyrant and a cruel dictator. He's ready to give up the Golan without demanding anything in return, just to distract attention from the economic failures of his government."

In Washington, the members of the peace team are a bit worried as they read the translation of the article Nahum Barnea has just published in *Yediot Ahronot*: "After his latest tribulations in the Knesset, the Israeli prime minister is of the opinion that he does not have a mandate for allowing the Syrians to dip their feet in Lake Tiberias."[71] It seems, then, that Barak would reject Assad's demand that the Israelis withdraw to the line of June 4, 1967, a demarcation coinciding with the eastern part of the sea for several hundred meters. Uri Saguy, who has just spent a whole night talking with Barak about the upcoming accord, reports the following exchange:

Barak: Tell me: What I'm suggesting, what you're suggesting to me, what we're discussing, do you think it will be accepted [in public opinion]?

---

71. Barnea, 1999b, p. 1.

Saguy: Yes!

Barak: Why?

Saguy: Because it's beyond belief! You and I both know what peace with Syria means. And then, personally, I know the Golan, I fought there, I have family in that area.[72]

Barak, Saguy continues, is surely aware of the strategic significance of a peace agreement with Syria. For this former head of military intelligence, there is no doubt that an accord with Hafez el-Assad would clear the way to a negotiated withdrawal from South Lebanon and would open Israel to other Arab countries, reduce the intensity of the conflict between Israel and Iran, and have a positive influence on the negotiations with the Palestinians. Barak, a great fan of polls, shows him the most recent survey of Israeli public opinion. An overwhelming majority of the respondents are in favor of peace with Syria, but only 13 percent agree that there should be a total withdrawal from the Golan.[73] "I'll never be able to sell [a total withdrawal] to the Israelis," Barak tells one of his advisers the following day.

On December 15, the prime minister's plane lands in Washington. Assistant Secretary of State Martin Indyk is on the tarmac for the official reception: "I went out to meet him at the airport," Indyk would later report:

He called me on the plane, and we sat down, and, well, everybody else was waiting at the bottom of the stairs, and he said, "I can't do it," and I said, "What? What do you mean? You were ready to do it, you were ready to have us convene the Syrians!" And he said, "Well, this law

---

72. Videotaped interview with Uri Saguy, March 25, 2002, Tel Aviv.

73. See Drucker, 2002, p. 71. Raviv Drucker is the political correspondent of Galei Tsahal, the radio station of the Israeli army.

just passed in the Knesset. My people wouldn't understand. It's all too quick, and they will not understand. . . . I have to prepare my public for a full withdrawal from the Golan, and I have to take time."

I remember going out of the plane, meeting up with Secretary of State Albright and Dennis Ross, who were having dinner before going to the formal meeting with Barak, and I walked in, and I said, "Houston! We have a problem!"[74]

Dennis Ross has this to say about Barak's attitude at the time: "I think Barak found out that, politically, it would be harder than he thought. He'd done all he could to have this meeting [in Washington], and when he got there he wasn't sure anymore that he was in a position to reach an accord. He drew back; it was an extremely paradoxical situation."[75]

The mood is tense at the ceremony in the White House. Bill Clinton has asked Farouk al-Shareh and Barak to keep their speeches very short. The Syrian minister has discreetly let it be known that he does not want to shake the Israeli prime minister's hand in public. Not now—later, when the agreement is signed.

Ehud Barak has the floor. He speaks for less than a minute:

We have come here to put the horrors of war behind us and to move forward toward peace. We are fully aware of [the importance of] this opportunity, but also aware of the need for responsibility, seriousness, and determination to move forward, with our Syrian partners,

---

74. Videotaped interview with Martin Indyk, February 19, 2002, Washington. At Barak's request, Indyk was once again named US ambassador to Israel. In his final comment, he is quoting astronauts calling from space.

75. Videotaped interview with Dennis Ross, February 19, 2002, Washington.

toward a Middle East in which nations will live side by side in mutual respect, as good neighbors with peaceful relations. We are determined to do all we can to put an end [to the horrors of war] and to fulfill the dreams of children and mothers of the entire region for a better future on the threshold of a new millennium. Thank you very much.

Farouk al-Shareh surprises Clinton. He takes a long speech out of his pocket. The text is sometimes hard on Israel, but, for the first time from the mouth of a Syrian diplomat, it involves a genuine promise of peace:

As you mentioned in your letter of October 12, 1999 to President Assad, the issues were spelled out, the problems defined. This is why these negotiations should succeed just as quickly, which is what we all wish, [given that] no one can be unaware of what has been accomplished and what remains to be done.

It goes without saying that, for Syria, peace means the return of all its occupied land, while, for Israel, peace will mean the end of the Israelis' sense of fear, fear that is a result of the occupation. [This occupation] is, without any doubt, the source of the wars and the misfortunes. The end of the occupation will overcome the barrier of fear and anxiety, and a shared aspiration for peace and security will take its place.

We are coming closer to the moment of truth, and . . . each of us understands that a peace treaty between Syria and Israel means the end of a history of wars and conflicts. This could be the beginning of a period marked by a dialogue of civilizations, an honorable competition in various domains: political, cultural, scientific, and economic. Peace will surely raise new issues for the Arab side, which, after fifty years, must ask itself this question:

Has the conflict with Israel merely posed a challenge to Arab unity, or has it stood in its way? In the course of the past half century, the world has completely ignored the way in which the Arabs see their sufferings, and this is because of a lack of interest on the part of the media. . . . As the most recent example, in these last four days, [the media] tried to arouse the sympathy of the international community on behalf of several thousand Golan settlers, arrogantly ignoring over half a million Syrians living in dozens of villages on the Golan that, today, have been totally destroyed, though these were villages where their ancestors had lived for thousands of years.

The Western image of Syria is that it is an aggressor, a Syria that would bomb [Israeli villages in the Galilee] from the Golan Heights. These statements are false. As Moshe Dayan himself explained in his memoirs, it was the other party that provoked the Syrians until they responded and were then accused of being the aggressors.[76]

Now, many years later, President Assad has stated that peace is Syria's strategic option. And we hope the same is true for the others today, so that we may bequeath to future generations a region that is not torn apart by wars, a region whose sky will not be polluted by the odor of blood and destruction. We all agree that we are on the threshold of a historic occasion, a precious opportunity

---

76. Al-Shareh is citing Dayan's November 22, 1976 interview with the journalist Rami Tal, published on April 27, 1997 by *Yediot Ahronot*. Here Dayan states that more than 80 percent of the incidents with Syria were provoked by Tsahal:

"This is how it was: we'd send a tractor into an area where nothing could grow, into the demilitarized zone, knowing in advance that the Syrians were going to open fire. If they didn't, we'd give the order to the tractor driver to move forward until the Syrians got nervous and started shooting. Then we'd bring in the artillery, then, later, the air force."

for Arabs and Israelis, for the United States and the entire world.

The Israelis pick up on the criticisms, the polemical tone, the absence of a handshake. "And we're supposed to make peace with people like that?" Barak will pointedly ask the Americans a little later. But the tone changes in the hushed atmosphere of Blair House, the presidential guest residence. Here Israelis and Syrians shake hands and negotiate in earnest, to the great relief of Clinton's advisers, still upset by Barak's announcement that he would not conclude an agreement. "Maybe the dynamics of the negotiation will make him change his mind after all," they hope.

Forty-eight hours later, on December 17, 1999, Bill Clinton reveals that a new round of negotiations will take place in the United States on January 3, 2000. The problems have been defined. The methodology has been worked out.

Not a good idea, says Uri Saguy, who sees failure looming on the horizon. Let's not get involved in these kinds of talks, he tells Barak: "The formula that's been adopted isn't symmetrical from the point of view of representation. As prime minister, you do not have to negotiate with a minister of foreign affairs. Let's keep on with the secret meetings. They're much more productive than these media events."

Barak rejects the argument: he wants to be there. And, in spite of this disagreement, it is in a mood of optimism that the Israeli delegation heads for Shepherdstown, West Virginia, where, as planned, negotiations with the Syrians will take place on January 3. As Gadi Baltiansky, Barak's spokesman, relates:

We had the feeling that peace with Syria was just around the corner. Even before we left for the United States, I'd prepared headlines for the Israeli press in the case of a positive outcome. I also had material to react to a pessimistic scenario. I didn't use it. The last headline I suggested, which was published by one of the biggest Israeli dailies, was: "Parties Anticipate a Peace Treaty in the Spring." I spoke in terms of spring because it has a positive connotation of optimism, flowering.[77]

But the negotiation soon takes a turn for the worse. Farouk al-Shareh wants the four committees set up at Blair House (border, security, water, and normalization) to negotiate simultaneously. Barak refuses. As Uri Saguy would later explain, "This was a tactical maneuver that was supposed to last two days. But when the Syrians found out that the committees weren't meeting, they expressed their anger, as did the Americans. Rightly so, in my opinion. From this point of view, [it could be said that] the Shepherdstown meeting led to the re-emergence of mistrust."[78]

Clinton, very distressed, will have to wait four days to get an account of the Israeli gambit. According to Dennis Ross, "The Syrians were moving ahead on all fronts, and Barak wasn't getting anywhere. This was a fundamental problem. We didn't know how to pursue the process. At the final meeting, Farouk al-Shareh said, 'I'm going to have to go back and tell my leader [about the failure],' and I felt . . . knowing the system [in place in Syria], and what he would have to tell Assad. . . . President Clinton said to him, 'No, don't tell President Assad before I've had a chance to speak with him.'"[79]

Uri Saguy is critical of the American mediation in these negotiations. As he sees it, Bill Clinton should not have intervened so soon in the discussion. As for the "non-paper"

---

77. Videotaped interview with Gadi Baltiansky, July 5, 2001, Jerusalem.

78. Videotaped interview with Uri Saguy, March 25, 2002, Tel Aviv.

79. Videotaped interview with Dennis Ross, February 19, 2002, Washington (verbatim).

presented to the parties by the peace team, it was, he says, useless and premature; this type of initiative is appropriate only once the positions on both sides have come closer. The American document Saguy is referring to notes the parties' respective positions by marking them "I" and "S." The day after the close of the conference, it is leaked to the press. *Al-Hayat*, the Arabic-language daily appearing in London, publishes extracts from it on January 9, 2000: "S: . . . Syria recognizes that the line of June 4 is not a border and has not been marked out, and it therefore agrees to participate in the determination of this line." This is a major concession on Syria's part, one that should clear the way for later concessions when the boundary between the two countries is drawn. Damascus also undertakes "to prevent attacks against Israeli citizens," meaning that the Syrians will neutralize Hezbollah in South Lebanon.

On January 13, the Israeli newspaper *Haaretz* publishes the document in its entirety. This is very embarrassing for Hafez el-Assad, since it appears that the Israelis still do not accept the principle of a return to the line of June 4, 1967, which has been the Syrian condition for any negotiation with Israel since the beginning of the peace process in 1993. Over time, Damascus had let this requirement become diluted into the ambiguity typical of diplomatic formulations, as in the version just cited.

On January 15, Bill Clinton has a long phone conversation with Assad, who has decided to break off all contacts with Israel. Clinton fails to persuade him to send the Syrian delegation to Washington to resume the negotiations scheduled for January 19. James Rubin, the spokesman for the State Department, says on the 15th: "With regard to the publication in *Haaretz*, we think that [this kind of initiative] is especially useless, that it infringes on the confidentiality of the negotiations. This makes our work even harder and complicates the quest for peace." Today, in 2002, Uri Saguy is convinced that the Syrians sincerely wanted to negotiate an accord at Blair House and later at Shepherdstown.

THE PALESTINIANS BECOME MISTRUSTFUL

The Palestinians are impatient. The timetable for the Sharm el-Sheik accord has not been observed, and the negotiations Barak is conducting with Syria are doing nothing to relieve their anxieties. On December 21, Barak had met Arafat once again at the Erez barricade and told him, "You know, I'm very busy with the Syrian matter. Our talks don't have to be interrupted, but I'd like to reach an agreement with Assad." Oded Eran, head of the Israeli delegation, has to confront mounting difficulties. "Frankly, I didn't like this idea of according priority to Syria," he will report. "I had long discussions with Barak about this. I told him it was the Palestinian problem that was at the center of the Israeli–Arab conflict. And that therefore, if it wasn't settled, there'd be no chance of finding a solution to the conflict and signing an accord with the Syrians. The Syrian question is secondary in relation to the Israeli–Palestinian conflict."[80]

Mistrust is setting in. Barak is leading the Palestinians to believe that negotiations with them are of lesser importance. The deadlines specified by the accords have not been observed, as was the case back in Netanyahu's time. And, most important, construction in the settlements is going forward at the same pace as in the preceding year. Since Barak came to power, and up to the end of December 1999, his government has issued 3,196 new invitations to tender bids for construction in the settlements. His response to Palestinian protests and the Israeli left is this: "These are commitments undertaken by the previous government. If we cancel them, we may

---

80. Videotaped interview with Oded Eran, November 1, 2001, Jerusalem.

be called before the Supreme Court. If we reach a final agreement, everything will be taken care of."

Uri Savir, who was the architect of the Oslo accords in 1993 and, like Shimon Peres, has been excluded from the negotiations with the Palestinians by Barak, is especially critical: "Of all our prime ministers, Barak is the one who least understood the Palestinians. After three years of dealing with Netanyahu's procrastinations, and when they were placing so much hope in the man who would be Rabin's successor, to stake everything on Syria was an error with disastrous consequences."[81]

In Barak's circle, the primary opponent of negotiations with Syria is none other than Ami Ayalon, the boss of Shin Bet. Ayalon is afraid of a catastrophe, of the collapse of the peace process. This is his analysis:

After the attacks of February 1996, the new young leaders of Fatah saw that the struggle against Islamic terrorism didn't lead to new territorial concessions on Israel's part. On the contrary, it was only after the riots following the opening of the tunnel near the Wailing Wall that the Israelis carried out their withdrawal from one part of the city of Hebron. And leaders like Marwan Barghouti [the head of Fatah on the West Bank] keep on saying, "The only thing the Israelis understand is force."[82]

During the last months of the Netanyahu government, the Palestinians, backed by the Americans and the Israeli left, had resisted the temptation to react to Israeli provocations: the attempt of the outgoing prime minister to close Orient House (the headquarters of the PLO in Jerusalem) and his decision to suspend implementation of the Wye

---

81. Videotaped interview with Uri Savir, December 9, 2001, Jerusalem.

82. Personal communication from a source wishing to remain anonymous.

River accords. In return, Yasir Arafat expected gratitude and, above all, a swift resumption of the peace process. Palestinian leaders will be disappointed on both counts. And now the Palestinian street is showing signs of increasing exasperation in the face of the blocked negotiations, with the risk, as Ami Ayalon sees it, of a Palestinian uprising in the event of an emergency.[83]

The attitude of the Israeli army is equally troubling to some intelligence experts, for Tsahal is gearing up to confront a new intifada, this time an armed one. Military leaders are convinced that the Palestinians are going to start using weapons. Arrangements for Operation Field of Thorns are being speeded up. For its part, the Palestinian leadership is convinced that, should negotiations fail, the Israelis could decide to reconquer the autonomous territories. They are preparing for such an event, and Shin Bet is receiving more and more information on arms smuggling, forbidden by the accords, especially in Gaza.

Raviv Drucker, the political correspondent for Galei Tsahal, the Israeli army radio station, reports that not only Ami Ayalon but also Ephraim Halevy, the head of Mossad, and Amos Malka, head of military intelligence, are advising Barak not to give priority to the talks with Syria. But Ayalon is the harshest:

Ginosar and I had a hard time getting the Palestinians to trust you. Now it's all no good. If you think you can evacuate 10,000 to 15,000 [settlers] from the Golan— which will take you to the brink of civil war—and then evacuate tens of thousands of others from Judea–Samaria, then you don't understand anything about the reality in Israel. Because you'll inflict wounds, traumas

---

83. Personal communication from a source wishing to remain anonymous. See also Drucker, 2002, pp. 68–69.

that [a society] can't easily recover from. It would also be a political error.[84]

The redeployment of the Israeli army planned for November 15, this time involving 5 percent of the West Bank, has not yet taken place. The Palestinians had rejected the map for this action, feeling that all they were being granted was some very small areas. This issue of the Israeli redeployments on the West Bank is of fundamental importance for the Palestinian leaders. What they fear is that, in the context of talks on the definitive status, they will have to renegotiate about territories that were to have reverted to them by virtue of the interim accord.

Finally, after several minor concessions on Barak's part, the withdrawal occurs on January 4, 2000. From now on, the Autonomous Authority will control 11.1 percent of the West Bank and will exercise civil administration over 28.9 percent of the territory under Israeli security control. The third and last phase of this second Israeli redeployment, involving an additional 6.1 percent of the West Bank and scheduled for January 20, is now being postponed to a later date.

On January 17, Yossi Ginosar invites Yasir Arafat and Ehud Barak to his home, Barak being his neighbor in Kochav Yair, near the demarcation line. Arafat explains that he must be able to present his people with genuine gains. The next Israeli withdrawal, for example, must include a Palestinian area near Jerusalem. "We'll see," replies Barak, who, as he is leaving, tells Arafat, "As for the third and last redeployment, there's no point going ahead with it. We'll talk about it during the negotiations on the definitive status." Ginosar is deeply shocked. Once again, he has to persuade Arafat that an agreement with Barak is possible—not an easy job.

---

84. Drucker, 2002, p. 69.

On February 3 there is a new meeting at the Erez checkpoint. Arafat rejects the map the Israelis offer him; the 6.1 percent he is supposed to receive does not include Abu Dis, the Palestinian suburb in East Jerusalem. Ten days later, the 13th, is the date set for the conclusion of the framework accord on the definitive status. That event is nowhere in sight. Negotiations have been suspended.

The Palestinian population is becoming increasingly uneasy. The smallest incident may degenerate into a pitched battle. The numerous rival security services—there are twelve different Palestinian security services—confront one another on a regular basis, but no real news leaks out. The Autonomous Authority, and often passersby, prevent television crews from filming these inter-Palestinian clashes.

On February 26 Lionel Jospin, the French prime minister, pays the price for this tension. During a visit to Bir Zeit University, near Ramallah, he is attacked by dozens of stone-throwing students enraged at the declaration he had made two days earlier: "Hezbollah is a terrorist movement." This statement, echoed on all Arab television stations via satellite, scandalized Palestinian youth. Chanting "Bir Zeit! Beirut! Same battle!" the students claim the right to struggle against Israel, against the Israeli soldiers they pass at the checkpoints near their houses and see in South Lebanon on their television screens.

On March 22, just as Pope John Paul II is leaving the Dehaysheh refugee camp near Bethlehem, violence breaks out between the people's committee of the camp, comprised of Fatah militants and the Popular Front, and the Palestinian police in charge of the pope's safety. Fifty-five people will be injured. Ami Ayalon, the head of Shin Bet, tells Dennis Ross that there is reason to fear a spontaneous explosion of violence in the Palestinian territories, directed against the Autonomous Authority or against Israel. Both possibilities exist.

A meeting between Barak and Arafat at Ben-Gurion Airport in Tel Aviv, late in the evening of March 7, only serves to deepen the crisis. Two days later, the two leaders meet in Sharm el-Sheik at the home of Hosni Mubarak, who persuades them to resume negotiations on the definitive status and suggests reaching a framework accord before the end of May.

BACK TO DAMASCUS

Ehud Barak has not given up the idea of concluding an agreement with Syria. Ever since the failure of the Shepherdstown negotiations, he has been discussing this regularly with Bill Clinton and the members of the peace team and has finally drawn up the new Israeli proposal. The basic idea is to give the Syrians back more than the whole of the Golan, 101 percent to be exact, but without access to Lake Tiberias. Territory to the north of the lake that would not be evacuated is offset by concessions elsewhere. Barak suggests that the president of the United States invite Hafez el-Assad to a summit and present him with the Israeli proposal.

Clinton is willing, although none of his close advisers has been to Damascus since Shepherdstown. On an official trip to India, he phones the Syrian president and announces, "You'll be interested in what I'm going to tell you!" An appointment is made for March 26 in Geneva. Madeleine Albright offers to go to Syria to prepare for the meeting. But as soon as he hears of this, Barak phones Clinton: "She must absolutely not go to Damascus," he says, "because Assad will think the Israeli positions she presents aren't definitive and are subject to negotiation. So he'll ask for additional concessions."

Clinton accepts Barak's argument. According to General Uri Saguy, head of the Israeli delegation to the talks with

Syria, who is not authorized to go to Geneva, Assad is certain that he is going to conclude the agreement. The Syrian president takes rooms in the Hotel Intercontinental,
accompanied by nearly a hundred experts who are to participate in drawing up the peace treaty.[85]

But the conference ends soon and suddenly. Clinton
begins to read aloud the six pages Barak has sent him. A few
lines in, when he mentions "the agreed-upon boundary,"
Assad leaps to his feet: "What agreed-upon boundary? Is
this the line of June 4, 1967?"

> *Clinton:* Let me continue! . . . Israel will retain sovereignty
> along Lake Tiberias and a strip of territory . . .
> *Assad:* The Israelis don't want peace! There's no point in
> continuing!

Clinton interrupts his reading to go into an explanation
of the difficulties Barak has to deal with: his shaky parliamentary coalition, Israeli public opinion, and so forth:
"Without sovereignty over the lake, Barak will never be able
to sell the agreement [to the Israeli public]!"

> *Assad:* That's not my problem! My problem is arriving at
> a just peace, not Barak's difficulties!
> *Clinton:* Farouk al-Shareh explained to us at Shepherds-
> town that, since the line of the 1923 border[86] and the
> 1967 line aren't very different on this part of the lake,
> this is about surface area, not principle. There are only
> ten meters of difference.

---

85. Present are Farouk al-Shareh; Butheina Shaaban, Assad's official translator; Madeleine Albright; Dennis Ross; and Gamal Hillal, the translator from
the State Department.

86. This is the boundary line according to the Sykes–Picot treaty of 1923, dividing the region between France and Great Britain.

Assad turns to his minister of foreign affairs: "You said that?"

Al-Shareh: What I said is that even the 1923 border isn't acceptable to us.
Assad: I remember that that's just where the cease-fire line was. I sometimes used to go swimming there.
Clinton: I'm sure the prime minister will give you permission to go swimming there again.

But Assad is no longer listening to Clinton, who is nonetheless trying to go on reading the document. The Syrian president repeats: "Barak does not want peace!" The two presidents eventually decide that Albright and Ross will read the Israeli proposal to Farouk al-Shareh. Al-Shareh suggests the publication of a joint communiqué. Clinton phones Barak, who refuses.

The conference is over. The Americans declare that the ball is now in the Syrians' court. According to Dennis Ross, "For a brief period of time [in January], Assad was ready to conclude an agreement. Barak made a decision that he wasn't able to implement politically. Assad lost confidence in the peace process." When, in March, Barak wanted to reach an agreement, Assad was no longer ready.

OF MAPS AND MEN

The Palestinians are growing more and more impatient. The planned withdrawal from the West Bank has still not occurred. Barak is under equal pressure from the Clinton administration, which fears an increase of tension in the area. A gesture has to be made to Yasir Arafat.

The heads of the General Staff and the Ministry of Defense suggest including in the next transfer of territories the small Palestinian village of Anata, north of Jerusalem. Anata is already in Zone B, administered by the Autonomous Authority. On March 15, the ministers of the security cabinet approve its transition to Zone A. But this is met with an uproar. The major daily newspaper *Maariv* addresses the people living in the districts north of Jerusalem: "[From now on] terrorists will be able to shoot into your living rooms!"

The campaign is led by Ariel Sharon, who suspects Barak of wanting to divide the capital of Israel. Ministers from the religious parties and Shcharansky's Russian-language movement, twenty-eight of the seventy deputies in the government coalition, now present Barak with an ultimatum: redeploy from Anata, and we go over to the opposition. Barak gives in. That very day, he rescinds his decision. Saeb Erekat reacts: "Every time we move ahead in a serious effort to resume the peace process, the government launches a political trial balloon involving us. This is an attack on the peace process."

The American peace team decides to intervene in the negotiations in order to resolve the impasse. Oded Eran and Yasir Abed Rabbo are invited to pursue their discussions, away from the press, at Bolling Air Force Base near Washington on March 21. Abed Rabbo reports:

The Americans wanted us to brainstorm without any commitments on either side. I played the role of the Israeli negotiator, but, I must say, not very well: I made a lot of concessions to the Palestinians. Seriously, though, some interesting ideas were examined, for example on the question of the Palestinian refugees. The Israelis didn't want to hear about a "right of return" but only about "family reunification."

Now today there are almost no families in need of reunification. We explained that the question of the refugees in Lebanon was fundamental for us. We put forth a plan envisioning the integration into Israel of several thousand refugees a year.

For the first time, we seriously discussed Jerusalem. The Israelis told us they could show flexibility outside the Old City. Inside it, they spoke of shared sovereignty, a "zone of cohabitation" in which each of the parties could consider itself to have sovereignty. We found this formula interesting.[87]

On March 31, the settlers in Hebron get a message from Ehud Barak congratulating them on the thirty-second anniversary of the founding of their settlement. The prime minister affirms

the right of the Jews to live in safety, protected from any attack in the City of the Patriarchs. The test, for the re-emerging Jewish community and for the Arab majority, will be their ability to establish relations of neighborliness and mutual respect. We would like to believe that the establishment of peaceful relations between us and our Palestinian neighbors throughout the territories will be the basis for such relations between the Jewish community and its Arab neighbors.

The message will be extensively reported in the Palestinian press.

The meeting at Bolling did not lead to a resumption of negotiations between Yasir Abed Rabbo and Oded Eran, and the Palestinian street concludes that the Israelis could not care less about reaching an agreement. As for Israeli public opinion, it maintains that the Palestinians are making undue demands. On May 4, the crisis erupts when the

---

87. Videotaped interview with Yasir Abed Rabbo, May 16, 2000, Ramallah.

talks resume in Eilat, the Israeli port on the Red Sea. Oded Eran describes what happened:

We were having endless discussions on the question of the border between the two states. The Palestinians were saying, "Obviously, in accordance with Resolution 242, it's the line of 1967." I asked them, "And what about Jerusalem? There are large Jewish areas on the other side of the 1967 line." They answered clearly and warmly that those areas could remain under Israeli sovereignty within the framework of an agreement.

I went further: "And Gush Etzion?"[88] I asked them. "Gush Etzion was inhabited by Jews up until the 1948 war." I offered them the following formula. The border would be determined on the basis of three criteria: the line of 1967, demographic factors, and security.

I suggested this to Barak, and he said, "It's out of the question to talk about the line of 1967!" But then there was the problem of the Tulkarm sector, where we had no choice but to draw the border on the basis of the 1967 line. Barak accepted this argument, but he asked me to modify my formula so that security came first, then demography, and finally the 1967 line. The Palestinians did not agree to this.

During the Eilat negotiations I went to see Ehud Barak at midnight, in Tel Aviv, to tell him it was time for me to submit a map of the final status to the Palestinians. He agreed, and I was authorized to present a map, without any names whatsoever, dividing the West Bank into three sectors. Sixty-six percent would be immediately transferred to the Palestinians within the framework of the ac-

---

88. This is a group of settlements located near the Israeli border southeast of Bethlehem.

cord, 20 percent would be annexed by Israel, and 14 percent would remain under Israeli control for an indefinite period.

The Palestinian delegation took this very badly. They began shouting, cursing in English, Hebrew, and Arabic, and then they walked out.[89]

Dennis Ross, who was present at the negotiations, describes his response to the Palestinians: "I went to them and I said, 'You want to be angry with them, fine. You don't like what he presented, that's fine. But you don't walk out on me. You walked out on me. You want me to be here for the negotiations, you stay in the negotiations, and if you aren't prepared to do that, I'm leaving.'"[90]

This was Abed Rabbo's reaction:

Dennis Ross asked, "Why did you leave? I was going to ask you questions about it." "OK. You can ask us questions by letter, but not in front of us. And what kind of questions?" He said, "One question I wanted to ask is why the Israeli area here, east of Jerusalem, is so big, why it's not smaller." "Thank you very much for this question. Keep this question for yourself, sir. I will not allow this question even to be asked in my presence."[91]

"They came back in the afternoon," Oded Eran relates. "I said to them, 'Listen, we're negotiating; this is our proposal, present yours.' And, for the first time, they expressed a clear position on the issue. They proposed to leave 4 per-

89. Videotaped interview with Oded Eran, November 1, 2001, Jerusalem.
90. Videotaped interview with Dennis Ross, February 19, 2002, Washington.
91. Videotaped interview, May 10, 2000, Ramallah.

cent of the West Bank under Israeli control, on condition that this be offset by an exchange of territory."[92]

For Yasir Abed Rabbo, the Israeli map was nothing less than the materialization of the old project of Ariel Sharon, who, in 1991, had wanted to cut the West Bank into three cantons encircled by settlements.

Since the last redeployments planned for the West Bank have not taken place, Eran feels he must offer concrete measures if he wants to win the trust of his Palestinian partners. What about freeing Palestinian prisoners? In Israeli prisons there are thirty-five of them who have Jewish blood on their hands and have already served most of their sentences. Eran recommends that Barak release some of these. The security services say no.

Early in April, Gilead Sher decides to re-enlist in the peace process. He sets aside his legal practice temporarily to take charge of the secret negotiations that are to begin, parallel to the official talks.

On May 5, the first meeting of what will later be known as the "Stockholm channel" takes place at a secret location in Jerusalem. The discussion focuses on the future of the settlements. Gilead Sher and the minister of internal security, Shlomo Ben Ami, are there, opposite Abu Ala and Hassan Asfur.

The next day, there is another secret meeting in the hotel of a kibbutz near Jerusalem. Present along with Dennis Ross is Robert Malley, the assistant to National Security Adviser Sandy Berger and later Clinton's adviser on Israeli–Arab affairs. Abu Ala sets forth his position on the refugee issue and Jerusalem:

First of all, the solution must be based on Resolution 194 of the General Assembly of the United Nations.

---

92. Videotaped interview with Oded Eran, November 1, 2001, Jerusalem.

Then a committee must be formed, bringing Israelis and Palestinians together with representatives of the United States, Canada, Europe, and Japan, as well as the countries that took in refugees. This committee would prepare a questionnaire to be given to the refugees, but the questions should be drawn up in such a way that those replying that they wish to return to Israel would be a minority.

On the subject of Jerusalem, we have looked at the question only in a general way, with regard to the creation of the Palestinian State. We do not need to discuss the question with you; we do not need anyone's agreement to proclaim our State.

The Americans are satisfied: a genuine negotiation is underway.

On May 10, the secret negotiations begin in Sweden. Abu Ala, Hassan Asfur, Shlomo Ben Ami, and Gilead Sher have left the night before from Ben-Gurion Airport on board the Swedish prime minister's private plane. The Swedish security services escort them to a government retreat two hours from Stockholm. Discussions are held around the clock.

The Palestinians insist on seeing the map of the West Bank as envisioned by Israel after the conclusion of a treaty, and it is shown to them. According to Gilead Sher, the Palestinians would receive 76.6 percent of this territory, 10.1 percent would be security zones, and 13.3 percent would become part of Israel. Sher tries to mitigate the Palestinians' reaction: "This isn't a proposal, just a simple illustration." Abu Ala replies, "This completely destroys our wish to pursue these negotiations. We're under intense pressure to go back home [immediately, without results]."

News comes from Israel about a hunger strike being held by the Palestinian prisoners in Israeli jails. The unrest spreads to the occupied territories. On May 14, Dennis Ross joins the discussions. Despite the differences of opinion between the two delegations, things seem to be going well. In the evening, however, the negotiators learn that Yasir Abed Rabbo has resigned his post as head of the official delegation, in protest against the existence of this secret channel of negotiations.

On May 15, the Palestinians observe Nakbah, the anniversary of the "catastrophe of 1948," the Arab defeat by Israel. As with the Israeli tradition according to which, on Holocaust Memorial Day, Israeli Jews observe a moment of silence, sirens sound on the West Bank and in Gaza at 11 A.M. Cars stop. Three million Palestinians stand at attention.

A few hours later, demonstrations get out of hand. In Ramallah, hundreds of young people come to the intersection at the City Inn Hotel to throw stones at Israeli soldiers guarding a barricade. The soldiers respond with rubber-coated bullets. People are wounded. Someone suddenly opens fire, and shots are exchanged. Similar scenes unfold at other barriers near Jenin and on the Gaza Strip. By the end of the day, four Palestinians have been killed, 200 wounded. Eight of the soldiers are injured, one of them by a bullet. Ehud Barak is furious. He calls Arafat to demand that he restore calm immediately.

This violence has occurred at a bad time: as it happens, Barak has finally agreed to include three Palestinian suburbs of Jerusalem in the redeployment of the Israeli army: Abu Dis, Azaryeh, and Sawahara. That morning, he had had the transfer agreement voted on by his government. Fifteen ministers voted in favor and six against, the opponents being the four representatives of the Sephardic Orthodox party Shas, Nathan Shcharansky of the Russian Party, and Yitzhak Levy of the National Religious Party.

Levy: I'm going to propose that my movement quit your coalition. From now on, I am no longer a member of the government.

Barak: We have no interest in annexing thirty Palestinian villages to Jerusalem or placing them under Israeli
sovereignty. In my experience, this kind of transfer of
territories has always worked in favor of our security.
In 1992, there were 2,400 anti-Israeli attacks in Judea–
Samaria, and last year only 140. [Turning to Yitzhak
Levy] I empathize with all those who are worried by
this withdrawal, but we also know what will happen if
we don't reach an agreement.

Levy: This is the beginning of a dangerous process that
threatens the integrity of Jerusalem. We cannot assume responsibility for such a gesture.

A stormy debate then takes place in the Knesset. The
government has decided to ask for a vote of confidence.
Barak announces that, because of the unleashing of violence
in the territories, the implementation of the transfer agreement for the three suburbs will be postponed. But deputies
on the right retort, "The Palestinians are shooting at us, and
you're giving them Abu Dis!"
Ariel Sharon is equally harsh:

When you've given them Abu Dis, they'll be able to shoot
from their rooftops at Jerusalem. Is that what you call
separation from the Palestinians? When we broke the
blockade of Jerusalem fifty years ago, we never imagined
that we'd have to confront the siege of our city again, but
this time a siege imposed by a Jewish government. This
is the first time since 1967 that a foreign power is coming right up to the borders of Jerusalem to surround it.

Barak is not to be outdone: "Knights of the Wailing Wall
tunnel and Joseph's Tomb, don't give us lessons in matters
of security. Jerusalem will not be destroyed because Abu Dis
and Azaryeh are no longer part of it. Jerusalem has been

destroyed in the past because of hatred among Jews, because of internal struggles."

The vote of confidence passes, 56 to 48. Nine of the seventeen deputies of Shas vote with the opposition and are joined by the National Religious Party.

In front of the Knesset 10,000 demonstrators, including religious people, secular people, settlers, kibbutz dwellers, and supporters of both Netanyahu and Barak are protesting a possible withdrawal from the Golan and demanding the prime minister's resignation. Some members of the government are there: with Yitzhak Levy are Nathan Shcharansky and Yuli Edelstein from Yisrael Ba'Aliyah and Eliahu Suissa from Shas.

On May 17, the delegates from Sweden return to the Middle East. Their respective leaders are briefed. Shlomo Ben Ami tells Barak that the main problem in these negotiations is that "the Palestinians want to go forward only on secondary questions, while Israel wants an agreement on principles."

On May 20, even greater unrest breaks out in the West Bank and Gaza. Ehud Barak is in a threatening mood: "If Arafat doesn't restore calm, the negotiations with the Autonomous Authority will simply be suspended. In the meantime, Abu Dis, Azaryeh, and Sawahara will remain under Israeli control." Sandy Berger, who is on tour in the region, meets with Yasir Arafat that evening and asks him to put a stop to the violence. Arafat replies that he is doing all he can, but that the patience of the Palestinian street is at an end.

THE EVACUATION OF SOUTH LEBANON

On May 21, 2000, Ehud Barak postpones his trip to Washington: he has decided to accelerate the withdrawal of the Israeli army from Lebanon. Hearing the news, Abu Ala rushes to the home of Uri Savir, with whom he has stayed in contact. "We're against your occupation of South Lebanon," he tells Savir,

> but the question is how you're going to leave. What will the Palestinians say? That the Israelis negotiated an agreement with us in which we gave them security, that we, the Autonomous Authority, are killing Palestinians for Israel's security, and that, when all is said and done, we don't get anything except the report of a territorial redeployment. Hezbollah has killed Israeli soldiers, and now they're getting Israel's withdrawal to the lines of 1967. The message for every Palestinian will be clear: "Kill Israelis, and you'll get the land."

Abu Ala goes on to warn Savir: "If this is how the withdrawal is going to take place, sooner or later there will be an explosion of violence." Uri Savir rushes to Barak's house to give him this message. The prime minister rejects these arguments.

Over the course of the preceding days, Tsahal and the South Lebanon Army (SLA), the Israeli-controlled military force fighting Hezbollah, have withdrawn from two of their outermost positions in the northern and eastern sectors. Since the departure of the Israeli liaison unit, SLA soldiers have been taking off their uniforms and going back home. Now, during the night, the group leaders conclude a treaty with Hezbollah, which is deployed only at the border of Druse villages.

The next day, the SLA collapses even faster. At Bint Bjbeil the Shiite battalion dissolves in a few hours, a part of its men going over to Hezbollah, the officers and NCOs fleeing to Israel with their families. Tsahal, which had originally anticipated a gradual withdrawal lasting until July, is ordered to speed up the operation.

In the absence of an agreement with the Lebanese government, SLA, Israel's ally since 1970, is simply abandoned to its fate. As the day wears on, the soldiers' departure begins to look like desperate flight. In some command posts, Israeli liaison officers are telling their Lebanese friends, "You've got only a few hours. Take your families and what you can carry with you, and get to the border fast." A long waiting line quickly forms at the Fatima Gate. To avoid infiltration of Hezbollah agents into Israeli territory, each fugitive, each family, each suitcase is searched.

Meanwhile, Tsahal is continuing its withdrawal. Its positions in South Lebanon are dynamited one after another, while Hezbollah moves its troops into the evacuated sectors at the same pace as the retreat. By the morning of August 25, it's all over. In their hurry to get to the border, the SLA soldiers and their families have left everything behind; now their cars and personal effects are being pillaged by the men of Hezbollah. Six thousand Lebanese take refuge in Israel. Barak has kept his word.

One week later, worried that the Palestinians got the wrong message from this hurried withdrawal, General Shaul Mofaz, the chief of staff, invites Mohammed Dahlan to Tel Aviv. "Make no mistake," he warns Dahlan. "The IDF has not lost its powers of dissuasion!" To which the Palestinian colonel replies, "You're going to take revenge on us for the humiliation you suffered in Lebanon."[93]

BACK TO SWEDEN

The negotiations in Sweden resume on May 19. At first they move along quickly. On the 20th, the sixth version of a

---

93. Interview with Mohammed Dahlan, September 27, 2002, Gaza. See also Kaspit, 2002a.

"non-paper" is written, entitled "Framework Agreement on Permanent Status" (FAPS). Here are excerpts, with the notations "I" or "P" marking Israeli and Palestinian positions:

Preamble

The Government of the State of Israel (Israel) and the Palestine Liberation Organization (PLO), acting as the sole legitimate representative of the Palestinian people [("the Parties")]:

Reiterating   their commitment to the United Nations Security Council Resolutions 242 and 338 and confirming that the FAPS provides the mechanism for the implementation of these resolutions;

[P: Recognizing the inadmissibility of the acquisition of territory by war and the obligation of states to conduct themselves in conformity with the UN Charter and the norms of international law, and the right of the Palestinian people to self-determination];

Reaffirming   their determination to put an end to decades of confrontation and conflict and to live in peaceful coexistence, mutual dignity, and security based on a just, lasting, and comprehensive peace settlement and historic reconciliation through the agreed political process;

Recognizing   each other's right for a peaceful and secure existence of their respective territory and peoples, within secure and recognized boundaries free from threats or acts of force;

Confirming that the FAPS is concluded within the framework of the Middle East peace process initiated in Madrid in October 1991 and the Israeli–Palestinian Declaration of Principles concluded on September 13, 1993; . . .

[I: *Therefore* [the conclusion of the FAPS] marks the end of the conflict between the Parties and the beginning of a period of reconciliation and peace]. . . .

In the rest of the text, the Palestinians offer to conclude the comprehensive agreement on the permanent status, an agreement that is supposed to issue from the FAPS by September 13, 2000 at the latest. The Israelis propose this as the date of the proclamation of the Palestinian State.

Article 2 defines relations between Palestine and Israel:

6. The State of Israel shall recognize the State of Palestine upon its establishment; the State of Palestine shall recognize the State of Israel.
7. Israel and Palestine shall establish full diplomatic relations.
8. Based on political and security separation, relations between Israel and Palestine shall be founded on peaceful coexistence. . . .
10. The legislative bodies of Israel and Palestine shall develop programs for cooperation and coordination. . . .
12. Israel and Palestine shall encourage cooperation among their civil societies and local authorities.

Paragraph 13 is especially interesting:

13. Israel and Palestine shall not enter into any military [I: economic or political] union or confederation with

Third Parties whose objectives are directed against the interests of the other party without consultation with and agreement of the other party.

The document continues:

14. The parties will respect the interests of each other in their bilateral and international relations. . . .
16. Israel and Palestine shall create the appropriate atmosphere for lasting peace by promulgating laws to put an end to incitement for terror and violence.

With regard to Palestinian prisoners being held in Israel, the negotiators propose the following compromise:

44. *Compromise suggestion for consideration*—Upon the conclusion of the CAPS[94] all Palestinian and other security prisoners shall be free persons. The majority of those prisoners shall be free persons upon the conclusion of the FAPS. The rest of the prisoners shall [P: be transferred to the responsibility of Palestine] [I: remain in the custody of Israel].

Another possibility put forth is that the Palestinian prisoners will be released in two phases upon conclusion of the FAPS:

47. Phase one of the release of prisoners shall comprise of [P: all those who were arrested before May 4, 1994 and] [I: the majority] of Palestinian prisoners [I: who are members of the organizations] who [I: publicly]

---

94. Comprehensive Agreement on Permanent Status.

support the peace process. Phase two of the release of prisoners shall concern all remaining prisoners [I: except for those who oppose the peace process or pose a security threat.]

Article 7 discusses the refugee question for the first time:

49. Taking into consideration the suffering caused to [P: Palestinian refugees] [I: individuals and communities] as a result of the 1948 [I: Arab–Israeli] War and recognizing that a just, humane, political, and realistic solution to their right. The Parties are determined to put an end to their suffering based on UNSCR 242 [P: and leading to the implementation of UNGAR 194] is essential to put an end to the Israeli–Palestinian conflict.[95]

The negotiators propose the creation of an international commission consisting of Israel, the PLO, Egypt, the countries hosting refugees (Jordan, Syria, and Lebanon), the United States, the European Union, Japan, the Russian Federation, and Norway. Paragraph 53 states that "the Commission shall prepare a special Form that will be filled out by all Palestinian refugees," ascertaining whether each individual wishes to:

a. [P: return to their homes in Israel with compensation];
b. return to Palestine with compensation;
c. remain in his current place of residence with compensation; or
d. move to a third country with compensation.

---

95. There is no final version of the Stockholm "non-paper," and the wording is unclear at some points.

The discussion of the refugee problem continues:

54. Every Palestinian [household] defined as refugee in 1948 may attach its entire property claim due to the 1948 War to one Form to be submitted to the Commission. . . .
55. [I: As a matter of Israeli sovereign discretion, Israel may facilitate phased and particular family reunification of [XX] Palestinian Refugees with their families in their present place of residence in Israel. Family reunification shall be carried on based on humanitarian grounds and conditioned by acceptance of Israeli citizenship and waiver of refugee status.]

The document goes on to state that an international fund for compensation of the refugees will be established.

But the tone changes during the final hours of the Stockholm meeting. Abu Ala is getting a lot of calls from Ramallah and Gaza on his cellphone. The more tense he grows, the harder his negotiating position becomes. The Israelis learn that there have been leaks about the Stockholm negotiations in the Palestinian press, and that their Palestinian counterpart is being strongly criticized in Arafat's circles. Nevertheless, Gilead Sher and Shlomo Ben Ami return to Israel convinced that major progress has been made. As is his custom, when Arafat gets Abu Ala's report he does not react. But Abu Ala will tell Dennis Ross that the Stockholm "nonpaper" is an *Israeli* document.

THE AMERICANS ARE WORRIED

On June 10, the Middle East is shaken by the news that Hafez el-Assad is dead. One of the major players on the political scene in the region for thirty-five years has vanished. His son Bachar succeeds him as the leader of Syria. Since the new president must, of course, first consolidate his power, negotiations with Israel will remain stalled for a long time. Arafat attends the funeral of the man who was his chief enemy in the Arab world. The Israelis no longer have a choice: they will have to carry on negotiations with Arafat.

On June 12, at Andrews Air Force Base near Washington, the Israeli delegation is briefed by the Americans Dennis Ross; his assistant Aaron Miller, state department adviser for the Middle East negotiations; and Robert Malley.

Aaron Miller: We had a discussion yesterday with the Palestinians: Abu Ala, Hassan Asfur, and Mohammed Rashid. And, at the same time, with Saeb Erekat and Dahlan. Arafat ordered Saeb to discuss the generics[96] and told Albright he'd done so. Abu Ala is against this; according to our analysis, he thinks it casts a slur on him. As far as we know, Saeb is just supposed to ask questions and not present the Palestinian position.

They have no intention of going forward. The president [Clinton] is going to offer Arafat two options: directly negotiate the framework accord or the third redeployment, that is, a new interim accord. If Arafat chooses this latter option, the president will lose interest in it.

Bill Clinton is approaching the end of his presidency, and he isn't going to waste his prestige and his time negotiating an interim accord. If Arafat decides to go ahead in the direction of the framework accord, then the president will commit himself to the negotiations. If Arafat is drawing the right conclusions from

---

96. The negotiators used the English word "core" to refer to the fundamental issues: East Jerusalem, the Palestinian refugees, territory, and security. Issues arising from the core were called the "generics."

Assad's death, he'll realize that there's no other alternative. Maybe this is what Assad has bequeathed to Arafat: [that he harden his positions and demand a retreat to] the line of June 4, 1967!

Dennis Ross: I met with Abu Ala yesterday. He wants to explain to Arafat that the discussions were serious and deep, and he wants to suggest various options to him, but for that there would have to be several more days of negotiations. Abu Ala is accusing you of having gone back on your positions regarding the eastern border.[97] He says you're insisting that it remain under your sovereignty.

Shlomo Ben Ami: That's not true. We never presented such a position. We've always stated that we would not consider the eastern and western borders in the same light.

Ross: We told Abu Ala we wouldn't present an American proposal [for mediation] during these talks. He asked us, three times, if that was going to be the case. We didn't understand if, when he did that, he was asking us to go forward, or if he just wanted to take note of our answer. The mood isn't healthy. Abu Ala is very vulnerable; he's not the man he used to be. What he wants isn't clear.

Ben Ami: This is going to be a negotiating summit, not a trap for the Palestinians.

Ross: The Palestinians are afraid that Barak and the president [Clinton] are going to form a unified front and present them with a take-it-or-leave-it proposition.

Robert Malley: It's important to know whether a summit is possible. The president isn't convinced yet.

Ross: The president is ready to roll up his sleeves and work to reach an agreement.

---

97. The Jordan Valley.

Miller: The Palestinians aren't sure that the suspension of the third redeployment is working in their favor, so it'll be hard for us to persuade them that it's in their interest. The president promised them the villages [around East Jerusalem].[98] The fact that they didn't get them undermines our credibility.

Ross: The window of opportunity in which the president can make a change will close on July 31. A summit could still be held after that, but the mood wouldn't be as favorable as it is now. I don't think we can get very far with Abu Ala. Dahlan is very angry. He doesn't trust Barak anymore. The idea of an exchange of territory has to be taken into consideration if we want to finalize the accord.

The same day, Gilead Sher and Gidi Grinstein are received in the White House by Sandy Berger. What Berger tells them is this:

It's impossible to know in advance whether a summit will succeed or fail. All we can do is prepare for it carefully. Failure wouldn't be a disaster for our administration, but for Barak it would mean the end of any hope of reaching an accord. Any summit will entail risks, and the president is willing to take them. But they have to be calculated. If a summit fails, that would be a heavy blow for the peace process and would set it back. We have a sense of urgency, just like Barak.

Two things have to be done: give Arafat something to get him to put aside the issue of the third redeployment. The president's credibility with Arafat is very important. Clinton promised him that the transfer of the villages would occur on a certain date. This is the first time the

---

98. See pp. 140–141. The promise was made in the name of Ehud Barak.

president has made a commitment to Arafat and not kept his promise.

We have to think about what to do. The president will have to step in at the end of the summit. On most topics the differences can be overcome, but on Jerusalem the chances of reaching an agreement seem to me to be nil. We have to figure out how to get Arafat to postpone the Jerusalem question, and only this question. But isn't an agreement without Jerusalem doomed to failure?

On June 14, Ehud Barak convenes his security cabinet in Jerusalem. He has decided to reduce the area of land that will be returned to the Palestinians at Abu Dis and Azaryeh near Jerusalem, and he announces a gesture toward the Autonomous Authority: three Palestinian prisoners will be freed. When he hears the news, Abu Ala will hurl angry words at his Israeli counterparts: "It would have been better if you hadn't freed any of them! This is an insult!"

This will be the only measure aimed at establishing trust before the Camp David summit.

On June 15, Bill Clinton receives Yasir Arafat at the White House.[99] Right from the start, Arafat makes it clear how dissatisfied he is. He accuses Barak of not honoring any of his commitments: not on the third redeployment of the Israeli army on the West Bank, not on the freeing of Palestinian prisoners, not on the transfer to the Autonomous Authority of the three Palestinian suburbs of Jerusalem:

Barak told me he'd consulted the Knesset about this. I asked him, "Why did you do that?" He answered that it was at the suggestion of one of his advisers. I told him I'd throw an adviser like that into jail.

---

99. Saeb Erekat is present, as is Sandy Berger on the American side.

Mr. President, Saeb's and Abu Ala's negotiations haven't gotten anywhere. I'm deeply grateful for your efforts and your role in the peace process. We want to finish what we began in Madrid. We're bound by the agreements concluded with Israel, by the process that was begun on May 7, 1994 and was supposed to end in September 1999. In this context, you'll always find us very cooperative. We want to reach a definitive accord so as to put an end to the conflict and establish a comprehensive peace. . . .

Mr. President, no negotiation can succeed without total adherence to the agreements already concluded. This is why I'm reminding you of the importance of the third redeployment, which, I may add, is mentioned in all the agreements reached up to now, agreements you countersigned [as witness]. It isn't a question of percentages [of territory on the West Bank] but of trust between the two parties. In these circumstances, what the Israelis want to negotiate with me in the framework of the permanent status isn't in accordance with the agreements. That's bad faith on their part.

You ought to do everything you can to help us get what was provided for in the agreements. Saeb has spoken with Oded Eran about this. To no avail. Nothing on the [Palestinian] prisoner issue. I have the impression that we're expected to keep quiet and wait for Mr. Barak to decide what's good for him and for us. In fact, I'm afraid that what this man, Barak, wants to do is drive us into a corner and make us look like the guilty party.

We need a lot of preparation, multiple exchanges, but I'll tell you my position on Jerusalem anyway [at this time]. Jerusalem must be the capital of the two states, and there can be no peace if Jerusalem is not the capital of the two states. I'm willing to take their needs into account, to think about the idea of an open city. . . .

With regard to borders, we're for [implementation of] Resolution 242. If there's a question of minor changes in the borders, we're prepared to consider them. On the refugee issue, yes, there's Resolution 194 [of the UN General Assembly], but we have to find a happy medium between the Israelis' demographic worries and our own concerns. . . .

With regard to the settlements, you are aware, Mr. President, of their destructive influence on the peace process (you've said that yourself), especially around Jerusalem and Bethlehem. For the Palestinians, the fact that the settlement policy as a fait accompli is still continuing means there's no more hope. It poisons the peace process. Mr. President, the settlements are at the root of the whole problem.

Sir, I'm positive that the government of Israel isn't aware of the historical importance of my ideas. I don't think Barak understands what I mean when I say we can go ahead with the rectification of borders. I don't think he understands the deep significance of my proposal: "Jerusalem, capital of two states," or when I say that a compromise must be found that can do justice to his anxieties and to our demands with regard to the refugees.

Unfortunately, Mr. President, I think Barak has decided to put us in the position of the guilty party, and I need your promise that, wherever we go with the negotiations, you won't shift the blame for failure onto us and won't back us into a corner.

"I appreciate what you've just told me," Clinton replies. "We'll see what the Israelis are going to do about the third redeployment, but I don't want to make any big promises. As for the prisoners, they ought to do something to help you. We should focus on more important topics. But I promise you that under no circumstances will I place the blame for failure on you."

A few hours later, Sandy Berger receives the Israeli team at the White House.[100] He tells them he is worried after what he has just heard Arafat say:

Berger: Even though Arafat is always playing the victim, the meeting between the president and the Palestinian leader was very tough, more than in Netanyahu's time. When Rob Malley came back from his tour of the Middle East, he submitted a report from which I erased the following sentence: "Arafat has lost all trust in Ehud Barak."

I was wrong. Rob was right. Arafat draws his strength from his position as victim. The promises weren't kept. What makes Arafat go ahead is the president. But peace will be concluded between Barak and Arafat. We can't make peace for you. The peace process is in bad shape; we're holding onto it by a hair. The parties aren't playing the same game. We're in the final act; the Palestinians are off the field.

In the next two or three weeks, Shlomo Ben Ami should continue his work, and we should ease the mistrust. We aren't against a summit, but it's ten to one that it would end in failure. So I'll advise the president not to go to Camp David. I strongly hope for such a meeting, but I know that, as things stand now, it would wind up as a failure. Abu Ala knows how to make progress, so Arafat has to be urged to give him a mandate to negotiate. You have to be creative.

Shlomo Ben Ami: There's a lack of trust between Arafat and Barak. Arafat isn't staying in touch. I've asked the

---

100. Present are Sandy Berger, Dennis Ross, Robert Malley, Shlomo Ben Ami, Gilead Sher, Shlomo Yanai, and Gidi Grinstein.

prime minister to transfer the villages. He said that he will if he has a government coalition [to support him]. If the political situation in Israel becomes more stable.

Berger: Trust is based on acts, not words. If the Palestinians had gotten the villages, they'd feel differently about things.

Gilead Sher and Shlomo Ben Ami are convinced that Arafat was not informed about the concessions they feel they made during the negotiations in Sweden. They ask to meet with him. On June 25, Saeb Erekat, urgently recalled to Jerusalem, is summoned to Nablus, where he joins his president. It is 8:30 P.M.

Yasir Arafat: Shlomo Ben Ami is coming here to try to get me to agree to the summit. These people don't want to negotiate anymore.

Saeb Erekat: Barak turns out to be a true Middle Eastern leader: no one dares to cast doubt on his judgment. . . .

Arafat (joking): I hope that's how it is with you where I'm concerned!

Erekat: Sir, thousands of people see through your eyes, hear through your ears, and speak through your mouth. You don't need me to behave like that.

Abu Mazen and Abu Ala arrive ten minutes later. The group goes to the home of Ghassan Shaka'a, the mayor of Nablus. Ben Ami and Sher are already there.

Shlomo Ben Ami: We've exhausted what can be done through negotiations. Agree to go to Camp David. You'll get 78 percent of the West Bank, and another 10 percent will gradually come under your control. As for Jerusalem, you and Barak have to decide. Solutions exist. With regard to the refugees, you must understand that no one in Israel, not now, not tomorrow, not even fifty years from now, will accept the refugees' right of return. I think we've come to the end of negotiations, and you should agree to the summit, because it's time to make decisions.

Arafat: We're not ready. We haven't even talked about Jerusalem or the refugee issue. . . . You're headed for failure. Go back with Abu Ala, with Saeb; negotiate for one more month.

Ben Ami then launches into a long speech about the state of the negotiations. He mentions the Stockholm "non-paper" and the Bolling talks. Arafat remains inflexible and, throughout the entire dinner, keeps on repeating, "Let's negotiate before convening a summit."

For the Israelis, the case is closed: the summit is definitely going to happen. In the course of several meetings, the last held in Tel Aviv on June 26,[101] they tell the Americans what they think should be done in order to ensure success:

Make a list of topics to be put on the agenda. Divide it in half. On one side, put the issues where you think there's agreement. On these points, if the parties aren't able to write a joint text, do so yourselves. Present the result to the parties, and include it in the final document. As for the issues where there are differences, draft a text on the basis of the statements on both sides and what you know about the negotiations. Check that this is each side's understanding about the other's position. Keep on

---

101. Present are Dennis Ross, Robert Malley, Gilead Sher, and Gidi Grinstein.

cross-checking on the respective positions. That way you'll gradually develop the outlines of the framework accord.

On June 28, at the Jerusalem Hilton, the Israelis and the Americans take stock of the situation.[102]

Dennis Ross: The president [Clinton] will set the schedule. There are still differences between the parties where this is concerned. The Palestinians want two weeks of negotiations before the summit meeting. The prime minister [Barak] would be willing as of right now [to set a date for the summit], with a few days beforehand for preparations. . . . We're looking for ways to influence the dynamics, wondering whether the gap between the respective positions can be bridged. On the issues of territory and the Palestinian refugees, there are solutions.

Gilead Sher: When can we reasonably expect the announcement of the summit?

Dennis Ross: Not before the beginning of next week. Wait for phone calls from the president.

Sher: Is he going to consult with other leaders—Mubarak, for example?

Ross: Apparently not.

Robert Malley: We have to find a compromise between an immediate summit, which is what you're asking for, and a summit in two weeks, as the Palestinians are proposing. I don't think it will be possible to make substantial progress in the context of a new round of negotiations. We're thinking of sending out an invita-

---

102. The participants are Dennis Ross, Gamal Hillal, Martin Indyk, Robert Malley, Gilead Sher, and Gidi Grinstein.

tion to a single summit preceded by several preparatory sessions.

Madeleine Albright meets with Yasir Arafat at Ramallah,[103] where Arafat tries to persuade her that it is much too soon to organize a summit at Camp David. Albright replies that she will inform Clinton of these objections. The press conference held after this meeting shows the extent of the differences between the two parties:

> *Question:* Ehud Barak has just repeated his non-negotiable points: no concession on Jerusalem, no return to the border of 1967. Do you think that, in the course of negotiations, the Palestinians could come closer to the Israeli positions?
>
> *Madeleine Albright:* I didn't hear Prime Minister Barak's statement, so I won't comment on it. The important point is that the parties must work together to overcome their differences. Israelis and Palestinians must now make some very important decisions. The United States will do what it can, but it is the leaders themselves who must decide.
>
> *Yasir Arafat:* Why did [Barak] implement Resolution 425 in South Lebanon? Why did he implement Resolution 242 with the Egyptians and the Jordanians? Even with Syria they committed themselves to the restoration of all the territories and the evacuation of all the settlements, as was the case in the Sinai. . . .

Albright announces that the parties will hold two weeks of intensive negotiations in Washington. She then goes on

---

103. Also taking part are Abu Mazen, Abu Ala, Saeb Erekat, and, on the American side, Ross, Miller, and Malley.

to Jerusalem, where Ehud Barak is not pleased to hear the news. Dragging things out is not what he wants: his governmental coalition is crumbling; the polls look bad. Better to have it over and done with. He phones Bill Clinton, who also thinks the summit should take place in mid-July, before the Republican and Democratic conventions in the United States.

A decision is made. The Palestinians, unpleasantly surprised, are informed by telephone. Clinton reassures Arafat that he has nothing to fear; in no case will he be blamed for a failure.

It will take all of Hosni Mubarak's powers of persuasion to get Arafat to agree to take part in the Camp David meeting. Still, Arafat is annoyed, and he convenes the central committee of the PLO in Gaza. On the agenda is the proclamation of the Palestinian State planned for September 13, the outside date for the signature of the definitive accord with Israel.

On June 29, Ehud Barak consults with his ministers in Jerusalem. In the event of a unilateral proclamation of the Palestinian State, Israel will take appropriate measures. There is talk of deploying the army in Zones B and C. Military leaders present the various scenarios under consideration should there be a failure at the summit. General Shaul Mofaz, the chief of staff, and General "Bogi" Yaalon, his deputy, state that an outbreak of violence can be expected. Tsahal, they say, must be prepared for this. Several variants of Operation Field of Thorns are devised.

The news filters to the press and confirms the fears of Arafat and his circle: "The Israelis are contemplating the retaking of the autonomous territories!"

On the West Bank, and especially in Gaza, various Palestinian organizations, the Autonomous Authority itself, and the security services it controls get ready to face the Israeli army if the peace process breaks down. Training sessions for the use of weapons are drawing thousands of college and high-school students. Handling the Kalashnikov becomes the major activity in Palestinian summer camps. All of this, amply filmed by Israeli and foreign television cameras, confirms the fears of the Israeli general staff: "The Palestinians are getting ready for their war of independence!"

On July 1, a bloody vendetta occurs in Ramallah as two clans confront one another. The Palestinian police have a great deal of difficulty restoring order. In the next three weeks, several incidents will claim victims in Gaza and on the West Bank.

On July 5, Clinton phones Arafat, inviting him to the United States to take part in the summit that is to begin at Camp David six days later. The members of the Palestinian negotiating committee are summoned to Ramallah. Gloom prevails. "This is a trap for us!"Arafat tells his delegates, who agree that there has not been enough preliminary groundwork for the summit. A crisis is inevitable. But the Palestinians have no choice: they can't refuse an invitation from the president of the United States.[104]

In Israel, Barak's parliamentary problems are becoming more acute. The first to rebel is Nathan Shcharansky's right-wing Russian-language party. Shcharansky demands that the prime minister form a government of national unity before the coming negotiations. Otherwise, he says, Barak will yield to American pressure and make important territorial concessions. The National Religious Party joins this movement. Both leave the coalition as soon as the summit is officially announced on July 5.

Then there is Shas, the Sephardic Orthodox party representing right-wing voters. Its head, Eliahu Ishai, demands that Barak make clear his non-negotiable points, the limits

---

104. Videotaped interview with Saeb Erekat, October 28, 2001, Jericho.

to the concessions he has in mind. Barak refuses, and, two days later, the seventeen Shas deputies leave the governmental coalition, which now has only forty-two members. On July 10, the opposition passes a motion of censure in the Knesset with a simple majority of 54 out of 120 votes. Barak is in the minority, but, according to law, he does not have to resign. On the same day, David Levy, the foreign minister, announces that he will not go to the United States. He, too, is considering going over to the opposition. Shlomo Ben Ami will replace him, thereby becoming minister of both internal security and foreign affairs.

THE DAYS BEFORE THE SUMMIT

The negotiators arrive in Washington on Sunday, July 9, and an initial session of talks takes place in the Madison Hotel, where the Israelis are staying.[105]

Shlomo Ben Ami: The prime minister is coming here with the intention of getting results. Don't be fooled by the political situation in Israel. We want an agreement, but not at any price. The accord, if we reach one, will be submitted to a referendum.

Abu Ala: How do you propose to work?

Ben Ami: We promised Arafat that this would be a negotiation summit. We'll meet in parallel work groups. The leaders will make the decisions.

Abu Ala: Are we going to start from square one or begin where we left off?

Ben Ami: No point reinventing the wheel. Let's determine the points of agreement. No point going back to square one.

---

105. The participants are Abu Ala, Hassan Asfur, Shlomo Ben Ami, Gilead Sher, Shlomo Yanai, and Gidi Grinstein.

Abu Ala: We'd reached an agreement on some general principles. The accord will be based on Security Council Resolution 242 and will go on from there, no subject will be set aside, and so forth. Let me review them quickly. There are four main subjects. The generics should not claim our attention for the moment. Saeb will be here [and will handle that].

Gilead Sher: We're at the stage we were at on May 21 in Sweden. Let's start off with the items we agreed on. Let's identify the points of agreement and disagreement and then submit them to our respective leaders. Let's go forward wherever we can.

Abu Ala: On the core topics, there are no points of agreement. We'll need the green light from our leaders. Let's go back to the document that was drawn up in Sweden to see how we can do what we have to do. I'm not willing to undertake simultaneous discussions on security and borders. If your answer on the issue of the eastern border is negative, there won't be any negotiations. But if your answer is positive [and if you agree to our demands], Dahlan will discuss security. Why begin with the negotiation of the framework accord on the status of the Palestinian territories, and not with the comprehensive accord on the permanent status?[106]

That evening, Madeleine Albright invites everyone to dinner at the state department.[107] On the American side, the

---

106. The negotiators use the English acronyms FAPS (Framework Agreement on Permanent Status) and, for the following stage, CAPS (Comprehensive Agreement on Permanent Status). CAPS is supposed to lead to the conclusion of a peace treaty between Palestine and Israel.

107. Abu Ala, Hassan Asfur, Mohammed Dahlan, Mohammed Rashid, and Saeb Erekat, who has just arrived in Washington, are there, along with Shlomo Ben Ami, General Shlomo Yanai, Gilead Sher, and Gidi Grinstein.

entire peace team is seated at the table. Albright opens the discussion:

> The president knows that relations between Prime Minister Barak and Chairman Arafat are not what one would wish. There is work to be done. At Camp David, we'll have the time to promote better understanding and make progress on other topics. This will be a working summit. We greatly admire your leaders: they're men who have done a great deal for their people. They know one another well. We're beginning this summit with the sense that we've been offered a unique opportunity. It will not be easy, and, like you, we want to help you succeed.

Albright goes on to ask the delegates whether they think they can write up a document presenting their respective positions.

> *Ben Ami:* We began work on such a document in Sweden, but we stopped. . . . We have to work along several axes at the same time. Putting the respective positions down on paper is less important than deciding about the main subjects. Obviously, the document should present all the issues, but once the leaders are here we'll be able to get on to the main topics.
> *Dennis Ross:* We'll have to combine the [different] levels of negotiation and move ahead toward the central element of the agreement. Getting the details right will take time, but it can be done.
> *Abu Ala:* President Arafat will want to consult the members of the central committee of the PLO.[108]
> *Albright:* The president [Clinton] will make that decision. Such a meeting could also take place at the State De-

---

108. This would entail infringing the isolation of the summit.

partment in Washington, so that it gets maximum publicity. . . . But this summit must absolutely be protected against any leaks. As for the core [of the agreement]: once we get to it, the rest will come naturally. The positions of the two sides on the issue of Jerusalem are very far apart, and, without an agreement on the principles, it won't be possible to go any further. Once we agree on the core, we can write up a document with I's and P's.

Ben Ami: This is a procedural matter. Do we have to settle the question of the core and postpone the discussion of the other topics, or do we have to discuss everything simultaneously? For us, security is part of the core, but the Palestinians have refused to talk about it. After Sweden, the Palestinians have refused to negotiate on security.

Albright: There are a variety of techniques. In some situations, we'll be discussing all the topics simultaneously.

Abu Ala: That's not technique; that's substance.

Saeb Erekat: Ready or not, we're here. Look, we can't let ourselves make this summit a one-time show that would raise too many hopes. Why not plan another summit in August or September? I'm worried about Barak's attitude. I think he's speaking honestly, but he's calculating wrong.

Saeb Erekat is watching the faces and eyes of the Israelis and the Americans. He has the feeling that what he is being told is: "You haven't come here to reach an agreement." By mentioning another summit after Camp David, Erekat has just rekindled the Israelis' mistrust. But he himself is absolutely certain that the chances of reaching an accord are slim, given the deadlines that have been set and the coming election in the United States.

The next day, while awaiting the arrival of Ehud Barak and Yasir Arafat later that evening, the delegations set out by car for Camp David. The Palestinians very soon regret not having asked the State Department to provide clear directions: no maps show the presidential retreat. For four hours they wander around in Maryland before turning to the local police, who escort them to their destination safe and sound.

Chapter 4

Camp David

On July 11, 2000, one of the oddest episodes of the peace process gets underway. The president of the United States, his secretary of state, his adviser for national security, the head of the CIA, and a team of crack experts in the history of the Middle East are going to try to settle the Israeli–Arab conflict in a few weeks, finding a solution to the problem of East Jerusalem, where Muslim, Christian, and Jewish holy places are claimed by both the Israelis and the Palestinians. For 3,000 years, the Holy City has been besieged by forty different armies and occupied twenty times. Hebrews, Assyrians, Babylonians, Egyptians, Greeks, Seleucids, Romans, Byzantines, Persians, Arabs, Seljuks, Crusaders, Mongols, Mamelukes, Turks, British, and Jordanians have fought to control the city of monotheism. At Camp David, what is at stake is nothing less than opening a new chapter of humanity.

The project gets off to an especially bad start. Ehud Barak wants to have the matter over and done with. On the eve of his departure for the United States, he receives several of his advisers in Jerusalem and tells them that the summit is the very last stage of the negotiations. When Gadi

Baltiansky, his spokesman, points out that advances might be made that call for new talks, Barak stands a pen upright on the table and replies, "If there is no accord, everything will fall down." The pen falls.

The Israeli prime minister believes more strongly than ever in his theory of the Titanic and the iceberg. If a peace treaty cannot be concluded on terms acceptable to him, if the region is heading toward an explosion, then the ship Israel will collide with the Palestinian iceberg unless the country gains the support of the international community. And, at all costs, Israeli society must not be shaken by a confrontation between the left and the right. In short, he is prepared for failure and sets very strict boundaries for the negotiation.

First of all, nothing must be concluded as long as there remains even one point of difference. To avoid having the Palestinians transform Israeli positions into a firm commitment, his proposals will be submitted to the Palestinians through American mediation. He himself will not have any face-to-face meetings with Arafat, who might seize on some minor verbal discrepancy and have it influence the talks.[109] On several occasions, at critical moments of the summit, his advisers will suggest that he speak directly with Arafat. Barak will refuse. At meals he will regularly and openly ignore him, an attitude that the Palestinians will take as an insult and an unwillingness to negotiate.

Barak arrives at Camp David in the worst possible circumstances for him. In Israel, his popularity rating is at an all-time low. He no longer has a majority in the Knesset, where one motion of censure follows another. The American diplomats who greet Gilead Sher are nonplused: "When your prime minister came to Shepherdstown for the negotiations with the Syrians, he surprised us by announcing that

---

109. Barnea and Shiffer, 2000, p. 4.

he couldn't make any concessions because he was 'tied up politically by his coalition.' And now he's coming to Camp David at the head of a minority government, but that isn't preventing him from discussing much more important ideas."[110] Barak intends to circumvent his opposition by submitting a possible accord to a referendum.[111]

Yasir Arafat is convinced that he has been brought to Camp David to have an agreement imposed on him, one that will force him to make concessions on East Jerusalem and the Haram al-Sharif. On this point he feels he can't give an inch. Several weeks earlier, King Fahd of Saudi Arabia had reminded him that Islam's third most holy place belongs to all Muslims. Besides, Arafat does not want to be the first Arab leader to fail to get back all the territories occupied by Israel in 1967. From the opening negotiating sessions on, he is highly mistrustful of the proposals submitted to him. As Martin Indyk will say, it is as though he is shut up in a bunker.

The delegations get settled in their quarters, cottages that are named after trees. Arafat is in Birch, where Israeli Prime Minister Menahem Begin had stayed during the first Camp David summit in 1978. At that time, Anwar El-Sadat was in Dogwood; today, Ehud Barak is lodged here. Bill Clinton's cottage, Aspen, is midway between them. The committees will be meeting in Holly.

At 2:15 in the afternoon, Bill Clinton takes the microphone in the Camp David meeting room:

---

110. Sher, 2001, p. 65.

111. According to Robert Malley, on the question of Palestinian sovereignty over a part of Jerusalem Barak told the Americans right from the beginning of the summit that all he could accept was a limited symbolic presence. Barak had also issued a warning to the effect that, if Arafat was going to claim 95 percent of the West Bank, there would be no agreement. The peace team would take this to be his starting position.

Clinton: This summit is a historic opportunity to reach an agreement on the permanent status. The negotiators have made progress. We want to reach a just solution for the benefit of both parties. If we fail, the parties will lose. Are we ready to make historic decisions, decisions that will be yours, not ours?

But here are the rules. We must proceed as quickly as possible. On each side there are good political reasons not to conclude an agreement. The prime minister faces serious problems at home, as does Chairman Arafat. Both parties have grievances, and we'll try to overcome them. There will be a complete blackout as far as the press is concerned. Only the American spokesmen will issue statements, with the agreement of both parties, and nothing of substance will be said. I'll stay here for as long as it takes to reach an agreement. . . .

Yasir Arafat: I would like the Russian Federation and the European Union to be associated with this process. Likewise the Arab countries, Morocco and Jordan. This is very important, [since that way] the whole world will support what we decide here.

Ehud Barak: We have come to Camp David in a spirit of responsibility. Seven years after the Oslo accord, nine years after the Madrid conference, thirteen years after the Intifada. The time has come for us to live side by side, to make an honorable peace, to work for a better future. . . . I have great respect for the Russian Federation and the European Union, but no one can take the place of the United States and President Clinton.

Arafat: What the prime minister is saying is very important. The contribution of the president of the United States to the success of the summit is crucial, and we hope to reach an agreement, as was the case when Egypt and Israel negotiated at Camp David.

Clinton explains that a summit held later, in the middle of the electoral campaign in the United States, might not have gotten congressional support. "An agreement in July could be supported by a large coalition, Republican and Democratic," he says. Arafat replies, "I want to resolve all the problems. Now, here, with your support."

Arafat and Barak embrace. Clinton announces that he will converse privately with each of the two leaders. The meeting with Barak, a brief one, takes place at 5 P.M. Barak is accompanied by Danny Yatom; when they see this, the Palestinians decide that Arafat will not go alone to the meeting with the president. He will be accompanied by his chief of staff, Nabil Aburdeineh. There will be no small concessions.

On a pathway at the presidential retreat, Shlomo Ben Ami meets Yasir Abed Rabbo. During the conversation, he assures Abed Rabbo that he is against any agreement that would exclude Jerusalem.

At 7 P.M., Clinton and his team[112] tackle the refugee issue with Yasir Arafat; Abu Mazen and Nabil Aburdeineh are also present. "We want the principle of the right of return to be laid down," Arafat announces, "and afterward we can talk about the practical details of its implementation. It's impossible for all the refugees to come back, since some of them are settled in the countries they live in."

At 10 P.M., Clinton and his team meet with Arafat and Saeb Erekat.

Clinton: I don't know what to do about Jerusalem.
Arafat: It's simple. East Jerusalem for us, West Jerusalem for the Israelis. It will be the capital of the two states, and there will be a joint commission for water, roads, electricity. . . .

---

112. Madeleine Albright, Sandy Berger, Dennis Ross, and Robert Malley attend the meeting.

Clinton: Israel will never give up sovereignty over East Jerusalem.

Erekat: The Israelis are contradicting themselves. How can they explain their refusal to allow refugees to return to Israel, when at the same time they want to annex 250,000 Palestinians living in East Jerusalem? The American position has always been *corpus separatum.* With no solution on Jerusalem, it will be impossible to reach an accord.

Arafat: I was in Togo for the Arab summit. I spoke in Arabic, and when I mentioned the Haram al-Sharif, everyone understood and all the Muslim delegates applauded.

Clinton: Barak has a lot of problems when it comes to Jerusalem. He can't go backward. He wants an open city, an enlarged Jerusalem under Israeli sovereignty. The solution would be extended city limits including the two capitals. You would have the rights over the Islamic holy places and also certain districts.

Arafat: The Christian and Islamic holy places are connected.

At this point, Arafat demands sovereignty not only over the holy mosques but also over the Christian holy sites in East Jerusalem. "Can you administer those sectors that the Christians are running themselves?" Clinton asks. Arafat and Erekat understand that, as the discussion proceeds, the status of Christian and Muslim districts will be linked.

Clinton turns to the matter of the Jordan Valley: "You can have the eastern boundary, but international forces, including American, will be deployed west of the Jordan." This Israeli concession, already discussed in the framework of the Stockholm channel, is mentioned for the first time at Camp David. Arafat realizes that Clinton is suggesting a kind of trade-off, the Jordan Valley in exchange for Palestinian concessions on East Jerusalem. "Nothing can be substituted for Palestinian sovereignty over East Jerusalem," he states.

Clinton mentions that the Israelis have told him about concerns on the part of Jordan, which, they say, would prefer to have a common border with Israel, not with the Palestinian State. Arafat ignores the remark and launches into a long disquisition, comparing the situation of the Palestinians to that of the Vanda people in South Africa. Clinton's aides will spend hours on the internet in search of the Vandas.

Clinton then asks the Palestinian leader to name his negotiators for the three committees he has decided to form. Arafat replies immediately: for Jerusalem, Yasir Abed Rabbo and Saeb Erekat; for borders, security, and the settlements, Abu Ala, Asfur, and Dahlan. Abu Mazen and Nabil Shaath will discuss the refugee issue.

Soon afterward it is Ehud Barak's turn to have a conversation with Clinton. The two men are alone. According to an Israeli source, they have a long discussion on the status of Jerusalem, the idea of two capitals in a single city, and access to holy sites.

When Arafat gets back to his lodgings, he convenes his delegation and tells Yasir Abed Rabbo: "We have to do something to explain our position on Jerusalem to Clinton, because he said to me, 'Don't worry, the Palestinians in Jerusalem will remain as they are today and will be connected to your authority.' I said I didn't want to separate the Palestinians of Jerusalem from their city. That would make Palestinians foreigners in their own city."

WEDNESDAY, JULY 12

The first meeting on the borders of the future Palestinian State begins with a brief conversation between Madeleine

Albright and the Palestinian negotiators. Albright says right from the outset that the Americans will be submitting a working document to the parties. She asks the Palestinians to give her some ideas that she can draw on.

> *Abu Ala:* What is the American position on the exchange of territories? We're prepared to discuss an exchange of territories if they're substantial, but the Israelis first have to accept the principle of a withdrawal to the line of June 4, 1967. After that, we'll discuss the equivalence of territories!
>
> *Madeleine Albright:* Israel wants to remain present in the Jordan Valley for a certain period of time.
>
> *Saeb Erekat* (who has joined the meeting): The Israeli–Jordanian border is 625 kilometers long from Eilat. Only 140 kilometers separate Palestine from Jordan. Why do the Israelis want a presence there? When they talk about a threat from the east, what do they have in mind? There are almost no Israeli soldiers between Eilat and the Dead Sea.

The Israeli negotiators[113] arrive and things quickly take a turn for the worse. Shlomo Ben Ami presents the Israeli demands: creation of settlement blocks on the West Bank, bringing together 75 to 80 percent of the Jewish settlers; definition of special arrangements in favor of 50,000 additional settlers, but for a limited time; and recognition of the Israeli presence until the western border is returned to the Palestinians—in twenty or thirty years. The Palestinians protest and refuse to discuss this proposal.

---

113. Israel Hasson, Gilead Sher, Amnon Lipkin-Shahak, and Shlomo Ben Ami.

Abu Ala: Will you accept the June 4 border [as the basis
of discussion]? Will you accept the principle of the exchange of territories?

Shlomo Ben Ami: The Palestinian State will be created in
the context of the agreement. This will be the solution
to the refugee and Jerusalem problems. It will create
a new situation, including various elements [that could
play a role in the] exchange of territories.

Mohammed Dahlan (with Saeb Erekat translating from
Arabic to English): We're entering the final week of a
negotiation that has lasted five years. I know time isn't
on our side. Will you accept Abu Ala's position on the
subject of the line of June 4, 1967? We don't trust the
way the Israelis are approaching the negotiation. You
demand positions in Palestinian territory, we accept,
and when all is said and done we wind up as strangers
in this territory. We know what you want, but I don't
think we can go further if you don't recognize the June 4
line. After that, it will be possible to discuss modifications of the border and raise the question of the
settlements. But this can't be done unless there's an
agreement on the '67 line and [recognition of] the concept of an exchange of territories.

Ben Ami: We'll see that on the maps. But we've always
taken the '67 line as a basis. The percentages of territory [that must be evacuated by the Israeli army] in
the framework of the interim accord[114] are on the West
Bank, that is, on the basis of the '67 line.

Dahlan: We're claiming the '67 line as a reality; it's not
just a slogan for us. I reject on principle any agreement
that will then be torpedoed in its implementation.

---

114. Signed in Washington on September 28, 1995.

Albright: The Palestinians aren't clearly explaining their demands in the negotiation, and that makes the Israelis' task difficult. There has to be more depth in the presentation of your demands.

Hassan Asfur: When the Israeli party puts obstacles in the way of the principle of exchange of territories, this makes it impossible to discuss other topics. . . .

Saeb Erekat: If Shlomo had said, "I take note of your position," we would have been able to get the discussion underway.

Ben Ami: I don't understand, since it's clear that we're going to discuss all the topics. The question of exchange of territories shouldn't get in the way of the discussion of the main subject.

Dahlan (annoyed): You came to Camp David to sabotage the meeting. What you want to do is shift the blame for the failure of the negotiations onto us. The only basis for discussion is the border of June 4, 1967. You don't understand the language of peace.

Dennis Ross: Both parties know that we're going to present a working document, and this isn't making them eager to reveal their margin of flexibility. . . . For the time being, the best plan is to work separately.

Albright: On several occasions we've encouraged you to draw up a working document with the I's and the P's. You didn't do so. The president [Clinton] will leave if no progress is being made. Neither party is going to get 100 percent of what it's asking for. There will be a comprehensive agreement.

Arafat, who has been informed of the tone of the discussion, goes to see Clinton in the company of Saeb Erekat. "Were we invited to Camp David so that we could be blamed for failure?" he asks. And Arafat is violently critical of Ehud Barak: "Let me remind you that he voted against Oslo. He wants to form a government of national unity in Israel with the Likud."

THURSDAY, JULY 13

There is a sense of caution in the air on July 13. Ehud Barak is more mistrustful than ever. "The Palestinians," he tells one of the Israeli negotiators, "have come for the sole purpose of taking note of the Israeli positions. They don't want to conclude an agreement in the course of this summit. Proof: Saeb Erekat has mentioned the possibility of holding other summit meetings." In the committees, the only topic of discussion is the American document that is to be presented that evening. An initial version of this text had been given orally to Barak by Dennis Ross; Barak immediately rejected it. According to this "non-paper,"[115] the Palestinian position was that Israel must retreat to the line of June 4, 1967.

Bill Clinton chairs a meeting of the borders committee. He asks each side to be patient.

Saeb Erekat: The gulf between the different positions is still very important, and the American working document might complicate things further. This document has to be thought through before it's written.

Gilead Sher: No, we're ready to accept such a document, including the I's and P's. Listen, Saeb: you'll have a role in the drawing up of the document, and, in the end, you'll find you've come out ahead every time. No one loses everything, no one gains everything.

---

115. This is one of the few documents written during the Camp David summit. The Israelis did not submit a document; their proposals were made orally to the Palestinians and were generally presented as "American ideas."

Erekat: I agree that that's what we want to wind up with, but what about Jerusalem?

Sher: There will be a special administration, a functional autonomy.

Erekat: Oh, come on! You really think forty million Jews will control and dominate the rights, the history, and the religion of billions of Muslims and Christians? If this is the way you see the solution to the Jerusalem problem, the Palestinians are going to be fighting you for the next thousand years.

Sher: Is that a threat?

Erekat: Don't exaggerate, Gilead. I'm not threatening. I'm telling the truth. You want to continue the occupation; you want the Palestinians to recognize the occupation of East Jerusalem.

Clinton breaks in: "I understand what Saeb means with regard to the working document. I'd like to see Chairman Arafat."

Shortly before dinner, Clinton has a brief conversation with Shlomo Ben Ami. Ben Ami tells him that, in order to bring 80 percent of the settlers together into settlement blocks, Israel would have to annex 6 to 8 percent of the West Bank. Soon afterward, Amnon Lipkin-Shahak and Shlomo Ben Ami, who became minister of foreign affairs after the resignation of David Levy, meet Mohammed Rashid, Arafat's financial adviser, and Mohammed Dahlan. Ben Ami will later report that Rashid and Dahlan were complaining about the lack of boldness in "the old Palestinian leadership"; they themselves, the younger men, were ready to "take the plunge." Dahlan will strenuously deny that these phrases were uttered.

Late, at half past midnight, Yasir Arafat and Saeb Erekat are received by Bill Clinton.

Clinton: I've met with Barak, and I want to go over certain ideas with you.

Arafat: What do you propose with regard to Jerusalem?

Clinton: Mr. Chairman, this document will record your position, namely that you want Jerusalem to be the capital of the Palestinian State, and we'll mention that Israel claims Jerusalem as the undivided capital of the State of Israel.

Arafat: I don't think I can accept a document including [the Israeli] positions. This is contrary to the reference terms of the peace process.

Clinton: This isn't binding on you. Look [the document] over, and tell me what you don't like.

Clinton announces the formation of four committees: the Palestinian refugees, borders, Jerusalem, and security. They are to present a report on their work at 6 P.M. tomorrow. Arafat promises him that his delegates are fully authorized to negotiate. Clinton repeats that the gulf between the respective positions is very deep.

Waiting. Mohammed Dahlan is especially uneasy. In the course of the day, he has been trying to persuade Clinton to let him see his proposals before submitting them to Arafat: "If certain elements come as a surprise to Chairman Arafat, he'll reject them. Don't give him anything without letting us have a look at it first, because he may not accept it."

At two in the morning Dahlan is called by Dennis Ross, who hands him the American document. Dahlan examines it and advises Ross not to let it reach Arafat. Ross refuses and asks that Arafat be told about it.

A few minutes later, this second version of the American "non-paper" is presented to Ehud Barak, who reads it quickly and jumps to his feet: on the Jerusalem issue, Article VI, Paragraph 4 stipulates that "the Jerusalem municipal area will host the national capitals of both Israel and the Palestinian State." For Barak, this means that the new Jewish quarters of Jerusalem will not be included. Dennis Ross corrects by hand, so that the first words are: "the expanded area of Jerusalem." The Israeli team examines this document and rejects it.

Saeb Erekat goes to see Arafat in order to look over the text. He translates into Arabic the passage concerning Jerusalem. These are the positions:

Article VI—*Jerusalem*

1. The Parties recognize the unique status of Jerusalem as a holy city for Judaism, Islam, and Christianity and reaffirm their commitment to the freedom of worship and religious practice in the city.

2. The Parties are committed to enhancing the status of Jerusalem as a City of Peace and to establishing arrangements that will address the needs and interests of both of their citizens in the life of the city.

3. [P: The Palestinian State will have sovereignty over East Jerusalem with special arrangements for settlements, the Jewish Quarter, and the Western Wall, and will provide a corridor for assured Israeli access to the Western Wall. The No-Man's-Land areas will be under shared sovereignty. Therefore, on the basis of the above, Jerusalem will remain an open and undivided city.]
   [I: Jerusalem will remain open and undivided, with special agreed security arrangements for the city as a whole and assured access to holy sites. The Zone of Jerusalem will consist of the territory within the municipal boundaries of Jerusalem and the adjacent Pal-

estinian and Israeli populated areas. The Zone will consist of Israeli Territories, Palestinian Territories, and areas in East Jerusalem that will be subject to Special Arrangements under Israeli sovereignty.]

4. The expanded area of Jerusalem will host the national capitals of both Israel and the Palestinian State.

With regard to the refugees, Paragraph 3 of Article V states:

As part of the international effort Israel will [I: as a matter of its sovereign discretion] facilitate the phased entry of _____ refugees to its territory [P: per year on the basis of the refugees' exercise of their right of return] [I: on humanitarian grounds provided they join their families in their present place of residence in Israel, accept Israeli citizenship, and waive their legal status as refugees]. In addition, in the context of pledges made by the international community, Israel will make an annual financial and/or in-kind contribution [of $_____] to the international program and/or to Palestinian efforts to deal with the refugee problem.

For Saeb Erekat, who does not know that the document has already been rejected by Barak, it is clear that this text was written in collaboration with the Israelis. In any case, it is unacceptable to Yasir Arafat, who summons Nabil Aburdeineh: "Nabil! Wake up Abu Ala! Wake up Abu Ala! Call Abu Mazen! Call Dahlan!"

The discussion begins. The Palestinian delegation is in unanimous agreement that there is no way this document can be considered a possible basis for the negotiations. Arafat flings the paper to the ground and orders Saeb Erekat to bring it back to the Americans.

Erekat: To whom?
Arafat: To Clinton!
Erekat (looking at his watch): Sir, it's 2:30 in the morning. I'm not going to wake up the president of the United States at this hour!
Arafat: Whom can we wake up?
Erekat: Maybe Albright.
Arafat: Go ahead!

Erekat calls the secretary of state and tells her he is coming over. Twenty minutes later, accompanied by Abu Ala, he arrives at Madeleine Albright's house.

Erekat: Madam Secretary, we reject this document, because, in our opinion, it puts us in an impossible position from the start. But we do not want to be blamed for this.
Albright: It's in no way an attempt to put you on the defensive or embarrass you. We aren't trying to annoy Chairman Arafat. What we're interested in is moving things forward.
Erekat: Secretary Albright, please! When I say that something is premature, you accuse me of rejecting the proposal. Please: we absolutely must draw up this kind of document together. You've written it with the Israelis.
Albright: The Israelis contributed by putting forth some ideas; you didn't.

Meanwhile, the Israeli delegation is meeting in Ehud Barak's apartment. Barak is dissatisfied:

The Americans informed us that they were going to present one kind of document, and then they went and presented another kind. If this is supposed to be the basis of negotiations, we're off to a bad start. The Palestinians haven't changed any of their positions. They mention the exchange of territories. They recall their demand for a return to the line of June 4, 1967. There's the problem of the western border. We have to draw the Americans' attention to page 12 of the document, on the subject of Jerusalem: this is not our position.

We have to write our comments on the paper, so that this document will not serve as a basis for negotiation. Negotiation is a process in which obstacles are overcome one after the other, not the prior recording of reasons for failure. What I see here is a ploy to introduce certain positions into the negotiation. The starting positions can't be the ones [that will be established] at the end. It's possible to define a special status for the Temple Mount. A more expansive definition of Jerusalem would include our territories and theirs and would define the city as a Jewish capital and, at the same time, an Arab capital.

Barak wants the American document to stipulate explicitly that "Jerusalem will be an open city, undivided, placed under Israeli sovereignty."

FRIDAY, JULY 14

At 2 P.M. Bill Clinton goes to see Yasir Arafat, who tells him straight out: "Mr. President, your aides have made a mistake. The text Dahlan brought me yesterday is the same as the one he got from the Israelis." According to a witness, Clinton does not get the joke. "I know who came yesterday evening," he says, "and you can rest assured that this document was taken from the negotiation." He announces that he has changed the organization of the talks. There will be not four but three committees: security and borders, Jerusalem, refugees. Clinton continues: "That said, this evening we'll have a dinner party with you and the Israeli delegation. Keep in mind that they say certain prayers on Friday evening; I should tell you about that." And Clinton then explains to Arafat about the kiddush, the Jewish blessing.

"Mr. President," Arafat replies, "you aren't embarrassing me. I respect Judaism. As a Muslim, I believe in Christianity and Judaism. It will be an honor for me to be at your dinner party."

Soon after this, Clinton will tell Ehud Barak that Arafat rejects the American paper on the grounds that it is too "soft" on the subject of Jerusalem. Eighteen months later, Dennis Ross will admit his error:

> We made a mistake in withdrawing our "non-paper." We'd defined a strategy for this summit, but when we ran into opposition from one party, we backed off. Our idea, from the beginning, was to turn the differences [between the parties' positions] into variables. Then the negotiations would proceed within the limits of these variables. Barak was against this method, and the president [Clinton] didn't want to put pressure on him. Barak was the one who was offering the most. The problem is that, when you give up this way, you aren't doing anybody any good. Later we stood firm, and that's when Barak moved forward.[116]

At 3 o'clock, the Jerusalem committee holds its meeting. Yasir Abed Rabbo is in charge of the Palestinian delegation. Dan Meridor, his Israeli counterpart, says right from the start that any agreement on the Holy City must be made public and accepted by the government of national unity he wants to form in Israel. Everything concerning Jerusalem is

---

116. Videotaped interview with Dennis Ross, February 10, 2002, Washington.

subject to negotiation, he says, except the issue of sovereignty: "The division of sovereignty over Jerusalem is an idea that won't be accepted in Israel."

Abed Rabbo then sets forth the difference he sees between an open city and a unified city. Two sovereign entities can agree on the principle of an open city: "We won't accept any solution that puts off dealing with the Jerusalem problem. That would be the time bomb that would blow up any future arrangement."

At the shared dinner, Elyakim Rubinstein, a religious Jew, says the kiddush at the beginning of the sabbath meal. All the members of the Israeli delegation are wearing *kippas*, the skullcaps worn by observant Jewish men.

That evening, the committee on borders and security makes its report to Bill Clinton. Shlomo Ben Ami presents the Israeli position:[117]

We've offered you territories, and, of course, you're within your rights to refuse. But we have to get a coherent counter-proposal from you. We can't accept the demand for a return to the borders of June 1967 as a precondition for the negotiation. What would happen if we accepted this principle, and then we didn't reach an agreement? We'd be left with a situation in which you got recognition of the principle and we didn't get an agreement. This is why I refuse to accept the principle of a return to the 1967 borders.

Sandy Berger accuses the Palestinians: "You aren't working on the dynamics of the negotiation the way the president asked." That afternoon, the Palestinians had interrupted the

---

117. Present are Amnon Lipkin-Shahak, Shlomo Yanai, Shlomo Ben Ami, Abu Ala, Hassan Asfur, Mohammed Dahlan, and, on the American side, Dennis Ross and Sandy Berger.

session, angrily protesting the Israelis' announcement that they intended to maintain control of the border between Gaza and Egypt.

Shlomo Ben Ami will state that Clinton told him he would accept "the Israeli position on the borders and the refusal to return to the line of June 1967. The settlement issue," Clinton had said, "is different on the West Bank in relation to the Golan. It's important to place 80 percent of the settlers under Israeli sovereignty."

At 7 P.M. Yasir Abed Rabbo, Saeb Erekat, Dan Meridor, and Gilead Sher meet with Clinton to give him a progress report on their discussions: there has been no progress. Clinton has no ideas on the subject of East Jerusalem. Obviously, his administration is unprepared on this issue: "I don't know how to resolve it. I'm asking you Palestinians to tell me your concept of Palestinian sovereignty over East Jerusalem."

An hour later, Clinton receives the negotiators from the work group on the refugees,[118] who present their report:

Nabil Shaath: We've examined the problem. If we're going to achieve peace and an agreement to cancel all claims, it's essential that we find a just solution. We can't live under the threat of new demands for compensation. Resolution 194 of the UN General Assembly, which stipulates return and reparations for the refugees, constitutes the basis of a just solution. We have to discuss the right of return.

Reparations must involve:
(1) items registered by the Israeli department of abandoned property (we have a copy of their list);

---

118. Abu Mazen and Nabil Shaath for the Palestinians, Elyakim Rubinstein and Gidi Grinstein for the Israelis. Madeleine Albright, Sandy Berger, Aaron Miller, and Robert Malley are also present.

(2) compensation to be paid to individuals; and
(3) public property abandoned by the Palestinian community.

We have other claims to present, in connection with the suffering inflicted on the refugees, their relocation, and the like.

Our first two claims, on the matter of abandoned property and individual damages, will be addressed solely to Israel. In accordance with the solution to the refugee problem, UNRWA[119] will gradually cease to exist.

Although we are aware of the demands for compensation made by Jewish refugees who left Arab countries, it is our opinion that these claims can in no case be equated with the Palestinian claims or cancel them out. . . .

We have a moral and legal responsibility. For us, this is a historic moment. Just as the Jews suffered horrible crimes during the Second World War and have presented claims for reparations, even in Switzerland, we likewise think that the Palestinian claims must be taken into consideration. Israel's recognition of its responsibilities in the refugee problem would be a historic gesture.

Elkayim Rubinstein: Can the problem be resolved? We agree [with the Palestinians] that it has to be. We've had a good conversation, but very important discrepancies remain between us on our concept of history and the concrete aspects of the problem. Our [the Israeli] vision is a humanitarian one. On the historical level, we can't agree to be held responsible for the refugee problem. What happened in 1948 is the sub-

---

119. The United Nations agency set up to help the Palestinian refugees.

ject of controversy, and the peace process shouldn't be
the arena in which historical truth is pronounced. We
want to do our part toward a solution that will put an
end to the refugees' suffering, but we're not going to
get there by imposing the right of return.

The discrepancies can be overcome. . . . Concretely,
with regard to the entry of refugees into Israeli territory, we're prepared to specify an agreement that
would allow a small number of them to move to Israel
in the framework of family reunification. The compensation of refugees should not be a punishment imposed on Israel. We don't have the wherewithal, and
we don't consider ourselves to blame. But we will
most certainly participate in financing the international
fund for the compensation of refugees.

Clinton: Are you in agreement on the four possibilities [of
individual solution] offered to the refugees?

Rubinstein: We have to be cautious. The problem is to
know what's feasible, concretely.

Clinton: I asked that question because, if you participate
in the international fund, and if we reach an agreement
that the fund will finance all the reparations, I'll get
together the necessary amount. But will *you* make a
commitment to do what you have to do to settle all the
claims?

Rubinstein: Yes, but with caution.

Clinton: . . . If the Palestinians accept the principle that all
claims for compensation will be examined by the international fund, and the Israelis agree to contribute to
it, that will lighten a part of the burden that could
be imposed on Israel. The budget of the international
fund should reach ten billion dollars, maybe more.
Israel obviously can't underwrite that large a sum.
But I don't think Israel will find it in its interest to
refuse to make a minimum contribution. An agree-

ment on this issue should cover all the demands for compensation.

Rubinstein: I understand why the Palestinians are comparing their claims to those of the Jews in Europe, but, when you get right down to it, the problem is totally different.

Clinton: Of course there's no comparison. If an agreement is reached on the specification of a maximum amount in view of these reparations, will you make the archives available?[120]

Rubinstein: . . . We're committed to having Jordan take part in resolving this problem. Palestinian refugees are 40 percent of the Jordanian population. . . . An agreement would imply the disappearance of refugee status in Palestine, Israel, and everywhere else. The international fund, or a similar organization, should make it possible to settle the problem of Jewish refugees from Arab countries.

Clinton: There we have a basis for going ahead on a solution. I'm asking you to make progress in two directions: (1) find a common language that will enable you to overcome your philosophical differences; (2) on the concrete level, reduce your secondary differences.

The final agreement will be judged by what it brings individuals. [It should be] explicit on this. Try to move forward on the concrete aspects.

Shaath: You clearly see what's involved in the problem of compensation, but, for us, the concept of return is very important. Only 10 to 20 percent of the refugees would want to have their right of return acknowledged. . . .

Rubinstein: Ten to 20 percent of the refugees amounts to between 400,000 and 800,000 people!

---

120. This is the register of all property abandoned by the Palestinian refugees in 1948.

Abu Mazen (tugging on Nabil Shaath's sleeve): No, no! That's not the case. We have to agree on the number of refugees . . . !

Rubinstein: There should not be very many of them. We have to reach an agreement on compensation without moving away from the principle of family reunification.

Sandy Berger: We have four days to reach a compromise.

SATURDAY, JULY 15

Arafat had awakened feeling anxious. "The Americans have withdrawn their working document," he tells the members of his delegation, "but the limits to the solution they have in mind are obvious": there will be no complete Palestinian sovereignty over East Jerusalem, and, as for the refugees, they'll have to rest content with financial compensation.

The Jerusalem committee meets at 10 A.M. There is an impasse. The Israelis seem to reverse direction: Dan Meridor announces that he rejects the principle of two municipalities in Jerusalem. Gilead Sher states that, while he does not reject the idea of a Palestinian municipal police force in the western part of the city, it can't be put in place until there is a decision on the territorial extent of the Palestinian municipality.

Yasir Abed Rabbo replies: "We didn't come here to discuss municipal affairs but to find a political solution. What we have to deal with are not basic social or administrative rights in Jerusalem, but political rights." The discussion gets bogged down, and Dan Meridor soon takes Abed Rabbo aside: "This is the toughest subject. I'm going to tell Barak that he handed the most complicated task to me, and that he's going to have to resolve it with Arafat. I can't go on with this mess. When he reaches a solution with Arafat, I'll decide whether or not I can accept it."

"I also got stuck with the most difficult task," says Abed Rabbo.

There are bonds between negotiators.

Meanwhile, at 11 o'clock, Madeleine Albright pays a visit to Yasir Arafat. She asks him to show flexibility. President Clinton, she says, is flying off to Japan the following Wednesday, come what may. Then, in a sudden burst of optimism, she tells the head of the PLO, "You will have a state!"

Arafat: I have always had a state! Barak doesn't want a solution. Fine! We'll wait another twenty years before reaching a solution like [the one found in] South Africa.

Albright: You'll have our economic and financial support for your future state.

Arafat: When I have that state, the whole world will support me. I don't need your money.

The committee on borders and security is also meeting. Shlomo Ben Ami has presented a map that outrages the Palestinians. Ten percent of the territory is colored orange, areas in which the Israelis intend to retain land on a long-term lease. Abu Ala can count: the Israelis intend to annex 14 percent of the territory; with the additional 10 percent, all that will actually be left for the Palestinians is 76 percent of the West Bank (in yellow on the map).

Bill Clinton, Madeleine Albright, Dennis Ross, and Sandy Berger come to see how the discussion is going. Clinton, too, criticizes the map: "I realize that this map is unacceptable. There's an orange line on the Jordan; the Jerusalem area under Israeli control reaches the Jordan Valley; and the Ariel settlement region, in the west, is greatly expanded." Clinton asks Abu Ala to comment on the Israeli map. The Palestinian refuses: "The Israelis must first accept the principle of the exchange of territories. Besides," he says, "for

the Palestinians, international legitimacy means Israeli retreat to the border of June 4, 1967."
   Now Bill Clinton explodes. He literally yells:

> Sir, I know you'd like the whole map to be yellow. But
> that's not possible. This isn't the Security Council here.
> This isn't the UN General Assembly. If you want to give
> a lecture, go over there and don't make me waste my
> time. I'm the president of the United States. I'm ready
> to pack my bags and leave. I also risk losing a lot here.
> You're obstructing the negotiation. You're not acting in
> good faith. You never submit a counter-proposal.

The quarrel is so violent that the delegates on the Jerusalem committee, meeting next door, come to see what is
going on. Abu Ala does not say a word. He lowers his head
and leaves the room. Later, running across Lipkin-Shahak
and Meridor, he will ask them, "What does Clinton want
from me?"
   When Arafat hears the story, later on, he does not comment. He just says to his delegation: "All of you go to bed."
But Hassan Asfur is not about to nap in the middle of a
summit. He asks Arafat, "What should we do?" "What do
you want to do," Arafat replies, "get down on your knees
to them?"
   Asfur gets the point and goes to lie down.
   At 6 o'clock in the evening, the negotiators who have
been discussing Jerusalem present their report to Clinton.

> *Yasir Abed Rabbo:* We [the Palestinians] want two open
> cities, with East Jerusalem placed entirely under Pal-
> estinian sovereignty.
> *Gilead Sher:* What we should discuss is [municipal] pow-
> ers, not the problem of sovereignty.

Dan Meridor says that, as far as he is concerned, there should be only a single municipality in Jerusalem, the Palestinians being granted all municipal powers—but not, however, power over planning and zoning.

Yasir Abed Rabbo: For 30 years your aim has been to prevent the Palestinians from building in East Jerusalem.

Clinton (interrupting): Specify the powers you're thinking of transferring to the Palestinians in the context of a Palestinian municipality.

Gilead Sher: Let's talk about principle and not details. We're willing to discuss all the powers with the exception of security, planning, and zoning. Those issues can be settled later. The present city limits of Jerusalem should be extended. That way there would be a second municipality, a Palestinian one, at Abu Dis, which could be entrusted with certain administrative powers in East Jerusalem. But this municipality, which would be that of Al-Qods,[121] would cover a different city.

Sandy Berger (to the Palestinians): Why wouldn't you agree that a certain number of Jews could pray on the Plaza [of the Mosques]?

Abed Rabbo (shaken by the question): What you're saying is very dangerous. We came here to make peace, not to set off another war of religions. It's as though I were to claim the right of Muslims to go and pray in front of the Wailing Wall. Can you imagine what would happen then?

The Israelis have been following the exchange in silence.

---

121. Al-Qods is the Arabic name for Jerusalem. This idea of two municipalities in Jerusalem was mentioned for the first time in the Beilin–Abu Mazen plan of November 1995.

Abed Rabbo (to Gilead Sher): Explain to him that what
he's saying is very dangerous. Why aren't you saying
anything? [turning to Clinton] On the Haram al-Sharif,
today, we accept the Israeli rules that forbid any foreign individual to pray on the Plaza of the Mosques.
Why do you want things to change after the conclusion of an agreement?

Clinton (trying for a diplomatic tone): I don't know how
we're going to solve the problem of Jerusalem. I'm
asking you Palestinians to present your concept of
Palestinian sovereignty over East Jerusalem. The Israelis will present their concept of East Jerusalem on the
basis of the way they're running the city today. We'll
see whether there are points of agreement, and what
the elements of disagreement are.

On his way out of the room, Yasir Abed Rabbo has a
brief conversation with Robert Malley, who tells him that
Sandy Berger did not intend any harm in putting this idea
forward, and that it should not be taken as the position of
the United States; it's just, he says, that certain Israelis had
suggested it to him. "Tell Sandy, your boss, that this proposal is very dangerous," Abed Rabbo replies. "I don't even
want Arafat to know about it."

In point of fact, the idea of reserving a space on the
Temple Mount for Jews is not a new one. It had been raised
during informal discussions at the Stockholm negotiations.
At that time, the Israelis had suggested that two sites be arranged: to the north of the plaza, where the Koranic schools
are located, and in the building of the "Mahkameh" overlooking the Wailing Wall. Both areas, which belong to the
Waqf, the department of Muslim property, are adjacent to
the Islamic holy site. But this is the first time the idea has
been officially presented at Camp David, in this case, according to Robert Malley, at the request of Ehud Barak.

Yasir Abed Rabbo will rush to tell Arafat about it, and it will become one of Arafat's favorite topics.

The Temple Mount/Haram al-Sharif is the most sensitive issue at the Camp David talks. Not only the Israelis but also the members of the peace team and Bill Clinton himself bridle each time Arafat, while accepting the principle of Israeli sovereignty over the Wailing Wall, declares that "the Jews have no claim to the whole area of the Haram al-Sharif. They [the Israelis] excavated everywhere, and they didn't find a single stone from the Temple, just some stones from the Temple of Herod."[122] And Saeb Erekat adds: "The fact is that, today, no such thing as a Temple Mount exists. What's there is a mosque. We're dealing with realities. There's no such thing as sovereignty over history. History is in our books, in our memories."

At dinner, Clinton reveals to the Palestinians: "I told Barak that, like Arafat, he bears responsibility for the lack of progress [in the negotiations]."

That evening, Saeb Erekat and Arafat are at Clinton's house.

Clinton: Mr. Chairman, we have to move forward. As of now, we're going nowhere. Listen, I have an idea. I want two of your delegates. Choose the ones you have most confidence in. I want you to give them a formal mandate. Give them the freedom to think freely, without restrictions, so that they can put forward ideas. I want this meeting to begin at midnight tonight. I'll give them my office, and they'll stay there with the door shut for twelve hours.
Arafat: Good idea. I choose Saeb and Dahlan.
Clinton: Barak has named Shlomo and Gilead.

---

122. Videotaped interview with Yasir Arafat, February 2, 2002, Ramallah.

At around 11:30 P.M. Robert Malley informs Gilead Sher that

Yasir Arafat is demanding a swap of territories, and he won't be satisfied with a symbolic swap in exchange for the 8 or 10 percent of the West Bank whose annexation by Israel he can accept. We have to reach an agreement on Jerusalem, present ideas, all possible options. Arafat is looking for a pretext. As for the eastern border, all of the Jordan must be Palestinian. That's the right solution.[123]

Before this, Sandy Berger had had a stormy conversation with Gilead Sher: "Your prime minister is the one who wanted this summit! He put pressure on us, and now he's reversing himself and is being incredibly rigid in his positions. Starting tomorrow, I'm not going to spend any more of my time on the peace process. What I'll be doing is working on President Clinton's behalf."

SUNDAY, JULY 16

Shortly before 1 A.M., the Palestinian delegates meet with Arafat. They are convinced that a confrontation with the American administration is at hand. The atmosphere is tense. "The most important thing for me is the Haram al-Sharif," Arafat tells Saeb Erekat and Mohammed Dahlan. They will receive no other instructions.

The scene is surrealistic. Shlomo Ben Ami, Gilead Sher, Saeb Erekat, and Mohammed Dahlan settle down in Laurel, the cottage where the president of the United States has a conference room and a personal office. There, arranged

---

123. Sher, 2001, p. 171.

on the table, are his family snapshots and his computer, on
which, early in the morning, Sher's assistant Gidi Grinstein
will try in vain to print a text. Employees of the State Department are posted at the exits. But they did not predict the
ingenuity of the negotiators from the Middle East: Saeb
Erekat and Gilead Sher will discover a French window that
they will use, around 6 A.M., to return to their respective
lodgings, take a shower, and inform their leaders of the status of the discussions.

According to Saeb Erekat, the Israelis submitted a proposal right at the outset:

Shlomo Ben Ami: The Arab districts in the outer ring
of Jerusalem would come under Palestinian sovereignty. They are: Kalandia, Semiramis, Kufr Akab,
Dalat el-Barid, a part of Al-Ram, Beit Hanina,
Shuafat, Sawahara el-Garbyeh, and Umm Tuba. The
other Arab districts: Ras el-Amud, Silwan, Sheik Jerrah, and Jabel Mukaber, would enjoy functional
autonomy, but their municipal services would proceed from Al-Qods, the municipality of Arab Jerusalem, which would be located outside the present city
limits of Arab Jerusalem. In the Old City, the Muslim, Christian, and Armenian districts would have a
special administration, to be discussed, but would
remain under Israeli sovereignty.

The Haram al-Sharif, the Temple Mount, would be
placed under Palestinian jurisdiction, the United Nations and Morocco granting the Palestinian State custody of this Muslim holy site, over which Israel would
retain limited sovereignty.

Gilead Sher: Israel will annex 10.5 percent of the territory
[of the West Bank]. In exchange, you'll receive a protected passage between the West Bank and Gaza,
without barricades or checkpoints. You will also re-

ceive docks left entirely at your disposal in the port of
Ashdod, as well as a terminal at Ben-Gurion Airport
[near Tel Aviv]. On the eastern border, for reasons of
security, we shall retain control of a piece of land representing 10 percent of the West Bank—land located
along the Jordan—for a period of twenty years. Israeli
withdrawal from this zone will take place gradually.
Moreover, we wish to retain five positions on the West
Bank, connected with one another by roads that, in
case of emergency, would be placed under Israeli control. Palestinian airspace will remain under Israeli control. The Palestinian State will be demilitarized.

The Israelis repeat that they refuse the right of return of
the Palestinian refugees to Israel. But they feel that they
have made concessions, and that the talks will be able to go
forward on the basis of this new proposal.

For Saeb Erekat and Mohammed Dahlan, none of this
is acceptable. They cannot agree to the annexation of 10.5
percent of the West Bank or to the occupation, for twenty
years, of an additional 10 percent in the Jordan Valley. Besides, they know very well that Arafat will reject any solution that does not grant the Palestinians sovereignty over
the Haram al-Sharif. Erekat therefore tells the two Israelis that their proposal would mean continued Israeli occupation of Jerusalem, especially, he adds, since "with the
five military positions you intend to keep, you could, in
case of emergency, cut the West Bank into five cantons."
The Israelis immediately conclude that he does not have
a mandate to make any concession whatsoever, which
Erekat formally denies. The only instruction he received
from Arafat, he says, is not to give in on the Haram al-
Sharif.

Dawn is breaking. The negotiators' nerves are on edge.
Exhausted, Saeb Erekat wants to lie down in the anteroom.

Shlomo Ben Ami raises his voice: "Are you people stupid, or what? This is our last chance, and you're tired! That's not what's meant by work! . . . Don't you want a state?"[124] Robert Malley, who has been following the situation from outside the room, calms Ben Ami down and awakens Erekat.

Israel Hasson, who has come at Sher's request to take part in the discussion, now speaks up for Dahlan, who intends to go and say his morning prayers against the better judgment of the watchdogs from the State Department. In the end, he is allowed to leave. Sher and Erekat disappear through the secret door they discovered during the night. Back after their escapade and a good shower, around 6:30 in the morning, they settle themselves in the presidential office to try to put together a document including the famous I's and P's.

The negotiators are exhausted and irritable. Saeb Erekat has sent for Gaith el-Omari, a young lawyer who is the legal counsel for the Palestinian delegation. Almost as soon as he arrives in the conference room, el-Omari has an exchange with Shlomo Ben Ami, who has been getting annoyed with Saeb Erekat: Erekat continues to reject the idea of shared sovereignty over the Temple Mount and evades any talk about the end of the conflict and the canceling of all Palestinian claims. "I'd like to understand why the Palestinians refuse to proceed toward the cancellation of all claims," Ben Ami tells el-Omari.

El-Omari: Because there's one topic that hasn't been discussed yet.
Ben Ami: Which one?
El-Omari: Compensation for the years of occupation.
Ben Ami (exploding): Your leaders don't deserve to have a state! They don't know how to seize an opportunity!

---

124. Sher, 2001, p. 173.

They're obsessed by public opinion! They're not equal to this historic moment!

Although Saeb Erekat seems to have been unaware of this incident (he was, he says, in the adjoining room), it further increases the mistrust of the Israeli negotiators. The Palestinians had first raised the issue of compensation for the years of occupation five months earlier, during the negotiations led by Oded Eran. The subject has not come up since then. On that earlier occasion, the Israelis had told the Palestinians that Ehud Barak could never persuade the Israeli public to accept an agreement that would not only fail to bring an end to the conflict, but would result in a demand for compensation.[125] The Palestinians feel they can discuss the end of the conflict and the definitive cancellation of all Palestinian claims only after they have obtained satisfaction on the other topics.

After twelve hours in Clinton's office, the negotiators go back to their respective delegations. To a man, they are pessimistic. Shlomo Ben Ami and Gilead Sher believe they took a step forward by offering to share the Temple Mount. The Palestinians, they say, have not given anything in exchange and have refused to accept the framework set up by Ehud Barak, who had expected that they would agree in principle to end the conflict and would present their demands in the context of his positions.

Barak analyzes the situation: "The Palestinians aren't taking a single step toward us. This game simply can't go on. Each side has to make a commitment. We're heading for a confrontation."

Early in the afternoon, Barak gets bad news from Israel. A right-wing meeting, held in Rabin Square in Tel Aviv, has

---

125. In fact, this subject will be examined one month later, during secret negotiations between Gilead Sher and Saeb Erekat.

been a success. There were 250,000 demonstrators according to the organizers, 150,000 according to the police. Hundreds of buses brought the whole slew of West Bank settlers, who marched under the slogan: "We are the majority!" Ariel Sharon made a tough speech:

> Barak's peace is a false and bad peace. A temporary peace. We have to talk about what Arafat is ready to give. I want to hear that, at Camp David, Arafat gave up East Jerusalem and the Old City, that he gave up the Jordan Valley and the airspace over Judea and Samaria. I don't want to hear—and you don't either, I'm sure—you don't want to hear that Israel is making concession after concession.

Saeb Erekat and Mohammed Dahlan report to Arafat. The Israelis, they say, want to annex 12 percent of the West Bank and get a 12-to-30-year lease on 10 percent of additional land in the Jordan Valley, where they will retain control of security. The border itself, on the river, would remain under Israeli sovereignty. The Palestinians would not have access to the Dead Sea. Four settlement blocks would be created on the West Bank, but 63 Jewish settlements would be preserved in the Palestinian State. The city limits of Jewish Jerusalem would be extended to the east. According to the two negotiators, the Israelis have offered nothing new except the proposal of a special government for the Old City of Jerusalem. The Muslim quarter would be granted a special status, but, they add, Sher and Ben Ami have once again claimed for the Jews the right to pray on a part of the Haram al-Sharif.

Arafat, very agitated, announces that he is going to talk with the Americans: "I'll tell them that this is no way to negotiate."

Clinton receives Arafat that afternoon. The meeting lasts half an hour.

Arafat: The Israelis have said again that they want to pray on the Haram. This is very dangerous. I don't mind their praying, but it would lead to an Islamic revolution. I can't accept that.

Clinton: OK! Present your objections and say no! But if we don't somehow reach a solution in the next few days, we'll all go back empty-handed. It seems that Barak, at least, has taken a step.

Arafat: It makes no sense to say that Barak has taken a step, because this step has to do with the districts outside Jerusalem that he wants to separate from.

Clinton: I'm asking you to bring in answers to three questions: (1) What is your reaction to Barak's wanting to annex 10.1 percent of the West Bank? (2) Do you accept a limited Israeli presence on the border with Jordan? (3) Do you accept a provision stipulating that this agreement would signify the end of the conflict?

The Palestinian delegation meets and decides to clarify its position in a letter to be sent to Clinton:

The aim of the negotiations is the implementation of Resolutions 242 and 338 of the United Nations Security Council, that is, Israel's withdrawal to the line of June 4, 1967. We are willing to accept adjustments of the border between the two countries, on condition that they be equivalent in value and importance. As for the refugee problem, we want to settle it on the basis of Resolution 194 of the United Nations General Assembly. With regard to Jerusalem, we want the eastern part of the city to become the capital of the Palestinian State. We are willing to discuss the concept of an open city between East and West Jerusalem, and to take into account the status of the Jewish quarter and the Wailing Wall, which could come under Israeli sovereignty. The proclamation of the end of the conflict will come only after the establishment of the mechanism for implementing the accord on the permanent status. Security arrangements cannot be the [sole] responsibility of the Palestinians. . . . We express our interest in other security arrangements with Egypt and Jordan. . . .

In this document, the Palestinians repeat that they oppose any Israeli presence on their borders, in the Jordan Valley, and between Gaza and Egypt. They demand access to the Dead Sea and accept the principle of an exchange of territories amounting to 3 or 4 percent, but on condition that this not involve any inhabited Palestinian areas and not affect the territorial integrity of the West Bank.

Mohammed Dahlan returns from a meeting with Shlomo Ben Ami. The latter has announced that all the settlements in the Gaza Strip will be evacuated if there is an accord.

Arafat goes to see Clinton. Saeb Erekat, who is with him, translates the letter from Arabic into English. If Erekat is to be believed, the mood was pleasant, with Clinton simply listening to Arafat's protest against the Israelis' most recent territorial proposal: 20.5 percent of the West Bank to remain in Israel's hands, 10.5 percent to be annexed outright, and 10 percent to be under military occupation for twenty years.

Sandy Berger will offer another version of the meeting. The discussion between Clinton and Arafat, he will say, was very difficult. Never had the president been so tough with Arafat. He asked him to reply to at least one of the three basic questions. "If you don't," Clinton said according to Berger, "there's no point staying at Camp David until Tuesday, when I'm leaving for Japan," whereupon Arafat, under pressure, accepted the principle that settlement blocks housing 80 percent of Israeli settlers would remain on the West Bank.

As evening approaches, Danny Yatom phones Martin Indyk: "Barak isn't about to go on like this. He plans to go back to Israel when Clinton leaves for Okinawa."

The mood is tense at dinnertime. Ehud Barak is seated between Yasir Arafat and Chelsea, Clinton's daughter. During the two hours that the meal lasts, he does not once turn toward the head of the PLO.

Sensing that the summit is about to fail, the Americans decide to put pressure on the two delegations. At 10 P.M. Clinton pays a visit to Barak. He has the impression, he says, that Arafat is ready to move forward on the territorial issue, that he could accept the annexation by Israel of 8 to 10 percent of the West Bank. Barak is asked to draw up a document on this basis.

At 10:30 P.M. Madeleine Albright meets with the Palestinians. She announces that, tomorrow, Clinton will be shuttling back and forth between the two delegations, and she reveals that Clinton is talking about an annexation by Israel of only 8 percent of the West Bank.

MONDAY, JULY 17

In the morning, the Americans inform the Israeli delegation that "Clinton has never been so hard on Arafat. Arafat was trembling. Clinton charged him with three tasks. He has to complete at least one of them, otherwise there'd be no point staying until Tuesday. The president believes the Israelis have made significant progress, while the Palestinians haven't budged."

Clinton is now talking with Ehud Barak. Madeleine Albright, though, is holding a discreet conversation with Abu Mazen. She asks him how he would feel if there were a difference of opinion between himself and Arafat. Would he join the Americans, or would he support Arafat? And what if he himself were in disagreement with Arafat: Would he confront him publicly?

Abu Mazen: No, I wouldn't go against him. If I disagree with his positions, I'll resign!
Albright: What about a partial accord? Would you accept it?
Abu Mazen: No, I won't accept any partial solution! Any agreement without Jerusalem would endanger Arafat's life!

This is not the first time that the Americans will try to do an end run around Arafat.[126] Less than a year later, the George W. Bush administration will contact Abu Mazen and Farouk Kaddoumi and awkwardly mention similar possibilities to them. They will not have any greater success.

Ehud Barak takes advantage of a pause to put through several phone calls to Israel. He talks with Dalia Itzik, the minister of the environment, and Avraham Burg, the president of the Knesset, who, with his authorization, will report his message: at Camp David, negotiations are close to an impasse; he might come back empty handed; the Israeli press is portraying the summit in much too rosy a light.

In the following days, other Israeli ministers will be party to similar confidences from Barak, who has established his communications operation on the only phone line available to the Israeli delegates. Several days later, Barak will tell Steve Cohen, the American academician who has been a mediator in the Middle East since the 1980s, that the thinking behind his persistence is this: if the summit ends in a historic agreement, public opinion in Israel should be pre-

---

126. An American diplomat denies that Madeleine Albright ever made such an appeal to Abu Mazen. Palestinian negotiators maintain that this did in fact occur.

pared for it; in the contrary case, the aim is twofold: avoiding the breakdown of Israeli society into right and left camps by persuading the international community that blame for the failure lies with Arafat, and making sure the doves in Israel understand that, despite his all-out effort, an accord with Arafat was impossible.

Barak's communications team consists of three men: Eldad Yaniv, the prime minister's personal assistant, and his spin doctors Moshe Gaon and Tal Zilberstein, heads of advertising agencies who are veterans of the 1999 electoral campaign. Yaniv has set up his headquarters in the firefighters' school in Emmitsburg, near Camp David. From there, he oversees the team of spokespeople from the Israeli Embassy in Washington and puts in regular appearances at the press-corps center in Thurmont, where the international press, including Israeli and Arab correspondents, is staying.

Gaon and Zilberstein spend long hours at the ministry of defense in Tel Aviv, which is linked telephonically with Barak's quarters in Camp David. An Israeli negotiator will say, with a certain cynicism, that an agreement would surely have been reached if Barak had spent as much time talking with Arafat as he did with Gaon.

The manipulation of the press, especially the Israeli press, is made all the easier by the fact that Camp David is hermetically sealed. Information must therefore pass through the single telephone line that Barak has available. As a result, journalists have no way of verifying what they are being told by Yaniv and the official spokespeople, who are staying in the same motel in the town of Frederick where the Israeli press is quartered.

One morning, in my presence, Meirav Parsi Tsadok, who is officially in charge of communications for the prime minister's office, receives a piece of information from Camp David that she immediately transmits to the correspondent of Israeli radio. A few minutes after the broadcasting of this news item, an official from the State Department phones Ms. Parsi Tsadok, who coolly denies being the source of the scoop.

At midday, Ehud Barak has a long telephone conversation with Eldad Yaniv. He describes his profound pessimism about the chances for success at the summit. Yaniv immediately contacts Gaon, and the two of them decide that it is time to prepare public opinion for a failure. Yaniv then gives the scoop to two star journalists at *Yediot Ahronot*. "Summit Fails. Prime Minister to Return to Israel" will be tomorrow's banner headline on page one of this daily newspaper. Gaon and Yaniv's reasoning is simple: if there is no crisis and the negotiations succeed, the paper and its correspondents will be blamed for the false news. For now, just sound the alarm.

At 1 o'clock in the afternoon, the Israeli delegation gets together for a discussion that will last until 6 the following morning. Everyone is there, including Gidi Grinstein, the delegation's assistant. They all have the sense of a historic mission. No political or electoral campaign argument is mentioned.

Oded Eran reminds the group that, in Jerusalem, there are "sectors with no historical or religious value: the whole northern part of the city up to Shuafat, south and east of Har Homa [Djebel Abu Ghneim]. Our message, he says

should be to avoid the annexation to Israel of 100,000 Arabs. But then there's the inner part of the city. The Temple Mount, the Old City, the commercial triangle north of the Temple Mount, and the surrounding area to the west, which includes the Mount of Olives and Augusta Victoria. These areas have to receive special treatment. I'm against the division into districts, and what I propose is a joint administration, representative, placed under a common municipality.

Yossi Ginosar: When it comes to Jerusalem, there's sym-
metry between the Israeli and Palestinian positions on
the importance of the city and also on the image that
the people who live there have of it: "See the Temple
Mount, the Old City." There can't be any give and
take on this issue. The Palestinians are being surpris-
ingly firm in refusing to understand the importance of
the Temple Mount for the Jews and Israel. It's amaz-
ing how they just can't see what matters to us. The
members of the Palestinian delegation all seem to have
closed minds here.

The Palestinians' order of priority is as follows: sovereignty over the Temple Mount, the Old City, and
the first circle of Arab districts; as for the outer circle
of Arab districts, the Palestinians believe we're interested in getting rid of them, and so they're not demanding them. Even the moderates around Arafat
won't support a solution that doesn't provide for [Pal-
estinian] sovereignty over East Jerusalem. . . .

What Arafat is interested in is Jerusalem, and this
is why he's hardening his positions on the other subjects. Arafat doesn't want just some small foothold on
the Temple Mount, though certain Palestinians are
mentioning other possibilities, like shared sovereignty
in the Old City, or the absence of sovereignty on the
Temple Mount, or the establishment of international
sovereignty over the Old City. Arafat won't be able to
accept an accord that grants him only partial sovereignty over the Temple Mount. He's demanding it all
[all of East Jerusalem], with the exception of the Jewish quarter and the Western Wall. Arafat actually considers himself the representative of the Muslim world
in everything having to do with the holy places. The
Christians have told him, "Get lost," but he doesn't

care. He attaches great importance to what the Saudis and the Egyptians say, and also the Italian government, King Abdallah of Jordan, and others. We should think about when to appeal to Mubarak.

Shlomo Ben Ami: This is a historic moment, the most important for a prime minister since 1967. What we have to do is come to a decision under very difficult conditions. Can any meaningful progress be made with the Palestinians? I knew that [Camp David] would be the Jerusalem summit. There are two aspects to this topic, concrete and mythological. Jewish Jerusalem has never been so extensive, and we've never had such complete control over the city.

Ehud Barak: Is time on our side? History consists of one wave after another, and the whole key to understanding politics is knowing what direction they're moving in. From the 1920s on, Zionism developed without making any mistakes. But the Palestinians have taken the wrong path at all the great crossroads of history. Later we made mistakes on a number of counts. One of the sources of our mistake in 1973[127] was viewing our situation at that time on the basis of past experiences: our victories of 1948, 1956, and 1967. We were sure, in 1973, that the Arabs were going to lose again. In 1967, Israel secured the bare minimum needed to guarantee its national interest. Today the real question is this: Should we take action now that the water [the situation] is calm, and put an end to the conflict, or should we run into the iceberg and react?

---

127. Barak is alluding to the error made by the intelligence services and the Israeli government, who misinterpreted the warning signs of a war and were surprised by the Syrian–Egyptian offensive in October 1973.

With these words, the prime minister is addressing a recurrent question in Israeli politics: Why negotiate when there is no emergency?

> *Ben Ami:* The agreement should take into account the mythical aura Jerusalem has for the Palestinians. Something impossible to quantify, but sucess depends on it. We have to deal with the question of Jerusalem. We have to get rid of slogans of the "Peres is ready to divide Jerusalem" type. Jerusalem has [already] been divided. On the Temple Mount, we have to strengthen the present arrangement by getting recognition for a benign Israeli sovereignty. As far as the inner districts are concerned, there won't be any agreement without mention of Arafat's sovereignty over the Old City.
>
> *Amnon Lipkin-Shahak:* We should move ahead on all the other topics before discussing a withdrawal in Jerusalem. What's our line in the sand when it comes to Jerusalem? Important parts of the present city aren't part of my Jerusalem. I have no problem with giving up Tsur Bakher. It's in Israel's interest to place as many Palestinian citizens as possible under Arafat's responsibility. It would be a huge mistake to increase in any significant way the number of Arabs under Israeli sovereignty.
>
> Ultimately, it's a good thing that we didn't invest more in East Jerusalem. We'd have many more Arabs today in the city and its surrounding areas. What separation [from the Palestinians] are we talking about here? In normal relations among states, there's no absolute control over people's movements. Control can't be exercised at roadblocks. We'll have to prevent the passage of Arab populations from the Palestinian territory to the State of Israel, and in order to do that we'll have to develop much more sophisticated instruments.

The State of Israel came about through a pragmatic Zionism that was prepared to make important compromises. We can't give up sovereignty over the Temple Mount. It's the heart of Jewish culture, whether we control it or not. And so sovereignty in the deeper sense is ours by right. We can't give the Temple to Arafat. But without Jerusalem, without something of the Old City [for the Palestinians], there won't be an agreement.

We have to find a way to grant the Palestinians a more or less ample space in the Muslim quarter of Jerusalem. There they can enjoy the kind of status that the churches and embassies have. . . . It's not clear that this will satisfy them. It's possible that, even if we go about it this way, we won't find a solution for Jerusalem. And then we're back at square one.

Dan Meridor is opposed to any concession on the present city limits of Jerusalem. Arafat, he says, is not interested in Beit Hanina: "What he wants is the Temple Mount. If Israel gives up the outer Palestinian suburbs, it will break a thirty-three-year-old line of defense without getting anything in exchange. Once this line is broken, we'll no longer be able to build a new line of defense on the walls of the Old City."

Elkayim Rubinstein: This debate is very hard for me. It's the moment of truth. If we want to enlarge the city limits of Jerusalem, all we have to do is make a governmental decision. But if what we're talking about here is reducing them, then there has to be a referendum. We have [a whole range of] resources to meet the humanitarian and religious needs [of the Palestinian population]. But the means are much more limited when it comes to a national question. We have to take the bull by the horns and decide.

The Arab situation is getting worse. We have to try to include as few Arabs as possible under our control, both in Jerusalem and in the settlement blocks. We can wholeheartedly accept a formula that would free us of the Arab villages around Jerusalem. If, on the one hand, we negotiate [with the Palestinians] on the return to Israel of thousands of refugees over a period of ten years, on the other hand we should free ourselves of control of 130,000 Arabs [in Jerusalem], all this in the framework of an agreement on security. As for the Temple Mount, we'd have to reach an agreement with the Waqf, arranging a space for Jewish prayer and the control over archeological digs. . . .

Gilead Sher: There may be no point of possible agreement between our fundamental interests and theirs. What we're aiming to do, in the long term, is separate [Palestinians and Israelis], especially in Jerusalem, and increase the Jewish population of the city. . . . Two cities, two municipalities working side by side. From the point of view of the present negotiations, we should try to reduce the number of issues in contention. Maybe we should develop a different system of conflict management.

Sher suggests that, at the last minute, Barak personally conduct the negotiation on the Jerusalem districts and do so in a context that would guarantee success.

Sher: This historic debate is difficult, because it touches on the heart of the matter. The major problem has to do with sovereignty and the Temple Mount. Clinton is the one who will arrive at a definitive solution, not the parties. All this should be decided in the course of a discussion with Clinton. I'm afraid that what will be said here will just amount to the beginning of new negotiations. But we absolutely have to come to a successful conclusion. Let's try to begin the negotiation on Jerusalem with the Old City and move outward from there.

Ehud Barak: This debate is gut-wrenching. Thirteen people far from the scene are supposed to make decisions on which the fate of millions of human beings depends, and make those decisions in calm waters, while we don't notice the iceberg in front of us. These decisions are like the ones that had to be made when the plan for the partition of Palestine was accepted in 1947, or those that led to the Yom Kippur War [in 1967]. Begin precisely understood the direction the process was heading in, and what his decisions would mean. It's no accident that he sent Jimmy Carter a letter in which he repeated the [famous] prayer: "If I forget thee, O Jerusalem." Rabin and Peres, too, perfectly grasped the importance of certain formulations in the Oslo accord: one jurisdiction, the concept of a single territorial entity. Words get results. We're coming to the end of the road, six months after the deadline. . . .

This is a historic moment, and we shouldn't shy away from it. . . . I don't know a prime minister who would be willing to sign his name to the transfer of sovereignty over the First and Second Temple [the Temple Mount], which is the basis of Zionism. The same isn't true for Tsur Bakher, but that's also the case for the other party [the Palestinians]. Palestinian sovereignty over the Old City would be as hard [for us to bear] as mourning. Without separation from the Palestinians, without an end to the conflict, we're headed for tragedy.

The situation isn't the same as in 1973, when some people could say they didn't see the iceberg coming. Anyone reading over the transcripts from April and

May 1973 knows that those who did see the iceberg refused to make decisions! Now, we can't say we don't
see the iceberg getting closer. We understand the question before us. We will not conclude an agreement at
any price. On certain subjects, we're prepared to refuse,
ready to face the world, like Ben-Gurion, who in his day
proclaimed Jerusalem the capital of the Jewish State—
which the international community has never accepted.

Israel Hasson then lists the various possible options for
the Old City: A special regime? An internationally recognized archeological site? He even foresees a limited presence
for the Palestinian police in the Muslim quarter.

While the Israelis are taking stock of the situation, Clinton
and Arafat have their first discussion of the day. The Palestinian leader repeats his position on Jerusalem and the
settlements. Clinton listens to him, then reveals: "I've spent
half the day looking at these problems with Barak. And I'll
be spending the coming night on them; it's going to be
Jerusalem Night. For the first time, the Israelis have accepted the principle of the exchange of territories. What will
be involved is a sector near Gaza."

Arafat returns to his quarters, satisfied. He had been able
to set forth his positions in detail, and, besides, he has the
sense that pressure from the Americans, which he has been
experiencing since the beginning of the summit, is easing up.

In the evening, Clinton and Sandy Berger chat with
Yasir Abed Rabbo:

Clinton: I understand that Arafat has to come back with
a solution that's acceptable to the people around him,
both Palestinian and Arab.
Berger: I've spoken with a lot of people who took part in
the first Camp David summit. They all told me that
we can't ignore this factor.

Clinton: I've become an expert on Jerusalem! I'll be the next mayor of Jerusalem, no doubt about it: I know everything there is to know on the subject. Tomorrow we can start working on the texts of the agreement.

After its internal discussion, the Israeli delegation gets down to work. While Gilead Sher, Shlomo Ben Ami, Saeb Erekat, and Mohammed Dahlan continue their talks, documents are being drawn up in Barak's quarters. Drafts are written by Ben Ami, Sher, and Grinstein. Elyakim Rubinstein and other delegates make corrections, so that "these documents will be unassailable." The result is a rapid hardening of the Israeli position, which Gilead Sher will describe as follows: "I sometimes had the impression that certain members of the Israeli delegation were trying to get the imprimatur of the settlement council."[128]

TUESDAY, JULY 18

Shortly after midnight, the diplomats who are not sleeping at Camp David are awakened by an incident that could have ended badly. Shouts ring out from the living room of Barak's suite. The prime minister's secretary yells, "Quick! A doctor, a doctor!" Everyone rushes in: Barak is choking: he had swallowed some peanuts the wrong way. Gidi Grinstein grabs him by the waist and performs the Heimlich maneuver. The head of the Israel government is saved. Clinton's personal physician, who has hurried over along with some marines, has nothing to do but tell Barak to be careful with peanuts from now on. Elyakim Rubinstein insists on saying the blessing: "Thanks to the Almighty for having saved a life."

---

128. Sher, 2001, p. 185.

Hearing about the incident in the morning, the Palestinians have a good laugh at Barak's expense, punning on the word *peanuts* in the colloquial American sense of "a trifling amount": "The man who wants to give us peanuts will choke on peanuts," says Yasir Abed Rabbo. Clinton enjoys the joke but makes the Palestinians promise not to let the Israelis get wind of it.

At 1:30 in the morning, Barak, who has recovered, presents his team's work to Clinton, whose advisers find it odd that the Israelis waited until they were at Camp David to discuss the Jerusalem issue. Clinton is dismayed. The Israeli delegation has taken a step backward: no concession is offered on Jerusalem, and the amount of territory that Israel wants to annex on the West Bank is far greater than 12 percent. All of the Jordan Valley is to remain under Israeli sovereignty, a demand Barak had given up the previous evening.

Annoyed, Clinton exclaims: "I can't go see Arafat with a retrenchment! You can try to sell it [to the [Palestinians]; there's no way I can. This is not real. This is not serious. I went to Shepherdstown [for the Israeli–Syrian negotiations] and was told nothing by you for four days. I went to Geneva [for the summit with Assad] and felt like a wooden Indian doing your bidding. I will not let it happen here!"[129]

Barak returns to his quarters. The document has to be redone. At 3 A.M. he hands his text to Clinton. This time, a certain flexibility has been introduced on the subject of the districts in the outer ring of East Jerusalem. For Clinton, this isn't enough: "I still can't present this document to the Palestinians. You have to accept a special status for the holy sites; without that, I can't negotiate a compromise between you."

"On the set of topics [under discussion]," Barak replies, "I can't morally or politically allow myself to go further than the document I've handed you. Nevertheless, Mr. President,

---

129. Malley and Agha, 2001, p. 60.

it's up to you to assess the situation and determine whether the respective positions are close to one another and can lead to an agreement. In any case, I ask that you be careful not to let the Palestinians make a record of the positions we're presenting in the negotiation."

Back in his quarters, Barak tells several members of his delegation: "There are issues that go beyond the mandate I got from the voters. If I take this step, I'll destroy the political and moral foundations of a possible agreement. . . . Clinton seems to understand this. He'll try to see whether the respective positions can converge."[130]

Bill Clinton receives Yasir Arafat and Saeb Erekat. Arafat protests. He is being asked to make intolerable concessions: "The Egyptians insisted on getting the last kilometer of the Sinai at Taba. Between Israel and Lebanon, there are heated discussions about each house in the village of Rajar in South Lebanon. And I'm supposed to give up Jerusalem?"

Clinton submits his latest proposal:

Israel will annex or retain under its control from 15 to 20 percent of the border on the Jordan River and will do so for twelve years. In this sector, international forces may be deployed. Furthermore, on the western border of the West Bank, Israel will annex 9 percent of the territory and in exchange will grant the Palestinians the equivalent of 1 percent of the area of the West Bank in land bordering Gaza.

On the subject of the Palestinian refugees, Clinton speaks of a "satisfactory solution," but what is most important is that, for the first time, he suggests offering the Palestinians full and entire sovereignty over the Muslim and Christian

---

130. Sher, 2001, p. 186.

quarters of the Old City of Jerusalem, with the Armenian and Jewish quarters coming under Israeli sovereignty. The other Arab districts in the city center would be granted functional autonomy under Israeli sovereignty. On the issue of the Haram al-Sharif, Clinton suggests a "sovereign custodianship" for the Palestinians, with the Israelis keeping "a residual sovereignty" over the primary holy site of Judaism.

Several hours later, Arafat will let it be known that he cannot accept these proposals: "I'm not about to have Israeli occupation replaced by Israeli sovereignty."

At midday, the Israelis are informed of the most recent American initiative. Ehud Barak is furious. In his view, this document, put together by Dennis Ross, goes way beyond the Israeli positions, and, at 6 o'clock, he decides to reject it. But matters do not end there.

The driver from the Israeli embassy in Washington, who brings the daily diplomatic mail and coded messages addressed to the prime minister, goes back with a document and detailed instructions for Eldad Yaniv. The result: leaks in the Israeli press a few hours later. Thus *Haaretz* will reveal that

the negotiators have arrived at an understanding on the American proposals, which must still be approved by Yasir Arafat. . . . The agreement being drawn up respects the three nonnegotiable demands spelled out by Ehud Barak: a unified Jerusalem under Israeli sovereignty; the annexation by Israel of blocks of territory in which the settlements will be brought together; and return of the Palestinian refugees limited to family reunification, without Israel's assumption of responsibility for the refugee problem. In exchange, Israel agrees to grant considerable autonomy to the Palestinians of East Jerusalem. Under a new juridical category, the Palestinians will have sovereignty over the roads leading to the settlements. Moreover, Israel will agree to accept 100,000 refugees into its territory, with those living in the settlement blocks being granted a special status. The talks may end in a partial accord, the solution to the problem of Jerusalem being postponed to a later date.[131]

It is 7 P.M. Abu Mazen, Abu Ala, and Abed Rabbo are having a conversation with Madeleine Albright, who is accompanied by Dennis Ross and Martin Indyk.

Albright: The problems are complex. The Israelis have submitted some ideas, but you haven't. All you do is state that East Jerusalem should revert to you, and that's all. This is no way to negotiate!

Ross: The Israelis have proposed that the Palestinian suburbs to the north and south of Jerusalem be transferred to the Palestinian Authority. A part of the Old City would be placed under Israeli sovereignty, and municipal powers would be negotiated between the two parties. The Muslim quarter would be placed under Palestinian sovereignty. In the Christian quarter, a distinction would be made between the holy sites and the quarter itself.

The Palestinians (protesting): This is very complex. You're talking about a sector with an area of one square kilometer, and you're proposing five different systems! This isn't realistic, and it runs the risk of complicating things still further.

Albright (tired, annoyed): We didn't get any sleep last night, but you people slept! According to Dennis's formula, the ordinary Palestinian will have control over his

---

131. Ben and Horowitz, 2000, p. 1.

own affairs and won't have Israel's hand over his head. *He* couldn't care less about the concept of sovereignty.

Yasir Abed Rabbo: We know better than you what the ordinary Palestinian wants. For him, sovereignty isn't an abstraction but the ability to live, move about freely, pray freely, marry and start a family freely.

Ross: Are you expecting an American proposal? Is that what you want?

Martin Indyk: The Israelis can't go as far as you'd like. No one can go that far.

Albright: We've reached an impasse. If we leave Camp David without a solution, violence is going to break out.

Ross: This question of Jerusalem is very hard. We can't bridge the gap between the two positions.

Abu Ala: We can't accept a solution without Jerusalem, and we can't accept solutions granting the Israelis sovereignty over East Jerusalem and leaving us only municipal powers. That would make it even harder for the people in the city to lead their lives. They'd live under two [different] systems: the municipal powers for the Palestinians and the real power for the Israelis.

Indyk: David Ben-Gurion created a state without Jerusalem.

Abed Rabbo: Ben-Gurion created a state with a cease-fire line that didn't include Jerusalem. We will create a state whose borders will include East Jerusalem.

Indyk (in a surge of optimism): We'll have an accord tomorrow!

Abed Rabbo: I'll bet you a meal for ten people in the best restaurant in Israel that there won't be an accord.

After dinner, the Palestinians have a brief conversation with Bill Clinton and Madeleine Albright. "Why don't you proclaim a state without Jerusalem?" Albright asks pointedly. "Impossible!" is the reply.

Clinton announces that he will be seeing Arafat that evening. He says he is thinking over a formula for arriving at an agreement.

At 8 P.M. Sandy Berger visits Barak to suggest that he postpone looking at the Jerusalem issue for two years: what has to be done now is sign an accord on the other negotiating points, where there seems to be more chance of success. The Israeli delegation considers the idea. Shlomo Ben Ami, Amnon Lipkin-Shahak, and Gilead Sher feel that the solution to the problem must not be put off. The prime minister agrees with them.

At 9 o'clock, Mohammed Dahlan brings Arafat a new proposal from Clinton, received a few minutes earlier from Ross: the Palestinians would become the custodians of the Haram al-Sharif. Did Abu Mazen try to avoid a new crisis by preventing this document from reaching Arafat, who, he knew, would reject the idea once again? Be that as it may, information to this effect will reach the Israeli delegation. Mohammed Dahlan will deny it.

The meeting with Clinton takes place around 10 P.M. Nabil Aburdeineh accompanies Arafat.

Clinton: I have a proposal, and I think this is the best deal. You will be the custodians of the Haram al-Sharif with the approval of the United Nations Security Council and Morocco,[132] who will entrust you with the administration of the Muslim holy places. The Palestinian flag will fly over the Haram, but under Israeli sovereignty. The same will hold true for the Christian holy sites. In the Old City, the Armenian quarter will be placed entirely under Israeli sovereignty. Likewise, outside the

---

132. Morocco heads the Al-Qods commission.

city walls, for districts like Sheik Jerrah and Salah a-Din, but Barak will grant them more independence in certain areas of municipal administration, for example, certain aspects—but not all—of planning and zoning, also certain aspects of security and certain juridical powers.

Between 80 and 85 percent of the border in the Jordan Valley will be Palestinian. The Israelis will maintain a military presence there for twelve years. Eight percent of the West Bank will be annexed by Israel in order to create settlement blocks there. There will be an exchange of territories of 1 percent. A satisfactory solution will be found for the Palestinian refugees. Finally, a formula will be developed to indicate the end of the conflict. . . .

Arafat (furious): Mr. President, this proposal is Dennis Ross's invention. I've already gotten it from Barak via Dahlan. I'm telling you, and I'm saying this in front of Sandy Berger and Albright, that Dennis Ross is in league with the Israelis. He's working with them, not with you.

According to a witness, Clinton manages to stay calm.

Back in their lodgings, the Palestinian negotiators are confused. They don't fully understand the details of this American proposal and send Mohammed Dahlan to verify certain aspects with Gamal Hillal, the official translator of the State Department, who was present at the conversation. Late in the evening, Hillal gives the Palestinians a somewhat different version: 9 percent of the West Bank will be annexed by Israel in exchange for 1 percent of Israeli territory. The Israeli military presence will occupy between 15 and 20 percent of the border of the Jordan Valley, where international forces will be deployed. The Palestinian quarters of East Jerusalem will be granted functional autonomy, with certain powers in the area of planning and zoning.

All of which Arafat rejects. He decides to send Clinton a letter.

WEDNESDAY, JULY 19

This is another day of crisis. Yasir Arafat has sent his message to Clinton. He formally rejects Clinton's latest proposals and suggests that the summit be suspended for two weeks, during which time there would be an attempt, with the participation of American diplomats, to bridge the gap between the two sides.

Ehud Barak is now convinced that Arafat wants to use the Jerusalem issue to torpedo the summit. He, too, sends a letter, meant for publication, to Clinton:

> To my great regret, I have come to the conclusion that the Palestinian side is not negotiating in good faith and is not willing to negotiate in a serious manner so as to achieve a permanent peace between us. If matters remain as is, the Palestinians will have to face the tragic consequences of this missed opportunity. My government has worked unremittingly to put an end to the Israeli–Palestinian conflict, but, to my great regret, the Palestinian side has been unwilling to make the historic decisions [called for] at this stage.

The letter will be transmitted by telephone, at 3 P.M., to the Israeli spokespeople who are waiting in the nearby town of Frederick. Barak announces that the Israelis are leaving. The delegates, along with the journalists who are to return on the prime minister's plane, are asked to prepare for departure. Everyone starts packing.

Ten o'clock. This is the first of six stormy meetings between Clinton and Arafat. Clinton has decided to up the pressure on the Palestinian leader: "I'm very disappointed. You're going to lose my friendship. You're going to ruin the opportunity to conclude an agreement for twenty years. Barak will form a government of national unity. You're making me lose eight years of effort."

> *Arafat:* I can't conclude an agreement without Jerusalem. I will not betray Jerusalem. . . . The proposals you're submitting to me are ones Dahlan brought me from Barak. I won't betray either the Christians or the Palestinians. I'm not to blame for the failure. I asked that this summit be better prepared for, and that we not repeat what happened with Assad in Geneva, but you didn't listen to me. I suggested that international forces be deployed [in the Jordan Valley], and you came and asked me for 20 percent of border territory.

Clinton talks about the fall of the Barak government and the formation of a cabinet of national unity with the Israeli right, which would mean a halt to the peace process.

> *Arafat:* What can I do? If I have to, I'll wait another twenty years. I'm asking you to continue the negotiations. And if your proposal is the final one, I'll consult with the Palestinian leadership and tell them: this is what we're being offered; it's up to you to decide.
> *Clinton:* What you're saying makes sense. Do you want to stop the negotiations now and consult with the Palestinian leadership?
> *Arafat:* When it comes to Jerusalem, and taking into account the fact that the solution we've been offered to all intents and purposes gives Israel sovereignty over the city . . . , and that Israel would [de facto] annex

Jerusalem in its totality, I have to consult with the entire Arab world, not just the Palestinians.

Clinton: Why won't you talk directly with Barak to find
the best way to resolve these problems?

Albright (breaks in): The Israelis have made progress.
You haven't taken a single step forward!

Arafat: That's not true! We've demonstrated a lot of flexibility, but Barak keeps on pretending. What is he offering? The annexation of Jerusalem. Right now I have
control over the Muslim holy places in Jerusalem,
under Israeli sovereignty. What will change? What difference will there be? Just words! Words!

At noon, Albright suggests that Clinton announce the
end of the summit at 4 P.M. by declaring that the parties
have made progress and that this will serve as a fulcrum for
future negotiations. The question of the status of Jerusalem
will be postponed for future talks between the State of Palestine and Israel. To which Arafat replies, "I'm not postponing the question of Jerusalem for one second." He again
suggests suspending the summit for two or three weeks.
"Clinton has new ideas he'll tell you about in an hour,"
Albright says.

As soon as she takes leave of her host, the phone begins
to ring in Arafat's suite. Calls come in from Amr Moussa,
the Egyptian minister of foreign affairs; Saud el-Faisal, head
of the Saudi foreign ministry; and the chief of staff of the
president of Egypt, all of whom inquire about the status of
the negotiations.

Amr Moussa will later relate that the first telephone call
from Clinton to Mubarak went like this:

Clinton: Mr. President, can you help us?

Mubarak: Yes, of course. What's this about?

Clinton: Put pressure on Arafat to accept my latest proposal!

Mubarak: Which is?

Clinton: I can't tell you![133]

In fact, Ehud Barak had personally asked Clinton not to tell Mubarak about the proposals discussed at Camp David, fearing that they might be leaked. Clinton will later disregard Barak's prohibition, and the Egyptian president will be put in the picture: what is involved is shared sovereignty over the Haram al-Sharif/Temple Mount. Mubarak will tell Clinton that no Arab leader could take on such a responsibility, since changing the status of this Muslim holy place might have serious consequences for the entire region.

King Abdallah of Jordan asks Arafat what he thinks of the proposal to deal with all the other problems and leave the question of Jerusalem pending for two years. "If all Arab countries, all Arab and Muslim leaders, agree to leave the question of Jerusalem pending," Arafat tells him, "then I'll agree too!" Clinton, of course, is up against a flat refusal. No Arab leader is about to advise the Palestinians to give up sovereignty over the third holiest place of Islam.

At 5:15, Clinton goes to visit Arafat.

Clinton: I've suggested to King Abdallah and President Mubarak that the negotiation on Jerusalem be postponed for two years. They think this is a good idea. I'm worried for Barak. He's facing internal problems. His concessions on Jerusalem are more important than I expected.

Arafat: I haven't found anything new in his position.

---

133. Videotaped interview with Amr Moussa, November 21, 2001, Cairo. An American diplomat involved in the talks denies that the conversation went this way.

Clinton: You've gotten a lot and offered nothing in exchange.

Arafat: I've given a lot. [Still,] we can go on with these negotiations for two weeks. We'll keep you informed.

Clinton: Can you wind things up successfully in two weeks?

Arafat: Yes! In fact, for me, the real negotiation began just two or three days ago.

Clinton: I have to leave for the G8 in Japan. Give me an agreement in principle on my proposal of yesterday, if need be with your objections. . . . Otherwise, you're risking the loss of my friendship and the friendship of the United States. Washington's doors will be closed to you.

Arafat: We're in a position of weakness. I appreciate your friendship, your efforts, but I can't betray my cause. . . .

Albright again brings pressure to bear on the Palestinians. "The Israelis have presented some very creative ideas," she tells Abu Mazen, Abu Ala, and Yasir Abed Rabbo:

They're going back to Israel to form a government of national unity. They'll hold the expected elections. The solution is for you people to begin to negotiate. Otherwise, it's all over. There won't be the two more weeks of preparatory talks that you asked for. And you'll have let the chance to conclude an accord slip away. All I can see is a disaster looming in front of us. This is the saddest day [of those we've spent together].

The Palestinians insist, repeating that they are demonstrating sufficient flexibility, and suggest again that the summit be suspended for two weeks, during which the negotiators would prepare draft agreements to be submitted to their leaders.

Dennis Ross: You've pushed Barak as far as he can go with his concessions. He can't give any more. The only way to deal with this is for you to talk directly with the Israelis.

Albright (angry): I'm not going to have dinner with you. Go talk to the Israelis. Talk to them. This is a very sad day.

Mohammed Dahlan and Hassan Asfur, who have had almost nothing to eat all day, go to the dining room, where they meet Amnon Lipkin-Shahak and Shlomo Ben Ami. The four men have a brief discussion and are in agreement: it would be a shame to end the summit like this. Clinton, too, is there. Asfur and Dahlan go over to him and tell him they hope to stay on. The president listens but does not answer.

The two Palestinians then go back to Arafat's quarters and tell him about their conversation. A few minutes later, the phone rings. It is Clinton, and, instinctively, Arafat wishes him *bon voyage* in French. Clinton does not notice the politeness and announces that he is coming to talk to him after dinner.

What Clinton suggests is that the talks be pursued in Israel and in the Palestinian territories: "But you have to agree to continue the discussion on the basis of my latest proposal and do no more than raise objections with regard to sovereignty over the Haram al-Sharif."

Arafat: Mr. President, thank you very much for your efforts. I'll send you an invitation to my funeral after my assassination, if you insist on this point.

Clinton: I don't want the same thing to happen to you that happened to Rabin and Sadat.

Arafat: We are willing to continue to negotiate and will keep you informed.

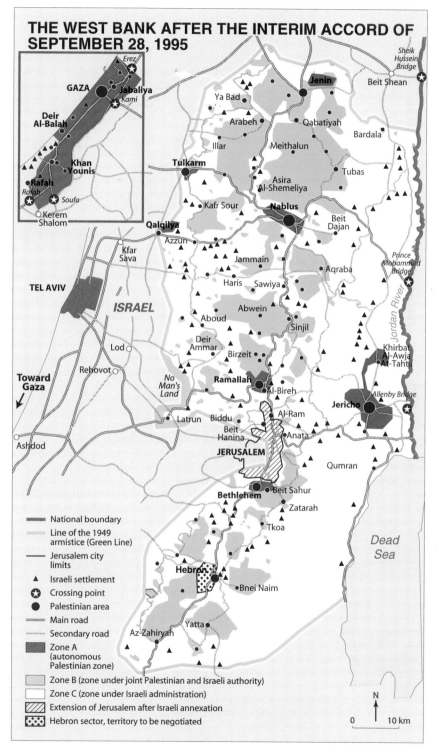

THE WEST BANK AFTER THE INTERIM ACCORD OF SEPTEMBER 28, 1995

Legend:

- National boundary
- Line of the 1949 armistice (Green Line)
- Jerusalem city limits
- ▲ Israeli settlement
- ✪ Crossing point
- ● Palestinian area
- Main road
- Secondary road
- Zone A (autonomous Palestinian zone)
- Zone B (zone under joint Palestinian and Israeli authority)
- Zone C (zone under Israeli administration)
- Extension of Jerusalem after Israeli annexation
- Hebron sector, territory to be negotiated

Map labels: Erez, GAZA, Jabaliya, Kami, Deir Al-Balah, Khan Younis, Rafah, Rafah, Soufa, Kerem Shalom, Sheik Hussein Bridge, Beit Shean, Jenin, Ya Bad, Arabeh, Qabatiyah, Bardala, Illar, Meithalun, Tulkarm, Tubas, Asira Al-Shemeliya, Kafr Sour, Nablus, Beit Dajan, Qalqilya, Azzun, Kfar Sava, Jammain, Aqraba, Prince Mohammad Bridge, TEL AVIV, Haris, Sawiya, ISRAEL, Abwein, Aboud, Sinjil, Jordan River, Deir Ammar, Lod, Birzeit, Khirbat Al-Awja At-Tahta, Rehovot, No Man's Land, Ramallah, Al-Bireh, Allenby Bridge, Jericho, Toward Gaza, Latrun, Biddu, Al-Ram, Beit Hanina, Anata, Ashdod, JERUSALEM, Qumran, Bethlehem, Beit Sahur, Zatarah, Tkoa, Dead Sea, Hebron, Bnei Naim, Az-Zahiryah, Yatta

N, 0 — 10 km

Source: Charles Enderlin, revised from Franck Debié and Sylvie Fouet. La paix en miettes. Presses Universitaires de France, 2001

THE TABA MAPS OF THE WEST BANK

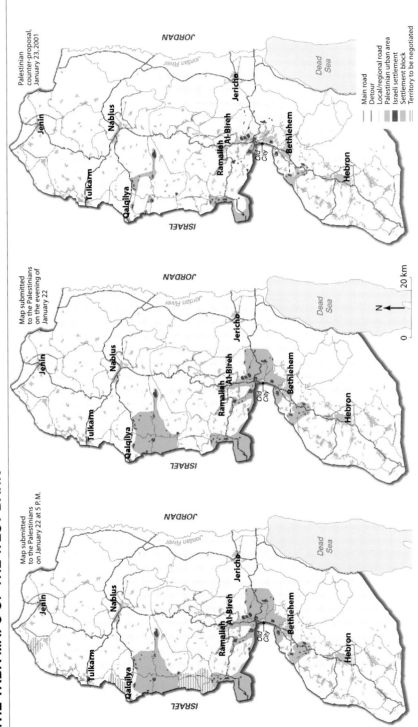

Source: Orient House (Palestinian Headquarters, Jerusalem)

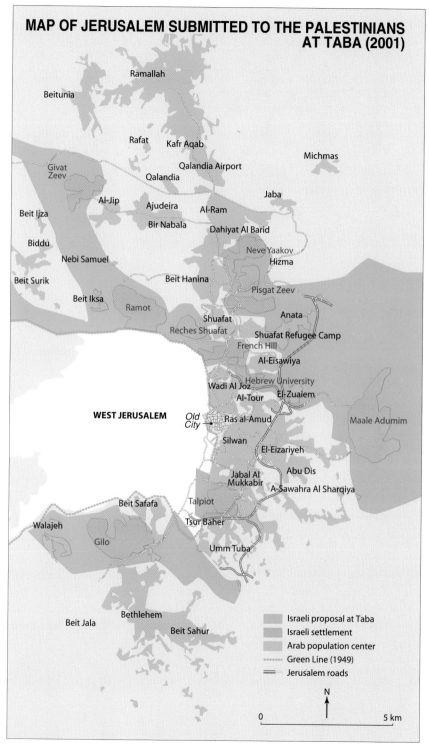

MAP OF JERUSALEM SUBMITTED TO THE PALESTINIANS AT TABA (2001)

Ramallah

Beitunia

Rafat

Kafr Aqab

Michmas

Givat Zeev

Qalandia Airport

Qalandia

Al-Jip

Ajudeira

Al-Ram

Jaba

Beit Ijza

Bir Nabala

Dahiyat Al Barid

Biddu

Neve Yaakov

Nebi Samuel

Hizma

Beit Surik

Beit Hanina

Pisgat Zeev

Beit Iksa

Ramot

Anata

Shuafat

Reches Shuafat

Shuafat Refugee Camp

French Hill

Al-Eisawiya

Hebrew University

Wadi Al Joz

El-Zuaiem

WEST JERUSALEM

Al-Tour

Old City

Ras al-Amud

Maale Adumim

Silwan

El-Eizariyeh

Jabal Al Mukkabir

Abu Dis

A-Sawahra Al Sharqiya

Beit Safafa

Talpiot

Walajeh

Tsur Baher

Gilo

Umm Tuba

Bethlehem

Beit Jala

Beit Sahur

	Israeli proposal at Taba
	Israeli settlement
	Arab population center
·····	Green Line (1949)
═══	Jerusalem roads

N

0 ————— 5 km

Reproduced from Orient House (Palestinian Headquarters, Jerusalem)

According to this map, the Jewish neighborhoods built in occupied territory at Ras al-Amud and Har Homa (opposite Umm Tuba) would be restored to the Palestinians.

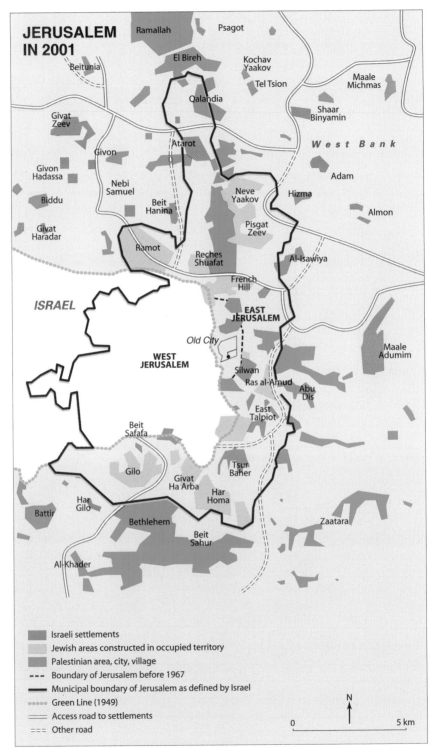

JERUSALEM
IN 2001

Ramallah   Psagot

Beitunia   El Bireh   Kochav
Yaakov
Tel Tsion   Maale
Michmas

Qalandia   Shaar
Binyamin

Givat
Zeev

Givon   Atarot   *West Bank*

Givon
Hadassa   Nebi
Samuel   Neve
Yaakov   Adam

Biddu   Beit
Hanina   Hizma   Almon

Givat
Haradar   Pisgat
Zeev

Ramot   Reches
Shuafat   Al-Isawiya

French
Hill

ISRAEL   EAST
JERUSALEM

Old City   Maale
Adumim

WEST
JERUSALEM   Silwan
Ras al-Amud   Abu
Dis

East
Talpiot

Beit
Safafa

Tsur
Baher

Gilo   Givat
Ha Arba   Har
Homa

Har
Gilo

Battir   Zaatara

Bethlehem   Beit
Sahur

Al-Khader

Israeli settlements
Jewish areas constructed in occupied territory
Palestinian area, city, village
Boundary of Jerusalem before 1967
Municipal boundary of Jerusalem as defined by Israel
Green Line (1949)
Access road to settlements
Other road

N

0   5 km

Source: Charles Enderlin. Revised from www.monde-diplomatique.fr/cartes/jerusalemdpl2000

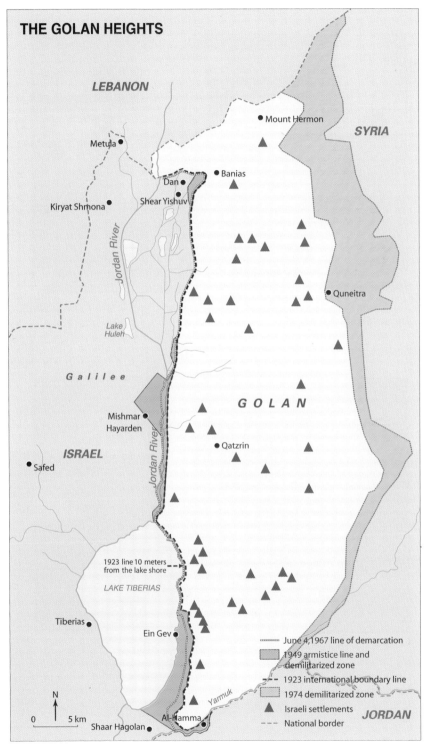

THE GOLAN HEIGHTS

LEBANON

• Mount Hermon

SYRIA

Metula •

• Banias
Dan •
Shear Yishuv

Kiryat Shmona •

Jordan River

• Quneitra

Lake Huleh

Galilee

GOLAN

Mishmar Hayarden •

Jordan River

• Qatzrin

ISRAEL

• Safed

1923 line 10 meters
from the lake shore

LAKE TIBERIAS

Tiberias •

Ein Gev •

⋯⋯ June 4, 1967 line of demarcation

1949 armistice line and
demilitarized zone

— ⋯ 1923 international boundary line

1974 demilitarized zone

▲ Israeli settlements

--- National border

JORDAN

N

0 ⎓ 5 km

Yarmuk

Al-Hamma •

Shaar Hagolan •

Source: Charles Enderlin

The historic handshake between Yitzhak Rabin and Yasir Arafat at the White House, September 13, 1993

The last working session at Wye River, October 22, 1998
Bill Clinton and Benjamin Netanyahu are in the foreground. Standing without a jacket is Secretary of the Israeli Cabinet Danny Naveh. Gamal Hillal is talking to Yasir Arafat, who is examining the draft of the agreement while Nabil Shaath, be-hind Arafat's left shoulder, looks on. Standing behind Clinton is Nabil Aburdeineh, advisor to Arafat.

Bill Clinton looks on as Yasir Arafat and Ehud Barak shake hands during the first days of Camp David in July of 2000

A working session at Camp David, July 2000
Clockwise from lower right: Saeb Erekat, Mohammed Dahlan, Gamal Hillal, Martin Indyk, Madeleine Albright, Aaron Miller (behind Albright), Shlomo Ben Ami, Gilead Sher, General Shlomo Yanai, Amnon Lipkin-Shahak, Hassan Asfur, Abu Ala.

Ehud Barak, Madeleine Albright, and Yasir Arafat at Camp David in July 2000

Gilead Sher (back to camera) and Saeb Erekat conduct a secret meeting at the Jerusalem office of France 2, January 31, 2001

It is pouring in Maryland. The Palestinians have packed
their bags and are ready to leave. The luggage is loaded
onto a van, but, oddly enough, the security forces prevent
them from setting out for Andrews Air Force Base, near
Washington. Time passes. The delegates try to get some
rest.

The Israeli delegation has gathered in Barak's quarters.
Yossi Ginosar describes the Palestinians' mood:

When we took our leave, some of them had tears in
their eyes. They're really distressed. Suddenly they realize what's happening. They're looking for some way to
resume the negotiations. This is all very hard for them.
[Turning to Barak] Yes, all of it! That you're imposing
the method on them, the summit itself, its date, the form
of negotiation. . . . The American team is almost entirely
Jewish. And the Palestinians have no doubts about our
influence on Clinton's positions.[134]

At 11:30 P.M., a cry rings out in Arafat's quarters:
"Clinton is at the door!"

Clinton: I've revised my position. If we stop the summit
like this, the results will be negative and the consequences [very] dangerous on the ground. I'm asking
you to stay here. I'm leaving for Japan and will be back
Sunday. I'm authorizing Madeleine Albright to continue the negotiations. But, please, try to find a solution for the Temple Mount, the Haram al-Sharif. It's
not necessary to put everything down on paper. Open
the subject up. Think about this question and others.
I've spoken with Barak.

---

134. Sher, 2001, p. 194.

Arafat: I take what you've just said as an order, and I accept it.

Asfur and Dahlan go back to the dining room, where there is an outburst of joy: embraces with Lipkin-Shahak, Ben Ami, and Sher. Most of the Israeli delegates had advised Barak not to leave Camp David.

At 1 A.M. Bill Clinton has a final meeting with Barak before taking the plane to Okinawa.

THURSDAY, JULY 20

Under the leadership of Madeleine Albright at Camp David, the delegates are able to work at a less frenetic pace. They take advantage of Clinton's absence to rest and walk in the park. Hours go by, and Arafat asks Albright: "Where are the Israelis? I solemnly promised Clinton that we were going to work. We can't lose time like this!"

Albright suggests that Mohammed Dahlan and General Shlomo Yanai discuss issues of security. Arafat replies that the questions of territory and security are connected.

Albright: Barak told me he wanted to go forward on the basis of the American document.
Arafat: Forget that! It's just a game! What you're suggesting is a political joke! I don't see how you can ask that one of Islam's holiest sites be placed under Israeli sovereignty.

Albright seems annoyed. By way of apology, Arafat kisses her hand six times, first on one side, then on the other. When he returns to his quarters, some of the delegates josh him: "Please, Mr. President, don't do that kind of thing in front of us; we've been among men for two weeks!"

Finally two committees meet, one on the refugees and the other on security and territory—according to the Palestinians, in vain.

At dinner Madeleine Albright takes the floor. She announces the times when meetings will be held tomorrow and says that the various American documents are no longer on the agenda.[135] Yasir Abed Rabbo notes that his neighbor at the table, Dan Meridor, is looking at Barak and smiling as Barak returns to the dining room. "I'm glad, because I was against the American proposal, in that it called for Palestinian sovereignty over a part of the Old City. That could bring about the fall of the government," Meridor whispers to Abed Rabbo.

Then something happens that greatly embarrasses the Israeli delegates who are present. Arafat heads for Barak, who is entering the dining room. The prime minister turns away without greeting him and sits down beside Madeleine Albright. Arafat, surprised, says nothing and goes to sit down on the other side of the secretary of state. The Palestinians will interpret this incident as further proof of Barak's arrogance toward the head of the PLO.

Later that evening, Barak and several of his advisers study the Palestinians' tactics. Ginosar accuses him: "You're stepping all over Arafat. He's afraid of you. We could get more flexibility from the Palestinians if the atmosphere weren't so tense and depressing. Does shock treatment really work? As it is, those Palestinians who are against an accord are delighted."[136]

---

135. The American documents contained the Israeli proposal and the one submitted by the Palestinians that claimed sovereignty over part of the Old City.

136. Sher, 2001, p. 199.

FRIDAY, JULY 21

The meeting of the committee on security and borders begins at 1 A.M.[137] The discussion proceeds very slowly. At 2:30, at the request of Gilead Sher, the Palestinians for the first time present a map of the West Bank as they envision it after the conclusion of an accord. For the occasion, Samih el-Abed, the Palestinian cartographer, has been allowed to come to Camp David. Sher will describe the scene as follows: "[In the past] the Palestinians had never given us a map admitting the existence of Jewish settlements in the territories. However, the [settlement] blocks weren't blocks, but instead spots linked by virtual 'laces'. . . . El-Abed explained that, this way, the settlement "blocks" wouldn't include many Palestinian towns, as was the case with the Israeli map."[138] The Israelis reject the Palestinian proposal: the blocks do not involve a large enough number of settlers.

At 11 A.M. Albright attends the discussion on the refugees. The negotiators have accomplished very little thus far. Elyakim Rubinstein says Israel is ready to accept the return of several hundred refugees for a long period of time. Several thousand, if they stayed for a shorter time. Yasir Abed Rabbo restates the Palestinian position. The secretary of state takes notes.

Ehud Barak does not go to lunch but stays in his quarters. He is furious. He has learned that the Americans are putting no pressure on Arafat to negotiate in the context of Clinton's most recent proposal. He, Barak, had agreed to negotiate on this basis if Arafat would do likewise. As Dennis Ross would later explain, "This was a real misunder-

---

137. Present are Gilead Sher, Israel Hasson, Shlomo Yanai, Mohammed Dahlan, and Abu Ala.

138. Sher, 2001, p. 202. When he speaks of "spots linked by virtual 'laces,'" Sher is referring to small Israeli enclaves connected by roads.

standing. Barak had stayed on at Camp David because, he thought, Arafat had accepted Clinton's ideas. But Arafat thought the only point to the negotiations was that the ideas he considered important were going to be examined. When we understood [the reasons behind] Barak's anger, we apologized."[139]

In the evening, Madeleine Albright invites the delegates to attend the screening of a film in the president's comfortable movie room. It is *U 571*, the story of a German submarine during the Second World War.

Before the film is over, an aide comes looking for Saeb Erekat, who is wanted by Arafat. "No, I want to know how it ends! Who won the war?" Erekat protests facetiously. But it turns out that the Americans have just scheduled a meeting at which the text of the agreements is to be written. Shlomo Ben Ami, Gilead Sher, Saeb Erekat, and Erekat's assistant, Gaith el-Omari, compare versions for several hours, without success.

SATURDAY, JULY 22

The delegates spend the day in discussions. Madeleine Albright invites Yasir Arafat to visit her farm. In the evening, the negotiators are treated to another film, *Gladiator*.

SUNDAY, JULY 23

In the morning, while Madeleine Albright takes Ehud Barak to visit the battlefield at Gettysburg, not far from Camp David, Yasir Arafat has a discussion with George

---

139. Videotaped interview with Dennis Ross, February 19, 2002, Washington.

Tenet. "Where is Barak?" he asks. "Why won't he meet
with me or talk to me? I came to an agreement with Clinton
so that we could use these days profitably and move
ahead."

The meeting of the security committee is presided over
by Tenet. Israelis and Palestinians feel that some progress
has been made; unfortunately, one of the delegates will report, the Americans did not follow up on this. Saeb Erekat,
Shlomo Ben Ami, and Israel Hasson discuss East Jerusalem. The Israelis are offering to give Arafat a "presidential
compound" in the Old City, with the Palestinians exercising sovereignty only over the outer districts. Erekat notes
that, for the first time, Ben Ami uses the term "sacred basin."
This is the sector to the south and east of the Old City that
includes the ancient cemetery of Silwan and the Mount of
Olives.

Clinton returns to Camp David in the afternoon. Saeb
Erekat immediately hands him a letter from Arafat: "Since
your departure, the Israelis have [de facto] suspended work
in the committees, and we have lost two days."

At 9:30 P.M., Clinton meets with Arafat for ten minutes
and announces that, together with two delegates from each
side, he is preparing to lead the negotiations: "I'm going to
intervene personally. We'll begin with security so as to take
advantage of George Tenet's presence, and, besides, I hear
there's been some progress on this question, as well as on
the refugee question."

At 11:30 a new discussion on security matters, presided
over by Clinton and Tenet, gets underway. Abu Ala and
Mohammed Dahlan represent the Palestinians, Gilead Sher
and General Shlomo Yanai the Israelis.[140] Clinton wants to
finish up. In order to move things forward, he suggests that

---

140. Madeleine Albright, Dennis Ross, Sandy Berger, and Robert Malley are
also present.

they begin with the issues that seem to be the easiest to resolve. First will be the problem of the warning and detection stations the Israelis want to maintain on the West Bank.

Dahlan: We agree to only two stations. The Israelis don't
need three, and this whole business is of concern only
to the Israelis, not to us.

Tenet (infuriated): If we can't reach an understanding on
such a simple topic, we aren't going to get anywhere.
You know perfectly well where these stations are to be
set up, and the only question that matters is how to
have access to them and ensure their defense!

Dahlan: We're not against that.

Clinton goes on to the next subject: airspace.

Yanai: The question here isn't sovereignty over Palestinian airspace but the conditions under which Israel
could use that space. There would be a single system
of air control, perhaps allowing for the presence of a
Palestinian liaison officer in the control center. Between us, we would coordinate the air corridors the
way the authorities in question do in different countries, the way it's done between us and Jordan. It's a
simple problem.

Dahlan (annoyed): We've never agreed to that. I'm not
an expert. We'd have to hand the matter over to experts. You're creating an artificial sovereignty here.
You don't need warning and detection stations and, at
the same time, [to guarantee yourselves freedom of
flight over our territory by] your air force.

Gilead Sher states that, during the Stockholm negotiations, Abu Ala had agreed to Israeli control over the airspace. At Camp David, however, Abu Ala is suggesting

that the civilian and military aspects of the problem be separated.

Yanai: We have to let the experts set up a coordination plan for airspace and airwaves in a context of mutual respect.

Yanai also mentions the other Israeli demand: maintaining five sectors of emergency deployment of Tsahal, with provision for the storage of heavy weapons.

Clinton: Who will define an emergency situation? When I have a migraine, you can't tell me I don't have a headache.

Yanai: A certain measure of trust would have to be established between the two states.

Tenet: While we're on this subject, are you willing to accept some form of American control?

Yanai: When it comes to our national security, we can't trust anyone but ourselves.

Gilead Sher will later say that he did not agree with Yanai. In his opinion, the Israeli refusal of all American control was unjustified.

Dahlan: We accept the principle of a presence of American forces in these five sectors for a specified time.

Clinton (replying to the Palestinians): We're ready to do a great deal to promote an agreement, but what you're asking me for there is something very different. [Turning to the Israelis] You have to be careful not to infringe on Palestinian sovereignty. In addition, the nature of an emergency situation should be clearly defined. With these two conditions, there should be no problem.

They go on to the issue of the demilitarization of the Palestinian State.

Clinton: We've always maintained that the demilitarization would be permanent, but we also have to take into consideration the necessary defense of the Palestinian State in the face of an attack by other Palestinians who don't come under its sovereignty. We can't disregard the dangers that will threaten the new state.

Yanai: The Palestinians should get guarantees of security, from us and the Americans, that would be included in the accord. Besides, the Palestinians will have to acquire nonmilitary means of defense. Finally, a regional defense pact, joined by Egypt or at least Jordan, will have to be set up.

Dahlan: We don't need tanks or fighter planes. We want to ensure the livelihood of our hungry citizens, but we don't want you Israelis to ensure our defense.

Sher: Let's define the term "powerful police forces."

Dennis Ross: Actually, we should also look at what kind of weapons this police force would have and also define threats like terrorism, which is a danger for both sides, and when we Americans should intervene. . . .

Dahlan: We're ready to enter into any form of cooperation, but we [also] have to get our people to understand that their daily lives have changed.

Abu Ala: We'll be responsible in our homeland, not you!

Clinton raises another problem: control of border posts between Palestine, Egypt, and Jordan. The Israelis explain that they do not intend to get control of these crossing points but only want to be able to observe them on a permanent basis, so as to verify the demilitarization of the Palestinian State. They suggest that a third party be on the scene.

Dahlan (annoyed): You've been controlling us for six years. We do not accept this situation. You Israelis are the ones who should be controlled now. We don't agree to any Israeli presence at the border posts, but we accept the principle of complete coordination with you.

Abu Ala: If you're not sure that we'll do our job right at the border posts, we're prepared to consider the presence of a third party.

Yanai: Counting on oneself isn't enough in this case. We've given in on our initial demand for control of the border posts, but this is a fundamental problem for our security.

Clinton (impatient): The question of border posts calls for additional discussions. Let's move on to the Jordan Valley.

Yanai describes the deployment that the Israelis have in mind for the Jordan: an electric fence; the possibility of intervening in the west and, if necessary, of conducting a manhunt; six to ten observation posts; and a special security administration for a period of time to be determined, in which 800 men would patrol the length of the shoreline.

Dahlan: You're thinking up all kinds of security pretexts to keep us from having our own state. Your concept is smothering us. We'll take care of our border with Jordan by ourselves. We don't want any presence of yours in the Jordan Valley.

Yanai: We can consult together about a reduction in our presence. In any case, this arrangement would be for a limited period.

Sher: This discussion is only about defense. We shouldn't forget that it has nothing to do with issues of sovereignty and borders. We'll make sure that the text of the accord stipulates that.

Clinton (to the Israelis): In the past, you've suggested the deployment of an international force on the Jordan, and your prime minister told me he has no objection to that. The presence of an international force is the condition for putting a security agreement into effect.

Sher: We'll look into that. It should be possible, if the international force is deployed alongside Tsahal and not independently of it.

Clinton: OK, think about it. Since we're about to do a lot on behalf of Jordan in the context of this agreement, please see if it's possible to consider an accord for Palestinian–Jordanian–Israeli cooperation, [providing for the deployment of] an international force for a certain period of time, maybe even on both sides of the river. The Israelis have raised legitimate issues, and I understand the logic of their position better now, but I also understand the fears this arouses in you Palestinians.

The discussion ends there. Gilead Sher will describe how Barak, when he gets his delegates' report, decides that "with regard to airspace, we must demand responsibility for security control; in the border posts, we have to discuss how the demilitarization of the Palestinian State is to be monitored. In the Jordan Valley, we'll consider the conditions under which an American or international force could be deployed alongside Tsahal."

In the course of the evening, the Palestinians draw up a balance sheet and feel shortchanged. Dahlan and Abu Ala say that, on the basis of the latest proposals they have received, Israel would want to annex 9 percent of the West Bank, in exchange for which Palestine would get 1 percent of Israeli territory. The Israelis want to keep three warning and detection stations and five positions for emergency military deployment, connected by road to Israeli territory. This would be in addition to the famous 10 percent of territories from the banks of the Jordan, which, like the airspace, would remain under Israeli control. Erekat considers that, under these conditions, the Palestinians would get only 82 percent of the West Bank.

MONDAY, JULY 24

3:15 A.M. The discussion of security and border questions continues in Bill Clinton's office.

Clinton (reviewing the issues): The warning and detection stations will be set up on relatively few sites. They're necessary for Israel's security.

Dahlan: We accept in principle that these stations will be set up on heights. We have no special feelings about their personnel and functioning. But, given the way we see the matter, we have to be shown a kind of moral argument: Why not provide for the presence of an American, or other, representative?

Clinton (to the Palestinians): With regard to airspace, there will be only a single air control, insofar as this space is very limited. So you have to make sure that there's no interference with your civilian flights, and then you also have the right to make sure you're not disturbed by noise and low-altitude flights.

Sher: We must be assured that responsibility in matters of air security remains in Israel's hands and takes precedence over civilian flights in all cases.

Abu Ala: We accept this principle, on condition that our commercial flights aren't disturbed and that our airport continues to function.

With regard to the sectors of emergency deployment of the Israeli army in the Jordan Valley, Abu Ala announces that Arafat wants an international force, and not Tsahal, to be stationed on the Jordan.

Clinton: Please tell your chairman that, in the present case, the Israelis' arguments are justified. As for you Israelis, you have to define the word "emergency." Regarding demilitarization of the Palestinian State, that's accepted in principle by both parties, and now we have to specify the composition of the Palestinian forces and their weapons. And we also have to give them a name that the Israeli negotiators can present to their public.

[To the Palestinians] For the border posts with Egypt and Jordan, think of an arrangement in the customs area. An Israeli observer could be stationed in your customs house, and, in exchange, the Israelis would allow a Palestinian observer to be placed in their own customs houses.

Sher: After discussions with the prime minister and the chief of staff, Israel's reply to your suggestion to deploy an international force in this sector is positive, on condition that the whole of the security agreement is approved.

Dahlan: In this sector, I don't want to share anything with Israel, Egypt, or Jordan. The Palestinian police and the United States are quite enough.

Clinton: Give it some thought. Israel has accepted a formula that takes your concerns into account as much as possible, and I won't send American forces unless I can ensure their defense. They'll draw fire by their very presence, which is what happened in East Timor, where I sent 500 men and then had to rush in an additional 3,000 soldiers to ensure their defense.

During this time, a final discussion on the refugee question is taking place. According to the Americans, it ends badly. A highly placed Palestinian will later explain that, in the absence of progress on Jerusalem, Arafat had forbidden Nabil Shaath to discuss the functioning of the international compensation fund for the refugees. This, however, was the subject on which the talks had seemed to be making the most progress. According to several Israeli delegates, the question of the refugees' right of return to Israel was the Palestinians' final card in the negotiation. They were not going to give in on this point until agreements were concluded on all the other pending issues.

Gilead Sher will later report that, on the concrete aspects, a broad understanding had been reached, especially on the creation of the international fund. Sher relates how Mohammad Rashid, Arafat's financial adviser, had told him in the course of an informal discussion that any solution to the refugee problem had to include three elements: prompt attention to the Palestinian refugees in Lebanon, timely and effective compensation, and the housing in evacuated Jewish settlements of the refugees returning to Palestine.[141] All Arafat did is repeat that, should there be an agreement, he would make sure Israel would not have to confront a demographic problem.

Before the meeting at which Erekat is to present Arafat's response to Clinton's proposals, Clinton asks Ben Ami if he plans to suggest dividing the Old City into two districts under Israeli sovereignty and two under Palestinian sovereignty. Ben Ami replies that this idea is now null and void. In the meantime, George Tenet is meeting with Arafat in a final attempt to persuade him to accept Clinton's proposals.

---

141. Sher, 2001, p. 227.

At 9 P.M., Bill Clinton receives Yasir Arafat. Madeleine Albright, Sandy Berger, George Tenet, and Robert Malley are present. Arafat is accompanied by Abu Ala and Saeb Erekat.

Arafat: I can't betray my people. Do you want to come to my funeral? I'd rather die than agree to Israeli sovereignty over the Haram al-Sharif. . . . I won't go down in Arab history as a traitor. As I've told you, Jerusalem will be liberated, if not now then later: in five, ten, or a hundred years. . . .

Clinton (exploding): Barak has made so many concessions. And you've made none! You could have gotten sovereignty over the Christian and Muslim districts of the Old City and full jurisdiction over the Haram al-Sharif. This is a political question, not a religious one. You missed an opportunity in 1948 and let another one go by in 1978, at [the first summit at] Camp David. And now here you go again! You won't have a state, and relations between America and the Palestinians will be over. Congress will vote to stop the aid you've been allocated, and you'll be treated as a terrorist organization. No one in the Middle East will look you in the eye. The Muslims will know that you could have received the custodianship of the Haram al-Sharif and founded a state, and you refused. Barak has come a long way [toward the conclusion of an agreement]. You haven't budged; all you've done is pocket what Barak was giving.

Saeb Erekat asks Arafat for permission to reply. He then launches into a passionate diatribe:[142]

---

142. What follows is the transcript of his speech.

Erekat: Mr. President. It doesn't cost you anything to blame and threaten us. We don't have a lobby that can influence the situation in Washington. We understand your strategic alliances, your alliance with Israel, that Israel is a participant in political life in the United States. . . . We are not hostile to Israel. We have recognized Israel. But what I want you to understand is that we are against the Israeli occupation. . . .

Mr. President, you are the leader of the world: don't threaten my president, treat us fairly. The Palestinian people, under the leadership of Yasir Arafat, have accepted and recognized the State of Israel, [which occupies] 78 percent of historical Palestine. Never in the history of the Palestinians has a leader recognized the State of Israel this way and agreed to base the [Palestinian] State on 22 percent of the land! Now you're saying that Arafat did not come a long way! . . . He agreed to the 22 percent because the preceding American administration, and the one before that, and Europe along with them, said they would support those who worked for peace. Well, that's exactly what I expect of you, Mr. President.

The Israelis want to drag concessions out of us: to satisfy their public opinion, for historical reasons, and in reaction to opinion polls, sometimes for their security or [to take care of] the psychology of the Israeli people. I can't do that. I can't negotiate one day for the settlers, the next day for History, another day for the generals, for the psychology of the Jews, then for the exceptional nature of the Jewish people. I can't. I'm trying to negotiate peace.

The Palestinian people are resisting the Israeli army. They won't let themselves be intimidated by the occupation. If we don't achieve peace, Mr. President, if there is no peace between Israelis and Palestinians, there won't be peace for anyone. I'm speaking to you with a broken heart. I'll go back and ask the Palestinians' forgiveness for what I've done for the last twenty-one years of my life: advocate for peace.

This summit has enabled us to accomplish a lot. I would never have thought that one day I'd be discussing Jerusalem, borders, security, and the refugee problem with an Israeli government. Please, Mr. President, don't let this summit fail. If you present it as a failure, the light will go out in the region, and I don't know when it will come back on.

Clinton (to Arafat, who has remained silent): You're a man of faith. You're an honest, honorable man. You've shown firmness in defending your positions. For that, I respect you, as I respect your demands. We'll have one more discussion on Jerusalem. Barak will send Ben Ami; give me a negotiator.

Arafat: Saeb Erekat will go.

One hour later, the final session of talks at Camp David begins.[143]

Saeb Erekat: Madeleine [Albright] holds me personally responsible [for blocking the smooth progress of the negotiations], because I told her, on July 11 in her office, that this summit should not be a unique event, that we shouldn't lead people to expect white smoke from it. Mr. President, 80 percent of the taboos between Israelis and Palestinians have been broken in the course of this summit. This summit is a great success; it must be followed up. We must build on what has been accomplished here. Please! Get a commitment

---

143. Taking part are Bill Clinton, Saeb Erekat, Shlomo Ben Ami, Madeleine Albright, George Tenet, Sandy Berger, Dennis Ross, and Robert Malley.

[to continue the negotiations] from Barak and Arafat. Don't cast blame on anyone, don't point a finger at anyone, because that will lead to bloodshed!

Clinton: I asked you to come here to listen to your suggestions on how we can get out of this crisis.

Erekat: I suggest the publication of a trilateral communiqué highlighting the progress made at Camp David and emphasizing that many taboos were broken, but that certain problems call for new negotiations, and that the two parties have decided to continue the talks under the supervision of the United States so as to implement Security Council Resolutions 242 and 338 and arrive at an accord by September 13.

Clinton (to Shlomo Ben Ami): What is your point of view?

Ben Ami (to Erekat): You're only four million Muslims, and you claim to represent a billion Muslims on the Temple Mount. The president's [Clinton's] proposals are a historic opportunity that you're letting slip by again. Arafat is putting the Muslim question at the top of his priorities, even before Palestinian national interests. Your national interest is becoming the hostage of Islam, and you're going to pay a high price for that. If Camp David ends without an agreement, it will mean the collapse of the peace process, the collapse of the peace camp in Israel, the fall of the Barak government, and maybe the formation of a cabinet of national unity with Sharon.

Erekat: Yes, and that's why we mustn't talk about a failure but emphasize what's been accomplished, so as not to destroy the peace camp on one or the other side. We have to continue negotiations.

Clinton: No arguments. There are four possibilities. (A) a trilateral statement announcing the continuation of the negotiations; (B) a communiqué announcing the collapse of the peace process; (C) postpone the Jerusalem question to a later date and resolve all the other problems; (D) postpone studying the issues concerning certain parts of Jerusalem for two years.

Erekat: (C) and (D) are unacceptable. (B) would be a disaster for the region.

Clinton: I'll decide what option to choose. Let's have another look at your proposals on Jerusalem.

Ben Ami: We're suggesting that the outer districts of [East] Jerusalem be placed under Palestinian sovereignty. Inside, one or two districts will also be placed under Palestinian sovereignty. The others will enjoy limited sovereignty. In the Old City, a special regime will apply to the Muslim, Armenian, and Christian quarters. Security will be ensured conjointly in the Old City. A compound for the use of the Palestinian government will be placed under Palestinian sovereignty. The Palestinians will have custodianship of the Temple Mount, and a Palestinian security force [will ensure its protection]. You must acknowledge that Israel has residual sovereignty over this holy place. We also want a specific area to be guaranteed on the plaza, where Jews will be able to pray.

Erekat: You're retreating on the positions we already discussed. This is your traditional way of negotiating. You make a good beginning, then you take it back.

Clinton (interrupting): There are two proposals I haven't discussed with Barak.

First proposal: the outer districts [of East Jerusalem] would be placed under Palestinian sovereignty, the inner districts under limited Palestinian sovereignty, so that the city can remain open. A special regime under Israeli sovereignty would apply to the Old City. A compound for the use of the Palestinian presidency would be placed under its sovereignty. On the

Temple Mount, the Palestinians would exercise custodial sovereignty over this holy site, Israel being accorded a residual sovereignty and an area for Jewish prayer on the plaza.

My second proposal is as follows: the outer districts would be placed under Palestinian sovereignty, the inner districts under limited sovereignty for the Palestinians. In the Old City, the Muslim and Christian quarters would be placed under Palestinian sovereignty, the Jewish and Armenian quarters under Israeli sovereignty. With regard to the Temple Mount, the United Nations Security Council would pass a resolution that would entrust it to the Palestinians, with a residual sovereignty for the Palestinians and a place of prayer for the Jews on the plaza.[144]

Erekat: Sir, there are other proposals. What you're talking about there is what you got from the Israeli side. For the first time, we offered them sovereignty over the Wailing Wall and the Jewish quarter. And we've had discussions with them on the Israeli settlements in East Jerusalem, in the framework of an exchange of territories. That's a genuine proposal.

Clinton: Saeb, please, I'm not expecting a response on your part. Give [these proposals] to Arafat and come back.

The Palestinian delegation meets briefly. Yasir Arafat writes a letter to Clinton: "I appreciate your efforts . . . , but these proposals could not constitute the basis for a historic reconciliation. . . ."

---

144. An American witness says that, on this occasion, Bill Clinton did not mention the establishment of a Jewish place of prayer on the Haram al-Sharif plaza.

TUESDAY, JULY 25

It is 2:30 A.M. Saeb Erekat hands Arafat's message to the president of the United States, who has been waiting for it in his lodgings. He reads it, then folds the paper and, with a glance all around the room, where Madeleine Albright and Sandy Berger are sitting, says, "I am profoundly saddened by the fact that we haven't concluded an agreement." After a few seconds of silence, Clinton, his expression inscrutable, declares, "I don't like to fail, and especially in this area." He has not slept for forty-eight hours.

Early in the morning, Clinton convenes the Israelis and the Palestinians for one last time. Ehud Barak is accompanied by Danny Yatom, Yasir Arafat by Saeb Erekat. Sandy Berger is also present.

Clinton: I am very displeased that we haven't concluded an accord. But I note that great progress has been made; on both sides the positions have moved forward. I would like you to continue negotiations so as to reach an accord by mid-September.

Arafat: Mr. President, I am entirely in agreement with you. I am at your service, as are all my negotiators.

Barak: We must not let the peace process fail. We would hope to reach an accord, and we must make every effort to do so.

The Israelis and the Palestinians undertake the writing of a final communiqué. It will be read by Bill Clinton.

The Palestinians are packing their bags. In their rooms, the televisions are on. Special broadcasts are being devoted to the failure of the summit. American and Israeli sources are accusing Arafat "of not having made any concessions," while Ehud Barak "risked his political career by agreeing to the re-dividing of Jerusalem." Saeb Erekat is furious. He phones Dennis Ross: "What's going on? What does this mean?" Why is the sword being raised over our head?"

Ross: Barak needs this so he can face his internal difficulties in Israel.

Erekat: You're destroying everything! You're destroying everything!

And he hangs up.

Chapter 5

Checkmate

Robert Malley, Clinton's special assistant for Israeli–Arab affairs, compares Ehud Barak to Stefan Zweig's brilliant chess player, Mr. B., who could play his own side and his opponent's at the same time but breaks down when his opponent doesn't make the move he had anticipated: "Barak knew how he was going to play his side, and he predicted Assad's and Arafat's moves. When he found he couldn't, the process collapsed."[145]

Barak was playing a subtle game of encouragement and stimulation, but also of retreats and attacks, and he was gambling on the logic of succession to the leadership of Syria. He hoped Arafat would turn his attention away from the territorial problem. "With Arafat," Malley says, "Barak believed that this same system would work, and that Arafat would move his pawns according to his, Barak's, game. In point of fact, because the Palestinians didn't have the same strategic vision, or had other interests that Barak had underestimated, the game didn't go as he'd anticipated."

Barak had prepared for a failure at Camp David, analyzing the various possible scenarios together with his commu-

---

145. This and the following citation are from a videotaped interview with Robert Malley, February 22, 2002, Paris.

nications advisers. During simulations held before the summit,[146] Moshe Gaon and Tal Zilberstein had concluded that blame for a possible failure absolutely had to be placed on Arafat.

Now, before leaving the presidential retreat, Barak has a final conversation with Bill Clinton. He says once again that he has taken considerable political risks. He is returning to Israel, he says, where his government no longer has a majority in the Knesset. He will very likely have to form a cabinet of national unity with Ariel Sharon's Likud. Clinton, who is closely following Israeli polls, promises to look into the possibility of transferring the United States embassy in Tel Aviv to Jerusalem, a move that could enhance Barak's rating in Israeli public opinion.

The Israeli delegation leaves Camp David and goes to the motel in the nearby town of Frederick, where the Israeli and international press are waiting in the banquet room. Barak reads his carefully prepared speech. Everything is there: the justification for his taking part in the summit, accounts of the concessions that he was ready to make on Jerusalem and that aroused very strong reactions from the right, and a message that, according to one of his advisers, was directed at Arafat and the Palestinian people. The peace process is over, Barak says:

We were not willing to sacrifice any one of these three principles: the security of Israel, what is sacred for Israel, and the unity of our people. If we were forced to choose between yielding on one of these principles and entering into a confrontation, we would have no hesitation.

We have been able to deal with such situations in the past, and we can confront them in the future. But if we

---

146. One of these simulations has been published in Drucker, 2002, p. 284.

plunge into confrontation, we will be able to look our children squarely in the eye and tell them we did all we could to prevent this. Faced with these dangers, . . . we must forget our differences and unite.

All my life I've fought for Israel's security, and, I repeat, I will not agree to sacrifice Israel's vital interests. I will not agree to stop strengthening Israel and Greater Jerusalem, ensuring a solid Jewish majority for future generations.

Israel was prepared to pay a high price in order to put an end to the conflict, but not any price whatsoever. We tried to reach a stable balance, to ensure peace for the generations to come without worrying about the headlines in tomorrow's papers. . . . Today we can look in the mirror and say that, during the past year, we have exhausted all the possibilities for ending the hundred-year-old conflict pitting us against the Palestinians, but, unfortunately, the conditions were not favorable enough. . . . Arafat was afraid of making the historic decisions [that were called for] to put an end to the conflict. It is Arafat's positions on Jerusalem that prevented the conclusion of an accord. . . .

To a question on the Holy City, this is Barak's verbatim reply:

We had in mind—and ideas were put forth in this direction—to make Jerusalem bigger and stronger than ever before in history, to annex to the city localities in the West Bank, beyond the 1967 border, such as Maale Adumim, Givat Zeev, and Gush Etzion. In exchange, we would have given the Palestinians sovereignty over certain towns or small [Palestinian] localities that were annexed to Jerusalem right after 1967. These ideas were discussed. But, since the summit proceeded according to the principle "nothing accepted until everything is concluded," even these ideas are now null and void.

The summit, then, failed on account of the Jerusalem issue, not the refugee problem. Barak will say nothing about the refugee problem on this day, mentioning it only later, when the conflict with the Palestinians grows more intense.

Almost at the same moment, in the Thurmont press center, Bill Clinton is speaking to the press. The issues that "revolve around Jerusalem," he says,

> go to the heart of Palestinian and Israeli identity. . . . Prime Minister Barak has made some very brave decisions, but, when all is said and done, we were unable to bridge the gap between the positions [of each side]. I think this will eventually be possible, because we have no choice. . . .
>
> Let me be more explicit. We made progress on the main topics. With a number of them, we even made substantial progress. The Palestinian negotiators worked hard on a good number of issues. But I think it is fair to say, at this point in time, perhaps because he prepared more, perhaps because he thought it over more, that Prime Minister Barak moved further ahead than Chairman Arafat, especially on the question of Jerusalem. . . .
>
> My comments should be taken for what they are, not so much as criticism of Chairman Arafat, because [negotiation] is really difficult and has never been tried before, but as praise for Barak. He came here knowing that he was going to have to take courageous steps, and he did so. And you should understand what I'm saying here more as a tribute to him than a condemnation of the Palestinian position.

ARAFAT: HERO AND GUILTY PARTY

A few months later, Robert Malley will make his mea culpa: "We welcomed Barak's proposals with unjustified enthusiasm. The United States was thinking in terms of the distance Israel had come, instead of the distance that remained to be covered in order to arrive at an acceptable compromise."

For the Israeli and international press, the subject is closed: Arafat is to blame for the failure at Camp David. The head of the PLO is completely overtaken by events. His entire communications system consists of several Palestinian leaders who have set themselves up in the business club of the luxurious Ritz Carlton Hotel in Washington's Pentagon City. He thinks he has escaped the trap set for him at Camp David, and that negotiations will resume under conditions more favorable to him. And so he leaves the capital without making a speech. It will be nearly a year before Abu Ala gives the press a full account of the summit.

Arafat makes his first appearance before the cameras in Cairo, after a brief meeting with Hosni Mubarak on July 26, 2000. "The American side," he says, "told us they were going to continue [to negotiate] with us. We reached an accord at Sharm el-Sheik in anticipation of pursuing the talks until September 13, the independence day for our state with Jerusalem as its capital, like it or not. Whoever doesn't like it can drink the [briny] waters of the Dead Sea!"

Arafat returns to Gaza, where thousands of Palestinians give him a triumphant welcome. On one banner are the words: "Welcome Arafat, war hero and peace hero." On another: "Jerusalem is before our eyes; tomorrow it will be in our hands." Arafat resisted pressure, people feel; he did not give in. A few hours earlier, hundreds of Islamic militants had marched, calling for renewal of the armed struggle against Israel. For the Israelis, these images justify Barak's accusations: Arafat did not want the historic accord Barak was offering him.

At almost the same moment, the prime minister is arriving at Ben-Gurion Airport in Tel Aviv. His ministers are waiting for him there, along with militants from the Labor Party. Barak's political situation has deteriorated. According to one poll, 57 percent of Israelis believe he made too many concessions at Camp David, and only 30 percent approve. He delivers a speech:

A peace treaty can't be signed at any price whatsoever, but there will be no peace [if we don't agree to pay] a certain price, one that will make us sick at heart and will be difficult to pay. . . . Agreement with the Palestinians is so close and yet always so out of reach. . . . I must say, and it grieves me to do so, that if we did not succeed, it is because we were not sitting opposite a partner who was ready to make difficult decisions on all the topics before us. . . .

The next day, Bill Clinton grants an interview to Israeli television. He makes a long speech declaring friendship toward Israel and condemnation for Arafat:

Relations between Israel and the United States are very strong. But, in the light of the courageous positions taken by the prime minister and the Israeli negotiating team, and in the light of the retreat from South Lebanon, I think these relations should be reconsidered and increased. I foresee a complete review [of our treaties], so as to strengthen our strategic relations. We shall look at what we can do to help Israel maintain its qualitative advantage, modernize its army, and prepare the army for the new threats that, along with other countries, Israel will have to face in the twenty-first century.

Clinton announces concrete measures: an agreement to expand military aid to Israel and increase economic assistance. And, as though putting the Palestinians on notice, he says this:

> I have always wanted to transfer our embassy [from Tel Aviv] to West Jerusalem. We already have a plot of land. I didn't do it because it might jeopardize the negotiation of a just and lasting peace between the Israelis and the Palestinians. But, in the light of what has happened, I'm going to re-examine that decision and do so before the end of the current year. . . . Arafat would be making a big mistake if he unilaterally proclaimed the Palestinian State in September. If that were the case, the United States would certainly reconsider its relations with the Palestinians.

NEGOTIATIONS RESUME, POSITIONS HARDEN

The peace team will find it hard to persuade Bill Clinton not to make good his threat to transfer the American embassy to Jerusalem: this would clearly mean the end of the peace process. But, although the White House is lowering its tone, it is not in Washington but in Jerusalem that, on July 31, Saeb Erekat and Gilead Sher resume contact.

Over the past year, the Palestinian and the Israeli have gotten to know and respect one another. What they want to do is draw up a list of all the points of agreement reached at Camp David and try to find a compromise on the question of East Jerusalem. They have a long discussion in a Jerusalem restaurant. Erekat figures they have two months in which to try to reach an accord. They will have forty meetings by September 28; a new channel of secret negotiations has been established. As Sher describes the situation, the Palestinians felt the Israelis were haggling as though they were in the souk. Even those [Palestinian leaders] who thought we'd gone right up to our lines in the sand [and could not make further concessions] had trouble maintaining their position. There was always someone who would tell them: hold off a little longer; the Israelis are getting ready to loosen up a bit.

The Palestinians felt that the absence of Shlomo Ben Ami, who until Camp David had been in the center of the process, was proof that we didn't really want a successful outcome. That we wanted to have these negotiations fail and blame it on them. The truth is that Ben Ami was overloaded with work, too busy with diplomatic activity and communications.[147]

From our perspective, the Palestinian negotiators didn't have a real mandate. Erekat felt that the mandate he and Dahlan got from Arafat was vague and meaningless. He had the sense that his hands were tied, and that he didn't really have the support of Abu Ala and Abu Mazen. Not to mention Arafat himself, this man who could just casually wave away everything his representatives agreed on.[148]

In the absence of a trusting relationship between the two leaders, understanding the way Arafat made decisions was always one of the major problems faced by Barak's negotiating team. One of Clinton's Camp David advisers had exclaimed, with a touch of regret in his voice, "Too bad Shimon Peres isn't here! At least *he* would have spent all day and all night talking to Arafat and wouldn't have let him go to bed without getting an accord out of him!"

---

147. In Hebrew, *hasbara*, which can also mean "propaganda."
148. Sher, 2001, pp. 241–242.

To go back to the metaphor of the Titanic, Barak is getting ready to collide with the iceberg—in other words, with the total collapse of the peace process and an explosion of violence. To confront it, Israeli society will once again have to come together in the crisis and win the support of the international community. Inside Israel itself, the public has accepted Barak's explanation of the Camp David failure all the more easily because it was corroborated by Bill Clinton, and because the Palestinians are not reacting to Barak's accusations.

Barak has launched a full-fledged campaign to persuade foreign leaders. He is spending hours on the telephone: all the European heads of state are contacted, from Luxembourg to Sweden, Spain, and Great Britain. When Arafat arrives in Paris on July 29, he finds that President Jacques Chirac himself is preoccupied with Barak's parliamentary difficulties.

The scene is the Elysée Palace, at 4 in the afternoon:

Arafat: The Camp David summit was convened prematurely, at the insistence of Ehud Barak, even though the official and secret negotiations hadn't allowed for the definition of the terms of an agreement. This was a risky approach. The Israeli and American proposals on Jerusalem were totally inadequate. At best, what we were offered was a mandate according to which we would have the holy sites available to us and would administer them and have custodianship of them. Well, this issue doesn't involve us alone; it concerns all the Arabs.

Yasir Abed Rabbo: If we were to yield on this issue, we'd risk being accused of treason by the entire Muslim community.

Arafat: We're willing to give the Israelis sovereignty over the Jewish quarter [of the Old City of Jerusalem] and over the Wailing Wall. But the Israeli demands for controlling the border with Jordan are unacceptable. They want to maintain exclusive control there, even though on the borders with Lebanon and Egypt they accepted the presence of international forces. And that's not all: the Israelis want to keep exclusive control of three early-warning stations. We are proposing the deployment of international forces [on the border with Jordan], including American and European units. We do not want any Israeli presence.

The Palestinians tell their host that progress was made on the subject of the Israeli settlements. Nevertheless, they feel that the blocks comprising 80 percent of the settlers should not represent more than 2 percent of the territory of the West Bank. With regard to the refugees, they report, disagreement continues on the question of the right of return. The Israelis have agreed to the return of Palestinian refugees to Israeli territory only in the context of family reunification involving 500 people per year. And Arafat speaks of what he sees as a fundamental injustice: 47 percent of Russian immigrants to Israel are not even Jewish, but, according to him, Christians, and yet Palestinians who were born in the Holy Land do not have the right to move back there.

Jacques Chirac ignores this argument and goes on to what he considers more essential:

Ehud Barak has given the impression of having taken important steps with regard to the positions he previously held, whether on territory, security, or the settlements. But, on the subject of the refugees, neither Barak nor any other Israeli prime minister is in a position to move forward to any significant extent. It's a question of political survival. On the subject of Jerusalem, a distinction has to be made between the issue of the holy sites and the issue of the western part of the city. It seems to me that it's impossible to settle the question of the holy sites before September 13. So thought must be given to another solution: a *corpus separatum*, a condominium.

Maybe the question is this: Can Barak make an effort on Jerusalem and you on the refugees? If there's no comprehensive accord, I'm afraid the hawks will prevail. Even though Clinton, at the end of his term, can resist the pro-Israel lobby [in Washington], this won't be the case with Bush or Al Gore.

Be careful when September 13 comes around. If you proclaim the Palestinian State, Barak could take retaliatory measures. Also, as Albright has just told [foreign minister] Hubert Védrine, inside the American administration, and in public opinion in the United States and Europe, there's the sense that Barak was forthcoming, while you remained stuck in your positions.[149]

On August 2, David Levy, the Israeli foreign minister, resigns. He is in absolute disagreement with Ehud Barak, who, a week later, entrusts Shlomo Ben Ami with the interim ministry. Ben Ami's first task will be to bring the gospel to European capitals in the form of a twofold message: Barak took a giant step; pressure must be put on Arafat.

THE MOSQUES AND THE TEMPLE

On August 2, 2000, Sher and Erekat reveal some details of their secret meetings to me. "We agreed," Erekat says,

that Israel would get 78 percent of historical Palestine, and we would get only 22 percent. And now the Israelis reject

---

149. Private communication.

this compromise. However, we've got to reach an accord that can be accepted, and not just by President Arafat and Prime Minister Barak, or by Sher and Erekat! I don't think an accord is possible if Palestinian sovereignty over the Haram al-Sharif isn't recognized. The Israelis ask me, "How can you disregard our thousand-year-old beliefs on this matter?" I respect everyone's beliefs. But the fact is that, today, there is no Jewish temple on the plaza. There is a mosque, the Dome of the Rock. The Grand Rabbi of Israel forbids Jews to pray there. My Israeli counterparts ask me not to deny their belief. I tell them: "If I don't deny what you believe, I'm denying my own religion!" This is one of the crucial aspects of the misunderstanding: for Islam, there was never a Jewish temple at Al-Qods but a "distant mosque."

I tell them: "You can have the Jewish quarter, control it. Control over the Wailing Wall [also]. But what you haven't done in all these years when you've had control of the Haram al-Sharif, don't ask me to do it now. . . . There's no such thing as sovereignty over history or memory.[150]

In the Palestinian territories, the people in charge of security are on the alert. Several Islamists in Gaza and on the West Bank are called in for questioning. At all costs, new anti-Israeli attacks must not cast a shadow on the peace process. And Colonels Dahlan and Rajoub are alarmed by the recent demonstrations against the Autonomous Authority and the calls for the revival of the intifada.

On August 9, Sher and Erekat meet again. Erekat arrives with a major piece of news: Arafat wants to conclude an accord. His political survival depends on it. Later Abu Ala

---

150. Videotaped interview with Saeb Erekat, August 2, 2000, Jerusalem.

joins these negotiations, as does Israel Hasson, the former number-two man at Shin Bet. Hasson and Erekat spend long hours poring over maps and aerial photographs of Jerusalem, and the discussion then turns to the other pending issues. Sher and Erekat believe it will take six to eight weeks to reach the accord.

The next day, Hasson and Erekat make a field visit to the Old City of Jerusalem. The Palestinian wears a cap so as not to be recognized. For several hours they inspect the area around the Western Wall, the part of the Armenian quarter that would remain under Israeli sovereignty. Hasson draws a line on an aerial photograph. As they leave the city, Erekat is greeted by some children: "Salaam Saeb!" So much for secrecy.

On August 14, Dahlan joins the negotiators. Forty-eight hours later, Shlomo Ben Ami, back from his tour of European capitals, also takes part in the meeting, which is held in a suite at the King David Hotel in Jerusalem. He quickly gets into an argument with Dahlan about the points of agreement reached at Camp David on the subject of security. Both parties decide to call in the Americans.

Dennis Ross is vacationing in Israel. Since there is no transcript of the summit negotiations, Ross has to consult his notes, and his conclusion will be that the Israeli version is closer to his own. With Martin Indyk, the United States ambassador to Israel, he will carefully follow the Sher–Erekat talks for several days.

The Egyptians are also on the scene. Muhammad Bassiouny, the ambassador to Tel Aviv, sends one report after another to his president, Hosni Mubarak, who has finally managed to convince the Americans that they were wrong not to have given him daily bulletins on the discussions at Camp David. Mubarak tries to make the Israelis and the Clinton administration understand that the Islamic world cannot tolerate Israeli sovereignty on the Haram al-Sharif.

Ehud Barak is worried. In a little over a month, the Knesset will be back in session, and the right-wing opposition is scoring points. On July 31, Labor had suffered a stinging defeat when Likud succeeded in getting one of its members, Moshe Katsav, former minister of tourism, elected head of state at a time when Shimon Peres had seemed to be a shoo-in. Barak needs an accord for his political survival, so he is keeping up pressure on Arafat and staying in telephone contact with foreign leaders.

On August 26, Ehud Barak has a phone conversation with Jacques Chirac:

Barak: Despite what is technically a failure, the Camp David summit brought us closer to the goal than we'd ever been. From here on, the conclusion of an accord is going to depend on the question of Jerusalem. Yasir Arafat is now trying to back off from his positions, no doubt for tactical reasons. Egypt is intervening on the Jerusalem issue, since the risk is that, as with Moses on Mount Nebo, the final step will not be taken.

I have taken unprecedented risks, I've staked my political career, but I'll go on to the end no matter what. . . . No Israeli prime minister will ever confer exclusive sovereignty over the Temple Mount [on the Palestinians]. It's been the cradle and the heart of the identity of the Jewish people for 3,000 years. A solution should be found that will grant the Palestinian State the custodianship and administration of the Plaza of the Mosques, while protecting the Temple Mount from any possibility of archeological digs by the Muslims.

The formula the Egyptians envision is unacceptable: "The Temple Mount to Islam and the Wailing Wall to the Jews." If the Palestinians keep on demanding exclusive sovereignty over this site, there isn't going to be any resolution. We're at the moment of truth. Arafat has to be helped to make a decision. History won't repeat itself.

Chirac: I agree with your analysis of how central the status of Jerusalem is in the perspective of an accord. Israel has never gone this far when it comes to the division of Jerusalem—namely, well beyond its lines in the sand. . . . Camp David showed that what the territorial division of Jerusalem and the future State of Palestine are coming up against is the question of the Plaza of the Mosques.

There's got to be another formula, one that doesn't involve exclusive state sovereignty for the Israelis or the Palestinians. Not just for the Plaza of the Mosques but for the entire Old City, shouldn't you be looking for a specific status based on co-sovereignty? The international community could be the witness and guarantor of the commitments on both sides.

Barak: France has a special role to play here: promoting the emergence of a moderate position. Contacts with President Mubarak and the King of Morocco are essential if the Muslim world is going to have a better understanding of Israel's attitude. France can help them realize that the holy sites are equally holy for Jews and Muslims. France has a legitimate right to weigh in on this issue.[151]

Chirac says that France is willing to pass along Barak's perspective, but that the basis of a solution has to come

---

151. Private communication.

from the United States. At the Elysée Palace and the Quai d'Orsay, maps of the Haram al-Sharif/Temple Mount are being pored over. How can there be shared sovereignty? How can the Mount be cut into pieces?

On September 6, Ehud Barak leaves for New York, where he is to take part in the ceremony at the UN General Assembly marking the new millennium. During the flight, he expresses his satisfaction to the journalists accompanying him: "I've put Arafat up against the wall, the way he was in Beirut in 1982. This is his last chance to conclude an accord with me. Arafat doesn't make decisions except under pressure."

As soon as the plane lands, these words are taken up by the Israeli media, and Arafat's entourage hears them almost immediately. In the forty-eight hours he will spend in New York, Barak will conduct what amounts to a campaign against Arafat among thirty heads of state, saying that he, Barak, broke all of Israel's taboos on the subject of Jerusalem and risked his political career, whereas Arafat made no concessions.

Arafat finds that some of his old friends are suddenly giving him a cool reception. His mood turns sour. Barak's negotiators have prepared huge files in anticipation of a new summit, but they leave them in their suitcases: Arafat is no longer willing now. The sole encounter between the two men occurs when, by chance, they find themselves waiting for an elevator in the United Nations building.

Bill Clinton has a long conversation with Arafat. He offers various new ideas toward a solution of the problem of the Haram al-Sharif. Arafat rejects them all. To the suggestion that the Temple Mount/Haram be placed under "divine sovereignty," Arafat replies: "That's meaningless—even the White House is under God's sovereignty! . . . My hands are tied. All the muftis in the Arab world have published fatwas forbidding any concession on this Islamic holy place."

In a conversation with Madeleine Albright, Arafat puts forth a new idea: "The Haram would be placed under the sovereignty of the Islamic Conference, which would entrust its custodianship to the Al-Qods committee chaired by the King of Morocco. All religions would have freedom of worship."

> *Albright:* How can you imagine that Israel will give up sovereignty over this site where the Temple of Judaism once stood?
>
> *Arafat:* So what? There are Roman ruins in Gaza, [yet] the Italians aren't claiming sovereignty there!

And he leaves in a rage, slamming the door. The secretary of state has spoken, in his presence, of the "Temple Mount" instead of "the Haram al-Sharif." The evening before, Arafat had left the CNN studio in the middle of an interview, hurt by the tone in which the journalist Christiane Amanpour was questioning him.

Still, Arafat finds that the situation is not such that he can proclaim the Palestinian State. He convenes the Central Council of the PLO in Gaza. Without fanfare, he has the declaration of independence, originally slated for September 13, postponed to an indefinite date. There is one less threat to the peace process.

Ben Ami and Sher have remained in New York, where they are meeting with the peace team, who, at the same time, are holding discussions with the Palestinians. Contrary to what the Israelis are saying, the Americans believe that Yasir Arafat wants to conclude an accord.

In Jerusalem, the Israeli ministry of housing publishes statistics indicating that, in the first six months of the current year, work has started on 1,924 dwelling units in the occupied territories. In the same period of 1998, the Netanyahu government had begun construction of 1,845 units. Barak, then, is building more extensively than his predecessor. He explains to the Palestinians, and to his own protesting ministers on the left, that this settlement policy appeases the rightists: "If we reach a definitive accord, all this won't matter anymore," he says.

FINAL ATTEMPTS AT COMPROMISE

The ideas Arafat presented to Madeleine Albright during their stormy conversation have gained ground. On September 15, Ehud Barak calls Jacques Chirac to talk about his meetings with Clinton, Albright, and Sandy Berger in New York on September 6. On the subject of the Temple Mount, new ideas were examined, he reports. But, he goes on to say, he prefers not to mention them publicly, because,

> presented by Israel, the Palestinians would consider them "contaminated." The United States is suggesting that the two parties shift their claims to the Security Council. Kofi Annan, with the agreement of the five permanent members, would then name a kind of governor who would administer the site. The secretary general would also designate a kind of advisory council including, among others, Muslim intellectuals and also Jewish and Christian ones, along with internationally respected jurists. They would recommend [the splitting up] of authority over the Temple Mount, [with] Palestinian sovereignty to ensure custodianship of the mosques and Israeli sovereignty beneath the ground.

Another solution, Barak says, would be to make no mention of sovereignty. Pragmatic arrangements would be made in the context of a functional status quo, with the international advisory council determining how responsibilities were to be divided.

> *Barak:* But these ideas are of interest only on condition that they're defined in detail, and especially that Arafat accepts them as a basis for negotiations. I wonder whether he's playing a strategic game, or whether he's so intoxicated by his international contacts that he's forgetting the practical side of things.
>
> *Chirac:* Arafat has been changing over the past two weeks. He's making a major effort by postponing the due date of September 13.
>
> *Barak* (before saying good-bye): Sovereignty [over the Temple Mount] devolving on an international Muslim organization is not acceptable to Israel.

On September 18, the negotiators examine the topic of security. According to Sher, Mohammed Dahlan refuses any concession with regard to Palestinian airspace and security arrangements in the Jordan Valley. Dahlan explains: "We agree to your demand that Palestine have no offensive military capability that would enable it to attack Israel, and we agree that Palestine will not form any alliance whatsoever with a third country mounting such an attack. And we are willing to make a commitment that, in Palestine, only the police will be armed. But this rule should apply equally to the settlers."

Erekat has learned from the Americans that they are working on a compromise proposal that could be presented to the parties very soon. He suggests getting them to hold back this initiative, since it could place a burden on both the Israelis and the Palestinians, and he asks Gilead Sher to head off the Clinton administration. Sher promises to bring him a quick response. Later, Dennis Ross will bitterly regret that he agreed to delay the presentation of the American document. "President Clinton's parameters" will not be made public until December 23, too late to save the peace process.[152]

On September 19, annoyed by the impasse in which the negotiations seem to be bogged down, Barak announces that he has decided to suspend them for awhile. Sher therefore cancels the meeting he had planned with Erekat, who immediately accuses the prime minister of giving up on the peace process. International reactions are strong. Sher is obliged to step in. He shifts the blame for the interruption of the talks onto the Palestinians: "After more than thirty meetings, we have not observed any willingness on the part of the Palestinians to arrive at a compromise. They've given no sign indicating that they would be prepared to discuss the ideas put forth by the Americans. As is the case for the other parties, we have the right to proceed to a re-evaluation of the situation." Shlomo Ben Ami, then on an official visit to Paris, thinks up a way to alleviate his hosts' concern: "This is just a technical interruption," he reassures them.

The next day brings a new session of talks. Sher and Erekat discuss the holy sites and decide to write a "non-paper."

On September 20, it is Yasir Arafat who telephones the Elysée:

Ambassador Bassiouny informed me yesterday of the resumption of the negotiations being conducted by Saeb Erekat, but, that afternoon, the Israelis announced that the meeting was being canceled. The Americans have let us know that they're preparing a document noting the positions of the two sides since Camp David. They're working through [United States ambassador] Martin Indyk, who is ensuring coordination between Washing-

---

152. Videotaped interview with Dennis Ross, February 19, 2002, Washington.

ton and Tel Aviv. As I see it, this American document will just be an Israeli paper.

Chirac uses the occasion to test an idea the state department and Quai d'Orsay have been working on:

Chirac: What do you think of the formula according to which you would have sovereignty over the Plaza of the Mosques and a certain below-ground depth? The Israelis would have sovereignty starting from the depth of the presumed ruins of the Temple.

Arafat (in terms brooking no appeal): We reject the horizontal division of sovereignty over the Haram because of the sanctification of this holy place and the absence of any trace of the Temple under the Plaza of the Mosques. For thirty-four years the Israelis have been digging without success.

Chirac (hardening his tone): This is a problem of principle for each of the two parties. Whether these ruins do or don't exist should not be taken into account. It's the idea of the ruins in the mind of the Israeli people that has to be reckoned with, not so much the ruins themselves. Either there's a willingness to make peace or there isn't. But neither party can be asked to give up what it regards as sacred. In this case, Palestinian sovereignty would be active over the entire space, and Israeli sovereignty passive, since it would pertain to an inert underground area.

Arafat (insistent): But the ruins of the Temple don't exist! Our studies show that these are actually Greek and Roman ruins.

Chirac (who seems to be running out of patience): This isn't a debate on the reality of the alleged substructure of the Temple but on the way the Israeli people hold it in their minds. Right now we've got all the elements of a historic peace agreement on the table. If it isn't concluded, the situation will become unstable again, and there'll be a return of terrorism and Israeli aggression against the Palestinians.

We have to think carefully, so that the decisions will be the right ones. Our sense is that Barak will never risk a compromise on the Temple Mount. You have three or four weeks in which to reach an accord and sign a historic peace treaty, or else find yourselves back in the worst kind of trouble. . . . You've shown courage under difficult conditions by postponing the September 13 due date. Now you have to go all the way. You'll go down in history, and rightly so.

A SECRET NEGOTIATION, FILMED LIVE

On September 24, Gilead Sher and Saeb Erekat allow me to videotape one of their secret meetings in the King David Hotel. Each of them takes stock of the negotiation thus far.

Sher: Because the Palestinians have hardened their positions, we haven't moved forward on most of the main topics. I hope they'll soon adopt positions aimed at seeking solutions.

Charles Enderlin: Is this the end of the process?

Sher: I don't think so. I don't think history will let us, the Palestinians and ourselves, miss this opportunity. We have a common history here, we have a common destiny, we share the same life. Daily life. In the name of future generations, we've got to try to resolve the conflict.

Enderlin: As a secular Jew, how do you accept the fact that the question of the Temple Mount could get in the way of concluding an accord?

Sher: A secular Jew isn't removed from his traditions, his history, and the heritage of his ancestors. My mother's family came to the Old City of Jerusalem in 1516, immediately after the expulsion [of the Jews] from Spain. So I have deep feelings about the Old City. And my paternal grandfather was killed in 1948 by Arab troops while he was escorting a Haganah convoy. The question isn't being secular or not. It has to do with respecting the dignity, the traditions, and the past of both sides. . . . We aren't extremists, but we have a tradition, a place of worship on which our ancestors prayed. This can't be brushed away with a wave of the hand.

Saeb Erekat is interviewed in his car:

I was twelve years old when the Israeli occupation began in 1967. The only thing I could do was throw stones and go to prison. Today I'm the father of four children, and I want them to have a different kind of life. . . . I never would have imagined that one day I'd be negotiating on Jerusalem. [He points to a street on the former line of demarcation.] Look: over here will be Palestine, over there Israel. What will happen in this street? I suggest that there be a combined Israeli–Palestinian police force. . . .

The main problem is the lack of trust between our two leaders. . . . The reason for this is that Barak hasn't stood by the commitments he made at Sharm el-Sheik. Arafat thinks he isn't serious. And yet he [Arafat] has offered him a thousand opportunities to become his partner. On the personal level, trust between them is at an all-time low. The Israelis want us to proclaim the end of the conflict and give up any future claim. They can't conclude an accord without be-

ing satisfied on these two points. These are the two
cards that we Palestinians are holding in our hand.

SHARON ON THE PLAZA

The Americans have invited the two delegations to
Washington. They would like Yossi Beilin, architect of the
Oslo accords and presently minister of justice, to take part
in the talks along with Osama al-Baz, Hosni Mubarak's adviser. Barak and Ben Ami say no to this suggestion.

Before the departure for the United States, a meeting
between Barak and Arafat is scheduled. It will be on September 25, in Barak's home at Kochav Yair. Daniel Abraham, the American billionaire who has been following the
peace process closely, has played a role in setting up this
summit.

The mood that evening is optimistic. Barak and Arafat
walk in the garden alone, arm in arm, for forty minutes:
the longest private conversation the two men have ever
had. In the living room, Israeli and Palestinian negotiators
are looking at one another. Maybe the ice has been broken, at last! Has Barak accepted the scenario his advisers
prepared for him? Who knows? During an interview with
me in 2002, Barak will say that the conversation was utterly uninteresting.[153]

According to Sher, what the prime minister was supposed to say to Arafat was this:

We've reached an impasse. We're at risk of letting a
historic occasion slip by. Dahlan, Erekat, and our team
are doing extraordinary, really creative work, and they're
trying hard to reach an accord. But we leaders are the

---

153. Videotaped interview with Ehud Barak, January 2, 2002, Tel Aviv.

ones who are responsible for setting forth principles to serve as a basis for negotiation. The presentation of the compromise the Americans are working on is not in our interest. A negotiated solution between us is preferable. We're at the moment of truth. . . . I'd like us to conclude the agreement that will lead to the end of our conflict. . . . You are the only one who can ensure the future of the Palestinian people. . . .[154]

In 2002, Yasir Arafat will report that he talked about the visit Ariel Sharon was planning to make to the Plaza of the Mosques in the Old City of Jerusalem: "I told Barak he had to do whatever he could to prevent this, because it could lead to a disaster!"[155]

What Sharon, the head of the Likud, wants to do is test the prime minister by showing that his government has only partial control of the Temple Mount, where the Waqf has been undertaking large-scale projects to the great dismay of Israeli archeologists and right-wingers. The Israelis who were at Kochav Yair that evening maintain that at no point was Sharon's name mentioned.

The meeting at Barak's house ends late. Arafat thanks Nava and Ehud Barak for their hospitality. He announces that his representatives have a formal mandate to negotiate. "I hope they'll succeed with your delegates," he says. "We are connected; it's our destiny."

Gilead Sher, Shlomo Ben Ami, and Israel Hasson, accompanied by Gidi Grinstein, leave directly for the airport, where they have to catch the plane for Washington. The Palestinian delegation consists of Saeb Erekat, Mohammed Dahlan, and Akram Hanieh. Gaith el-Omari, the jurist, will

---

154. Sher, 2001, p. 280.
155. Videotaped interview with Yasir Arafat, February 2, 2002, Ramallah.

be assisting them. So as not to lose time going from one place to another in Washington, the Israeli delegation is staying in the Ritz Carlton, the Palestinians' favorite hotel. The peace team will shuttle between the two sets of negotiators, keeping in mind the compromise that is to be presented to the parties.

Meanwhile, in Israel, Ehud Barak is trying to resolve the problem of Ariel Sharon's projected visit to the Temple Mount. Prohibition is out of the question: it would hand the right a crushing argument. From Sharon's perspective as head of the opposition, the exercise can only win points for him. By forbidding the visit, the government would demonstrate its weakness. But if allowed to survey the plaza, Sharon would send a message to the most nationalistic of his constituents: "The Temple Mount is the most sacred place, the very foundation of the existence of Judaism, and I am not afraid of any Palestinian riots."

Palestinian leaders put Barak on alert: the visit to the Haram al-Sharif of the man they consider the Butcher of Sabra and Shatila will inevitably heighten tensions.

Caught between one more incident in the long series of crises with the Palestinians, and, on the other hand, a new problem of internal politics, Barak decides to allow the visit. The Autonomous Authority is asked to do what it can. There is disagreement on what comes after that. In Washington, Shlomo Ben Ami, the Israeli minister of internal security, gets a phone call from Jibril Rajoub, head of preventive security in the West Bank, who tells him that, in his opinion, the visit can take place without any problems as long as Sharon does not enter the mosques. Later, Rajoub will swear he never said this to Ben Ami.[156] Faisal al-Husseini, the Palestinian leader of East Jerusalem, is also said to have issued warnings against

---

156. Videotaped interviews with Shlomo Ben Ami, June 17, 2001, Tel Aviv, and Jibril Rajoub, November 11, 2001, Ramallah.

Sharon's visit. As for the Israeli left, they are speaking in terms of an intolerable provocation.

On September 28, 2000, at 7:30 in the morning, Ariel Sharon, accompanied by Likud deputies and escorted by bodyguards and numerous police officers, visits the Plaza of the Mosques. He does not enter either Al-Aqsa or the Dome of the Rock but comes close to the new entrance of the underground mosque beneath Al-Aqsa, stays there for a few minutes, then makes a half-turn. Several hundred young protesters are being held back by border guards and a police unit. Led by Ahmed Tibi, some Israeli Arab deputies are protesting noisily.

Going back through the Maghreb Gate as he leaves the Temple Mount/Haram al-Sharif, Sharon declares, "I think we can live together with the Palestinians. I came to see what is going on here. . . . I have not committed any act of provocation." He then leaves. The police deal with some stone-throwing. The people in charge of security breathe again. The visit has taken place without undue incident.

Marwan Barghouti, head of Fatah on the West Bank, is disappointed. His call for a mass demonstration on the plaza has had little effect.[157] Some agitation around Jerusalem would have shown once again how attached the Palestinians are to their holy site. True, the Autonomous Authority is sending a mixed message on this issue: "Why go and confront the Israeli police and get hurt, when our leaders are negotiating the status of the city with the minister in charge of the police?" is what is being said in the Muslim quarter of the Old City. For everyone, the crisis is over. Tomorrow—Friday—a special force, barely augmented, will keep an eye out as Muslims leave their place of prayer.

---

157. Videotaped interview with Marwan Barghouti, November 11, 2001, Ramallah.

Chapter 6

Chain Reactions

September 29, 2000 is a Friday. In Jerusalem, as in Ramallah, people are getting ready to spend a relatively calm day. Nevertheless, Fatah has planned several demonstrations with stone-throwing, so that Ariel Sharon's visit to the Plaza of the Mosques will not go unnoticed. The Jerusalem police and Israeli forces on the West Bank have been told to be on the alert, but no particular security measures have been put into effect.

Early in the morning, there is a bloody incident near Qalquilya: a Palestinian police officer on a joint patrol opens fire and kills an officer of the Israeli border guards. The murderer is arrested by Jibril Rajoub's services. As a precaution, but also to force the Autonomous Authority to take the necessary measures, Tsahal immediately cancels all joint patrols. A few hours later their absence will be cruelly felt.

At midday, 20,000 worshippers attend prayers on the Haram al-Sharif. Yair Yitzhaki, the Jerusalem chief of police, has deployed several hundred men alongside the Western Wall and near the Lions Gate. But he has not forbidden all Palestinians under the age of forty to enter the plaza, as he does each time incidents are feared. Nor do the news services anticipate any special danger. As on all Fridays, only two Palestinian cameramen with minicams are stationed there.

As the crowd begins to disperse, about twenty young people start throwing stones at the police, and, down below, at the crowds in front of the Western Wall. Yitzhaki immediately evacuates the Jewish worshippers and mounts the slope leading to the Maghreb Gate. He is wounded when a stone strikes his head, and, his face bloody, is evacuated in an ambulance. His second-in-command, David Krauze, takes over. Israeli radio broadcasts the news and announces that Yitzhaki is seriously injured, with a fractured skull. The police officers deployed around the Haram precinct react very badly.

The rest is described by Shlomo Ben Ami, minister of both internal security and foreign affairs, in an interview taped in 2001 after his return from New York:

Ben Ami: During my absence, Prime Minister Ehud Barak made sure security would be covered in the interim. I had just gotten back when I learned that David Krauze had decided to enter the plaza in order to drive back the crowd that, according to him, was getting ready to go down and invade the sector of the Western Wall. Under this kind of pressure, this officer decided to enter the Temple Mount.

Charles Enderlin: We have the videotape of these few minutes. There were only about twenty stone-throwers.

Ben Ami: I can't go into the details. It was, in my opinion, a wrong decision. If Yair Yitzhaki had been there, nothing like this would have happened. It was a wrong decision, made by an officer on the ground while the chief of police, who normally goes to hot spots, wasn't there. He was going back home to Tel Aviv. This clearly shows that the national police command had no idea what was going to happen.[158]

The police open fire at short range with rubber-covered metal bullets as well as real ones, hitting several of the stone-throwers and people leaving the Al-Aqsa Mosque. The officers quickly lose control of some of their men, who are enraged by the wound inflicted on Yitzhaki. The clash turns extremely violent. Shots are aimed toward the interior of the mosque. This is a riot, and it will last several hours.

Other television crews arrive and film the scene. There will be four dead and 160 injured, some seriously, among the Muslims. Fourteen police officers are lightly wounded. Shlomo Ben Ami, who does not understand what is happening, still does not go to the plaza but chooses to be photographed at the bedside of Yitzhaki, who is in fact only slightly injured. Pictures of the suppression are immediately rebroadcast over Arab satellite channels, and the Palestinian territories erupt into violence.

At this point, spontaneous demonstrations are organized in all the towns of the West Bank. Military and police forces are attacked by stone-throwers more or less everywhere. They respond with rubber-coated bullets. At short range, these wound and kill. The Israeli army has only rarely used anti-riot equipment in the Palestinian territories. At the end of the day, the toll is high: six dead on the Palestinian side.

The stone that hit Yitzhaki has set off a regional chain reaction that nothing will be able to stop in the following months.

Military leaders and heads of security in Israel know that events of this kind on the Plaza of the Mosques always lead to violent reactions from the Palestinian population. The

---

158. Videotaped interview with Shlomo Ben Ami, June 17, 2001, Tel Aviv.

agitation looks as though it will last several days. At all costs, the events of the day of Nakbah, last May, must not be repeated. The implementation of some elements of Operation Field of Thorns is considered.

That evening, in Ramallah, Marwan Barghouti, the head of Fatah, convenes his staff. Tomorrow, he says, the demonstrations must be put under the control of his men. Shabiba, the Fatah youth movement, will take things in hand. Orders are sent to the militants during the night.

THE SECOND INTIFADA

September 30 is a turning point. At the checkpoint of the City Inn Hotel, in the northern part of Ramallah, hundreds of teenagers throw stones at Israeli border guards and soldiers, who respond with rubber-coated bullets and real ones. On the West Bank, four Palestinians are killed. Another drama unfolds at the military post defending the approaches to the Netzarim settlement in the middle of the Gaza Strip. This colony, occupied by around fifteen Israeli families, controls the main road crossing the region from north to south; this is why, for the Palestinians, it is a symbol of the occupation.

From the loopholes in the small fort, tear-gas grenades and bullets meet hurled stones and Molotov cocktails. At the intersection, trucks, taxis, and ambulances continue to pass through. Abdel Hakim Awad, head of Shabiba in Gaza, is on the scene. He tells Talal Abu Rahmeh, the France 2 correspondent in Gaza, that "these demonstrations will continue for two or three days. They are intended to show the Israeli government that the Palestinians will never give up Al-Aqsa."

Suddenly, bursts of fire from automatic weapons are heard. Who began shooting? The Palestinians will accuse the Israelis, who will issue a denial. Caught in the crossfire, Talal Abu Rahmeh runs to hide behind a van. He finds that a father and son have gotten there before him, trying to protect themselves behind what seems to be a drum of concrete. For several long minutes they seem to be safe. But then, all at once, they become targets. According to all witnesses, the bullets that will soon mortally wound the child come from the Israeli position. The father is seriously injured. Images of this tragedy will go around the world. Mohammed Al-Doura will become one of the symbols of the new Palestinian uprising.[159]

Four Palestinians meet their death in Gaza and six in the West Bank; members of the Palestinian police are among them. The Al-Aqsa Intifada is born. All the anger, all the frustration accumulated by the Palestinian population since 1996, erupts now. At the scene of the fighting, Israeli soldiers are allowed to open fire more freely and do so. Cries ring out at the funeral of the Palestinian victims: "Revenge!" and "With fire, blood, and spirit we shall defend Al-Aqsa!" Immediately after the burial, funeral processions form, and the crowd heads toward the nearest Israeli checkpoint, where a clash will claim new victims. Nothing will break this vicious circle.

Two years later, Ben Kaspit of *Maariv* will reveal that, during the first three weeks of the Intifada, the Israeli army fired 700,000 cartridges of different calibers on the West Bank and 300,00 in Gaza.[160]

---

159. Pressed for an explanation, the Israeli army will at first admit: "We can't rule out the possibility that, from the Netzarim post, the soldiers thought they saw threatening silhouettes behind the concrete drum." Later, General Yom Tov Samia, commander of the southern military region, will conduct his own inquiry with the intention of proving that his men were not responsible for the death of little Mohammed. His conclusion: "It is more likely that the child was the victim of Palestinian fire than of Israeli gunfire." (Interview of General Yom Tov Samia by Bob Simon (*60 Minutes*, CBS, November 12, 2000).

160. Kaspit, 2002b, p. 9.

By the end of the month, the balance sheet will speak for itself: 102 Palestinians and 10 Israelis have been killed.[161] This discrepancy, illustrated with pictures of children and teenagers confronting a well-equipped army, will be disastrous for Israel's image.

The Israeli chief of staff, General Shaul Mofaz, blames the Autonomous Authority and its security services for this outbreak of violence. Tsahal's own website, however, gives the following account:

The Palestinians claim that the disturbances were triggered by a visit by Likud leader Ariel Sharon to the Temple Mount, on 28 September, which they viewed as a provocation. However, before this visit there had been a marked rise in tensions. These tensions had previously manifested themselves in attacks on Israelis for several days. Actually, the causes of underlying Palestinian dissatisfaction and frustration can be traced back over a much longer period of time. Over the months preceding the disturbances, there was a growing sense of frustration among the Palestinian public, a sense exacerbated by an extended period of economic and political stagnation. Particularly disgruntled were the grassroots members of Yasir Arafat's Fatah organization and a paramilitary subgroup within the Fatah, known as the Tanzim. These groups felt they were not receiving adequate treatment from Arafat and the Palestinian Authority. . . .

Following the 29 September disturbances on the Temple Mount, and due to mounting Palestinian casualties, disturbances quickly spread throughout the West Bank and Gaza, as well as in Arab towns within Is-

---

161. See detailed statistics published by B'tselem, the Israeli Information Center for Human Rights in the Occupied Territories (http://www.btselem.org/). These figures include members of security personnel on both sides.

rael. . . . This recent outburst of violence . . . represents
a blatant and fundamental violation of the Oslo Agreement, in which the Palestinian Authority undertook to
prevent violence in areas under its control.[162]

Government officials in Egypt, afraid of a rapid escalation
with disastrous consequences for the region, are following
these events very closely and with great concern. On October 1, at the Waldorf Astoria in New York, Amr Moussa,
the Egyptian foreign mininster, has a working breakfast with
Madeleine Albright. His advice is that she immediately
present the Israelis and Palestinians with the compromise
proposal discussed a few days earlier in Washington:

I pleaded with Mrs. Albright, pleaded with her, that
this is the time to present your paper, or your ideas, or
your framework, or whatever you call it, but it's now and
not tomorrow. She seemed to be convinced, but there
were other forces that wanted to stall.

Speaking in November, 2001, Amr Moussa will refer to
the American compromise presented to the parties in December, 2000:

Had President Clinton offered his parameters six
months earlier, by December we would have reached the
framework agreement. But the question is: Why didn't he
offer his parameters earlier, and why were October and
November wasted time, without meetings or anything?
And why weren't the parameters announced before December 23?[163]

---

162. See http://www.idf.il/english/news/background_20nov00.stm.

163. Videotaped interview, November 21, 2001, Cairo. On the proposal, see
pp. 332–339.

The fact is that, in the first weeks of the Intifada, Ehud Barak will not consider a resumption of negotiations on the final status: "We don't want to reward Palestinian violence." And the peace team thinks it would be best to wait until things calm down.

On October 1, Barak takes stock of the situation with his advisers. All of them suggest that he meet in person with Yasir Arafat. Yossi Ginosar contacts the Palestinians, who agree in principle to a meeting. Then, several hours later, Barak changes his mind. Arafat will infer from this that, once again, Barak does not want to talk with him.

At Nablus, thousands of people attend the funeral of the mayor's oldest son, who was killed during confrontations the day before. The crowd then makes for the enclave of Joseph's Tomb, where Palestinian police and military men open fire on the Israelis guarding the Talmudic school established at this holy site. Shooting on both sides becomes heavier. An Israeli border policeman is seriously wounded. He cannot be evacuated and will die. Three Palestinians are killed. The agitation spreads like wildfire in the Arab community inside Israel itself. Violent protests break out in Israel at Umm el-Fahem, Nazareth, and Galilee, and the Israeli police are charged with restoring order. In several places in Galilee, they disperse demonstrators with rubber-coated bullets. But they also deploy sharpshooters, who open fire with real bullets.

The Palestinian problem is once again in the forefront of the international news. For better or worse, the Israelis are trying to justify the very harsh picture being broadcast around the world. Shlomo Ben Ami steps forward and holds a press conference in Jerusalem:

The Israeli government has done its utmost with regard to a compromise, and has paid a high price politically, in order to create the conditions for a peace agreement with our Palestinian neighbors. Such an agree-

ment remains possible. . . . Let this be clear: the events
at the Temple Mount were the direct result of massive
and dangerous attacks perpetrated by a Muslim crowd
gathered [on the plaza] and attempting to clash violently
with Jewish worshippers praying at the Western Wall,
before Rosh ha-Shana, the Jewish New Year. We are all
responsible for making sure confrontations like this, in
places like this, do not occur. . . .

As we have seen, Ben Ami will offer another explanation
later on.

According to Israeli spokesmen, the high toll of Palestinian victims can be accounted for by the fact that soldiers had
to shoot back at Tanzim gunmen hidden behind the demonstrators. But many independent journalists have ascer-
tained that the Palestinian fighters opened fire only after
several stone-throwers were wounded or killed. Israeli
sharpshooters play a more discreet role. As one of them has
revealed, they had been told to neutralize the ringleaders by
shooting them in the knee. Troops in armored personnel
carriers and tanks are deployed in Palestinian territories,
which are being encircled more heavily.

On October 2, the harshest fighting continues around
Joseph's Tomb and near Netzarim in Gaza, where, for the
first time, Tsahal brings in its combat helicopters. In Galilee, demonstrations are put down harshly. The police kill
five Israeli Arabs, some of whom had not even been among
the stone-throwers.

All discussions aimed at establishing a cease-fire end in
failure: the Palestinians want Israel first to stop shooting, to
withdraw its troops from points of friction, and, above all,
to agree to the setting up of an international commission of
inquiry charged with determining the origin of the crisis. Bill
Clinton phones Yasir Arafat, asking him to intervene and
calm the Palestinians down.

On October 3, while violent clashes continue near all Israeli positions on the West Bank and in Gaza, the Americans suggest that a summit be held in Paris, where Madeleine Albright is on an official visit. President Jacques Chirac is only too happy to cooperate. Hosni Mubarak, who has also been spending hours on the telephone with Clinton and Arafat, suggests that the accord reached in Paris be solemnly signed at Sharm el-Sheik in Egypt. His plan is approved by the parties.

THE SUMMIT IN PARIS

On October 4, 2000, at 8:30 in the morning, Yasir Arafat is the first to arrive at the Elysée. He shows Chirac the balance sheet for the past six days: 64 dead and 2,300 wounded on the Palestinian side. Nine Israeli Arabs have been killed as well, he reports, and continues:

> Ehud Barak made a major mistake in letting Sharon go to the Plaza of the Mosques. Palestinians, Arabs, and all Muslims saw his visit as a provocation. But I'd warned Barak, two days earlier, when we met at his house. It's Mofaz who's really behind all this. He's the one who encouraged Barak to use armed force against the demonstrators. Barak is going to pay a high [political] price for the number of Israeli Arab victims. More than 90 percent of this community voted for him.

Chirac refers to his phone conversation with Barak the previous evening:

> *Chirac:* Barak doesn't seem to be aware of how Israel's responsibilities are being perceived abroad. [But] the televised reports and dramatic pictures that have gone

around the world were clear. The Europeans and a good part of the international community are reacting very negatively to the provocation that led to the spiral of violence. France and Europe are in favor of setting up an international commission of inquiry. Bill Clinton and Madeleine Albright have indicated their agreement. Barak hasn't declared himself.

Arafat: I'm going to insist that the three-way meeting be expanded, and that you take part in it. This is the basis on which I agreed to come to Paris. Right now I don't know whether this meeting will take place; I'll know better after I meet with Madeleine Albright and Kofi Annan. The Israelis would first have to accept the three conditions mentioned two days ago with Barak: observance of the cease-fire, withdrawal of Israeli troops from points of friction, and establishment of a commission of inquiry. I could stand to lose a lot if my meeting with Barak doesn't lead to satisfactory results. Not only Palestinian public opinion, but opinion in all Arab and Islamic countries has to be taken into account.

Chirac: I understand your concerns. You should clearly communicate your legitimate demands to Madeleine Albright now, this morning, but you should also keep in mind that the international community wants this meeting to be held. As for me, I'm available. If worse comes to worst and you don't reach an agreement, you'll have to explain the Palestinian position in a strong speech reaffirming your wish for peace.

Meanwhile, Ehud Barak and his delegation are meeting with Madeleine Albright and Dennis Ross at the home of Felix Rohatyn, the American ambassador, in Rue du Faubourg-Saint-Honoré. George Tenet, the head of the CIA, has joined them.

Barak: For the first time, I'm not sure that Arafat wants to put an end [to these riots]. If you have any information that I don't . . . . Should we see this as a strategic move? A sort of corridor [of violence] before an agreement? Tell us! Otherwise we'll have to take action. Arafat must not take advantage of this situation. We're sure that he can put an immediate stop to this violence. At this stage of the political process, violence must not be rewarded. We have irrefutable evidence that the leaders of the Tanzim think Arafat wants the riots to continue, at least for the next few days. What we're seeing is the Palestinians' repeated violation of agreements and all the rules of the game. The Palestinian police are still opening fire. The Tanzim are out of control, and [illegal] arms are not being confiscated. Arafat has to control weapons in his territory, . . . especially [those held by] the Tanzim. If he can't, it's because he's a gang leader, not a political one. . . .[164]

General Bogi Yaalon (deputy chief of staff): Since Saturday morning we've been witnessing a meticulously planned offensive. It began after a meeting between Marwan Barghouti and Arafat. Our open lines with General Abdelrazik el-Majaida [head of the Palestinian forces in Gaza], Jibril Rajoub, and others are of no use. They can't go against the Tanzim. This is an armed gang, part of Fatah, whose leaders get their orders from Arafat himself. There's no point talking about a cease-fire. All we're doing is responding to their attacks.

Dennis Ross mentions the discrepancy in the death toll: Tsahal, he says, is reacting too brutally to Palestinian provocations. He is told about the debate that has been roiling the

---

164. Sher, 2001, p. 292.

prime minister's office in Jerusalem ever since the beginning
of the Intifada: several of Barak's advisers have openly accused the army of acting like a bull in a china shop. Each
new Palestinian victim makes the situation worse. The death
toll, the advisers are saying, must absolutely be decreased.

> *Ross:* This vicious circle has to be broken. The dynamics
> here are tragic. We all know that agreement is within
> reach.
> *Barak:* It's much easier for me to negotiate than to fight.
> But if I have to fight, I will. I won't give in to blackmail.

Here George Tenet intervenes. As he sees it, Arafat has
lost control of his troops. Barak breaks in: "No, he has not
lost control. All Arafat has to do is make two phone calls,
which is what he should be doing, and the whole thing will
end in twelve hours." Tenet is worried about the attitude of
Hamas and says he would like to meet with the heads of security from both camps.

> *Barak* (annoyed): The Israeli right was absolutely correct:
> Why give them arms? This is a gang, and the accord
> is meaningless to them! They don't control anything?
> Nonsense! . . . You should come to our part of the
> world. If Arafat doesn't play the peace card, we know
> what we'll have to do. We may be witnessing the fail-
> ure of a decade of negotiations. If, at this critical mo-
> ment, Arafat can't come to a decision, we'll know
> what to make of that.
> *Albright* (emphasizing that the killing must stop): We
> Americans are prepared to tell Arafat what he has to
> be told. But we're alone. You'll realize this when you
> meet with Jacques Chirac. The pictures of helicopters
> shooting missiles at residential buildings are dreadful.
> The mood here is against you. If things quiet down,

President Clinton will be able to meet with the negotiators on Tuesday. . . .

Ehud Barak is late in getting to the Elysée. It is noon. Before going into the room where the meeting is to take place, he had told Miguel Moratinos, the European emissary to the Middle East, and Hubert Védrine, the French foreign minister, that in no case did he want to see France or Egypt participating in an international commission.

Jacques Chirac takes the floor:

Chirac: There's a sense of anxiety in the air. We all know about the current situation and how serious it is. We should not focus on the past. There's no need for assigning blame. Each of the parties has its own version of the events. Instead, we have to find a way to get out of the crisis, restore peace, and renew the talks. . . .

    [Referring to his meeting with Arafat] Arafat told me how hard he finds it to accept such a trilateral meeting, but he will take part if three conditions are met: a cease-fire, a withdrawal by the Israeli army, and the formation of an international commission. It will be difficult to hold such a meeting if these conditions are not fulfilled.

Barak: I first want to indicate that, like the Palestinians, we Israelis are human beings. We understand the human tragedy that is being experienced in the Palestinian territories. But Israel is also in mourning for its dead.

    It's important that I clarify what led to this violence. Arafat is to blame. He has given orders to fire on isolated Israeli positions, and, even when he doesn't, he turns a blind eye when his men open fire. Palestinian policemen are taking part in the attacks alongside the demonstrators and the Tanzim. That's what happened at Joseph's Tomb in Nablus and at the Netzarim crossing.

All the Israeli army is doing is reacting at the scene. When Arafat orders a cease-fire, our reaction will stop. We have occupied new positions only in exceptional cases and with a single motive: improving our line of defense. When the violence stops, we'll withdraw.

Arafat has chosen to go from the negotiating table to armed confrontation. This attitude wins him the attention and the support of the international community, at the price of Palestinian blood. He has it in his power to stop the violence in less than twenty-four hours. If he can't control his armed forces on his own territory, what kind of leader are we dealing with? If he can't do this, he'll never be a respectable head of state but just a gang leader.

As I see it, Arafat is motivated by the wish to set off a new outburst of violence before focusing on the peace agreement. He thinks he'll improve his position this way. This is the optimistic hypothesis. According to a less optimistic one, Arafat has given up on peace and chosen confrontation. In neither case must he benefit from the violence. If he does, the door will be open to permanent blackmail.

Sharon's visit to the Plaza of the Mosques is a matter that stems from internal political dynamics in Israel. The initiative was directed not against Arafat but against me and my government.

We reject the idea of an international commission of inquiry, and we ask Europe, and France in particular, not to be influenced by public opinion and to act so as to strengthen the outlook for peace.

Amnon Lipkin-Shahak (minister of tourism and former chief of staff): I'd like to clarify our position. Sharon's visit to the Plaza of the Mosques had an internal political motive. I don't want to go into the details, but this visit had been organized in agreement with Pales-

tinian authorities and the Muslim administration. The
only thing we were asked is that Sharon not enter the
mosques. His visit was directed against Barak, to punish him for having made concessions on Jerusalem.

The situation is truly disturbing and frustrating.
Yes, we have suffered fewer losses than the Palestinians, but the numbers that have been mentioned are
inaccurate. Joseph's Tomb in Nablus, where our soldiers are, is surrounded by a Palestinian crowd, and
civilians are opening fire and throwing Molotov cocktails. If our soldiers hadn't responded with precise
shots, they would have been massacred.

Another [sensitive] spot is the Netzarim crossing in
Gaza, where the famous Palestinian boy fell. There,
our position is surrounded by buildings, high struc-
tures from which Palestinian submachine guns fire on
us. The only thing we can do is use combat helicopters, and this is never very pleasant to see.

We are convinced that violence would have broken
out in any event, even without Sharon's visit. We're in
a terrible dilemma: we're eager to make peace, but we
have to protect the lives of our soldiers. The violence
must stop, and negotiations must resume.

Barak (very agitated): I certainly want to move forward
on the road to negotiation, but I can't accept a situation in which the Palestinians benefit from violence.

Hubert Védrine: A gesture has to be made as a first step.
It would be good if, here in Paris, Israel made a gesture
toward Arafat. That would allow him to de-escalate the
violence and return to negotiation.

Barak: Today he's asking for one gesture, and tomorrow
he'll ask for another one! Every time we make a gesture, he demands more.

Arafat cannot and should not derive any benefit
whatsoever from violence. His attitude does an injus-

tice to all those who want peace. The Israeli right is celebrating, because its traditional argument has been validated: they've always told us we shouldn't arm the Palestinians, because, if we did, they would turn the arms against us. On account of Arafat, the peace camp in Israel has lost its bearings and has been put on the defensive.

We are against the idea of an international commission; accepting it would be to side with organized violence. If France and Egypt participate in this international investigation, I will not go to Sharm el-Sheik [to conclude the cease-fire accord].

Chirac: As I listen to you, it's clear that the situation is bad. I don't want to stand in judgment on actions that have been taken, and this is why, contrary to certain rumors, France has abstained and will abstain from issuing any statement today. But I would like to point out that no countries and no media subscribe to the Israeli version of events. The whole world shares the same feeling, even Mexico, if I'm to believe my recent conversation with its president.

After Camp David, I was the first to defend your political courage. I appreciated your commitment to peace. But Sharon provoked these incidents, and he did so with the agreement of your government. He pressed the detonator, and everything exploded. The discrepancies have to be considered: 64 Palestinians and 9 Israeli Arabs dead, 2,300 Palestinians wounded, while, on the Israeli side, only two civilians and one soldier were killed. No one can believe that the Palestinians are to blame for this chain of violence.

On the basis of my experience of guerrilla warfare in Algeria, I know how to interpret this kind of imbalance. Using combat helicopters against stone-throwers is not acceptable. If no agreement on a cease-fire is reached, it's up to the stronger party—and you are the stronger ones—to take the first step.

An Israeli diplomat slips into the room and hands a note to Ehud Barak. The prime minister winces: the situation in Nablus, around Joseph's Tomb, is deteriorating. Chirac continues:

If Israel rejects the international commission, it will give the impression that it wants to hide the reality of what's happening. So it's up to Israel to make the first gesture. It's a matter of noblesse oblige for the stronger party to hold out its hand.

I am for peace, and I am convinced that the Arab countries are as well. We have conjointly put pressure on Arafat to get him to come to Paris. He didn't want to come, but we persuaded him to. We aren't asking anything for ourselves: I did not intend to go to Sharm el-Sheik, and I shall not go. I don't know what the Egyptians want. Our role is to be your lawyers, to take notes and give good advice.

Barak (again): Arafat must not be rewarded for his behavior.

Chirac: Maybe history will not be written today.

By now, Arafat has arrived at Rue du Faubourg-Saint-Honoré. He has an initial discussion with Madeleine Albright, who suggests setting up an American commission headed by George Tenet, the head of the CIA, to oversee the implementation of a cease-fire.

Arafat: It's out of the question that there should be no commission of inquiry. With 2,300 wounded and 64 dead, I have a population that's asking me to be accountable. There is no way I can reconcile myself to the situation and pretend that Barak didn't order the army to shoot. I need a commission of inquiry, and it can't be exclusively American.

Albright: Do you really need the French? The United Nations? Do you really want us to go back to the time of useless commissions of inquiry?

Arafat is insistent. Albright says she will discuss this with Barak. It all has to be over, she says, around 3 P.M., when there will be a press conference to announce the agreement. In the meantime, while the meeting with the Israelis is taking place, Albright invites the Palestinians to have lunch at the embassy. Arafat has the feeling that the die is cast, that the Americans have completely given up the idea of a commission of inquiry. He gets up and announces to his entourage, "We're going to the hotel!"

In the car, Leila Shahid, the Palestinian representative in France, asks Arafat what has been going on. He replies, "Why stay? She [Albright] doesn't want a commission of inquiry. And if she doesn't, why would Barak? Am I supposed to forget all the dead and wounded? A commission of inquiry is the least I can do for the dead!"

Arafat asks Saeb Erekat to inform Dennis Ross that the Palestinians will not return to the negotiations, since the Americans favor a security commission and not an investigatory one. The 3 P.M. press conference is canceled. Erekat and Ross get busy. Barak and his delegation have returned from Felix Rohatyn's house and, at 3:15, have a work session with Madeleine Albright, who announces that, the way things stand, the Israelis are going to have to give in. "Arafat has a political problem," she says. "How can he restore calm after the death of over 70 Palestinians?" She suggests the deployment of international observers at hot spots in the Palestinian territories.

Around 5 P.M., Dennis Ross calls Arafat and tells him that, after a long discussion between Albright and Barak, there has been progress. Arafat and his entourage then go to Rohatyn's house. A long negotiating session begins. What has to be done is bypass the problem of the commission of inquiry and draw up the final statement that Albright is to read to the press in the evening.

The discussion is tense. Arafat addresses Barak: "Ehud! I warned you at that dinner at your house. I told you not to let Sharon go to the Plaza of the Haram. I told you he would use his visit against you in the electoral campaign, that he would set himself up as the defender of Jerusalem."

To which Barak replies, "You don't understand. Every Israeli citizen has the right to visit the most sacred site in Judaism!"

Hours pass. The negotiators go back and forth. The delegates who are not taking part in the writing of the accord kill time any way they can, walking through the residence, making phone calls, and so forth. Around 9 P.M., since Barak has not replied, and Albright has not been clear on the nature of the commission of inquiry, Arafat gets up and heads out the door.

Leila Shahid joins him: "What's going on?" "Come on," Arafat says. "We're leaving." They get into the car. Madeleine Albright learns that Arafat is about to escape. Gilead Sher describes the scene: "Like an American football player, the secretary of state charges into the hall and out the front door, shouting, 'Close the gate! Don't let him leave!' Someone calls to her, 'Please, please: don't run after him!'"

Albright goes over to the car. Arafat, unruffled, pretends not to see her. Leila Shahid opens her door, "Come talk to him from here." Albright walks around the car. "Why are you leaving?"

Arafat: Because this is going to go on forever! You aren't coming to a decision.
Albright: That's not so. We're making progress. Come on back.

Arafat gets out of the car and kisses Albright, who takes his arm and, holding him close to her and not letting go, leads him back to the room where the negotiations are taking place.

Shortly after 11 P.M. an agreement seems to have been reached. There will be two commissions. The first, set up to examine the technical aspects of a cease-fire, is to be headed by George Tenet and will begin work immediately. The composition of the second, the commission of inquiry, has yet to be determined. Barak is demanding that it be presided over by Bill Clinton, while Arafat wants Kofi Annan. A solution will have to be found before the signing at Sharm el-Sheik.

The delegations leave for the Elysée and bring the good news to Jacques Chirac.

Albright: An agreement has been reached on the security procedures needed to head off the return of violence in the territories. A document will be initialed tonight at the United States embassy. The formal signing will take place tomorrow at Sharm el-Sheik. President Clinton is offering to receive the Israeli and Palestinian negotiators in Washington on October 10.
Arafat: The accord on the security arrangements is consistent with what was concluded at Wye River. We agree to the establishment of an international commission of inquiry in liaison with the secretary general of the United Nations.
Barak: The establishment of a commission of inquiry is not the best way to restore trust and peace, but we

nevertheless agree to it. We could accept the presence on this commission of distinguished Americans.

Madeleine Albright confirms that an agreement has been reached with regard to the commission of inquiry.

Arafat: The accords to which we have subscribed are within the framework of the United Nations resolutions. I hail the presence here today of Kofi Annan. It's important to associate the United Nations with our efforts.
Chirac (who has congratulated Barak and Arafat): I know they've shown all their goodwill in finding a way out of the crisis. I'm encouraged by the fact that a document will be initialed after your next meeting at the American embassy. I hope calm will be restored. I'm told that the document will be signed tomorrow at Sharm el-Sheik with the Egyptian president standing by.

I want to express my admiration and support for Secretary Albright's efforts, and I am pleased with the remarkable job she has done here in Paris. We can all be pleased with the results. We must do all we can to get back to the peace process.

I know that you've done a lot of work these past few weeks under the auspices of President Clinton, and we should be able to establish a mechanism guaranteeing cooperation in matters of security. As for the international commission, it would be desirable for the secretary general of the United Nations to define and organize it.

The incident of September 28 must be the object of an investigation. An explanation must be offered to local and international public opinion. Reality must be faced without fear. When there is an accident, it must be acknowledged, and an investigation must follow. This is the voice of reason.

Kofi Annan: I've been in contact with all the parties. The accord that has just been reached is a good one. The violence and bloodbath must be stopped, and I am prepared to encourage this process.

Madeleine Albright: It's time for us to leave for the American embassy to initial the document. Dennis Ross and his team are putting the final touches to it.

As she leaves, Albright discreetly whispers a few words to Chirac on the doorstep of the Elysée. A few minutes later, Chirac speaks to Arafat and Leila Shahid. Shahid translates his question: "Are you ready to sign the document this very night?"

Arafat does not reply. He is tense, and, instead of going to the American embassy, orders his driver to take him to his hotel. During the ride, he says to Shahid: "Did you see the trick Albright pulled? She knows—I told her—that I want to sign in the presence of Hosni Mubarak." When he gets to his suite, Arafat sends Nabil Shaath and Saeb Erekat to the American embassy to work on the draft of the text that is to be signed the next day in Egypt.

The Paris summit has just failed. Madeleine Albright had asked Jacques Chirac to persuade Arafat to sign the accord that evening, not just to initial it as planned. Arafat saw this as a maneuver to impose a text on him that did not provide for the composition of the commission of inquiry.

The Israelis, who are waiting in Rue du Faubourg-Saint-Honoré, know nothing of this and suspect that Chirac is urging Arafat not to sign. Albright, who also has no idea why Arafat has not joined her, is irritated: "We'll never get to Sharm el-Sheik if that guy doesn't come here and sign! He thinks we're puppets."

At 2 A.M., Dennis Ross goes to see what is happening. He comes back at 4 o'clock and reports: "The Palestinians will stand by all their commitments in the domain of security, as they announced orally. They may have a problem accepting things in a written document. They may think they'll get more at Sharm el-Sheik."

Barak is furious: "I won't go to Sharm el-Sheik unless the Palestinians observe, on the ground, the commitments Arafat made."

When they leave, the Israeli delegation wrongly accuses Jacques Chirac of anti-Semitism that prevented the conclusion of the cease-fire the Jewish state needs so badly.

SHARM EL-SHEIK

October 5 is another day of violence. In Jerusalem, Palestinians shoot from Beit Jalla at Gilo, a Jewish district built on land occupied in 1967. At Netzarim, two Palestinians are killed, as are two others in the southern part of Jerusalem.

Meanwhile, Madeleine Albright and Yasir Arafat have been holding talks with President Mubarak at Sharm el-Sheik. As long as Barak is absent, none of this can make very much of a difference.

The next day, a Friday, new protests break out on the Plaza of the Mosques. This time, the police keep their distance. The demonstrators confront border guards and policemen outside the holy site. A police station is set on fire. One young Palestinian is killed. The clashes are equally violent on the West Bank and in Gaza, where eight Palestinians fall under Israeli bullets. On the border with Lebanon, tension mounts again: three Israeli soldiers have been kidnapped by Hezbollah and taken to Lebanon. The United Nations Security Council has voted a resolution "condemning the excessive use of force against the Palestinians," with the United States abstaining. Ehud Barak issues an ultimatum to the Palestinians: "If the riots have not stopped in forty-eight hours, Israel will consider the peace process dead and will take the measures necessary to restore order."

In the evening, enraged by scenes of the destruction of Joseph's Tomb in Nablus, several hundred Israeli demonstrators damage an abandoned mosque in Tiberias. In the course of the night, the unit besieged in Joseph's Tomb is evacuated by helicopter. And, as dawn breaks, a crowd demolishes the building, stone by stone.

October 9 is the fast day of Yom Kippur. The most violent confrontations occur at Nazareth, where Jews are struggling alongside the police to suppress the demonstrations of their Arab fellow citizens. There are two casualties, both Arabs.

Kofi Annan arrives in Israel in an attempt at mediation, and Barak agrees to extend his ultimatum. No date is set.

On October 10 and 11, the intensity of the confrontations seems to diminish. But on the 12th there is a disaster. Two Israeli reservists, Yosef Avrahami, 38, and Vadim Novesche, 33, lose their way and end up in the center of Ramallah. They are arrested by Palestinian policemen and taken to the police station near the central square. The news of their capture spreads quickly, and hundreds of angry young Palestinians gather in front of the building. They soon force their way in, and, with the help of some policemen, make their way to the room where the two men are being held. Some officers try to protect them but are shoved aside. This is a lynching. The Israelis are murdered. One of the bodies is thrown out the window and stomped on. The rioters, who are especially concerned that Tsahal not be able to identify them from the pictures being taken on the spot, attack the foreign television crews filming the scene. Videocassettes are seized, all except one from an Italian reporter. The video sequence will open television news programs all over the world.

Ehud Barak decides to react immediately. The Autonomous Authority was supposed to ensure the safety of the two men: it will pay the price for these murders. Combat helicopters shoot several missiles at the police station where the drama had unfolded, as well at other targets in Ramallah and Gaza. Fearing the bombardments, several prison wardens free their inmates, an act that greatly distresses the security services, who have to watch the most dangerous Islamists going free.

On October 14, after a number of contacts with the American administration and with President Mubarak, Yasir Arafat and Ehud Barak agree in principle on a new summit. Gilead Sher, who has just been appointed to head Barak's cabinet, reports his confusion in the face of a situation that is growing worse day by day: "I haven't spoken with my friend, Saeb Erekat, these past few days, because I can't talk to him when he's accusing me, on television, of committing genocide. . . . I'm very disappointed in the Palestinian [leaders]. Earlier on they didn't want to take control of the streets; now I'm not sure they're able to do so."[165]

The summit begins on October 16, 2000 at Sharm el-Sheik. King Abdallah of Jordan, Bill Clinton, and Kofi Annan are present alongside Hosni Mubarak. Arafat has been having problems with Mohammed Dahlan, head of security in Gaza, who is protesting the attitude of the Israeli army and refuses to come. As an exception, therefore, Yasir Abed Rabbo, the minister of culture and information, will participate in the negotiations on security issues: Arafat has named him a temporary general for two days. Abed Rabbo and Jibril Rajoub sit opposite Avraham Diechter, the head of Shin Bet, and General Shlomo Yanai, head of planning.

The meeting is chaired by George Tenet of the CIA and Omar Sliman, who is in charge of Egyptian special services. Abed Rabbo will later report as follows:

---

165. Videotaped interview with Gilead Sher, October 14, 2000, Jerusalem.

I am handed a working document and told that it's an "American–Egyptian" project. I glance at it and find that it is, in fact, an Israeli document. According to this text, Chairman Arafat was supposed to proclaim the end of the violence, ask his people to stop all acts of violence. The Israeli army would not conduct any reprisals, would no longer use combat helicopters. On the ground, buffer zones between the warring parties would be specified. . . .

[So] this would be done at our expense. All the clashes, after all, are occurring at the entrances to our towns. . . . Before Sliman and Tenet could begin their explanations, I told them, "Sorry, but I have a comment. I reject this document and will absolutely not discuss it." Sliman insisted, and I said, "No way. If this paper is the basis for the discussion, I'm getting up and leaving."

Then I turn to the Israelis and ask, "What do you think of this document?" They say, "We want to add two demands: the collection of weapons from the Tanzim and the arrest of the Ramallah murderers." "Anything else?" "No," they say. Then I turn to Tenet and say, "This isn't right. The Israeli delegation has obviously examined your document and studied it before coming here. You've been acting in concert with the Israelis. Don't play that game with us."[166]

During this time, the political committee has been meeting under the co-leadership of Madeleine Albright and Miguel Moratinos, the European emissary to the Middle East. Things are not going well. Shlomo Ben Ami rejects the idea of an international commission of inquiry. Saeb Erekat refers to precedents; he mentions Rwanda among other cases. Whereupon Ben Ami gets up and explodes:

---

166. Videotaped interview with Yasir Abed Rabbo, October 24, 2000, Ramallah.

"Are you accusing us of genocide? How can you?" Erekat also gets up and likewise raises his voice: "Watch what you're doing. . . ." "We're not on CNN here," Ben Ami replies, "so you don't need to ham it up!" The two men are about to come to blows. Madeleine Albright seems to be paralyzed in her chair. Moratinos intervenes and separates the belligerents.

The leaders spend the day in bilateral contacts. After a night of discussions, and with the active support of Javier Solana, the European Union's senior representative for foreign politics, who shuttles between the Israeli and Palestinian delegations, Bill Clinton concludes the accord. Each side has made concessions. The most important of these is that Ehud Barak has finally agreed to the establishment of an international commission of inquiry, as Arafat had demanded.

In the morning, Clinton convenes a plenary session of the conference. He makes a speech that constitutes the accord of Sharm el-Sheik, for no document will be signed:[167]

> [T]he greatest credit for the progress we have made today belongs to Prime Minister Barak and Chairman Arafat, who have had to overcome the difficulties of these last several days. And we all recognize that theirs was the primary decision to make.
>
> Our meeting has not been easy because the last two weeks have been so hard, with a tragic and terrible confrontation costing many lives and injuries, threatening everything that we have worked to achieve between Israelis and Palestinians and throughout the region over the past seven years now.
>
> Even as we meet, the situation in the territories remains tense. Yesterday again was violent.

---

167. The speech is reported verbatim.

This is a reminder of the urgency of breaking the cycle of violence. I believe we have made real progress today. Repairing the damage will take time and great effort by all of us.

When we leave here today, we will have to work hard to consolidate what we have agreed. Let me summarize what has been agreed so there will be no misunderstanding.

Our primary objective has been to end the current violence so we can begin again to resume our efforts towards peace. The leaders have agreed on three basic objectives and steps to realize them.

First, both sides have agreed to issue public statements unequivocally calling for an end of violence. They also agreed to take immediate, concrete measures to end the current confrontation, eliminate points of friction, ensure an end to violence and incitement, maintain calm, and prevent recurrence of recent events.

To accomplish this, both sides will act immediately to return the situation to that which existed prior to the current crisis, in areas such as restoring law and order, redeployment of forces, eliminating points of friction, enhancing security cooperation, and ending the closure and opening the Gaza airport. The United States will facilitate security cooperation between the parties as needed.

Second, the United States will develop with the Israelis and Palestinians, as well as in consultation with the United Nations Secretary General, a committee of fact-finding on the events of the past several weeks and how to prevent their recurrence. The committee's report will be shared by the US President with the UN Secretary General and the parties prior to publication. A final report shall be submitted under the auspices of the US President for publication.

Third, if we are to address the underlying roots of the Israeli–Palestinian conflict, there must be a pathway back to negotiations and a resumption of efforts to reach a permanent status agreement based on the UN Security Council Resolutions 242 and 338 and subsequent understandings. Toward this end, the leaders have agreed that the United States would consult with the parties within the next two weeks about how to move forward.

We have made important commitments here today against the backdrop of tragedy and crisis. We should have no illusions about the difficulties ahead.

If we are going to rebuild confidence and trust, we must all do our part, avoiding recrimination and moving forward. I'm counting on each of us to do everything we possibly can in the critical period ahead.

I am sure it will be a disappointment to some of you, but one of the things that all the leaders agreed was that our statement should stand on its own and we should begin by promoting reconciliation and avoiding conflict by forgoing questions today.

Thus a summit bringing together the head of the PLO, the Israeli prime minister, the presidents of the United States and Egypt, the king of Jordan, the secretary general of the United Nations, and the senior representative for foreign politics of the European Union ends with a speech by Bill Clinton. Not a single agreement is written down.

Back in Jerusalem, Ehud Barak orders an easing of the closure of Palestinian territories. From now on there will be less tension on the ground. But the Palestinians soon accuse the Israeli army of not fully implementing the accord. Certain checkpoints have not been removed. Orders from the political level are obviously not getting through. Not until 2002 will the story of this crisis between the Israeli government and its army leak out. As reported by Ben Kaspit in *Maariv*,

Ephraim Sneh, the deputy minister of defense, whom
Ehud Barak had put in charge of easing military measures
[against the Palestinians], has . . . found that clear written
orders from political circles, the government, or the prime
minister were for the most part blocked before they could
be carried out, or, worse, were not carried out to the letter, or, worst of all, were simply not carried out. . . .

The Israeli Defense Forces [IDF] had been getting ready
to confront the Intifada for years, and when it erupted they
vented their long frustration on the Palestinians, who did
not know what hit them. No one on either the Israeli or the
Palestinian side imagined that an event that, in the beginning, was supposed to be just a tough remake of the 1996
tunnel affair and would allow the Palestinians to demonstrate their attachment to their national struggle, would last
over two years and lead to thousands of deaths.

One hypothesis circulating in the government and the
defense community is that the IDF's destructive reaction,
the blows suffered by the Palestinians during the first weeks
of the Intifada, may have made the situation worse. "What's
wrong with you people?" the Palestinian leaders were asking their Israeli counterparts. "You're challenging everything we agreed on."

The IDF continued to open fire, especially with sharpshooters. The result was a balance sheet of death: the Palestinians had an overriding interest in causing Israeli losses,
equalizing the death toll, getting revenge.[168]

On October 19, a group of Israelis living in a nearby
settlement take a trip to Mount Grizim for a long-distance
view of Joseph's Tomb in Nablus. Palestinian fighters from
the nearby refugee camp think they are being attacked and
open fire on the bus and its accompanying patrol. The battle

---

168. Kaspit, 2002b, p. 9.

lasts five hours. One settler is killed, and several are hurt. One Palestinian will die in the hospital of a stomach wound. The next day, fighting will leave nine dead on the Palestinian side. Ehud Barak suspends contact with the Autonomous Authority.

Saeb Erekat comes to see me in Jerusalem:

My big fear is that Mr. Barak, as a Jewish prime minister, is wondering: "What will happen to me? Will I go down in history as someone who gave back Jerusalem, the West Bank, and Gaza? Or as someone who resisted, who gave nothing? But I have a third option: giving [the Palestinians] nothing and blaming them for the failure." I think this is Barak's strategy. I'm afraid because the worst hasn't happened yet. I'm afraid because I don't want the Israelis to elect someone who could kill more Palestinians and make us suffer even more. It's the fear you have when you've constructed a building and find that it's about to collapse.[169]

In Cairo, from October 21 to October 22, the Arab League meets in an extraordinary summit for the first time in five years. Heads of state and representatives of twenty-two Arab countries decide to suspend all regional economic cooperation with Israel and, in their final communiqué, do not mince words:

Israel has transformed the peace process into a war against the Palestinian people, using its military force to cordon off and isolate this population, holding it hostage on the West Bank and in Gaza. The summit hails the Intifada of the Palestinian people in the occupied Palestinian territories, [as an uprising] expressing bitterness

---

169. Videotaped interview with Saeb Erekat, October 20, 2000, Jerusalem.

and frustration after long years of waiting for a political settlement that has not borne fruit on account of Israel's intransigence and evasions. . . . Arab leaders consider the pure blood of the Palestinians to be the precious treasure of the liberation of the land. . . .

The summit pronounces in favor of the creation of an independent Palestinian State, with Jerusalem as its capital, the holy sites being placed under Palestinian sovereignty. In Israel, the minister of foreign affairs issues a statement denouncing the threat and warning against appeals to violence.

On October 24, I get a call from Saeb Erekat, who tells me: "You're going to interview me this afternoon around 4. You should also interview Yossi Beilin around the same time." Clearly, the Palestinian negotiator and the Israeli minister of justice have planned to do an end run around Barak's prohibition. Miguel Moratinos phones me a few minutes later. It was his idea to use interviews as a pretext for organizing a secret meeting in Jerusalem on the premises of France 2, French public television, the only place where the presence of the people in question will not arouse the curiosity of the press. (All the news services and most of the correspondents for television channels are located in the building where I have my office.) An hour later, Gilead Sher contacts me. He is going to see Saeb Erekat at around 6 P.M. Beilin must not be told of this.

The first meeting proceeds without a hitch. Yossi Beilin tells me:

My message to Saeb was that he should present our perspective on recent events to his people. We don't understand the Palestinians anymore. We don't understand why Arafat released the Hamas people from jail, and we don't understand why the Palestinian police are shooting at us. They don't understand why Sharon got permission to visit the Temple Mount, why Palestinians died there, why we're using so much firepower [against them]. There's real uncertainty and fear on both sides. We each have to try to understand the other side. At the end of this month of October 2000, we have two camps that are deathly afraid of one another. And fear leads to hatred. It's so easy to fear and to hate.[170]

An hour later, Saeb Erekat and Gilead Sher are in the CNN studio, where they take part in the same program, one after the other. In front of the journalists, they greet each other politely. After his portion of the program, Erekat says good-bye to his hosts and leaves. But instead of heading for the exit, he comes to my office on the fifth floor, where Sher soon joins him. The two men have a very long discussion, of which only Barak is informed.

IS ARAFAT GUILTY?

On October 30, the Israeli Knesset goes back into session. Ehud Barak makes a much-awaited speech:

We are not the ones who chose the path of violence. This, unfortunately, was the choice made by Yasir Arafat and the Palestinian leadership. We realize that we will have to pay a heavy price for peace. But we have never advocated peace at any price, a price of surrender. [We have never] agreed to all the demands of the other party. The Palestinians should know that we were ready to make some of their dreams come true, even at a heavy price. But they should [also] know that we too have dreams and vital interests that we will not give up: the security of Israel,

---

170. Videotaped interview with Yossi Beilin, October 24, 2000, Jerusalem.

the unity of Israel, and the holy places [of Judaism]. Since the Palestinians have decided to resort to violence, we are not dealing with a partner willing to make difficult decisions. In the name of the majority of the people of Israel, I am issuing an appeal to President Arafat: you should know that violence will get you nowhere. . . .

Ariel Sharon, the opposition leader, describes the dangers that, in his opinion, the country is facing:

> We are in a state of emergency. It would be important to form a cabinet of national emergency. It would be crucial to present to the outside world the image of a united and strong Israel. The Arab countries are uniting all around us. Threats are heard, coming from everywhere, and Israel seems weak despite its economic and military power. . . . In the course of my conversations with the prime minister, I've come to realize that he didn't intend to give up the ideas discussed at Camp David. I, for my part, cannot accept them. Imagine how hard things would be for us [today] if we had transferred part of the Old City to the Palestinians, as was proposed at Camp David. . . .

Thanks to an agreement reached with the ultra-Orthodox parties, Barak manages to avoid a vote on a new motion of censure. But his coalition is extremely fragile.

During the day, two Israelis are killed by Palestinians, and, in the evening, Tsahal helicopters bomb Fatah targets on the West Bank and in Gaza. The next day, at a loss for solutions, Barak agrees to let Shimon Peres try to negotiate a cease-fire with Arafat. And so, late in the evening of November 1, the Nobel prizewinner, accompanied by Gilead Sher, goes to meet Arafat in Gaza.

Barak has given him a very limited mandate. In the course of that night, Peres negotiates the implementation of the recent accord at Sharm el-Sheik. He gets back to Jerusalem very late. At 8 in the morning, Tsahal is to withdraw its tanks from the zones of tension. At 10, the people in charge of Israeli and Palestinian security will meet and resume their cooperation. Barak and Arafat will come to an agreement on the common announcement they are to issue at 2 P.M.

Everything indicates that a real cease-fire is on the horizon. But early in the morning the Palestinians claim that Israeli tanks have not been withdrawn everywhere. There are further incidents. Still, the announcement is being prepared, and Arafat convenes his cabinet in order to have the text approved. At 2 P.M., nothing has been announced. Barak and Arafat have a tense phone conversation. Arafat promises that the problem will be resolved in a matter of minutes. At 3, a booby-trapped car explodes near Jerusalem's Jewish market, Mahaneh Yehuda. There are two casualties, including the daughter of Yitzhak Levy, the chairman of the National Religious Party.

Jacques Chirac phones Barak, offering his condolences and telling him how urgent it is to resume the peace process. "This is intolerable," Barak replies. "That wasn't some salesclerk Arafat met with; it was Shimon Peres! I myself heard Arafat say: 'Six hours after the withdrawal of the tanks, we'll issue a declaration of cease-fire.' . . . Even more serious is the situation on the ground. We're under constant gunfire from Zone A. . . . Arafat's friends, like you, should tell him: 'We won't support you if you don't put an end to this violence!'"[171]

Several Palestinian leaders and heads of security then contact the Israelis: "The situation is extremely tense. We're doing what we can." In the past forty-eight hours, eight Palestinians have been killed on the West Bank and in Gaza. After the funerals, whole crowds have gone to confront the

---

171. Sher, 2001, p. 324.

Israeli army, and the Tanzim are becoming more and more active. In all, 165 people have lost their lives since the start of the Intifada.

The conflict on the ground is paralleled by a media battle. Faced with the disturbing pictures of Palestinian victims, Israeli authorities are eager to win over public opinion. The offensive is directed against Yasir Arafat personally, the party line being that he rejected "the Palestinian State generously offered by Ehud Barak" at the Camp David summit, thereby setting off a "war of liberation."

For long months to come, these accusations will distort the perception of events in the Middle East. For one thing, negotiations were not broken off at Camp David, which was only one stage in the peace process. Moreover, at no time was Arafat offered a Palestinian State on more than 91 percent of the West Bank and, at that, without recognition of his complete sovereignty over the Arab quarters of Jerusalem and the Haram al-Sharif/Temple Mount. This will come only later, in December, when Bill Clinton issues his final proposal, the one that was to have been submitted to the parties back in September.

Never, despite the claims of certain Jewish organizations, did the Palestinian negotiators demand the return to Israel of 3,000,000 refugees. The figures discussed in the course of the talks varied from several hundred to several thousand Palestinians to be allowed to return with Israel's authorization.

Nor was the Intifada triggered by Arafat. For more than a year, the head of Shin Bet, American diplomats, and Bill Clinton himself had been saying that they feared a spontaneous explosion of violence on the part of a Palestinian population enraged by the increasing number of settlements and checkpoints, and by their own diminished standard of living.

To be sure, Arafat was not displeased at the outbreak of the Intifada. It enabled him to regain a strategic advantage at a moment when his position had been considerably weakened by American and European support for Barak. And he thought the crisis would enable him to patch up Arab unity around the Palestinian cause.

Miguel Moratinos returns from Riyadh, where he met with Crown Prince Abdallah. "These were very difficult meetings," Moratinos will report:

> The Saudis have been very disappointed by [the negotiations in] these past three months. Nothing has been resolved, [they say]. They've been disappointed in the American administration, which was unable to get the results that had been anticipated. The Saudi leaders told me that, if the situation were to deteriorate, the stability of the entire region would of course be affected. Europe might face fluctuating oil prices. It would have consequences for the daily life of the Europeans.[172]

One month later, Terje Larsen, the United Nations coordinator in the Middle East, will issue a report on the effects of cordoning off Palestinian cities and territories: 110,000 people who worked in Israel have lost their jobs. The unemployment rate has reached 40 percent. More than 260,000 people are out of work on the West Bank and in Gaza, and 200,000 have lost their main source of income. A third of the population of the Palestinian territories is directly suffering from the impossibility of moving about freely. The poverty rate has increased 50 percent in three months. Between September 28 and November 9, 431 private dwellings, 13 public buildings, 10 factories or places of business, and 14 places of worship have been destroyed by the Israeli army. In addition, 69 orchards have been razed.

---

172. Videotaped interview with Miguel Moratinos, November 25, 2000, Tel Aviv.

On Election Day in the United States, Bill Clinton will name former senator George Mitchell to head the commission of inquiry into the events in the Middle East. It will include Souleyman Demirel, the former president of Turkey; Thorbjoern Jagland, the Norwegian foreign minister; and Javier Solana, the senior representative of the European Union for foreign relations.

CLINTON RISKS EVERYTHING

On November 9, Yasir Arafat meets with Bill Clinton in Washington. He tells the outgoing president that he wants to conclude an accord before Clinton leaves the White House in January 2001. Once again he sets forth his position. In East Jerusalem, all the Arab districts would be placed under Palestinian sovereignty, as would the Haram al-Sharif. Arafat also claims 98 percent of the West Bank. With regard to the right of return of the refugees, he says that the situation most urgently to be addressed is that of the Palestinians in Lebanon. Clinton understands that if this problem is resolved, especially by the international fund for the rehabilitation of refugees, the matter will be settled.

A few hours later, in Bethlehem, a combat helicopter fires two missiles at Atef Abayat, the local leader of the Tanzim; the Israelis had accused him of starting the shooting at Gilo. The same evening, Palestinians fire mortar shells at this Jewish quarter in the southern part of Jerusalem. The next day, Arafat calls for an international force to be set up in the Palestinian territories. He will present this demand to the UN Security Council in New York the day after that, without success. In the Palestinian territories, the death toll is mounting: seven killed on November 11, one on the 12th, three on the 13th.

Ehud Barak arrives in the United States three days later. Clinton tells him about his conversation with Arafat and confirms that Arafat is willing to accept an accord on this basis. Clinton believes that a solution can be found on the issue of the Temple Mount/Haram al-Sharif, and that the Palestinians will ultimately accept 95 percent of the West Bank if there is an exchange of territory to offset the area annexed by Israel. He suggests that the secret mission being conducted by Yossi Ginosar and Amnon Lipkin-Shahak be pursued with Arafat. This, he says, should be enough to bring about a cease-fire.

"Arafat," Barak replies, "is wrong in his analysis of Israel. There are things we can't do in the face of pressure and violence. That would represent a defeat, a surrender of Israel in the eyes of the Arab world. . . . At the Sharm el-Sheik summit, we heard Arafat accepting all the agreements, making promises. I sent Peres, Shahak, and Gilead to him, and no progress was made. We won't allow ourselves to be evicted from the West Bank and Gaza by force."[173]

The next day, November 13, the Israeli delegation learns that four Israelis have been killed by Palestinians in the last twenty-four hours. A total closure around Palestinian cities is once again imposed. On November 20, in the Gaza Strip, Palestinians fire mortar shells on a school bus from the Kfar Darom settlement: two pupils are killed and five maimed. For the first time, the Israeli air force uses F16 fighter planes to bomb buildings belonging to Fatah.

The Arab world sees this as a sign of escalation. Hosni Mubarak recalls his ambassador; when Mohamed Bassiouny leaves, the political scene in the Middle East loses one of the principal mediators of recent years, an advocate of peace and a man of great intelligence.

---

173. See also Sher, 2001, p. 327.

On November 22, Saeb Erekat tells me:

> Since my meeting in the France 2 office, I haven't met
> with any Israeli negotiators. They're dancing to the tune
> of Sharon's pipe and the pipe of the National Religious
> Party. On November 9, Clinton asked us if we were pre-
> pared to resume the talks with a view to a definitive accord.
> Arafat agreed. Barak refused. He demands that we first put
> an end to all violence. But violence can't be ended by re-
> mote control! We did all we could, but we don't even have
> a state. Barak should speak to the Palestinians and tell
> them: "You will have a state alongside Israel. This is our
> objective." The Palestinians would react accordingly.[174]

Two days later, Barak and Arafat have a phone conversation. Arafat is in Moscow, where he is holding meetings
with Vladimir Putin. On November 27, by a vote of 84 of
its 120 members, the Knesset passes a bill stating that it
must approve any territorial concession in Jerusalem by an
absolute majority of 61. In other words, given the balance
of power with the opposition on the right, Barak has no
chance of winning approval for an accord on Jerusalem.

The next day, feeling that he no longer has a choice, the
prime minister declares that he agrees on principle to early
elections. With 80 members voting, a bill to this effect is
promptly approved, 79 to 1. All that remains is to set the
date for the balloting. May 2002 is mentioned by some.
Gilead Sher tells me:

> What we're seeing now is a real effort on the part of
> the Palestinians to control the violence, to prevent it. The
> contacts Amnon Lipkin-Shahak and Israel Hasson are
> pursuing have to do with security only. At the present

---

174. Videotaped interview with Saeb Erekat, November 22, 2000, Jerusalem.

time, I don't believe we'll be able to conclude a comprehensive peace with the Palestinians. Over the last eighteen months we've heard everything and its opposite from them. Currently there are no secret contacts going on.[175]

BARAK RESIGNS, THE TALKS RESUME

December 9 is a Saturday. For several days, the polls have been looking bad for Ehud Barak. And if Benjamin Netanyahu declares his candidacy, he will definitely win: all the surveys are predicting a Netanyahu victory. How to block his path? Barak thinks he has found a way. If he resigns now, elections for the prime minister's office will have to be set in two months, in other words, before the elections to the Knesset. In this case, he would run against Ariel Sharon, the current opposition leader, an easier opponent to beat, Barak thinks. He consults his wife, Nava, and his brother-in-law. At 9 P.M. he holds a press conference and announces his decision. Most of his advisers, as well as the negotiators, think he is making a mistake: four months will be lost, during which an accord might be reached.

The next day, for the first time since September 27, the talks resume. A secret meeting takes place in a suite of the Hotel David Intercontinental in Tel Aviv.[176] The following morning, Yasir Abed Rabbo declares his optimism:

It happened at the Israelis' request. This time, and for the first time, I think they really want to conclude an accord, perhaps out of fear of a victory for the right in the coming elections. We should be able to finish up two or

---

175. Videotaped interview with Gilead Sher, October 14, 2000, Jerusalem.

176. Taking part are Shlomo Ben Ami, Gilead Sher, Israel Hasson, Yasir Abed Rabbo, Saeb Erekat, and Mohammed Dahlan.

three weeks from now. For the first time, they've accepted the principle of Palestinian sovereignty over the
Haram al-Sharif. The conversation took place in this
hotel near the Hassan Bek Mosque in Jaffa, where my
grandfather used to pray. Through the window, I could
see the colored lights that used to decorate the mosque
during Ramadan. I was moved, because I was going to
negotiate the definitive accord near this place where my
family had its roots.[177]

The news is sensational, but I am not able to broadcast
it, having agreed not to reveal anything about these interviews before the end of 2001. I rush to Tel Aviv, and, for
several hours, wait for Gilead Sher to leave the defense ministry, where he is accompanying Ehud Barak. Around
7 P.M., in his car, he sums up the situation: "I don't understand how the Palestinians could have believed we were
willing to give up sovereignty over the Temple Mount. I
never heard the prime minister say that, I've never said it,
and neither has anyone else." Then, after several remarks
interrupted by telephone calls, he continues: "The Palestinians should know that I am the only representative authorized by the prime minister."[178] After checking, it turns out
that this comment about the Temple Mount, which elicited
such a positive reaction from the Palestinian negotiators,
was made by Shlomo Ben Ami.

On November 14, there is a new meeting in Gaza, this
time in the villa of Mohammed Rashid, Arafat's financial
adviser.[179] The meeting gets off to a late start.

---

177. Videotaped interview with Yasir Abed Rabbo, December 13, 2000,
Ramallah.

178. Videotaped interview with Gilead Sher, December 13, 2000, Tel Aviv.

179. Present are Yasir Arafat, Shlomo Ben Ami, Yasir Abed Rabbo, Mohammed Rashid, Mohammed Dahlan, Saeb Erekat, Nabil Aburdeineh, Israel
Hasson, and Gilead Sher.

Ben Ami (to Arafat): Your relationship with Barak isn't good. But I want you to know that no one [no Israeli] before us, and perhaps after us, will go so far, so deep, in seeking an accord. We're pursuing the peace process despite our political problems. Even on the left, we're being accused of going too far. [You and we] are hostages, and we should be courageous in attacking the problems before us, like the issue of the Haram al-Sharif. It may be that, at Camp David, we weren't ready for that. . . . But we can't ignore the attacks by Hamas and Islamic Jihad. . . .

Arafat: Yes, we really do have very little time, and we should work quickly and seriously. The new American administration will need time to study the subject. It's been a very hard day today in Gaza.

In this day's clashes, four Palestinians have died: one in Gaza, three on the West Bank. Arafat and Ben Ami get up and go into an adjoining room. For about twenty minutes, they talk behind closed doors. According to the Palestinians, Ben Ami repeated to Arafat what he had told Yasir Abed Rabbo, namely that they would have sovereignty over the Temple Mount/Haram al-Sharif. Gilead Sher and Israel Hasson, who already have their suspicions, will find this confirmed during the following negotiations. Ehud Barak has officially forbidden this concession that, the Palestinians maintain, would have ended the deadlock. And, according to an Israeli negotiator, this initiative on Ben Ami's part caused problems for the rest of the talks, since Arafat and his representatives were sure they would ultimately get what the head of Israeli diplomacy had let slip.

The meetings continue in Tel Aviv. On December 17, two Fatah militants are killed on the West Bank. The movement blames Israel and promises to avenge them. The next day, Amnon Lipkin-Shahak reports on his conversations with Yasir Arafat during a meeting of the "peace cabinet," the ministers close to the peace process:

Arafat wants an agreement. I think he's willing to do what's necessary to reach one. But I have the impression that his negotiating team isn't telling him everything, that he doesn't have a full overview of the talks. The daily "liquidations" of the Fatah people are having a very negative effect on the Palestinians. This makes it impossible for there to be a dialogue with those [of the Palestinians] who would be ready for one.[180]

For Gilead Sher,

two groups are facing off against one another within Fatah. The hard-liners, encouraged by the Israeli withdrawal from Lebanon, are trying to draw Israel into more and more radical reprisals, so as to put the Palestinian issue at the top of the news. They think the senior members and the old guard are traitors. The other group is led by Marwan Barghouti and his men, who hold to a relatively moderate line at the same time as they keep up the violence in the territories, but only in the territories. And the Islamists are threatening Arafat with assassination if he tries to stop the Intifada.

THE AMERICAN PROPOSAL COMES TOO LATE

Dennis Ross has negotiated the continuation of Israeli–Palestinian meetings, this time at Bolling Air Force Base near Washington. He had met with Yasir Arafat in Mo-

---

180. Sher, 2001, p. 351.

rocco, where the head of the PLO was on an official visit. Bill Clinton has been having phone conversations with Arafat and Barak.

The delegates arrive in Washington on December 19. The negotiations are difficult. Both the Israelis and the Palestinians know that Bill Clinton is getting ready to make his proposals for resolution of the conflict. It's just a matter of time. The Bolling discussions are apparently intended to help the peace team determine certain parameters of those proposals.

On the Israeli side, there is a crisis: Israel Hasson does not appreciate the concessions Ben Ami is making to the Palestinians, obviously without Barak's authorization. He has threatened to resign and will not play a large role in the discussions. One evening, he comes downstairs to the meeting room and asks to be allowed to put questions in Arabic. He suggests the following formula to the Palestinians: "You will have sovereignty over the Haram al-Sharif, but we will write these words into the accord: 'We know that the Jews maintain they have a religious connection to what they regard as the Temple Mount.' You don't recognize anything! All you have to do is mention our position, without taking sides!" The Palestinians refuse. Hasson leaves in disgust.

On December 23, 2000, everyone is summoned to the White House. Bill Clinton presents his final proposal to the Israelis and the Palestinians.[181] He reads the text straight out, as follows verbatim:

---

181. Present are Madeleine Albright, John Podesta, Sandy Berger, Steven Richetti, Bruce Reidel, Dennis Ross, Aaron Miller, Robert Malley, Gamal Hillal, Saeb Erekat, Mohammed Dahlan, Samih el-Abed, Gaith el-Omari, Shlomo Ben Ami, Gilead Sher, Pini Medan, Shlomo Yanai, and Gidi Grinstein. On the Clinton plan see Quandt, 2001, p. 371 and the documents reproduced as Appendix 2, AA, and AB on http://www.brook.edu/dybdocroot/press/appendix/peace_process.htm.

Territory:

Based on what I heard, I believe that the solution should be in the mid-90%'s, between 94–96% of the West Bank territory of the Palestinian State.

The land annexed by Israel should be compensated by a land swap of 1–3% in addition to territorial arrangements such as a permanent safe passage.

The Parties should also consider the swap of leased land to meet their respective needs. There are creative ways for doing this that should address Palestinian and Israeli needs and concerns.

The Parties should develop a map consistent with the following criteria:

80% of settlers in blocks.

Contiguity.

Minimize annexed areas.

Minimize the number of Palestinians affected.

Security:

The key to security lies in an international presence that can only be withdrawn by mutual consent. This presence will also monitor the implementation of the agreement between both sides.

My best judgment is that the Israeli withdrawal should be carried out over 36 months while international force is gradually introduced in the area. At the end of this period, a small Israeli presence would remain in fixed locations in the Jordan Valley under the authority of the international force for another 36 months. This period could be reduced in the event of favorable regional developments that diminish the threats to Israel.

On early warning stations, Israel should maintain three facilities in the West Bank with a Palestinian liaison presence. The stations will be subject to review after 10 years with any changes in status to be mutually agreed.

Regarding emergency deployments, I understand that you still have to develop a map of the relevant areas and routes. But in defining what is an emergency, I propose the following definition:

Imminent and demonstrable threat to Israel's national security of a military nature that requires the activation of a national state of emergency.

Of course, the international forces will need to be notified of any such determination.

On airspace, I suggest that the state of Palestine will have sovereignty over its airspace but that the two sides should work out special arrangements for Israeli training and operational needs.

I understand that the Israeli position is that Palestine should be defined as a "demilitarized state" while the Palestinian side proposes "a state with limited arms." As a compromise, I suggest calling it a "non-militarized state."

This will be consistent with the fact that in addition to a strong Palestinian security force, Palestine will have an international force for border security and deterrence purposes.

Jerusalem and Refugees:

I have a sense that the remaining gaps have more to do with formulations than practical realities.

Jerusalem:

The general principle is that Arab areas are Palestinian and Jewish ones are Israeli. This would apply to the Old City as well. I urge the two sides to work on maps to create maximum contiguity for both sides.

Regarding the Haram/Temple Mount, I believe that the gaps are not related to practical administration but to the symbolic issues of sovereignty and to finding a way to accord respect to the religious beliefs of both sides.

I know you have been discussing a number of formulations, and you can agree on any of these. I add to these two additional formulations guaranteeing Palestinian effective control over the Haram while respecting the conviction of the Jewish people. Regarding either one of these two formulations will be international monitoring to provide mutual confidence.

1. Palestinian sovereignty over the Haram and Israeli sovereignty over [the Western Wall and the space sacred to Judaism of which it is a part] [the Western Wall and the Holy of Holies of which it is a part].

There will be a firm commitment by both not to excavate beneath the Haram or behind the Wall.

2. Palestinian shared sovereignty over the Haram and Israeli sovereignty over the Western Wall and shared functional sovereignty over the issue of excavation under the Haram and behind the Wall as that mutual consent would be requested before any excavation can take place.

Refugees:

I sense that the differences are more relating to formulations and less to what will happen on a practical level.

I believe that Israel is prepared to acknowledge the moral and material suffering caused to the Palestinian people as a result of the 1948 war and the need to assist the international community in addressing the problem.

An international commission should be established to implement all the aspects that flow from your agreement: compensation, resettlement, rehabilitation, etc.

The US is prepared to lead an international effort to help the refugees.

The fundamental gap is on how to handle the concept of the right to return. I know the history of the issue and how hard it will be for the Palestinian leadership to appear to be abandoning this principle.

The Israeli side could not accept any reference to a right of return that would imply a right to immigrate to Israel in defiance of Israel's sovereign policies on admission or that would threaten the Jewish character of the state.

Any solution must address both needs.

The solution will have to be consistent with the two-state approach that both sides have accepted as the way to end the Palestinian–Israeli conflict: the state of Palestine as the homeland of the Palestinian people and the state of Israel as the homeland of the Jewish people.

Under the two-state solution, the guiding principle should be that the Palestinian state will be the focal point for Palestinians who choose to return to the area without ruling out that Israel will accept some of these refugees.

I believe that we need to adopt a formulation on the right of return that will make clear that there is no specific right of return to Israel itself but that does not negate the aspiration of the Palestinian people to return to the area.

In light of the above, I propose two alternatives:

1. Both sides recognize the right of Palestinian refugees to return to Historic Palestine. Or,
2. Both sides recognize the right of the Palestinian refugees to return to their Homeland.

The agreement will define the implementation of this general right in a way that is consistent with the two-state solution. It would list the five possible final homes for the refugees:

1. The state of Palestine
2. Areas in Israel being transferred to Palestine in the land swap
3. Rehabilitation in a host country
4. Resettlement in a third country
5. Admission to Israel

In listing these options, the agreement will make clear that the return to the West Bank, Gaza Strip, and the areas acquired in the land swap would be a right to all Palestinian refugees.

While rehabilitation in host countries, resettlement in third countries and absorption into Israel will depend upon the policies of those countries.

Israel could indicate in the agreement that it intends to establish a policy so that some of the refugees would be absorbed into Israel consistent with Israel's sovereign decision.

I believe that priority should be given to the refugee population in Lebanon.

The parties would agree that this implements Resolution 194.

I propose that the agreement clearly mark the end of the conflict and its implementation put an end to all its claims. This could be implemented through a UN Security Council Resolution that notes that Resolutions 242 and 338 have been implemented through the release of Palestinian prisoners.

I believe that this is the outline of a fair and lasting agreement.

It gives the Palestinian people the ability to determine their future on their own land, a sovereign and viable state recognized by the international community, Al-Qods as its capital, sovereignty over the Haram, and new lives for the refugees.

It gives the people of Israel a genuine end to the conflict, real security, the preservation of sacred religious ties, the incorporation of 80% of the settlers into Israel, and the largest Jewish Jerusalem in history recognized by all as its capital.

This is the best that I can do. Brief your leaders and tell me if they are prepared to come for discussions based on these ideas. If so, I would meet them next week separately. If not, I have taken this as far as I can.

These are my ideas. If they are not accepted, they are not just off the table, they also go with me when I leave office.

After the meeting, Israel Hasson flings a question at the peace team: "Why so late? Everything would have been different if you'd submitted this proposal in September or at Camp David!" Several of Clinton's advisers look at him approvingly.

TABA

The Israelis return to Tel Aviv, certain that an accord is imminent. Shlomo Ben Ami is delighted. With a cease-fire at stake, he is sure that the February 6 election will turn into a referendum for peace. The "peace cabinet" therefore decides to accept Clinton's proposals as the basis for negotiations, but only on condition that Arafat do likewise. The ball is in the Palestinians' court. Time is of the essence. If Arafat says yes, a new summit can be organized very quickly, at Sharm el-Sheik, for example, with the heads of state of the moderate Arab countries and, of course, the president of the United States.

On December 28, the Israeli government as a whole approves the cabinet's decision. From Gaza, Arafat replies to Clinton on this same day. He thanks the president for his efforts and asks him to clarify and explain the basis for his initiative:

I need clear answers on a number of questions concerning the percentage of territories that would be annexed and exchanged; their exact location; the precise demarcation of the Wailing Wall, its boundaries and extensions; the consequences this would have for the notion of complete Palestinian sovereignty over the Haram al-Sharif.

It is our understanding that the idea of leasing additional territories is an option we have the right to reject, and that it is not included in your proposal. It is also our understanding that the zones of emergency Israeli deployment [on Palestinian territory] should also be negotiated and receive our approval. I hope your position is the same [as ours] on this matter.

I have a number of questions concerning the return of the refugees to their homes and towns. We have had a negative experience on this issue, during the interim period, with the return to the West Bank and Gaza of displaced Palestinians. Because the terms [of the return] depended entirely on an Israeli veto, not one single refugee was allowed to return in the context of the interim accord. A committee composed of Israeli, Egyptian, Jordanian, and Palestinian representatives was supposed to decide on such returns. Likewise, matters are not very clear on the subject of the compensation of the refugees for the land, property, and sums of money seized by Israel under the aegis of the Israeli administration of abandoned properties.

Mr. President, I think the periods you specify for the carrying out of the Israeli withdrawal are too long. They would give the enemies of peace the opportunity to undo the accord. Can the periods you envision in your proposal be modified?

Mr. President, I have a number of questions. I need details, clarifications, and maps to help me make the necessary decisions with my leaders and my people.

I hope you understand that I do not want to lose time. We need you in order to reach a just and lasting peace, thanks to your efforts and under your presidency.

Arafat ends his letter by stating that he is ready to go to
the White House as soon as possible. He then heads for
Sharm el-Sheik to consult with Hosni Mubarak. Mubarak
says he is waiting for the Israeli negotiators and asks Saeb
Erekat to remain. His conversation over, Arafat leaves.

Gilead Sher, Israel Hasson, and General Shlomo Yanai
arrive. Erekat does not attend this meeting but waits, alone,
in an adjoining room. Mubarak is assisted by Foreign Minister Amr Moussa and General Omar Sliman, the head of
special services. For three hours, the Israelis set forth their
positions, Sher and Yanai in English, Hasson in Arabic.
Maps of Jerusalem are analyzed in detail. Amr Moussa asks
what "the sacred space for Judaism behind the Western
Wall" is. Sher replies that this is a space beneath the Haram
whose exact location is unknown.

Mubarak says that, according to the map he was given of
the West Bank, the Israelis want to annex 8 percent of this
territory. Yanai tells him that Israel is willing to move its
position closer to the one set forth by Clinton: annexing
6 percent and leasing 2 percent for a given period. According to Saeb Erekat, who will be told the details of the discussion later on, the Israelis agree in principle to offset this
annexation by giving the Palestinians territories representing 3 percent of the area of the West Bank. Access to Jerusalem remains a problem. Nonetheless, the Egyptians tell the
Israelis that they are impressed by what they are hearing.

Omar Sliman invites everyone to dinner. In the restaurant, they find Saeb Erekat, who is having coffee at Sliman's
table.

But a few hours later, after taking another look at the
Israeli position and holding a phone conference with Arafat,
the Egyptian leaders contact the peace team in Washington.
Arafat believes that Barak is moving away from the Clinton
parameters allocating 94 to 96 percent of the West Bank to

the Palestinians and is instead asking for 8 percent of this territory. The Americans reply that the Palestinians are not obliged to go along with either the leasing or the swap requested by the Israelis. This discussion will delay Arafat's acceptance of Clinton's proposal.

On December 29, the Israeli army enters the political debate. During a meeting with the security cabinet, the chief of staff, General Shaul Mofaz, criticizes the American peace plan in no uncertain terms. Tsahal, he says, will not be able to defend the country against a threat from the east if it does not control the Jordan Valley: Israel should retain control of a security zone 15 kilometers wide in this sector. (This is Ariel Sharon's position as well.) Moreover, he says, "the settlements that will be landlocked within Palestinian territory will be very hard to defend. The Clinton plan leaves Israel very vulnerable. For security reasons, it must be rejected." This statement is published in the press, right in the middle of the electoral campaign.

At year's end, the balance sheet is dismal. Since the beginning of the Intifada, 279 Palestinians and 41 Israelis have been killed.[182] Thousands have been wounded. Suicide bombings have begun again, creating massive insecurity among Israelis already convinced that Arafat is wholly to blame for the crisis. The peace camp has been splintered. Only the Peace Now movement is trying to issue statements. They reveal that, in the past year, 6,045 housing units have been built in the settlements, the highest number since 1992. This means that Ehud Barak is the prime minister who, after Yitzhak Shamir, has most strongly promoted the settlements. He is also the one who has gone furthest in negotiations with the Palestinians.

---

182. B'tselem, the Israeli Information Center for Human Rights in the Occupied Territories. See http://www.btselem.org/.

Still believing that the Israelis want to annex 8 percent of the West Bank, Arafat hesitates to give his consent to the Clinton parameters. The Americans ask all friendly heads of state, government leaders, and foreign ministers of Europe and Asia who have relations with the PLO to intervene. Arafat's telephone is ringing off the hook. Even on New Year's Eve, a tipsy European prime minister advises him to say yes to Clinton's proposals. "Have you seen them?" Arafat asks. "No," his interlocutor replies, "but accept them!"

On January 1, 2001, Javier Solana and Miguel Moratinos come to deal personally with the problem. While they are talking with Arafat in his Gaza office, there is a phone call from Clinton. Arafat agrees to go to Washington to explain his reservations. He takes a plane later that morning. While they await his return, the two diplomats go to Barak's house in Jerusalem. At midnight, Barak and Clinton have a difficult phone conversation. Their raised voices can be heard out in the yard.

Clinton: Arafat wants to conclude an accord before I leave the White House. He wants to continue the negotiation.

Barak: Arafat is fueling the violence. It's being carried out by his security services. He wants to extort an internationalization of the conflict and new concessions from the two of us. I have to tell my public the truth. I have no intention of concluding any accord before the elections. . . .

The conversation with Solana and Moratinos is in the same vein.

I learn that the Palestinians are making a huge strategic mistake. Despite all the polls, they do not believe that Ariel Sharon will win the election. In Ramallah, Yasir Abed Rabbo tells me, "The Israelis won't elect the man who was responsible for Sabra and Shatila! What would they look like?" The Palestinians also seem to have great expectations for the new American administration. Several negotiators remind me of the pressure the first George Bush put on Yitzhak Shamir in 1991. And besides, they say, the Bush family is close to the oil interests and, therefore, to the Arabs.

Forty-eight hours later, the press in the United States announces that Yasir Arafat has responded positively to Clinton. The news will be denied in various ways. But, for now, Dennis Ross and Bill Clinton tell the Israelis that Arafat "can live with" Clinton's parameters. Barak wants more details and sends Gilead Sher to get them. Sher meets with Clinton and the members of the peace team, who confirm Arafat's agreement.

Sher then has a secret meeting with Mohammed Rashid, Arafat's adviser. He begins by issuing a warning: "The future of relations between our two peoples depends on your chairman's willingness to fight terrorism and violence. . . ." "Arafat," Rashid replies, "is ready to conclude an accord. He intends to make the necessary concessions. He understands perfectly. He's actually given up the right of return. All he needs now is something that will allow him to save face before the Arab world and his people. The territorial problem, especially, worries him. He should get clarifications on the maps, and proof that Palestine will not be fragmented. That will satisfy him. . . ."

The two men look closely at certain aspects of the accord under discussion. When Rashid leaves, he says that the Palestinians are perfectly aware that the failure of the negotiations could have consequences as serious for them as the lost opportunity in 1947.

Meanwhile, on January 7 in Cairo, George Tenet is chairing a meeting of the heads of security on both sides. An accord, the "Cairo Understanding," is reached:

(1) The two parties agree to an immediate resumption of anti-terrorist cooperation. Information about threats should be immediately transmitted and dealt with by both parties. Individuals suspected of plotting or participating in terrorist activities will be arrested.

(2) The Autonomous Authority must take immediate measures to stop, or permit a stop to be put to, shooting from Zones A, B, and C. Action and public statements are called for immediately.

(3) The Israeli services must take similar measures to stop the violence against the Palestinians. Action and public statements are called for immediately.

(4) Israel will open the main road in the Gaza Strip, the Rafah border post, and Gaza Airport on January 10. The Allenby Bridge [over the Jordan river] will be open on January 10, and those who hold VIP cards[183] will once again have freedom of movement. . . .

The agreement provides for the start of negotiations on January 14 to end the closure of all Palestinian cities. This measure will remain a dead letter: on the ground, violent clashes are continuing.

Sher returns to Israel, where he presents the results of his mission to the "peace cabinet." It is unanimously agreed that negotiations must continue so as to arrive at a joint declaration, the embryo of an accord that would enable the next administration to return to the path of peace. Yossi Ginosar, Yossi Beilin, and the head of Meretz, Yossi Sarid, who is taking part in the discussions even though he has resigned from his position as education minister, advise Barak to meet with Arafat.

The prime minister is undecided. In the midst of an elec-

---

183. These cards, given to Palestinian leaders and senior officers, allow them to pass freely through all Israeli checkpoints.

toral campaign, he thinks this might cost him still more points: all the polls are predicting a victory for Sharon. Nevertheless, marathon negotiations are planned.

On January 11, Yasir Abed Rabbo declares that Israel "is committing war crimes," and that "Barak should be brought before an international tribunal."

At midnight, the negotiators[184] meet at the Erez checkpoint. The Israelis refuse to begin the discussion until Abed Rabbo apologizes. After an hour of back-and-forth, Abu Ala says, "We withdraw Abed Rabbo's accusations." Sher finds that the Americans have not given him an accurate account of Arafat's replies to Clinton's proposal; they were, in fact, negative on several points. Erekat confirms this.[185]

The following day, January 13, the negotiators meet again at Barak's house. Barak does not think an agreement will be reached in the next few days. Lipkin-Shahak and Sher believe that an attempt must be made "to bring Arafat into the Clinton parameters." In the evening, Peres, Ben Ami, Lipkin-Shahak, and Sher go to meet with Yasir Arafat in Gaza. Mohammed Rashid, Abu Ala, Yasir Abed Rabbo, and Saeb Erekat are at Arafat's side. These are the Palestinians who are organizing the convoy between the Erez checkpoint and Arafat's office, and, because of the tension between Peres and Ben Ami, they make sure not to seat the two men in the same car.

Arafat: We have to do something before Clinton leaves. We've got six or seven days. . . . We won't stop nego-

---

184. Yasir Abed Rabbo, Abu Ala, Saeb Erekat, Amnon Lipkin-Shahak, Gilead Sher, and Shlomo Ben Ami.

185. According to Robert Malley, Arafat was afraid that, in the absence of an accord, he would be bound by "the Clinton parameters," with international resolutions retreating into the background. With a view toward future negotiations, Arafat preferred to keep the umbrella of the international resolutions instead of agreeing to the American proposals.

tiating after January 20, but at least he'll be able to say to his successor, "Here is my [peace] plan."

Ben Ami: We've learned that certain elements you're contesting aren't in the Clinton parameters. Under these circumstances, I don't think it's possible to conclude an accord in the time we have left.

Arafat: In their day, Begin and Sadat discussed everything!

The negotiation begins after dinner. Peres and Arafat have a private conversation and then rejoin the negotiators. But twenty minutes later, to the Israelis' great surprise, Shimon Peres announces that the session is over. The delegations will meet the next day, in a Jerusalem hotel.

January 15: in the Mawassi sector of Gaza, a Palestinian enclave in the Gush Katif settlement block, some settlers, enraged by the murder of one of their own, attack a town, burning houses and cars and destroying a plantation. The scene is filmed by Israeli television. This is also the day Ariel Sharon has chosen to pay a visit to the Negev, where the negotiators are considering the transfer of the Halutza sector to the Palestinians in the context of a possible exchange of territories. With heavy media coverage, the right-wing candidate declares that, as far as he is concerned, he will not give up an inch of Israeli territory: "The Jordan Valley must remain under Israeli control, the same goes for other security zones in Judea–Samaria, and Jerusalem is the eternal capital of Israel. No concession is possible here."

The next day, Barak convenes his cabinet and announces that he is going to proclaim the failure of the peace process. Lipkin-Shahak and other ministers protest vehemently: "That will just fuel the violence," they say. On January 17, Shlomo Ben Ami meets with Arafat in Cairo. He persuades Arafat to agree to marathon negotiations at Taba in Egypt, near the Israeli town of Eilat. Ehud Barak gives the go-ahead from his side.

The Taba negotiations begin on January 18, 2001. For the first time since Ehud Barak came to power, the Palestinians have the full "peace cabinet" opposite them: Shlomo Ben Ami, Amnon Lipkin-Shahak, Yossi Beilin, and Yossi Sarid, assisted by Gilead Sher, Israel Hasson, Pini Medan, and Avraham Diechter. Arafat's delegation consists of Yasir Abed Rabbo, Nabil Shaath, Hassan Asfur, and Mohammed Dahlan.

But no Americans are present at these negotiations. George W. Bush, the new president, and Secretary of State Colin Powell have decided not to get involved with the Middle East—at least not now. It is the European Union that lends a hand, in the person of Miguel Moratinos. Revenge is sweet: Moratinos will agree to keep certain American diplomats on the scene informed of the proceedings.

Two committees are formed. One will look at all the topics with the exception of the refugee problem, which will be discussed by the second committee, consisting of Yossi Beilin and Nabil Shaath.

Ehud Barak, worried about concessions his representatives might make, phones Sher and dictates a firm message to Shlomo Ben Ami and Amnon Lipkin-Shahak: "Whatever territorial combinations you discuss, we must keep 8 percent of the West Bank, including, if necessary, territories leased to the Palestinians for a certain period. When you talk about the exchange of territories, don't mention the Halutza dunes in the Negev."

On January 22, the positions seem to be moving closer together. The two parties present maps. The territorial limits of the Palestinian State are taking form. According to Yossi Beilin, the discussion on the refugees is also coming along well.

But the next day, the 23rd, two Israeli restaurant owners are murdered in Tulkarm. Barak decides to suspend the talks and recall part of his delegation to Jerusalem.

Twenty-four hours later, Israel Hasson takes advantage of the suspension of the talks to try to force destiny's hand: he gets permission from the Egyptian security services to cross the border with a car registered in Israel and drives Abu Ala and Mohammed Dahlan to a restaurant south of Taba. Gilead Sher and Pini Medan, another member of the Israeli delegation, join them. What they will try to do is determine, once and for all, each side's "lines in the sand."

Hasson: You're never going to face this kind of Israeli negotiating team. The whole left is here! All you have is a few days to reach an accord. After that, the idea of a Palestinian State may simply disappear. This is the moment of truth. The historical gains you can ratify here will go up in smoke. We can get you a plane or a helicopter so you can go and speak with Abu Ammar [Yasir Arafat]. Get him to conclude an accord!

Abu Ala: He doesn't want to.

The Palestinians who took part in this secret discussion will deny having been so positive on the subject of Arafat's intentions. But since the Egyptian security services were present at the meeting, I asked Osama al-Baz, Hosni Mubarak's adviser, what he knew: "Yes," al-Baz said, "Arafat was hesitating; he wanted to analyze his situation first. Before the elections in Israel, after the arrival of a new administration in Washington."

For his part, Saeb Erekat maintains that Gilead Sher told him, at the beginning of the Taba negotiations, that it would not be "ethically appropriate to conclude an accord so close to the elections in Israel."

The negotiations resume, but they make slow progress. The participants realize that they will not have time to conclude an accord, and they prepare a final statement. On

January 26, a Friday evening, the Israeli delegates invite the Palestinians to their Sabbath meal at the Princess Hotel in Eilat, on the other side of the border. Miguel Moratinos, too, attends what amounts to the farewell banquet of the peace process.

The Israeli press is criticizing the pursuit of these negotiations two weeks before the elections. Even within the government, left-wing ministers Haim Ramon from the Labor Party and, at Taba, Yossi Sarid believe the talks should be suspended. And, after a further conversation with Ehud Barak, Gilead Sher declares that it is "difficult to continue under these circumstances."

The next day, Sunday, Shlomo Ben Ami and Abu Ala read the final communiqué:

The Taba discussions are without precedent in the positive atmosphere in which they have proceeded and the mutual willingness to meet the fundamental national and security needs of each party. Because of circumstances and time constraints, it has proved impossible to come to an understanding on all the issues, despite substantial progress on each of the questions that were discussed.

The parties declare that they have never been so close to an accord. They believe that the remaining differences can be overcome when the negotiations resume after the elections in Israel. . . . The political calendar has prevented the conclusion of an accord on all the problems. . . . We are leaving Taba . . . aware of having set down the basis [of an accord] by establishing a climate of mutual trust, and of having made substantial progress on all the essential questions.

Gilead Sher and Saeb Erekat meet in front of my camera in a room at the Hilton. A few minutes earlier, Erekat had suggested that Miguel Moratinos write a report on these negotiations. In the following months, Moratinos and his diplomatic adviser, Christian Jouret, will prepare a document entitled "European Narrative of What Happened at Taba in January 2001 in the Israeli–Palestinian Negotiations on Permanent Status Issues." While the document is being prepared, Yossi Beilin and Abu Ala no doubt embellish the accounts of the understandings reached in the course of the negotiations. Gilead Sher, who was Barak's representative, will find this text unacceptable and reject it. It is, however, the last vestige of the peace process in the Middle East, and large excerpts are worth citing:

1. TERRITORY

The two sides agreed that in accordance with the UN Security Council Resolution 242, the June 4, 1967 lines would be the basis for the borders between Israel and the State of Palestine. Any modifications will be calculated from this baseline.

1.1. The West Bank
For the first time both sides presented their own maps of the West Bank. The maps served as a basis for the discussion on territory and settlements. . . . The Clinton parameters served as a loose base for the discussion, but differences of interpretations regarding the scope and meaning of the parameters emerged. The Palestinian side stated that it had accepted the Clinton proposals but with reservations.

The Israeli side stated that the Clinton proposals provide for annexation of settlement blocs. The Palestinian side did not agree that the parameters included blocs, and did not accept proposals to annex blocs. The Palestinian side stated that blocs would cause significant harm to Palestinian needs and rights, particularly for the Palestinians residing in areas Israel seeks to annex. . . . The

Palestinian side maintained that since Israel has needs in Palestinian territory, it is responsible for proposing the necessary border modifications. The Palestinian side reiterated that such proposals must not adversely affect the Palestinians' needs and rights.

The Israeli side stated that it did not need to maintain settlements in the Jordan Valley for security purposes, and its proposed maps reflected this position.

The Israeli maps were principally based on a demographic concept of settlement blocs incorporating 80% of the settlers. The Israeli side sketched a map presenting a 6% annexation of the West Bank, the outer limit of the Clinton proposal. The Palestinian illustrative map presented 3.1% of the West Bank in the context of a land swap.

Both sides accepted the principle of land swap but the proportionality of the swap remained under discussion. . . .

The Israeli side requested an additional 2% of land under a lease arrangement to which the Palestinians responded that the subject of lease can only be discussed after the establishment of a Palestinian state and the transfer of land to Palestinian sovereignty.

1.2. Gaza Strip

. . . . It was implied that the Gaza Strip will be under total Palestinian sovereignty. . . . All settlements will be evacuated. The Palestinians claimed it could be arranged in 6 months, a timetable not agreed by the Israeli side. . . .

2. JERUSALEM

2.1. Sovereignty

Both sides accepted in principle the Clinton suggestion of having Palestinian sovereignty over Arab neighbourhoods and Israeli sovereignty over Jewish neighbourhoods.

The Palestinian side, within the context of a land swap, affirmed that it was ready to discuss Israeli requests regarding Jewish settlements in East Jerusalem that were constructed after 1967, but not Jebel Abu Ghneim and Ras al-Amud. The Palestinian side rejected Israeli sovereignty over settlements outside the municipal borders of Jerusalem, such as Ma'ale Adumim and Givat Ze'ev.

The Palestinian side understood that Israel was ready to accept Palestinian sovereignty over the Arab neighbourhoods of East Jerusalem, including the entire Muslim, Christian and Armenian quarters of the old city of Jerusalem. The Israeli side understood that the Palestinians were ready to accept Israeli sovereignty over the Jewish Quarter of the Old City and part of the Armenian quarter.

2.2. Open City
Both sides favoured the idea of an Open City. . . .

2.3. Capital for Two States
Both sides accepted that the City of Jerusalem would be the capital of the two states: Yerushalayim, capital of Israel and Al-Qods, capital of the state of Palestine.

2.4. Holy/Historical Basin and the Old City
. . . The Israeli side expressed its interest and raised its concern regarding the area conceptualized as the Holy Basin (which includes the Jewish Cemetery on the Mount of Olives, the City of David, Kidron Valley). The Palestinian side confirmed that it was willing to take into account Israeli interests and concerns provided that these places remain under Palestinian sovereignty. Another option for the Holy Basin, suggested informally by the Israeli side, was to create a special regime or to suggest some form of internationalization for the entire area or a joint regime with special cooperation and coordination.

The Palestinian side did not agree to adopt any of these ideas, although the discussion could continue.

2.5. Holy Sites/Western Wall and the Wailing Wall

Both parties have accepted the principle of respective control over each side's respective holy sites by the two parties (religious control and management). According to this principle, Israeli control over the Western Wall would be recognized although there remained a dispute regarding the area covered by the Wall and especially the link to what is referred to in Clinton's ideas as "the space sacred to Judaism of which it is a part."

The Palestinian side acknowledged that Israel has requested to establish an affiliation to the holy parts of the Western Wall, but given its own reservations regarding the delineation of the Western/Wailing Wall, this issue has not been fully resolved.

2.6. Haram al-Sharif/Temple Mount

Both sides agreed that the question of Haram al-Sharif/Temple Mount has not been resolved. . . . An informal suggestion was raised that for an agreed period such as three years, Haram al-Sharif/Temple Mount would be under international sovereignty of the P5 [the five permanent members of the Security Council] plus Morocco (or another Islamic presence), whereby the Palestinians would be the "Guardian/Custodians" during this period. At the end of this period, either the parties would agree on a new solution or agree to extend the existing arrangement. In the absence of an agreement, the parties would return to implement the Clinton formulation. Neither accepted or rejected the suggestion.

3. REFUGEES

Non-papers were exchanged, which were regarded as a good basis for the talks. . . .

Both sides suggested, as a basis, that the parties should agree that a just settlement of the refugee problem in accordance with the U.N. Security Council Resolution 242 must lead to the implementation of UN General Assembly Resolution 194. Both sides maintained their respective narratives regarding the essence of UNGAR 194, namely the right of return versus the wish to return.

3.1. Narrative

The Israeli side put forward a suggested joint narrative for the tragedy of the Palestinian refugees. The Palestinian side discussed the proposed narrative and there was much progress, although no agreement was concluded. . . .

3.2. Return, Repatriation, and Relocation and Rehabilitation

Both sides engaged in a discussion of the practicalities of resolving the refugee problem. The Palestinian side reiterated that the Palestinian refugees shall have the right of return to their homes in accordance with UNGAR 194. The Israeli side expressed its understanding that the wish to return as per wording of UNGAR 194 shall be implemented within the framework of one of the following programs:

A. Return and Repatriation
1. to Israel
2. to Israel swapped territories [Israeli territory transferred to the Palestinians in a land-swap agreement], which will be over and above territories discussed in the territorial negotiations
3. to the Palestinian state

B. Rehabilitation and Relocation
1. Rehabilition in host country
2. Relocation to a 3rd country.

Preference in all these options shall be accorded to the Palestinian refugee population in Lebanon.

The Palestinian side stressed that the above shall be subject to the individual free choice of the refugees. . . . The Israeli side, informally, suggested a three-track 15-year absorption program. The first track referred to the absorption to Israel. No numbers were agreed upon, but with a non-paper referring to 25,000 in the first 3 years of the program (40,000 in the first 5 years of this program did not appear in the non-paper but was raised verbally). The second track referred to the absorption of Palestinian refugees into the Israeli territory that shall be transferred to Palestinian sovereignty, and the third track referring to the absorption of refugees in the context of the family reunification scheme.

4. SECURITY

4.1. Early Warning Stations

The Israeli side requested to have 3 early warning stations on Palestinian territory. The Palestinian side was prepared to accept the continued operations of early warning stations but subject to certain conditions. The exact mechanism has therefore to be detailed in further negotiations.

4.2. Military Capacity of the State of Palestine

The Israeli side maintained that the State of Palestine will be non-militarized as per the Clinton proposals. The Palestinian side was prepared to accept . . . [that Palestine] be defined as a state with limited arms. . . . Both sides agree that this issue has not been concluded. . . .

4.4. Timetable for Withdrawal from the West Bank and Jordan Valley

Based on the Clinton proposal, the Israeli side agreed to a withdrawal from the West Bank over a 36 month period with an additional 36 months for the Jordan Valley in conjunction with an international force. . . .

The Palestinian side rejected the 36 month withdrawal process expressing concern that a lengthy process would exacerbate Israeli–Palestinian tensions. The Palestinian side proposed an 18 month withdrawal under the supervision of international forces. As to the Jordan Valley the Palestinian side was prepared to consider the withdrawal of Israeli armed forces for an additional 10 month period. Although the Palestinian side was ready to consider the presence of international forces in the West Bank for a longer period, it refused to accept the ongoing presence of Israeli forces. . . .[186]

SHARON'S VICTORY

On January 28, Shimon Peres and Yasir Arafat meet at Davos, in Switzerland, where they are taking part in the World Economic Forum. The two Nobel Prize winners embrace warmly. Arafat then mounts the dais and gives his speech:

The Barak government, like its predecessor, the Netanyahu government, is practicing a politics of economic strangulation, blockade, and siege, as well as collective

---

186. The text is reproduced verbatim from the English translation of the original text. The version that appeared in the press is inaccurate.

punishment and starvation, against our Palestinian people. For four months, the present Israeli government has been waging a savage, barbarous war and fascist military aggression against our Palestinian people. To this end, it is using weapons forbidden by international conventions, arms containing depleted uranium. . . .

The entire speech is of this nature. Shimon Peres is dumbfounded. He takes the floor and begins to give the relatively moderate speech he had prepared. Then he speaks extemporaneously, saying that Israel has simply been defending itself against terrorism. The Israeli right will immediately use this affair in its electoral campaign: Arafat, they say, is not a credible interlocutor.

The final attempt to organize a summit between Ehud Barak and Yasir Arafat, this time in Sweden, takes place in the France 2 office in Jerusalem. Saeb Erekat and Gilead Sher have asked me to host the meeting. As a sign of the times, both men arrive with bodyguards, security agents who, after looking daggers at one another, will have a friendly conversation. This time, I am allowed to tape the beginning of the discussion. (In previous meetings on the France 2 premises, I'd had to be content with capturing the event on film without sound.)

> *Erekat:* We made a bet. If Sharon won the elections, I'd buy you lunch, and if Barak won, you'd have to pay. At the time, five weeks ago, I didn't think the Israelis would choose Sharon. [Now] I know he's going to win.
>
> *Sher:* You're going to lose, for sure. You people woke up too late. You've destroyed the peace camp in Israel.
>
> *Erekat:* What you're saying there is unfair!
>
> *Sher:* You wrecked it with these four months of violence.

Erekat: I told you that, if Sharon went up to the Haram, one man would be smiling after that visit and the rest of us would be weeping.

Sher: It's been four months now. You could have stopped [all that]. You didn't want to.

Erekat: All Barak is now is a chapter in a Greek tragedy.

At this point, the camera has to leave the room and continue filming through the picture window. The discussion, interrupted by phone calls to Barak, Arafat, and Lipkin-Shahak, who is in Gaza meeting with Arafat, will continue until 1 A.M. A document is prepared. The replies come in: No.

After a final cup of coffee, Gilead Sher and his bodyguard are the first to leave. Saeb Erekat leaves a few minutes later. This precaution is unnecessary: the corridors of the studio are empty. No journalist believes in a miracle anymore.

Sher and Erekat did not see one another again for months. After Barak's defeat, Sher left politics to return to his law practice, in which he focuses on freedom of the press. Erekat has stayed on as Arafat's negotiator. In July 2001, each of them asked me to set up a meeting. It took place in a discreet restaurant in West Jerusalem, in the presence of the writer David Grossman, who wanted to know why the peace process had collapsed.

On February 6, 2001, Ariel Sharon was elected prime minister of the State of Israel by an unprecedented majority of 62.39 percent of the votes to 37.61 percent for Barak, who regretfully left the political scene. He had his eye on the post of defense minister in the new government and had asked several important people abroad to intercede with Sharon on his behalf. All refused politely. His last political gesture was to write to all foreign governments, informing them that the proposals he had submitted to the Palestinians were henceforth null and void. In so doing, he swept away eighteen months of the peace process.

Yasir Arafat, who had negotiated with four Israeli governments since 1993, found himself opposite his old enemy, Ariel Sharon, who had thrown him out of Beirut in 1982. With the full support of the army and a public enraged by insecurity and terrorism, the new prime minister has triggered an even harsher war against Palestinian organizations, with the Autonomous Authority as its primary objective.

Dennis Ross has left the State Department for a research institute in Washington, where he is analyzing the decade he spent heading the peace process:

I think [our] biggest mistake was letting a huge gap develop between the reality on the ground and the reality around the negotiating table. The Palestinians have to stop inciting violence. They have to bring up [their children] differently. The Israelis have to stop . . . constructing settlements. I don't care if they build within existing locations, but no extensions. They have to stop destroying Palestinian houses and confiscating land, and [they have to] change their attitude at the checkpoints. Both sides have finally understood that they had to change reality.

The realities on the ground, the environment, had to support the negotiations, not undercut them. On the Palestinian side, they got used to the idea of engaging permanent incitement and socialization of the violence. And on the Israeli side, they constantly did things that created a sense of powerlessness in the Palestinians. From the very beginning, we should have held both sides accountable for the commitments they made. We did not. And there are always good reasons, but once the commitments didn't have to be fulfilled, it created a mindset that commitments could be made but they didn't mean anything.

We never did anything to prepare public opinion [for peace]. Holding negotiations come what may got us nowhere. If I could do it all over again, I'd do it differently.[187]

This mea culpa was late in coming. The conflict between Israelis and Palestinians is once again at the center of regional instability, and there is no longer any hope of reaching an accord in the foreseeable future. The Clinton administration was unable to complete the political process that Yitzak Rabin had begun without any American assistance. Because they did not understand that peace must first be made between nations and not solely between leaders, the peace team and the negotiators in both camps led the Middle East closer to hell.

This is a failure of politics, of diplomacy, and of a vision of the world.

---

187. Videotaped interview with Dennis Ross, February 19, 2002, Washington. This interview was conducted in English.

CHRONOLOGY OF
MAJOR EVENTS

1993

September 9–10: Mutual recognition between Israel and the PLO.

September 13: The "Oslo Accord," a declaration of principle between Israel and the PLO, signed in Washington.

1994

February 25: Hebron settler Baruch Goldstein kills twenty-nine Palestinians.

May 4: Accord on the autonomy of Gaza and Jericho signed in Cairo.

October 26: Peace treaty between Israel and Jordan signed in Ein Evrona in the Arava desert.

1995

January–July: Terrorist attacks in Israel by Hamas and Islamic Jihad. Ninety-five Israelis killed.

September 28: Interim accord (Oslo II) between Israel and the PLO signed in Washington, extending Palestinian autonomy to the main urban centers of the West Bank.

November 4: Yitzhak Rabin assassinated in Tel Aviv by Yigal Amir, a young religious far-rightist.

December 27–February 25, 1996: Israeli–Syrian negotiations at Wye Plantation in the United States.

1996

January 20: Palestinian general elections in the West Bank, Gaza, and East Jerusalem. Arafat elected chairman of the Palestinian Authority.

February 25: Suicide bomber kills twenty-six Israelis in a bus in Jerusalem.

March 3: Suicide bomber kills nineteen Israelis in a bus in Jerusalem.

March 4: Suicide bomber kills fourteen Israelis in front of a Tel Aviv mall.

March 6: Mass arrest of Hamas and Jihad activists by Palestinian security forces in the West Bank and Gaza.

March 13: Summit of "peacemakers" at Sharm el-Sheik in Egypt. Condemnation of Islamic terrorism.

April 11: Israeli army launches Operation Grapes of Wrath against Hezbollah in South Lebanon.

April 18: Israeli shells kill 102 Lebanese refugees in Kfar Kana, South Lebanon.

May 29: Benjamin Netanyahu elected prime minister in Israel.

September 23–October 1: Armed clashes between Israel and the Palestinians after the opening of the underground passageway at the Wailing Wall in Jerusalem. Eighty Palestinians and fifteen Israeli soldiers killed.

1997

January 17: Israel withdraws from part of Hebron.

July 30: Two Hamas suicide bombers kill thirteen Israelis in Jerusalem.

September 4: Three suicide bombers kill five Israelis in Jerusalem.

September 25: In Amman (Jordan), Mossad agents try to assassinate the Hamas leader Khaled Mashaal.

October 1: Sheik Ahmed Yassin, founder of Hamas, returns to Gaza after nine years in Israeli prisons.

1998

October 23: Wye River accord signed by Benjamin Netanyahu and Yasir Arafat in Washington.

December 14: Bill Clinton visits Gaza and addresses the Palestinian leadership. The revocation of the PLO charter is confirmed.

1999

July 7: Ehud Barak of the Labor Party, elected on May 17 over the right-wing leader Benjamin Netanyahu, takes office.

July 17: In talks with Bill Clinton in Washington, Barak gives himself fifteen months to reach a comprehensive peace in the Middle East.

September 2: Ariel Sharon is elected head of the major opposition party, the rightist Likud, in place of Netanyahu, who has resigned.

September 5: An ultra-Orthodox party (The Unified List of the Torah) leaves the government coalition, reducing its majority from seventy-three to sixty-eight deputies out of the 120 comprising the Knesset. Barak and Arafat sign the Sharm el-Sheik accord, opening the way to negotiations on a final peace settlement.

September 10: Israel transfers to the Palestinian Authority the administrative control of 7 percent of the West Bank.

November 8: Negotiations between Israel and the Palestinians begin in Ramallah.

December 15: Peace negotiations between Israel and Syria resume in Washington, after nearly four years of interruption.

2000

January 3: Israeli–Syrian negotiations at Shepherdstown in the United States, ending on January 10. On January 17, Damascus indefinitely postpones a third round of talks.

March 21: Israel withdraws from 6.1 percent of the West Bank, two months behind schedule.

March 26: Bill Clinton–Hafez Assad summit in Geneva.

May 10: Secret negotiations between Israel and the Palestinians begin in Sweden.

May 24: Hasty withdrawal of the Israeli army from South Lebanon, after twenty-two years of occupation.

June 21: The left-wing secular Meretz Party (ten deputies) leaves Barak's coalition.

July 9: Barak loses his majority in the Knesset with the departure of the ultra-Orthodox Shas Party (seventeen deputies), the National Religious Party (five deputies), and the Russian-language party Israel B'Aliyah (four deputies).

July 11–25: At Camp David, Barak and Arafat negotiate under the auspices of President Clinton but, because of major differences on Jerusalem, do not reach an accord.

July 31: Barak barely survives two right-wing motions of censure.

August–September: Israeli–Palestinian negotiations in Jerusalem, Tel Aviv, and Jericho.

August 1: Barak declares that he is prepared to consider all possibilities for constituting "the broadest possible emergency government."

August 2: Resignation of Foreign Minister David Levy. The Knesset adopts, on first reading, several motions from the right in favor of early elections.

September 28: Ariel Sharon's visit to the Haram el-Sharif/Temple Mount in Jerusalem leads to a wave of violence in the Palestinian territories and in Israel.

September 29: Violent clashes at the Haram el-Sharif/Temple Mount. Israeli police kill four Palestinians and injure 160. Beginning of the Al-Aqsa Intifada.

October 4: Madeleine Albright meets with Arafat and Barak in Paris.

October 12: Two Israeli soldiers lynched in Ramallah by Palestinian mob. Israel responds by bombing Palestinian Authority targets. Barak officially invites the Likud to join a "national emergency government."

October 16–18: Sharm el-Sheik summit between Barak and Arafat. Bill Clinton, Hosni Mubarak, Kofi Annan, and Javier Solana take part. The summit calls for ending the violence and resuming negotiations, and it establishes a commission of inquiry. Since the beginning of the Intifada, 127 Palestinians and eight Israelis have been killed.

October 21–22: Arab League summit in Cairo. On October 22, Barak announces an indefinite "pause" in the peace process.

October 23: Shas refuses to be part of a united government but promises to offer support from the outside.

October 30: The Knesset is back in session. Barak is temporarily rescued by Shas's decision to support him in the Knesset for one month.

November 12: Barak and Clinton meet to discuss ways of ending the violence.

November 20: Shas announces that it will withdraw parliamentary support for Barak at the end of the month. Sharon rejects Barak's appeal for a "government of national emergency."

November 21: Egypt recalls its ambassador from Tel Aviv.

November 27: The Knesset votes decisively in favor of a motion by the right-wing opposition intended to make any concessions to the Palestinians on East Jerusalem more difficult.

November 28: Barak agrees to hold early elections. With an absolute majority and on first reading, the Knesset adopts five right-wing motions for its dissolution and the holding of early elections.

December 1: Barak barely manages to get the support of the Labor Party, but the left wing of the party continues to challenge him, opposing the idea of holding early elections.

December 4: The Knesset, on preliminary reading, votes in favor of a motion forbidding any prime minister who lacks a parliamentary majority to sign international agreements.

December 6: The major political parties discuss the possibility of holding elections in May 2001. No agreement is reached. Though still saying that he is willing to hold early elections, Barak repeats his preference for a government of national unity with the Likud.

December 9: Barak announces his resignation.

December 10: The resignation is submitted to President Moshe Katsav. As stipulated by law, elections for the premiership will be held two months later. The Labor Party overwhelmingly declares Barak its candidate for re-election. Former Prime Minister Benjamin Netanyahu announces his candidacy for the leadership of Likud and for the office of head of government, possible only if the Knesset votes to dissolve itself or amends the electoral law.

December 23: Clinton presents the Israelis and Palestinians with his parameters for an agreement on the final status.

2001

January 1: Since the beginning of the Intifada, 227 Palestinians and forty-one Israelis have been killed.

January 18–28: Negotiations between Israel and the Palestinians at Taba in Egypt.

February 6: Ariel Sharon elected prime minister of Israel.

February 14: In Tel Aviv, a Palestinian bus driver ploughs his vehicle into a waiting queue, killing eight Israeli soldiers and civilians. Israel imposes a total blockade on the Palestinian territories.

May 14: Israeli troops kill five Palestinian policemen manning a checkpoint in the West Bank. (Israeli officials will later admit this was a mistake caused by misinformation.) Combat helicopters bomb security targets in the Gaza Strip.

May 18: A Palestinian suicide bomber kills himself and five Israelis in a shopping mall north of Tel Aviv. Israel retaliates by bombing targets in Ramallah and Nablus with F16 warplanes.

June 1: A suicide bombers kills nineteen young Israelis at a popular discotheque in Tel Aviv.

July 31: An Israeli combat helicopter launches rockets at the Hamas office in Nablus. The leading Hamas figure in the West Bank and two young children are among the eight dead. Hamas vows revenge.

August 9: A suicide bomber blows himself up in a Jerusalem pizzeria, killing fifteen Israelis and tourists. Hamas claims responsibility.

August 10: Israeli helicopters destroy the headquarters of Palestinian police and security in Ramallah. Israeli police seize Orient House, the headquarters of the PLO in East Jerusalem.

August 26: After a Palestinian attacked an Israeli army post in the Gaza Strip on the previous day, F15 and F16 planes destroy Palestinian security installations in Gaza and the West Bank

August 27: Abu Ali Mostafa, leader of the Popular Front for the Liberation of Palestine (PFLP), is killed in his office in Ramallah by an Israeli rocket.

October 17: Rehavam Zeevi, Israeli minister of tourism and head of the extreme right-wing Moledet party, is assassinated in a Jerusalem hotel. The PFLP claims responsibility, saying this is an act of retaliation for the killing of Abu Ali Mostafa.

October 2001–March 2002: Violence escalates. Repeated Palestinian suicide attacks create an atmosphere of deep anguish and insecurity in Israel, while Israeli retaliatory raids and incursions into autonomous areas in the West Bank and Gaza inflict a growing number of casualties on the Palestinian populations and wreak havoc on the Palestinian economy.

2002

March 27: A suicide bomber kills himself in a hotel in Netanya, north of Tel Aviv, killing twenty-nine Jewish guests who were participating in a Passover seder. Hamas claims responsibility.

March 29: Israel launches Operation Defensive Shield in the West Bank, reoccupying all the major Palestinian cities. In Ramallah, Israeli troops lay siege to Arafat's presidential compound.

March 31: A suicide bomber kills sixteen Israelis in Haifa.

April 2: Israeli tanks and infantry launch an attack on Bethlehem. Palestinian gunmen take refuge in the Church of the Nativity.

April 9: A fierce battle in the Jenin refugee camp leaves fifteen Israeli soldiers and 53 Palestinians dead.

April 12: A suicide bomber kills himself and six Israelis in a bus in Jerusalem.

April 15: Marwan Barghouti, the leader of Fatah in the West Bank, is captured in Ramallah by Israeli troops.

May 2: End of the siege of Arafat's compound in Ramallah.

May 10: End of the siege of the Church of the Nativity in Bethlehem. The gunmen are allowed to move to Gaza. Some are sent abroad.

June 5: A Palestinian suicide bomber detonates a car packed with explosives next to an Israeli bus in the Galilee, killing seventeen civilians and soldiers. In retaliation, Israeli helicopter gunships attack Palestinian targets.

June 6: Israeli tanks and bulldozers destroy part of Arafat's Ramallah headquarters. No building in the compound remains intact.

June 18: A suicide bomber blows himself up on a bus in Jerusalem. Twenty people are killed and more than forty wounded, including several schoolchildren. The Israeli government announces that it will reoccupy Palestinian territory in the West Bank and hold it indefinitely in reprisal for the bombing.

July 2: Yasir Arafat dismisses two of his most senior security officers, Jibril Rajoub, head of preventive security in the West Bank, and Ghazi Jibali, the Gaza police chief.

July 16: Eight Israeli settlers on the West Bank are shot dead as Palestinian gunmen open fire on a bus.

July 22: An Israeli jet launches a bomb on a residential area of Gaza City, killing the Hamas military leader Salah Shehadeh and fourteen other Palestinians, including nine children.

July 31: A bomb explodes in the Hebrew University cafeteria, killing four Israelis and five US nationals.

September 21–30: The Israeli army traps Arafat in his Ramallah compound for ten days. The siege is ended under pressure from the US.

September 30: Since the beginning of the Al-Aqsa Intifada, 1,599 Palestinians and 577 Israelis have been killed.

APPENDIX

RESOLUTION 194 (III)
OF 11 DECEMBER 1948

194 (III). Palestine—Progress Report of the United Nations Mediator

The General Assembly, having considered further the situation in Palestine

1. Expresses its deep appreciation of the progress achieved through the good offices of the late United Nations Mediator in promoting a peaceful adjustment of the future situation of Palestine, for which cause he sacrificed his life; and extends its thanks to the Acting Mediator and his staff for their continued efforts and devotion to duty in Palestine;

2. Establishes a Conciliation Commission consisting of three States, members of the United Nations, which shall have the following functions:

(a) To assume, in so far as it considers necessary in existing circumstances, the functions given to the United Nations Mediator on Palestine by resolution 186 (S–2) of the General Assembly of 14 May 1948;

(b) To carry out the specific functions and directives given to it by the present resolution and such additional functions and directives as may be given to it by the General Assembly or by the Security Council;

(c) To undertake, upon the request of the Security Council, any of the functions now assigned to the United Nations Mediator on Palestine or to the United Nations Truce Commission by resolutions of the Security Council; upon such request to the Conciliation Commission by the Security Council with respect to all the remaining functions of the United Nations Mediator on Palestine under Security Council resolutions, the office of the Mediator shall be terminated;

3. Decides that a Committee of the Assembly, consisting of China, France, the Union of Soviet Socialist Republics, the United Kingdom, and the United States of America, shall present, before the end of the first part of the present session of the General Assembly, for the approval of the Assembly, a proposal concerning the names of the three States which will constitute the Conciliation Commission;

4. Requests the Commission to begin its functions at once, with a view to the establishment of contact between the parties themselves and the Commission at the earliest possible date;

5. Calls upon the Governments and authorities concerned to extend the scope of the negotiations provided for in the Security Council's resolution of 16 November 1948[1] and to seek agreement by negotiations conducted either with the Conciliation Commission or directly, with a view to the final settlement of all questions outstanding between them;

6. Instructs the Conciliation Commission to take steps to assist the Governments and authorities concerned to achieve a final settlement of all questions outstanding between them;

7. Resolves that the Holy Places—including Nazareth—religious buildings and sites in Palestine should be protected

---

1. See *Official Records of the Security Council*, Third Year, No. 126.

and free access to them assured, in accordance with existing rights and historical practice; that arrangements to this end should be under effective United Nations supervision; that the United Nations Conciliation Commission, in presenting to the fourth regular session of the General Assembly its detailed proposals for a permanent international regime for the territory of Jerusalem, should include recommendations concerning the Holy Places in that territory; that with regard to the Holy Places in the rest of Palestine the Commission should call upon the political authorities of the areas concerned to give appropriate formal guarantees as to the protection of the Holy Places and access to them; and that these undertakings should be presented to the General Assembly for approval;

8. Resolves that, in view of its association with three world religions, the Jerusalem area, including the present municipality of Jerusalem plus the surrounding villages and towns, the most eastern of which shall be Abu Dis; the most southern, Bethlehem; the most western, Ein Karim (including also the built-up area of Motsa); and the most northern, Shu'fat, should be accorded special and separate treatment from the rest of Palestine and should be placed under effective United Nations control;

Requests the Security Council to take further steps to ensure the demilitarization of Jerusalem at the earliest possible date;

Instructs the Conciliation Commission to present to the fourth regular session of the General Assembly detailed proposals for a permanent international regime for the Jerusalem area which will provide for the maximum local autonomy for distinctive groups consistent with the special international status of the Jerusalem area;

The Conciliation Commission is authorized to appoint a United Nations representative, who shall co-operate with the local authorities with respect to the interim administration of the Jerusalem area;

9. Resolves that, pending agreement on more detailed arrangements among the Governments and authorities concerned, the freest possible access to Jerusalem by road, rail, or air should be accorded to all inhabitants of Palestine;

Instructs the Conciliation Commission to report immediately to the Security Council, for appropriate action by that organ, any attempt by any party to impede such access;

10. Instructs the Conciliation Commission to seek arrangements among the Governments and authorities concerned which will facilitate the economic development of the area, including arrangements for access to ports and airfields and the use of transportation and communication facilities;

11. Resolves that the refugees wishing to return to their homes and live at peace with their neighbours should be permitted to do so at the earliest practicable date, and that compensation should be paid for the property of those choosing not to return and for loss of or damage to property which, under principles of international law or in equity, should be made good by the Governments or authorities responsible;

Instructs the Conciliation Commission to facilitate the repatriation, resettlement and economic and social rehabilitation of the refugees and the payment of compensation, and to maintain close relations with the Director of the United Nations Relief for Palestine Refugees and, through him, with the appropriate organs and agencies of the United Nations;

12. Authorizes the Conciliation Commission to appoint such subsidiary bodies and to employ such technical experts, acting under its authority, as it may find necessary for the effective discharge of its functions and responsibilities under the present resolution;

The Conciliation Commission will have its official headquarters at Jerusalem. The authorities responsible for maintaining order in Jerusalem will be responsible for taking all measures necessary to ensure the security of the Commission. The Secretary-General will provide a limited number of guards to the protection of the staff and premises of the Commission;

13. Instructs the Conciliation Commission to render progress reports periodically to the Secretary-General for transmission to the Security Council and to the Members of the United Nations;

14. Calls upon all Governments and authorities concerned to co-operate with the Conciliation Commission and to take all possible steps to assist in the implementation of the present resolution;

15. Requests the Secretary-General to provide the necessary staff and facilities and to make appropriate arrangements to provide the necessary funds required in carrying out the terms of the present resolution.

At the 186th plenary meeting on 11 December 1948, a committee of the Assembly consisting of the five States designated in paragraph 3 of the above resolution proposed that the following three States should constitute the Conciliation Commission: France, Turkey, United States of America.

The proposal of the Committee having been adopted by the General Assembly at the same meeting, the Conciliation Commission is therefore composed of the above-mentioned three States.

RESOLUTION 242
OF 22 NOVEMBER 1967

The Security Council,

Expressing its continuing concern with the grave situation in the Middle East,

Emphasizing the inadmissibility of the acquisition of territory by war and the need to work for a just and lasting peace in which every State in the area can live in security,

Emphasizing further that all Member States in their acceptance of the Charter of the United Nations have undertaken a commitment to act in accordance with Article 2 of the Charter,

1. Affirms that the fulfilment of Charter principles requires the establishment of a just and lasting peace in the Middle East which should include the application of both the following principles:

(i) Withdrawal of Israel armed forces from territories occupied in the recent conflict;

(ii) Termination of all claims or states of belligerency and respect for and acknowledgment of the sovereignty, territorial integrity, and political independence of every State in the area and their right to live in peace within secure and recognized boundaries free from threats or acts of force;

2. Affirms further the necessity

(a) For guaranteeing freedom of navigation through international waterways in the area;

(b) For achieving a just settlement of the refugee problem;

(c) For guaranteeing the territorial inviolability and political independence of every State in the area, through measures including the establishment of demilitarized zones;

3. Requests the Secretary-General to designate a Special Representative to proceed to the Middle East to establish and maintain contacts with the States concerned in order to promote agreement and assist efforts to achieve a peaceful and accepted settlement in accordance with the provisions and principles in this resolution;

4. Requests the Secretary-General to report to the Security Council on the progress of the efforts of the Special Representative as soon as possible.

Adopted unanimously at the 1382nd meeting.

RESOLUTION 338
OF 22 OCTOBER 1973

The Security Council

1. Calls upon all parties to the present fighting to cease all firing and terminate all military activity immediately, no later than 12 hours after the moment of the adoption of this decision, in the positions they now occupy;

2. Calls upon the parties concerned to start immediately after the cease-fire the implementation of Security Council resolution 242 (1967) in all of its parts;

3. Decides that, immediately and concurrently with the cease-fire, negotiations shall start between the parties concerned under appropriate auspices aimed at establishing a just and durable peace in the Middle East.

Adopted at the 1747th meeting by 14 votes to none.[1]

---

1. One member (China) did not participate in the voting.

RESOLUTION 425
OF 19 MARCH 1978

The Security Council,

Taking note of the letters from the Permanent Representative of Lebanon[1] and from the Permanent Representative of Israel,[2]

Having heard the statement of the Permanent Representatives of Lebanon and Israel,[3]

Gravely concerned at the deterioration of the situation in the Middle East and its consequences to the maintenance of international peace,

Convinced that the present situation impedes the achievement of a just peace in the Middle East,

1. Calls for strict respect for the territorial integrity, sovereignty, and political independence of Lebanon within its internationally recognized boundaries;

2. Calls upon Israel immediately to cease its military action against Lebanese territorial integrity and withdraw forthwith its forces from all Lebanese territory;

3. Decides, in the light of the request of the Government of Lebanon, to establish immediately under its authority a

---

1. *Ibid.*, documents S/12600 and S/12606.
2. *Ibid.*, document S/12607.
3. *Ibid.*, Thirty-third Year, 2071st meeting.

United Nations interim force for Southern Lebanon for the purpose of confirming the withdrawal of Israeli forces, restoring international peace and security, and assisting the Government of Lebanon in ensuring the return of its effective authority in the area, the Force to be composed of personnel drawn from Member States;

4. Requests the Secretary-General to report to the Council within twenty-four hours on the implementation of the present resolution.

Adopted at the 2074th meeting by 12 votes to none, with 2 abstentions (Czechoslovakia, Union of Soviet Socialist Republics).[4]

---

4. One member (China) did not participate in the voting.

OSLO ACCORDS

Declaration of Principles on Interim Self-Government Arrangements

September 13, 1993

The Government of the State of Israel and the P.L.O. team (in the Jordanian–Palestinian delegation to the Middle East Peace Conference) (the "Palestinian Delegation"), representing the Palestinian people, agree that it is time to put an end to decades of confrontation and conflict, recognize their mutual legitimate and political rights, and strive to live in peaceful coexistence and mutual dignity and security and achieve a just, lasting and comprehensive peace settlement and historic reconciliation through the agreed political process. Accordingly, the two sides agree to the following principles:

ARTICLE I: AIM OF THE NEGOTIATIONS

The aim of the Israeli–Palestinian negotiations within the current Middle East peace process is, among other things, to establish a Palestinian Interim Self-Government Authority, the elected Council (the "Council"), for the Palestinian people in the West Bank and the Gaza Strip, for a transitional period not exceeding five years, leading to a permanent settlement based on Security Council Resolutions 242 and 338.

It is understood that the interim arrangements are an integral part of the whole peace process and that the negotiations on the permanent status will lead to the implementation of Security Council Resolutions 242 and 338.

ARTICLE II: FRAMEWORK FOR THE INTERIM PERIOD

The agreed framework for the interim period is set forth in this Declaration of Principles.

ARTICLE III: ELECTIONS

1. In order that the Palestinian people in the West Bank and Gaza Strip may govern themselves according to democratic principles, direct, free and general political elections will be held for the Council under agreed supervision and international observation, while the Palestinian police will ensure public order.

2. An agreement will be concluded on the exact mode and conditions of the elections in accordance with the protocol attached as Annex I, with the goal of holding the elections not later than nine months after the entry into force of this Declaration of Principles.

3. These elections will constitute a significant interim preparatory step toward the realization of the legitimate rights of the Palestinian people and their just requirements.

ARTICLE IV: JURISDICTION

Jurisdiction of the Council will cover West Bank and Gaza Strip territory, except for issues that will be negotiated in the permanent status negotiations. The two sides view the West Bank and the Gaza Strip as a single territorial unit, whose integrity will be preserved during the interim period.

ARTICLE V: TRANSITIONAL PERIOD AND PERMA-
NENT STATUS NEGOTIATIONS

1. The five-year transitional period will begin upon the withdrawal from the Gaza Strip and Jericho area.

2. Permanent status negotiations will commence as soon as possible, but not later than the beginning of the third year of the interim period, between the Government of Israel and the Palestinian people representatives.

3. It is understood that these negotiations shall cover remaining issues, including: Jerusalem, refugees, settlements, security arrangements, borders, relations and cooperation with other neighbors, and other issues of common interest.

4. The two parties agree that the outcome of the permanent status negotiations should not be prejudiced or preempted by agreements reached for the interim period.

ARTICLE VI: PREPARATORY TRANSFER
OF POWERS AND RESPONSIBILITIES

1. Upon the entry into force of this Declaration of Principles and the withdrawal from the Gaza Strip and the Jericho area, a transfer of authority from the Israeli military government and its Civil Administration to the authorised Palestinians for this task, as detailed herein, will commence. This transfer of authority will be of a preparatory nature until the inauguration of the Council.

2. Immediately after the entry into force of this Declaration of Principles and the withdrawal from the Gaza Strip and Jericho area, with the view to promoting economic development in the West Bank and Gaza Strip, authority will

be transferred to the Palestinians on the following spheres: education and culture, health, social welfare, direct taxation, and tourism. The Palestinian side will commence in building the Palestinian police force, as agreed upon. Pending the inauguration of the Council, the two parties may negotiate the transfer of additional powers and responsibilities, as agreed upon.

ARTICLE VII : INTERIM AGREEMENT

1. The Israeli and Palestinian delegations will negotiate an agreement on the interim period (the "Interim Agreement").

2. The Interim Agreement shall specify, among other things, the structure of the Council, the number of its members, and the transfer of powers and responsibilities from the Israeli military government and its Civil Administration to the Council. The Interim Agreement shall also specify the Council's executive authority, legislative authority in accordance with Article IX below, and the independent Palestinian judicial organs.

3. The Interim Agreement shall include arrangements, to be implemented upon the inauguration of the Council, for the assumption by the Council of all of the powers and responsibilities transferred previously in accordance with Article VI above.

4. In order to enable the Council to promote economic growth, upon its inauguration, the Council will establish, among other things, a Palestinian Electricity Authority, a Gaza Sea Port Authority, a Palestinian Development Bank, a Palestinian Export Promotion Board, a Palestinian Environmental Authority, a Palestinian Land Authority, and a Palestinian Water Administration Authority, and any

other Authorities agreed upon, in accordance with the Interim Agreement that will specify their powers and responsibilities.

5. After the inauguration of the Council, the Civil Administration will be dissolved, and the Israeli military government will be withdrawn.

ARTICLE VIII: PUBLIC ORDER AND SECURITY

In order to guarantee public order and internal security for the Palestinians of the West Bank and the Gaza Strip, the Council will establish a strong police force, while Israel will continue to carry the responsibility for defending against external threats, as well as the responsibility for overall security of Israelis for the purpose of safeguarding their internal security and public order.

ARTICLE IX: LAWS AND MILITARY ORDERS

1. The Council will be empowered to legislate, in accordance with the Interim Agreement, within all authorities transferred to it.

2. Both parties will review jointly laws and military orders presently in force in remaining spheres.

ARTICLE X: JOINT ISRAELI–PALESTINIAN
LIAISON COMMITTEE

In order to provide for a smooth implementation of this Declaration of Principles and any subsequent agreements pertaining to the interim period, upon the entry into force of this Declaration of Principles, a Joint Israeli–Palestinian Liaison Committee will be established in order to deal with issues requiring coordination, other issues of common interest, and disputes.

ARTICLE XI: ISRAELI–PALESTINIAN COOPERATION IN ECONOMIC FIELDS

Recognizing the mutual benefit of cooperation in promoting the development of the West Bank, the Gaza Strip and Israel, upon the entry into force of this Declaration of Principles, an Israeli–Palestinian Economic Cooperation Committee will be established in order to develop and implement in a cooperative manner the programs identified in the protocols attached as Annex III and Annex IV.

ARTICLE XII: LIAISON AND COOPERATION WITH JORDAN AND EGYPT

The two parties will invite the Governments of Jordan and Egypt to participate in establishing further liaison and cooperation arrangements between the Government of Israel and the Palestinian representatives, on the one hand, and the Governments of Jordan and Egypt, on the other hand, to promote cooperation between them. These arrangements will include the constitution of a Continuing Committee that will decide by agreement on the modalities of admission of persons displaced from the West Bank and Gaza Strip in 1967, together with necessary measures to prevent disruption and disorder. Other matters of common concern will be dealt with by this Committee.

ARTICLE XIII: REDEPLOYMENT OF ISRAELI FORCES

1. After the entry into force of this Declaration of Principles, and not later than the eve of elections for the Council, a redeployment of Israeli military forces in the West Bank and

the Gaza Strip will take place, in addition to withdrawal of Israeli forces carried out in accordance with Article XIV.

2. In redeploying its military forces, Israel will be guided by the principle that its military forces should be redeployed outside populated areas.

3. Further redeployments to specified locations will be gradually implemented commensurate with the assumption of responsibility for public order and internal security by the Palestinian police force pursuant to Article VIII above.

ARTICLE XIV: ISRAELI WITHDRAWAL FROM THE GAZA STRIP AND JERICHO AREA

Israel will withdraw from the Gaza Strip and Jericho area, as detailed in the protocol attached as Annex II.

ARTICLE XV: RESOLUTION OF DISPUTES

1. Disputes arising out of the application or interpretation of this Declaration of Principles, or any subsequent agreements pertaining to the interim period, shall be resolved by negotiations through the Joint Liaison Committee to be established pursuant to Article X above.

2. Disputes which cannot be settled by negotiations may be resolved by a mechanism of conciliation to be agreed upon by the parties.

3. The parties may agree to submit to arbitration disputes relating to the interim period, which cannot be settled through conciliation. To this end, upon the agreement of both parties, the parties will establish an Arbitration Committee.

ARTICLE XVI: ISRAELI–PALESTINIAN COOPERATION CONCERNING REGIONAL PROGRAMS

Both parties view the multilateral working groups as an appropriate instrument for promoting a "Marshall Plan," the regional programs and other programs, including special programs for the West Bank and Gaza Strip, as indicated in the protocol attached as Annex IV.

ARTICLE XVII: MISCELLANEOUS PROVISIONS

1. This Declaration of Principles will enter into force one month after its signing.

2. All protocols annexed to this Declaration of Principles and Agreed Minutes pertaining thereto shall be regarded as an integral part hereof.

Done at Washington, D.C., this thirteenth day of September, 1993.

Shimon Peres, for the Government of the State of Israel
Mahmud Abbas, for the PLO

Witnessed by:

Warren Christopher, for the United States of America
Andrei Kozyrev, for the Russian Federation

ANNEX I: PROTOCOL ON THE MODE AND CONDITIONS OF ELECTIONS

1. Palestinians of Jerusalem who live there will have the right to participate in the election process, according to an agreement between the two sides.

2. In addition, the election agreement should cover, among other things, the following issues:

(a) the system of elections;

(b) the mode of the agreed supervision and international observation and their personal composition; and

(c) rules and regulations regarding election campaigns, including agreed arrangements for the organizing of mass media, and the possibility of licensing a broadcasting and TV station.

3. The future status of displaced Palestinians who were registered on 4th June 1967 will not be prejudiced because they are unable to participate in the election process due to practical reasons.

ANNEX II: PROTOCOL ON WITHDRAWAL OF ISRAELI FORCES FROM THE GAZA STRIP AND JERICHO AREA

1. The two sides will conclude and sign within two months from the date of entry into force of this Declaration of Principles, an agreement on the withdrawal of Israeli military forces from the Gaza Strip and Jericho area. This agreement will include comprehensive arrangements to apply in the Gaza Strip and the Jericho area subsequent to the Israeli withdrawal.

2. Israel will implement an accelerated and scheduled withdrawal of Israeli military forces from the Gaza Strip and Jericho area, beginning immediately with the signing of the agreement on the Gaza Strip and Jericho area and to be completed within a period not exceeding four months after the signing of this agreement.

3. The above agreement will include, among other things:

(a) Arrangements for a smooth and peaceful transfer of authority from the Israeli military government and its Civil Administration to the Palestinian representatives.

(b) Structure, powers, and responsibilities of the Palestinian authority in these areas, except: external security, settlements, Israelis, foreign relations, and other mutually agreed matters.

(c) Arrangements for the assumption of internal security and public order by the Palestinian police force consisting of police officers recruited locally and from abroad holding Jordanian passports and Palestinian documents issued by Egypt. Those who will participate in the Palestinian police force coming from abroad should be trained as police and police officers.

(d) A temporary international or foreign presence, as agreed upon.

(e) Establishment of a joint Palestinian–Israeli Coordination and Cooperation Committee for mutual security purposes.

(f) An economic development and stabilization program, including the establishment of an Emergency Fund, to encourage foreign investment and financial and economic support. Both sides will coordinate and cooperate jointly and unilaterally with regional and international parties to support these aims.

(g) Arrangements for a safe passage for persons and transportation between the Gaza Strip and Jericho area.

4. The above agreement will include arrangements for co-ordination between both parties regarding passages:

(a) Gaza—Egypt; and

(b) Jericho—Jordan.

5. The offices responsible for carrying out the powers and responsibilities of the Palestinian authority under this Annex II and Article VI of the Declaration of Principles will be located in the Gaza Strip and in the Jericho area pending the inauguration of the Council.

6. Other than these agreed arrangements, the status of the Gaza Strip and Jericho area will continue to be an integral part of the West Bank and Gaza Strip, and will not be changed in the interim period.

ANNEX III: PROTOCOL ON ISRAELI–PALESTINIAN COOPERATION IN ECONOMIC AND DEVELOPMENT PROGRAMS

The two sides agree to establish an Israeli–Palestinian continuing Committee for Economic Cooperation, focusing, among other things, on the following:

1. Cooperation in the field of water, including a Water Development Program prepared by experts from both sides, which will also specify the mode of cooperation in the management of water resources in the West Bank and Gaza Strip, and will include proposals for studies and plans on water rights of each party, as well as on the equitable utilization of joint water resources for implementation in and beyond the interim period.

2. Cooperation in the field of electricity, including an Electricity Development Program, which will also specify the mode of cooperation for the production, maintenance, purchase, and sale of electricity resources.

3. Cooperation in the field of energy, including an Energy Development Program, which will provide for the exploitation of oil and gas for industrial purposes, particularly in the Gaza Strip and in the Negev, and will encourage further joint exploitation of other energy resources. This Program may also provide for the construction of a Petrochemical industrial complex in the Gaza Strip and the construction of oil and gas pipelines.

4. Cooperation in the field of finance, including a Financial Development and Action Program for the encouragement of international investment in the West Bank and the Gaza Strip, and in Israel, as well as the establishment of a Palestinian Development Bank.

5. Cooperation in the field of transport and communications, including a Program which will define guidelines for the establishment of a Gaza Sea Port Area, and will provide for the establishing of transport and communications lines to and from the West Bank and the Gaza Strip to Israel and to other countries. In addition, this Program will provide for carrying out the necessary construction of roads, railways, communications lines, etc.

6. Cooperation in the field of trade, including studies, and Trade Promotion Programs, which will encourage local, regional, and inter-regional trade, as well as a feasibility study of creating free trade zones in the Gaza Strip and in Israel, mutual access to these zones, and cooperation in other areas related to trade and commerce.

7. Cooperation in the field of industry, including Industrial Development Programs, which will provide for the establishment of joint Israeli–Palestinian Industrial Research and Development Centers, will promote Palestinian–Israeli joint ventures, and provide guidelines for cooperation in the textile, food, pharmaceutical, electronics, diamonds, computer, and science-based industries.

8. A program for cooperation in, and regulation of, labor relations and cooperation in social welfare issues.

9. A Human Resources Development and Cooperation Plan, providing for joint Israeli–Palestinian workshops and seminars, and for the establishment of joint vocational training centers, research institutes, and data banks.

10. An Environmental Protection Plan, providing for joint and/or coordinated measures in this sphere.

11. A program for developing coordination and cooperation in the field of communication and media.

12. Any other programs of mutual interest.

ANNEX IV: PROTOCOL ON ISRAELI–PALESTINIAN COOPERATION CONCERNING REGIONAL DEVELOPMENT PROGRAMS

1. The two sides will cooperate in the context of the multilateral peace efforts in promoting a Development Program for the region, including the West Bank and the Gaza Strip, to be initiated by the G-7. The parties will request the G-7 to seek the participation in this program of other interested states, such as members of the Organisation for Economic

Cooperation and Development, regional Arab states and institutions, as well as members of the private sector.

2. The Development Program will consist of two elements:

(a) an Economic Development Program for the West Bank and the Gaza Strip.

(b) a Regional Economic Development Program.

A. The Economic Development Program for the West Bank and the Gaza strip will consist of the following elements:

1. A Social Rehabilitation Program, including a Housing and Construction Program.

2. A Small and Medium Business Development Plan.

3. An Infrastructure Development Program (water, electricity, transportation, and communications, etc.).

4. A Human Resources Plan.

5. Other programs.

B. The Regional Economic Development Program may consist of the following elements:

1. The establishment of a Middle East Development Fund, as a first step, and a Middle East Development Bank, as a second step.

2. The development of a joint Israeli–Palestinian–Jordanian Plan for coordinated exploitation of the Dead Sea area.

3. The Mediterranean Sea (Gaza)—Dead Sea Canal.

4. Regional Desalinization and other water development projects.

5. A regional plan for agricultural development, including a coordinated regional effort for the prevention of desertification.

6. Interconnection of electricity grids.

7. Regional cooperation for the transfer, distribution, and industrial exploitation of gas, oil, and other energy resources.

8. A Regional Tourism, Transportation, and Telecommunications Development Plan.

9. Regional cooperation in other spheres.

3. The two sides will encourage the multilateral working groups, and will coordinate toward their success. The two parties will encourage intersessional activities, as well as pre-feasibility and feasibility studies, within the various multilateral working groups.

AGREED MINUTES TO THE DECLARATION OF PRINCIPLES ON INTERIM SELF-GOVERNMENT ARRANGEMENTS

A. GENERAL UNDERSTANDINGS AND AGREEMENTS

Any powers and responsibilities transferred to the Palestinians pursuant to the Declaration of Principles prior to the inauguration of the Council will be subject to the same principles pertaining to Article IV, as set out in these Agreed Minutes below.

B. SPECIFIC UNDERSTANDINGS AND AGREEMENTS

ARTICLE IV

It is understood that:

1. Jurisdiction of the Council will cover West Bank and Gaza Strip territory, except for issues that will be negotiated in the permanent status negotiations: Jerusalem, settlements, military locations, and Israelis.

2. The Council's jurisdiction will apply with regard to the agreed powers, responsibilities, spheres, and authorities transferred to it.

ARTICLE VI (2)

It is agreed that the transfer of authority will be as follows:

1. The Palestinian side will inform the Israeli side of the names of the authorised Palestinians who will assume the powers, authorities, and responsibilities that will be transferred to the Palestinians according to the Declaration of Principles in the following fields: education and culture, health, social welfare, direct taxation, tourism, and any other authorities agreed upon.

2. It is understood that the rights and obligations of these offices will not be affected.

3. Each of the spheres described above will continue to enjoy existing budgetary allocations in accordance with arrangements to be mutually agreed upon. These arrangements also will provide for the necessary adjustments required in

order to take into account the taxes collected by the direct taxation office.

4. Upon the execution of the Declaration of Principles, the Israeli and Palestinian delegations will immediately commence negotiations on a detailed plan for the transfer of authority on the above offices in accordance with the above understandings.

ARTICLE VII (2)

The Interim Agreement will also include arrangements for coordination and cooperation.

ARTICLE VII (5)

The withdrawal of the military government will not prevent Israel from exercising the powers and responsibilities not transferred to the Council.

ARTICLE VIII

It is understood that the Interim Agreement will include arrangements for cooperation and coordination between the two parties in this regard. It is also agreed that the transfer of powers and responsibilities to the Palestinian police will be accomplished in a phased manner, as agreed in the Interim Agreement.

ARTICLE X

It is agreed that, upon the entry into force of the Declaration of Principles, the Israeli and Palestinian delegations will exchange the names of the individuals designated by them as members of the Joint Israeli–Palestinian Liaison Committee.

It is further agreed that each side will have an equal number of members in the Joint Committee. The Joint Committee will reach decisions by agreement. The Joint Committee may add other technicians and experts, as necessary. The Joint Committee will decide on the frequency and place or places of its meetings.

ANNEX II

It is understood that, subsequent to the Israeli withdrawal, Israel will continue to be responsible for external security, and for internal security and public order of settlements and Israelis. Israeli military forces and civilians may continue to use roads freely within the Gaza Strip and the Jericho area.

Done at Washington, D.C., this thirteenth day of September, 1993.

Shimon Peres, for the Government of the State of Israel
Mahmud Abbas, for the PLO

Witnessed by:

Warren Christopher, for the United States of America
Andrei Kozyrev, for the Russian Federation

THE WYE RIVER MEMORANDUM

The following are steps to facilitate implementation of the Interim Agreement on the West Bank and Gaza Strip of September 28, 1995 (the "Interim Agreement") and other related agreements including the Note for the Record of January 17, 1997 (hereinafter referred to as "the prior agreements") so that the Israeli and Palestinian sides can more effectively carry out their reciprocal responsibilities, including those relating to further redeployments and security respectively. These steps are to be carried out in a parallel phased approach in accordance with this Memorandum and the attached time line. They are subject to the relevant terms and conditions of the prior agreements and do not supersede their other requirements.

I. FURTHER REDEPLOYMENTS

A. Phase One and Two Further Redeployments

1. Pursuant to the Interim Agreement and subsequent agreements, the Israeli side's implementation of the first and second F.R.D. will consist of the transfer to the Palestinian side of 13% from Area C as follows:

1% to Area (A)
12% to Area (B)

The Palestinian side has informed that it will allocate an area/areas amounting to 3% from the above Area (B) to be designated as Green Areas and/or Nature Reserves. The Palestinian side has further informed that they will act according to the established scientific standards, and that therefore there will be no changes in the status of these areas, without prejudice to the rights of the existing inhabitants in these areas including Bedouins; while these standards do not allow new construction in these areas, existing roads and buildings may be maintained.

The Israeli side will retain in these Green Areas/Nature Reserves the overriding security responsibility for the purpose of protecting Israelis and confronting the threat of terrorism. Activities and movements of the Palestinian Police forces may be carried out after coordination and confirmation; the Israeli side will respond to such requests expeditiously.

2. As part of the foregoing implementation of the first and second F.R.D., 14.2% from Area (B) will become Area (A).

B. Third Phase of Further Redeployments

With regard to the terms of the Interim Agreement and of Secretary Christopher's letters to the two sides of January 17, 1997 relating to the further redeployment process, there will be a committee to address this question. The United States will be briefed regularly.

II. SECURITY

In the provisions on security arrangements of the Interim Agreement, the Palestinian side agreed to take all measures necessary in order to prevent acts of terrorism, crime, and hostilities directed against the Israeli side, against individuals falling under the Israeli side's authority, and against their property, just as the Israeli side agreed to take all measures necessary in order to prevent acts of terrorism, crime, and hostilities directed against the Palestinian side, against individuals falling under the Palestinian side's authority, and against their property. The two sides also agreed to take legal measures against offenders within their jurisdiction and to prevent incitement against each other by any organizations, groups, or individuals within their jurisdiction.

Both sides recognize that it is in their vital interests to combat terrorism and fight violence in accordance with Annex I of the Interim Agreement and the Note for the Record. They also recognize that the struggle against terror and violence must be comprehensive in that it deals with terrorists, the terror support structure, and the environment conducive to the support of terror. It must be continuous and constant over a long-term, in that there can be no pauses in the work against terrorists and their structure. It must be cooperative in that no effort can be fully effective without Israeli–Palestinian cooperation and the continuous exchange of information, concepts, and actions.

Pursuant to the prior agreements, the Palestinian side's implementation of its responsibilities for security, security cooperation, and other issues will be as detailed below during the time periods specified in the attached time line:

A. Security Actions

1. Outlawing and Combating Terrorist Organizations

(a) The Palestinian side will make known its policy of zero tolerance for terror and violence against both sides.

(b) A work plan developed by the Palestinian side will be shared with the U.S. and thereafter implementation will begin immediately to ensure the systematic and effective combat of terrorist organizations and their infrastructure.

(c) In addition to the bilateral Israeli–Palestinian security cooperation, a U.S.–Palestinian committee will meet bi-weekly to review the steps being taken to eliminate terror-ists [cells] and the support structure that plans, finances, supplies, and abets terror. In these meetings, the Palestin-ian side will inform the U.S. fully of the actions it has taken to outlaw all organizations (or wings of organizations, as ap-propriate) of a military, terrorist, or violent character and their support structure and to prevent them from operating in areas under its jurisdiction.

(d) The Palestinian side will apprehend the specific indi-viduals suspected of perpetrating acts of violence and terror for the purpose of further investigation, and prosecution and punishment of all persons involved in acts of violence and terror.

(e) A U.S.–Palestinian committee will meet to review and evaluate information pertinent to the decisions on prosecu-tion, punishment, or other legal measures which affect the status of individuals suspected of abetting or perpetrating acts of violence and terror.

2. Prohibiting Illegal Weapons

(a) The Palestinian side will ensure an effective legal frame-work is in place to criminalize, in conformity with the prior agreements, any importation, manufacturing, or unlicensed sale, acquisition, or possession of firearms, ammunition, or weapons in areas under Palestinian jurisdiction.

(b) In addition, the Palestinian side will establish and vigorously and continuously implement a systematic program for the collection and appropriate handling of all such illegal items it accordance with the prior agreements. The U.S. has agreed to assist in carrying out this program.

(c) A U.S.–Palestinian–Israeli committee will be established to assist and enhance cooperation in preventing the smuggling or other unauthorized introduction of weapons or explosive materials into areas under Palestinian jurisdiction.

3. Prevention Incitement

(a) Drawing on relevant international practice and pursuant to Article XXII (1) of the Interim Agreement and the Note for the Record, the Palestinian side will issue a decree prohibiting all forms of incitement to violence or terror, and establishing mechanisms for acting systematically against all expressions or threats of violence or terror. This decree will be comparable to the existing Israeli legislation which deals with the same subject.

(b) A U.S.–Palestinian–Israeli committee will meet on a regular basis to monitor cases of possible incitement to violence or terror and to make recommendations and reports on how to prevent such incitement. The Israeli, Palestinian, and U.S. sides will each appoint a media specialist, a law enforcement representative, an educational specialist, and a current or former elected official to the committee.

B. Security Cooperation

The two sides agree that their security cooperation will be based on a spirit of partnership and will include, among other things, the following steps:

1. Bilateral Cooperation

There will be full bilateral security cooperation between the two sides which will be continuous, intensive, and comprehensive.

2. Forensic Cooperation

There will be an exchange of forensic expertise, training, and other assistance.

3. Trilateral Committee

In addition to the bilateral Israeli–Palestinian security cooperation, a high-ranking U.S.–Palestinian–Israeli committee will meet as required and not less than biweekly to assess current threats, deal with any impediments to effective security cooperation and coordination, and address the steps being taken to combat terror and terrorist organizations. The committee will also serve as a forum to address the issue of external support for terror. In these meetings, the Palestinian side will fully inform the members of the committee of the results of its investigations concerning terrorist suspects already in custody and the participants will exchange additional relevant information. The committee will report regularly to the leaders of the two sides on the status of cooperation, the results of the meetings, and its recommendations.

C. Other Issues

1. Palestinian Police Force

(a) The Palestinian side will provide a list of its policemen to the Israeli side in conformity with the prior agreements.

(b) Should the Palestinian side request technical assistance, the U.S. has indicated its willingness to help meet those needs in cooperation with other donors.

(c) The Monitoring and Steering Committee will, as part of its functions, monitor the implementation of this provision and brief the U.S.

2. PLO Charter

The Executive Committee of the Palestine Liberation Organization and the Palestinian Central Council will reaffirm the letter of 22 January 1998 from PLO Chairman Yasir Arafat to President Clinton concerning the nullification of the Palestinian National Charter provisions that are inconsistent with the letters exchanged between the PLO and the Government of Israel on 9–10 September 1993. PLO Chairman Arafat, the Speaker of the Palestine National Council, and the Speaker of the Palestinian Council will invite the members of the PNC, as well as the members of the Central Council, the Council, and the Palestinian Heads of Ministries to a meeting to be addressed by President Clinton to reaffirm their support for the peace process and the aforementioned decisions of the Executive Committee and the Central Council.

3. Legal Assistance in Criminal Matters

Among other forms of legal assistance in criminal matters, the requests for arrest and transfer of suspects and defendants pursuant to Article II (7) of Annex IV of the Interim Agreement will be submitted (or resubmitted) through the mechanism of the Joint Israeli–Palestinian Legal Committee and will be responded to in conformity with Article II (7) (f) of Annex IV of the Interim Agreement within the 12-week period. Requests submitted after the eighth week will be responded to in conformity with Article II (7) (f) within four weeks of their submission. The United States has been requested by the sides to report on a regular basis on the [steps] being taken to respond to the above requests.

4. Human Rights and the Rule of Law

Pursuant to Article XI (1) of Annex I of the Interim Agreement, and without derogating from the above, the Palestinian Police will exercise powers and responsibilities to implement this Memorandum with due regard to internationally accepted norms of human rights and the rule of law, and will be guided by the need to protect the public, respect human dignity, and avoid harassment.

III. INTERIM COMMITTEES AND ECONOMIC ISSUES

1. The Israeli and Palestinian sides reaffirm their commitment to enhancing their relationship and agree on the need actively to promote economic development in the West Bank and Gaza. In this regard, the parties agree to continue or to reactivate all standing committees established by the Interim Agreement, including the Monitoring and Steering Committee, the Joint Economic Committee (JEC), the Civil Affairs Committee (CAC), the Legal Committee, and the Standing Cooperation Committee.

2. The Israeli and Palestinian sides have agreed on arrangements which will permit the timely opening of the Gaza Industrial Estate. They also have concluded a "Protocol Regarding the Establishment and Operation of the International Airport in the Gaza Strip During the Interim Period."

3. Both sides will renew negotiations on Safe Passage immediately. As regards the southern route, the sides will

make best efforts to conclude the agreement within a week of the entry into force of this Memorandum. Operation of the southern route will start as soon as possible thereafter. As regards the northern route, negotiations will continue with the goal of reaching agreement as soon as possible. Implementation will take place expeditiously thereafter.

4. The Israeli and Palestinian sides acknowledge the great importance of the Port of Gaza for the development of the Palestinian economy, and the expansion of Palestinian trade. They commit themselves to proceeding without delay to conclude an agreement to allow the construction and operation of the port in accordance with the prior agreements. The Israeli–Palestinian Committee will reactivate its work immediately with a goal of concluding the protocol within 60 days, which will allow commencement of the construction of the port.

5. The two sides recognize that unresolved legal issues adversely affect the relationship between the two peoples. They therefore will accelerate efforts through the Legal Committee to address outstanding legal issues and to implement solutions to these issues in the shortest possible period. The Palestinian side will provide to the Israeli side copies of all of its laws in effect.

6. The Israeli and Palestinian sides also will launch a strategic economic dialogue to enhance their economic relationship. They will establish within the framework of the JEC an Ad Hoc Committee for this purpose. The committee will review the following four issues: (1) Israeli purchase taxes; (2) cooperation in combating vehicle theft; (3) dealing with unpaid Palestinian debts; and (4) the impact of Israeli standards as barriers to trade and the expansion of the A1 and A2 lists. The committee will submit an interim report within

three weeks of the entry into force of this Memorandum, and within six weeks will submit its conclusions and recommendations to be implemented.

7. The two sides agree on the importance of continued international donor assistance to facilitate implementation by both sides of agreements reached. They also recognize the need for enhanced donor support for economic development in the West Bank and Gaza. They agree to jointly approach the donor community to organize a Ministerial Conference before the end of 1998 to seek pledges for enhanced levels of assistance.

IV. PERMANENT STATUS NEGOTIATIONS

The two sides will immediately resume permanent status negotiations on an accelerated basis and will make a determined effort to achieve the mutual goal of reaching an agreement by May 4, 1999. The negotiations will be continuous and without interruption. The United States has expressed its willingness to facilitate these negotiations.

V. UNILATERAL ACTIONS

Recognizing the necessity to create a positive environment for the negotiations, neither side shall initiate or take any step that will change the status of the West Bank and the Gaza Strip in accordance with the Interim Agreement.

ATTACHMENT: TIME LINE

This Memorandum will enter into force ten days from the date of signature.

Done at Washington, D.C. this 23rd day of October 1998.

Benjamin Netanyahu, for the Government of the State of Israel

Yasir Arafat, for the PLO

Witnessed by:
William J. Clinton, for the United States of America

Time Line

Note: Parenthetical references below are to paragraphs in "The Wye River Memorandum" to which this time line is an integral attachment. Topics not included in the time line follow the schedule provided for in the text of the memorandum.

1. Upon Entry into Force of the Memorandum:

—Third further redeployment committee starts (I (B))

—Palestinian security work plan shared with the U.S. (II (A)(1)(b))

—Full bilateral security cooperation (II (B)(1))

—Trilateral security cooperation committee starts (II (B)(3))

—Interim committees resume and continue; Ad Hoc Economic Committee starts (III)

—Accelerated permanent status negotiations start (IV)

2. Entry into Force—Week 2:

—Security work plan implementation begins (II (A)(1)(b)); (II (A)(1)(c)) committee starts

—Illegal weapons framework in place (II (A)(2)(a)); Palestinian implementation report (II (A)(2)(b))

—Anti-incitement committee starts (II (A)(3)(b)); decree issued (II (A)(3)(a))

—PLO Executive Committee reaffirms Charter letter (II (C)(2))

—Stage 1 of F.R.D. implementation: 2% C to B, 7.1% B to A. Israeli officials acquaint their Palestinian counterparts as required with areas; F.R.D. carried out; report on F.R.D. implementation (I(A))

3. Week 2–6:

—Palestinian Central Council reaffirms Charter letter (weeks two to four) (II (C)(2))

—PNC and other PLO organizations reaffirm Charter letter (weeks four to six) (II (C)(2))

—Establishment of weapons collection program (II (A)(2)(b)) and collection stage (II (A)(2)(c)); committee starts and reports on activities

—Anti-incitement committee report (II (A)(3)(b))

—Ad Hoc Economic Committee: interim report at week three; final report at week six (III)

—Policemen list (II (C)(1)(a)), Monitoring and Steering Committee review starts (II (C)(1)(c))

—Stage 2 of F.R.D. implementation: 5% C to B. Israeli officials acquaint their Palestinian counterparts as required with areas; F.R.D. carried out; report on F.R.D. implementation (I (A))

4. Week 6–12:

—Weapons collection stage (II (A)(2)(b)); (II (A)(2)(c)) committee report on its activities

—Anti-incitement committees report (II (A)(3)(b))

—Monitoring and Steering Committee briefs U.S. on policemen list (II (C)(1)(c))

—Stage 3 of F.R.D. implementation: 5% C to B, 1% C to A, 7.1% B to A—Israeli officials acquaint Palestinian counterparts as required with areas; F.R.D. carried out; report on F.R.D. implementation (I (A))

5. After Week 12:

Activities described in the Memorandum continue as appropriate and if necessary, including;

—Trilateral security cooperation committee (II (B)(3))

—(II (A)(1)(c)) committee

—(II (A)(1)(e)) committee

—Anti-incitement committee (II (A)(3)(b))

—Third Phase F.R.D. Committee (I (B))

—Interim Committees (III)

—Accelerated permanent status negotiations (IV)

SOURCES

UN General Assembly Resolution 194 (III) of 11 December
1948. UN Information System on the Question of
Palestine (UNISPAL)
UN Security Council Resolution 242 of 22 November 1967.
UN Document Library
UN Security Council Resolution 338 of 22 October 1973. UN
Document Library
UN Security Council Resolution 425 of 19 March 1978. UN
Information System on the Question of Palestine
(UNISPAL)
Oslo Accords. US Institute of Peace Library through http://
www.access.gpo.gov/su_docs/locators/search/index.
html
The Wye River Memorandum. US Institute of Peace through
http://www.access.gpo.gov/su_docs/locators/search/
index. html

REFERENCES

Agence France Presse (1997). Wire story: AFP. MOA160. 201753GMT AVR97.

Barnea, N. (1999a). Shalom be pkouda. *Yediot Ahronot*, September 5, pp. 1, 23.

———— (1999b). Hakineret sheli yomar Barak. *Yediot Ahronot*, December 14, pp. 1, 23.

Barnea, N. and Shiffer, S. (2000). Camp David. Mabat mi bifnim. *Yediot Ahronot*, Mossaf Shabat, July 28, pp. 2–5.

Ben, A. and Horowitz, N. (2000). PM offers Arafat Temple Mount access. *Haaretz*, July 19, p. 1.

Benvenisti, M. (1998). The distorted symbolism of Mossad. *Haaretz*, December 17, p. 5.

Butler, L. (1997). Fresh light on the Syrian–Israeli peace negotiations: An interview with Ambassador Walid Al-Moualem. *The Journal of Palestine Studies*, 26.2, Issue 102 (Winter 1997), pp. 81–94.

Cordesman, A. H. (2001). Israel versus the Palestinians: The "second intifada" and asymmetric warfare. Working Paper, Center for Strategic and International Studies, Washington DC, October, pp. 163–164.

Drucker, R. (2002). *Hara Kiri*. Tel Aviv: Yediot Ahronot.

Enderlin, C. (1997). *Paix ou Guerres. Les Secrets des Négotiations Israélo–Arabes 1917–1997*. Paris: Stock.

Ford, G. (1975). Letter to Yitzhak Rabin. See http://www .usisrael.org/jsource/Peace/ford_rabin_letter.html.

Foundation for Middle East Peace, http://www.fmep.org.

Ha'etzni, E. (1999). Hostile media against Serbia. Arutz Sheva National Radio, March 29. See http://www. hebroots.org/hebrootsarchive/9904/9904_ll.html.

Hockstader, L. (1999). Israel uneasily wrestles with "genocide" in Kosovo. *The Washington Post*, April 1, p. A12.

Kaspit, B. (2002a). Ha tsava iakhlit ve yaasher. *Yediot Ahronot*, Mossaf Shabat, September 13, p. 9.

———— (2002b). Israel eina medina she iesh la tsava ela tsava shemesunefet la medina. *Maariv*, Mossaf Rosh Ha-shana, September 6, 2002, p. 9.

Lior, D., Shilo, D., and Melamed, E. (1995). Medina shel memshala raa hazo? Reprinted in *Dat ve medina be Israel 1944–1995*, pp. 121–123. Hamerkaz le-Pluralism Yehudi, Jerusalem 1996.

Malley, R. and Agha, H. (2001). Camp David: The tragedy of errors. *The New York Review of Books*, August 9, pp. 59–65.

Marcus, Y. (1997). Miskhak Be Esh Arafat. *Haaretz*, March 25, p. B1.

MEMRI (1999). See http://www.memri.org.

Mosko, Y. (1997). Interview of Amos Gilaad: Arafat lo natan or yarok. *Kol Ha Ir*, April 25, pp. 44–47.

Netanyahu, B. (1993). *A Place among the Nations*. New York: Bantam.

Quandt, W. B. (2001). *Peace Process: American Diplomacy and the Arab–Israeli Conflict since 1967*, revised ed. Washington, DC: Brookings Institution.

Rabinovich, I. (1998). *Saf ha-Shalom*. Tel Aviv: Yediot Ahronot.

Seale, P. (1999). *Al-Hayat* (London), November 21 and 22, p. 1.

Shavit, A. (1996). Interview of Benjamin Netanyahu. *Haaretz*, November 22, p. 18.

Sher, G. (2001). *Bemerhak Neguiya*. Tel Aviv: Yediot Ahronot.

Sigler, J. (n.d.). Conflict in the Middle East. Carleton University, Ottawa, Canada. See http://www.ulaval.ca.iqhei/circa/cm95-96/C_Sigler_f.html.

Simon, B. (2000). Interview of General Yom Tov Samia. *60 Minutes*, CBS, November 12.

Sprinzak, E. (1999). *Brother against Brother*. New York: Free Press.

Tal, R. (1997). Moshe Dayan. Kheshbon nefesh. *Yediot Ahronot*, Mossaf le Hag, April 27, pp. 2–6.

INDEX

Acknowledgments

This English version of *Le Rêve Brisé* was, for me, another adventure. Thanks to the talent and dedication of Susan Fairfield, *Shattered Dreams* is not merely a translation but another book, completely adapted for the American public. The enthusiasm and drive of Judith Feher Gurewich, Stacy Hague, and their team from Other Press made this project possible. I wholeheartedly thank them.

Charles Enderlin
Jerusalem
October 18, 2002